Planning for a
Sustainable Future

Sustainable development is now firmly on the planning agenda and is an issue neither practitioner nor academic can afford to ignore. *Planning for a Sustainable Future* provides a multi-disciplinary overview of sustainability issues in the land use context, focusing on principles and their application, the legal, political and policy context and the implications of sustainable development thinking for housing, urban design and property development as well as waste and transport. The book concludes by considering how sustainable and unsustainable impacts alike can be measured and modelled, providing real tools to move beyond rhetoric into practice.

Planning for a Sustainable Future is aimed at undergraduate and post-graduate students as well as practitioners – its mix of introductory and advanced chapters aims to provide something for everyone. Its editors and contributors all work at (or have close links with) the Bartlett School of Planning at University College London. **Dr Antonia Layard** is a lecturer at the Bartlett, where she teaches and researches on aspects of environmental and planning law and policy. **Simin Davoudi** is Professor of Planning and Environment and Director of the Centre for Urban Development and Environmental Management at Leeds Metropolitan University. **Dr Susan Batty** is a senior lecturer at the Bartlett where she teaches and researches on the politics and theory of planning and urban development.

Contributors to the book are: Professor David Banister, Professor Mike Batty, Dr Matthew Carmona, Professor Harry Dimitriou, Michael Edwards, Dr Nick Gallent, Professor Sir Peter Hall, Chris Marsh, Dr Stephen Marshall, Daniel Mittler, Robin Thompson, Mark Thurstain-Goodwin, Helena Titheridge and Jo Williams.

Planning for a Sustainable Future

Edited by Antonia Layard, Simin
Davoudi and Susan Batty

First published 2001
by Spon Press
11 New Fetter Lane, London EC4P 4EE

Simultaneously published in the USA and Canada
by Spon Press
29 West 35th Street, New York, NY 10001

Spon Press is an imprint of the Taylor & Francis Group

Typeset in Sabon by Keystroke, Jacaranda Lodge, Wolverhampton

Printed and bound in Great Britain by Biddles Ltd, Guildford and King's
Lynn

British Library Cataloguing in Publication Data
A catalogue record for this book is available from the British Library

Library of Congress Cataloging in Publication Data
Planning for a sustainable future / edited by Antonia Layard, Simin Davoudi,
Susan Batty.
    p. cm.
Includes bibliographical references and index.
    1. Sustainable development. I. Layard, Antonia. II. Davoudi, Simin
III. Batty, Susan.
HC79.E5 P525 2001
338.9'7–dc21   2001020710

ISBN 0–415–23227–9 (hbk)
ISBN 0–415–23408–5 (pbk)

Contents

Contents

Contributors

Professor David Banister is Professor of Transport Planning at the University of London and Director of Research at the Bartlett School of Planning at University College London. From 1994 to 1996 he was Visiting VSB Professor at the Tinbergen Institute in Amsterdam. His research interests lie in transport analysis and in particular the contribution that the social scientist can make to the investigation of these problems. Recent research has been on transport investment decisions and economic development, policy scenarios for sustainable mobility, transport and sustainable development (reducing the need to travel) and modelling energy and emissions from transport nodes in urban areas.

Professor Michael Batty is Professor of Spatial Analysis and Planning and Director of the Centre for Advanced Spatial Analysis (CASA) at UCL. In the 1980s he was Professor and Head of the Department of City and Regional Planning in the University of Cardiff, and before coming to UCL he was Director of the National Center for Geographic Information and Analysis at the State University of New York at Buffalo. His research interests are the use of computers in planning, spatial analysis, fractal cities and geographical information systems.

Dr Sue Batty is Senior Lecturer at the Bartlett School of Planning, University College London. She teaches urban and environmental politics and comparative planning, and also has research interests in planning institutions and town centre analysis. She is associated with the CASA Town Centres group and recent work with this group has included user testing and expert panel evaluation for the Department of Environment, Transport and the Regions' (DETR) Town Centres Project.

Dr Matthew Carmona is a Senior Lecturer in planning and urban design at the Bartlett School of Planning. He is an expert on the policy context for delivering better design quality in the built environment, having worked on a range of research projects examining design policies in local plans, residential design policy and guidance, delivering urban renaissance, and the value of urban design. Matthew teaches urban design at the Bartlett and is Director of the BSc and MSc/Diploma programmes in planning. His research interests lie in the areas of design control, urban design and urban regeneration.

Contributors

Professor Simin Davoudi is Professor of Planning and Environment and Director of the Centre for Urban Development and Environmental Management (CUDEM) at Leeds Metropolitan University. She has previously conducted research and lectured in the Bartlett School of Planning and Newcastle University. She has extensive research experience and has published widely particularly in the three areas of UK and European spatial planning, urban policy and regeneration and environmental sustainability and waste management. She is the co-author/co-editor of five books and has written several academic and professional articles. She has worked on a range of research projects funded by research councils, the European Commission, UK central and local governments and other public agencies.

Professor Harry Dimitriou is Bartlett Professor of Planning Studies at University College London and Head of the Bartlett School of Planning. He has been a consultant to several international development agencies and adviser to numerous government agencies throughout the world on transport and urban development issues. His research interests lie in the area of land use/transport planning, institution building for development, risk analysis in the planning of large-scale transport infrastructure investments, and Third World city development.

Michael Edwards studied economics in Oxford and planning at the Bartlett, then worked for Nathaniel Lichfield for some years before joining the Bartlett School of Planning. His work has mainly focused on property markets and how they interact with planning systems and practices – arguing that the two phenomena should always be studied and taught in an integrated way. He is currently working with Dr Emmanuel Mutale on a long-term study of urban change at King's Cross in London and on development processes in European cities.

Dr Nick Gallent is a lecturer at the Bartlett School of Planning at UCL. He has previously lectured and conducted research at the Universities of Manchester and Cardiff. His research is chiefly concerned with UK housing policy and, in particular, the problems of providing affordable housing via planning mechanisms. This work has been disseminated in various formats, both through academic and professional publications. Past research has included studies of housing requirements in the north of England. More recent work has focused on the relationship between housing providers and planners (for the Royal Town Planning Institute), housing pressure in rural Europe (for Scottish Homes) and the characteristics of sustainable suburban areas (for the Civic Trust).

Sir Peter Hall is Professor of Planning at the Bartlett School of Planning. From 1991 to 1994 he was Special Adviser on Strategic Planning to the

Secretary of State for the Environment. In 1998–99 he was a member of the Deputy Prime Minister's Urban Task Force. He is author or editor of nearly thirty books on urban and regional planning and related topics and holds seven honorary doctorates from universities in the UK, Sweden and Canada. He was a founder-member of the Regional Studies Association and the past Chairman of the Town and Country Planning Association. He has been a member of many British official committees. He is convener of the World Commission on Twenty-First-Century Urbanization and co-editor of its report, which was the subject of a major conference in Berlin in July 2000.

Antonia Layard is a lecturer at the Bartlett School of Planning, University College London. She is a qualified solicitor and has studied law, public policy and public health at the Universities of Oxford, Columbia (New York) and the London School of Economics. Antonia's research interests lie in environmental law and policy and her recent projects have focused on aspects of environmental justice and environmental rights. Her DPhil thesis was called *Environmental Victims: An Argument for Compensation* and is due to be published (in a format to be decided) in the near future.

Christopher Marsh is a surveyor and planner, active in research and practice and Head of the School of Estate Management at Westminster University. His current work emphasises sustainable property development and includes research on the impacts of London's Jubilee Line Extension. He contributes courses to the MSc in European Property Development and Planning which is a joint programme with the Bartlett.

Stephen Marshall graduated with a BEng in Civil Engineering from Glasgow University and a MSc in Transport Planning and Engineering from Leeds University. He was a transport planning consultant for five years in Edinburgh, with Acer Consultants and Halcrow Fox, and gained a Postgraduate Diploma in Urban Design from Edinburgh College of Art. For the last five years he has been undertaking research at the Bartlett School of Planning, where he is Research Fellow. His principal research interests are in the relationships between transport and land use planning, and the integration of transport and urban design through urban structure.

Daniel Mittler is an international campaigner at Friends of the Earth Germany (BUND) and is based in Berlin. He studied Politics, African Studies and Philosophy at Edinburgh University and Queen's University, Canada. Since 1997, he has been studying at the Bartlett School of Planning, University College London. He is writing a PhD thesis comparing the rhetoric and reality of local sustainability policies in Edinburgh and Wuppertal (Germany). Daniel Mittler has published widely on urban sustainability, Local Agenda 21, Scottish and German politics, as well as environmental philosophy. He is a

Member of the Sustainable Europe Research Institute, Vienna, and a Fellow of the Centre for Human Ecology, Edinburgh. His other publications can be downloaded from his website at http://www.seri.at/dme.htm.

Mark Thurstain-Goodwin is Senior Research Fellow in the Centre for Advanced Spatial Analysis at UCL where he runs the Town Centres group. He has extensive experience of property analysis in his previous role as research associate with Property Market Analysis, and his current work is focused on statistical analysis of large data sets. He is active in retail market research and spatial analysis, with particular emphasis on town centres.

Robin Thompson is Strategic Planning Director at Kent County Council and Visiting Professor at the Bartlett School of Planning. He has been involved in partnerships in the Thames Gateway since its inception, first as Director of Development in Southwark and then in Kent. He is a former President of the Royal Town Planning Institute and is the current President of the European Council of Town Planners.

Helena Titheridge is a Research Fellow at the Bartlett School of Planning, University College London. Her expertise focuses on the development of decision support tools for local authorities, and she is particularly experienced in transport and energy modelling. Since joining UCL in 1997 she has worked on a number of projects aimed at developing models to assist local authorities in siting new housing developments sustainably – examining land use, transport and sustainability with database analysis and spatial modelling. She played a key role in the development of ESTEEM (a GIS-based travel, energy and emissions model). Previously, Helena worked in the Energy and Environment Research Unit of the Open University, where she was involved with the development of a Dynamic Regional Energy Analysis Model (DREAM) and an information system to evaluate energy strategies and improve energy management in urban areas.

Jo Williams is a lecturer at the Bartlett School of Planning, University College London. She specialises in aspects of sustainable development in the fields of housing, travel and community and has produced a number of publications in these areas. She has also completed work focusing on the use of IT in promoting social inclusion and reduction travel. In addition, her research interests include alternative lifestyles and communities. Her PhD thesis focuses on the development of new design solutions to accommodate the growth of one-person households in the future, in a manner that reduces resource consumption and encourages the development of social networks. She is also actively involved in various governmental, academic and professional panels.

Preface and Acknowledgements

This book is a collection of papers by researchers and practitioners on the impact of sustainable development on planning. Their backgrounds are heterogeneous, their disciplines mixed. The one trait the authors all share is a commitment to bring greater clarity and understanding to the sustainable development agenda. They do not, of course, share a consistent view of what sustainable development means or what it requires. Indeed, in some respects, this collection can be seen as a reflection of the diversity of interpretations surrounding the principle and the difficulties implementation entails.

Given the scope of concerns that might fall under the 'sustainable' label, no single text could claim to be totally comprehensive. It is for this reason that the volume's authors take different perspectives, analysing sustainable development from their own disciplinary and professional standpoints. The collection is the Bartlett School of Planning's contribution to the debate on sustainable development and planning at the start of a new century.

The collection is divided into three parts. The first is concerned with principles of sustainable development and their theoretical, political, legal and policy context. The second focuses on contemporary debates on how best to implement sustainability in planning practice. The third part then presents some new ways in which the theory of sustainable development is being put to the test.

Putting this book together has been a remarkable experience in colleagiality. The idea for the volume came from David Banister and was enthusiastically taken up by all our colleagues. Initial seminars provided the intellectual framework where central ideas were discussed and debated. We would like to thank all those who attended the seminars and sharpened our thinking in this respect, in particular Dr Emmanual Mutale.

Once the chapters were written they were peer reviewed both internally and externally. We are grateful to all those who took time to comment on drafts; individual chapters contain their own acknowledgements on this point. Within the Bartlett School of Planning, some colleagues read all the papers – out of intellectual curiosity alone – and provided fruitful and constructive comments. For all of us the book has been a fascinating exercise in discovering the research interests and styles of all our colleagues, displaying a compelling range of expertise and interests. Like the Bartlett School of Planning where many of the contributors work, this book represents a real commitment to the interdisciplinary work that infuses planning, as well as consistently mixing theory and practice.

Finally, as the book neared production Emma Bailey and Rachael Coffey were once again quite simply brilliant. Reliable and calm, able to retrieve complicated computer images and deal with ever-mounting piles of paper, they ensured that the book did not falter at the last hurdle. It is here also that we would like to express our thanks and appreciation for all the hard work of Caroline Mallinder and Rebecca Casey at Spon Pross. They have dealt with our requirements exceptionally well and ensured that the book reached its intended audience as quickly as possible.

PART I

Introduction: Sustainable Development – Principles and Practice

Antonia Layard

Land use planning and sustainable development seem to be ever more inextricably intertwined. References to the ideas, principles and policies underpinning sustainability are everywhere – from planning policy guidance to good practice guides to inclusions in development plans. Yet it is also widely acknowledged that there is no single way forward to pursue sustainability. In fact, some even dispute that it is desirable at all; others disagree over what the concept means. Diverse views also exist as to its interpretation and implementation.

In practice, however, the principle has garnered widespread support. Even if it means different things to different people at different times in different places, it can provide a touchstone for reflection. Is cycling or driving a more sustainable form of transport? Should we build on green fields or brownfield sites to ensure that we meet the needs of current generations whilst protecting the interests of future ones? Even if we are unable to find a simple maxim to sum up the dictates of sustainability in a nutshell, we can simply and intuitively reflect on which of these two alternatives is the more 'sustainable' taking into account environmental, social and economic concerns. The answer may not be simple – driving has major ecological and safety effects but promotes mobility and personal freedom; greenfield developments reduce our open spaces but provide residents with a desirable place to live. By thinking about sustainability we can understand the tensions and dilemmas these issues pose, and we have an intuition of the outcome we wish to achieve. Sustainability is more than just 'quality of life' – it requires us also to consider the interests of 'strangers in time and space' as well as considering ecological limits and other species. It requires a holism that is often missing when we concern ourselves solely with the here and now.

To a large extent these are concerns that planners have always had to consider in a spatial context: they have long needed to balance social, economic and amenity issues, sometimes with an eye to environmental concerns as well. The new emphasis on sustainability, however, means that they must mediate between still more interests. There are new matters to be taken on board or concerns to resolve. This is a point stressed in Chapter 1 of this part by *Simin Davoudi* and *Antonia Layard*. If sustainability is to be more than merely a mantra on quality of life, spoken in the interests of electoral longevity, rather than long-term reform, we must integrate true concerns for intra- and inter-generational equity into our policies, in the spatial context and elsewhere.

The political context for such development is explored in Chapter 2 by *Sue Batty*. She analyses sustainability in its political context, considering how the principles can be used to inspire consensus rather than merely identifying causes. Sustainable development is more than merely a set of technical analyses, measuring emissions and absorptive capacities, depletion rates and waste generation statistics. The concept goes beyond these indices of measurement and assessment to call for ways to resolve the global political problem of the redistribution of scarce and limited resources. Scientific knowledge is also now more than merely technocratic – it empowers citizens and is no longer the prerogative of suited civil servants and scientists in white coats. Indeed, calls for sustainability now come from throughout the political spectrum, some see the consensual basis for sustainable development as implying bottom-up, participatory democracy, some even believe that anarchy holds the key to viable progress. Others hold more mainstream communitarian beliefs. In contrast, many believe that sustainable development is inevitably associated with the process of liberal democracy while others still opt for an element of authoritarian government or at least strong central regulatory powers. Advocates of sustainable development come from a broad range of political perspectives, and interpreting these is crucial if we are to understand what the political aspect of sustainability means, and how we are to implement it should we desire to do so.

Another key aspect of sustainability and one considered here is the legal dimension, as Chapter 3 by *Antonia Layard* explains. Laws can either underpin strategies by providing a legislative framework for subsequent policy development, or they can provide mandatory objectives and targets, requiring operators to reduce emissions or states to take responsibility for the harm they cause. There is, however, no central legal authority capable of implementing sustainability by legislative fiat. Under public international law countries need only make commitments on curbing greenhouse gas emissions or promoting equitable forms of trade if they wish to; should they refuse to sign up to such initiatives or breach laws once agreed, there is little the international community can do in law. It will be up to patient diplomatic negotiations or political persuasion to bring recalcitrant governments (back) into line.

On occasion, alliances can be set up, to promote sustainability and other goals, and these can be spectacularly successful. The most impressive of these is undoubtedly the European Union, where states have pooled sovereignty on an impressive scale adopting the guideline of subsidiarity, pursuing together what can best be achieved at the collective level while otherwise leaving governments to legislate alone. Here the pursuit of sustainability (so far focusing primarily on environmental protection) is steady and productive. Environmental standards have risen significantly throughout the Community as a whole, laggards have been brought into line and impacts on trade have generally been delicately defused. It is for this reason that the vast majority of United Kingdom law and legislation concerned with sustainability and environmental protection begins in Brussels.

Another key aspect of the political changes underway is an increased focus on public participation: it is widely accepted that sustainable development will not be achieved by 'top-down' approaches alone. And so the fourth chapter in this part is by *Daniel Mittler* who explains the origins and objectives of Local Agenda 21, analysing the extent to which these can be achieved in practice. There are real difficulties in achieving this end. Resources are lacking, institutional hierarchies are inflexible, planners prefer to stay 'on top' rather than being 'on tap' and it is much harder to actually implement progress than merely redefine it. And yet there are changes underway. The most important of these, Mittler submits, is the way Local Agenda 21 inspires and underpins calls for local empowerment. It provides a valuable focus to revisit relationships between local and central government and it is here that the potential for sustainable progress truly exists.

A further aspect of the political and legal framework for sustainability is the importance of institutions. The best principles and most coherent philosophies in the world cannot be introduced without effective and continuing institutions that both deliver and oversee implementation. This is a point stressed by *Harry Dimitriou* and *Robin Thompson* in Chapter 5. They refer to the work of Brinkerhoff and Goldsmith in developing a generic framework for understanding institutional sustainability. These authors believe that longevity alone is an insufficient goal for institutions; to be truly successful, two other aspects should be borne in mind. The first of these is that both an organisation's internal capabilities and its external environment matter, the second, that an organisation must chart a balanced course if it is to reflect its own internal strengths and weaknesses as well as external threats and opportunities. In the event of a mismatch between the two, it is said, institutional decline or demise will occur.

Dimitriou and Thompson broadly agree with this analysis and apply it to an urban development in the United Kingdom. The project they choose is the ambitious urban regeneration initiative in the Thames Gateway area on the premise that if the institution delivering the regeneration is itself unsustainable, then the outcomes of the project (sustainable regeneration) must themselves be in doubt. At first sight they certainly agree that the institutional arrangements in place for the regeneration strategy of the area represent a model of stability and sustainability in which an explicitly stated strategy is carried forward by a set of powerfully entrenched institutions. On closer analysis, however, they believe the initiative to have been characterised by institutional instability with many of the failing features evident in unsustainable institutions. Their analysis leads them to be cautious about the possibility of successful sustainable urban regeneration in the Thames Gateway area, though they note that improvements to the institutional structure can be, and are being, made.

The final chapter in Part I reflects two innovative theories on sustainability: that of a risk society (promulgated by the German sociologist Ulrich Beck) and the idea of ecological modernisation, a theory and practice developed largely in the Netherlands. Beck's risk society thesis argues that 'we are eye-witnesses – as subjects and objects – of a break within modernity, which is freeing itself from the contours of classical industrial society and forging a new form – the industrial risk society . . . Just as modernization dissolved the structure of feudal society in the nineteenth century and produced the industrial society, modernization today is dissolving industrial society and another modernity is coming into being' (Beck 1996: 9). Ecological modernisation, on the other hand, is an altogether more optimistic approach. Its advocates start 'from the conviction that the ecological crisis can be overcome by technical and procedural innovation' (Hajer 1996: 249). They 'propose that policies for economic development and environmental protection can be combined to synergistic effect . . . [and rather] than perceiving economic development to be the source of environmental decline, ecological modernisation seeks to harness to forces of entrepreneurship for environmental gain' (Gouldson and Murphy 1997: 94).

In Chapter 6 *Simin Davoudi* takes these two theories and considers their implications for sustainability in the planning context. Her conclusion is that they mirror two different forms and views of planning: one ideological, the other technocratic. Like these, the risk society thesis is moral; ecological modernisation meanwhile is rational. Her conclusion is that planning needs to take both these agendas into account. Both inspiration and application will be needed to implement sustainable development effectively in the spatial context.

4

Overall, then, the aim of Part I of this book is to provide an overview of sustainable development's central principles whilst also considering the concept's political, legal and planning context. The chapters are heterogeneous both in form and content, they make no attempt to provide a single definition of sustainability, nor do they advocate a single way in which to carry the idea forward. What they do, in conjunction with the other chapters in this collection, is to provide a snapshot of current thinking and analysis on the issue. The authors explore pivotal concepts and consider the issue critically. The idealistic and holistic worldview the notion of sustainable development incorporates provides a valuable focus, yet it is crucial to underpin this with analytical rigour if the vision is to provide a useful and tangible guide to future development. We often have a basic intuition about what is sustainable and what is not: these chapters illustrate some of the considerations on which these early (and often accurate) judgements are based.

1 Sustainable Development and Planning: An Overview

Simin Davoudi and Antonia Layard

This chapter addresses two issues. The first is the concept of sustainable development and its connection to prosperity and growth. Whether or not win-win solutions can be achieved, it is clear that policy-makers and politicians want to reach them. The most widespread recipe for sustainable development these days is a focus on 'quality of life'. Human wellbeing – particularly for voters – is central. Sustainability is packaged as an idea that can deliver better homes, workplaces and lifestyles and many (particularly governmental) definitions seem to suggest that there are no hard choices to be made. One group who should know is planners, and this is the second issue to be addressed. For however easy or difficult sustainability decisions are to make, it is they who must determine them in a spatial sphere and balance economic, social and environmental concerns. The question is whether the requirement and language of sustainability demand anything new, or if this is in fact what planners have been doing all along.

The Concept of Sustainable Development

The language of sustainability has certainly been around for some time. It emerged from forestry practices in eighteenth- and nineteenth-century Europe when foresters realised that they needed to plant enough trees to ensure that the wood fibre lost to harvesting was replaced. 'Scientific' or 'sustainable' forestry was to monitor the growth of wood fibre assessing what was needed to replace that lost to harvesting. And so right from the beginning, 'sustainability' showed a distinctive affinity with the older discourse of 'limits' (Batty, Mittler this volume).

Indeed, this notion of natural limits was taken up by the International Union for the Conservation of Nature when it prepared in its World Conservation Strategy in 1980. This stressed sustainability in ecological terms, calling for a strategy to ensure the sustainable utilisation of species and ecosystem (IUCN 1980). Its concern was the preservation of habitats, vital for conservation. Yet as critics noted, this was a narrow approach. Human activities are an integral part of the habitats conservationists seek to protect and neither should be seen in isolation from the other. The IUCN Report saw 'poverty and the actions of the poor . . . as one of the main causes of non-sustainable development, rather than recognizing that poverty and environmental degradation are both consequences of existing development patterns' (Soussain 1992: 24). As one analyst concludes, 'this lack of vision of the relationship between the economy and the environment led to a re-formulation of the concept of sustainable development to reflect concerns over what many commentators saw as an "anti-poor" bias in the IUCN Report' (ibid.).

In light of this growing critique, and as a reflection of changing times, the poor were a key focus of the seminal work by the World Commission on Environment and Development in 1984. This meeting, better known as the Brundlandt Commission after its chair, Gro Harlem Brundlandt, was convened in response to a United Nations General Assembly Resolution following up the Stockholm Conference on the Human Environment in 1972. Their 1987 report, *Our Common Future*, provided the most quoted definition of sustainable development of all time: 'development that meets the needs of the present without compromising the ability of future generations to meet their needs' (WCED 1987: 8). This incorporated two key concepts: justice within generations (intra-generational equity) and justice between generations (inter-generational equity) and here already was the focus on human wellbeing. For according to the Commission, the 'central rationale for sustainable development is to increase people's standard of living (broadly defined) and, in particular, the well-being of the least advantaged people in societies, while at the same time avoiding uncompensated future costs' (Turner 1993: 413). Sustainable development was an anthropocentric concept from the outset.

This call is powerful rhetoric, yet it is unclear how such ends are to be achieved. In particular, it is uncertain whether current economic processes are the problem or the solution to unsustainable ways. Are 'win–win' solutions – arrangements in which all parties benefit – possible here? Or are there inescapable trade-offs that have to be made? This is clearly a fundamental debate.

Indeed, as Michael Carley and Ian Christie (1992) have pointed out, there have been two responses to the Brundlandt Commission's call for sustainable development, broadly caricatured as 'growth' and 'no growth'. 'One advocates continuing economic growth, made much more environmentally sensitive in order to raise living standards locally and break the link between poverty and environmental degradation. The other calls for radical change in economic organisation, producing much lower rates of growth as we know it, or even zero or negative economic growth' (ibid.: 42).

Daly (1991) also distinguishes between the 'expansionist' and the 'steady state' view of sustainable development, a view also accepted by Rees (1999). The Brundlandt Commission though was certainly 'firmly in the first camp' (Carley and Christie 1992). They believed that it was vital to increase economic growth if sustainability were to be achieved; in other words, that 'the surest way to improve your environment is to get rich' (Beckerman 1995: 42).

However attractive, this pro-growth stance has come in for harsh criticism. From the South it is said that 'Western proponents of sustainable development "just don't get it"' (Nagpal 1995: 13). Critics point out that 'the debates on sustainability closely mirror those on development. By using terms of economic growth and efficiency, important issues are ignored: the urgency of nurturing human life and ecosystem health and the primacy of people, their communities, and the environment they depend on for their livelihood' (ibid.). From the North, meanwhile, it is said that development and economic growth are all very well, but only when certain limits, or ecological constraints, are observed.

These concerns resonate in the planning context as well. McLaren suggests, for example, that the 'principles of sustainability planning are (at least in theory) simple'. His view is that 'sustainable development can only be achieved if human capacity is kept within the constraints set by environmental capacity. If technical information is poor or lacking, then to locate those constraints, the precautionary principle must be applied. From such sustainability constraints, political planning processes are needed to set targets which can be met through the application of a range of appropriate policy tools' (in Buckingham-Hatfield and Evans 1996: 145–6). Growth, such analysts suggest, cannot be the answer unless it observes some very basic limitations.

This debate over limits has produced another distinction, this time between sustainability that is either 'strong' or 'weak'. And here the concept of 'constant capital stock' takes centre stage in a discussion again dominated by economics. Pearce *et al.* (1989) have famously suggested that one definition could be that if a society is to be sustainable, an undiminished per capita stock of capital should be passed from one generation to the next. Yet this begs the question, what form should this capital stock take? Are all goods 'substitutable'? Proponents of weak sustainability believe they are, and regard capital stock as the aggregate stock of human-made (such as machinery, infrastructure and even knowledge) and natural capital. They conclude that the latter can be substituted with the former (Pearce *et al.* 1989; Pearce and Barbier 2000) and argue that it is therefore of little consequence if natural capital assets are depleted, as long as these are invested in creating an equivalent value of manufactured capital.

Beckerman is one supporter of such thinking, in his provocatively titled book *Small is Stupid*. He maintains that the whole notion of sustainability is a red herring, concluding that ultimately sustainability becomes so weak a constraint that the only objective is standard micro-economic maximisation of welfare. And this, in his view, adds up to little more than 'the old-fashioned economist's concept of optimisation' (Beckerman 1995: 129). As he writes, given 'the acute poverty and environmental degradation in which many of the world's population live, we could not justify using up vast resources in an attempt to preserve from extinction, say, every single one of the several million species of beetle that exist. The cost of such a task would be partly, if not wholly, resources which could otherwise have been devoted to more urgent environmental concerns, such as increasing access to clean drinking water or sanitation in the Third World' (ibid.: 128).

The other side of the coin is presented by advocates of 'strong' sustainability. These analysts suggest that both natural and human-made capital should be held intact separately rather than being elided (Costanza and Daly 1992; Daly 1991; Rees 1990). They regard natural and manufactured capital to be complements rather than substitutes. As Rees puts it, 'more fish boats are no substitute for a depleted fish stock' (Rees 1999: 34). Or in the evocative words of the native American elder: 'only when you have felled the last tree, caught the last fish and polluted the last river will you realise that you can't eat money' (Shiva 1992: 193).

Ultimately the answer is probably to avoid absolutism whilst revering both the earth and its residents. Certainly analysts are keen to avoid a 'growth–no growth' dualism – there is no need for either–or. The World Bank, for example, conventionally a staunch promoter of economic development above all else, has cautioned that the type as well as the amount of any development matters. In its recent document *The Quality of Growth*, it argues that quantity alone is not enough (Thomas *et al.* 2000). Indeed, though critics quickly accused the institution of pandering to political correctness, maintaining that quantity is more important than quality (*The Economist* 2000b), the Bank has repeated this view. It countered that 'Quantity versus quality is a false dichotomy. The two are jointly determined and their interaction is what decides whether the results will be good, bad or indifferent' (Thomas 2000: 142).

Another attempt to reformulate the debate comes from Michael Jacobs at the Fabian Society. He argues that we should use the language of ecological modernisation rather than sustainable development. This, he believes, will be heard more favourably by government and public alike (Jacobs 1999). Certainly, ecological modernisation promotes a win-win approach: starting, as it does, 'from the conviction that the ecological crisis can be overcome by technical and procedural innovation' (Hajer 1996: 249; and see Davoudi,

Chapter 6, this volume). It proposes that 'policies for economic development and environmental protection can be combined to synergistic effect. Rather than seeing environmental protection as a brake on growth, ecological modernisation promotes the application of stringent environmental policy as a positive influence on economic efficiency and technological innovation. Similarly, rather than perceiving economic development to be the source of environmental decline, ecological modernisation seeks to harness forces of entrepreneurship for environmental gain' (Gouldson and Murphy 1997: 94). This certainly seems to suggest that the sustainability circle can be squared.

Whatever the language – be it sustainable development, quality growth or ecological modernisation – it is, perhaps inevitably, the 'win-win' philosophy that has been taken up by politicians. Here sustainable development is presented as a vision of a brighter future, where economic prosperity and environmental enlightenment go hand in hand (DoE 1994a; DETR 1999a). As Margaret Thatcher declared: Governments should espouse 'the concept of sustainable economic development. Stable prosperity can be achieved throughout the world provided the environment is nurtured and safeguarded' (cited in Pearce *et al.* 1989: 183).

Such mantras are widespread. The 1997 European Union Treaty of Amsterdam, for example, submits in Article B that sustainable development is to be achieved, amongst other ways, by promoting the single currency (reproduced in Rudden and Wyatt 1999). The World Trade Organisation exhorts its members to promote 'sustainable trade' and the 1992 international Convention on Biological Diversity signed in Rio espouses the principle of 'sustainable use' (see Layard, Chapter 3, this volume). Similarly, the current British Prime Minister, Tony Blair, makes almost no reference to environmental concerns in his foreword to the 1999 United Kingdom strategy on sustainable development, *Towards a Better Quality of Life*. Instead, he stresses that sustainable development is important to 'ensure that our economy thrives, so we can deliver the schools and hospitals we want, the jobs we need, and provide opportunities for all'. Economic growth must contribute 'to our quality of life, rather than degrading it'. 'And' of course, we must 'all share in the benefits' (DETR 1999a: foreword). Finally, in the guidance to Regional Development Agencies the Department of the Environment, Transport and the Regions states that sustainable development is 'a broad agenda, which includes tackling social exclusion, and increasing prosperity, while improving and protecting the environment' (DETR 2000a: 6). This is quite some list when social exclusion is defined as 'a shorthand term for what can happen when people or areas suffer from a combination of linked problems such as unemployment, poor skills, low incomes, poor housing, high crime environments, bad health, poverty and family breakdown' (Cabinet Office 2000a).

These formulations beg the question. Are such broad, holistic definitions of sustainable development still of use? Can their calls be practicable, their objectives achievable, when the key concerns of sustainability seem to be overridden and ignored in the rush to inclusiveness? It often seems as though quality of life for the current here and now is the priority, and that meaningful concern for intra- and inter-generational equity is increasingly scarce. The focus is domestic, for home-grown electoral consumption. Environmental considerations seem to become lost in a whole wish-list of broader concerns.

Indeed, despite the rhetorical speeches and the theoretical arguments, pollution and other unsustainable activities continue to have documented ill-effects, burdens which invariably affect the poor. Even with the widespread embracing of the sustainable development idea, at a time when average global per capita income exceeds US$5,000 a year, over 1,300 million people still live on less than US$1 a day (UNEP 1999: 2). More significantly, 'of the 4.4 billion people in developing countries, nearly three-fifths lack basic sanitation; a third have no access to clean water; a quarter lack adequate housing; and a fifth have no access to modern health services. About 20 percent of children do not complete 5 years of school, and a similar percentage does not receive enough calories and protein from their diet' (World Bank 1999: 26). In fact, though these are far less extreme, ill-effects are felt in richer economies as well. Air pollution – for example – has documented effects on health. Just one 1991 London incident was reported by the Department of Health to have caused between 100 and 180 excessive deaths (ENDS 1995). Cumulative effects are believed to be responsible for 12,000 and 24,000 advanced deaths and 10–20,000 hospital admissions each year, in addition to many thousands of instances of illness, reduced activity, distress and discomfort (COMEAP 1998). Indeed, the Committee on the Medical Effects of Air Pollutants (COMEAP) who quantified these estimates, stated with 'reasonable confidence' that they had underestimated the full effects (ibid.: 59). Such uncertainty has also been echoed by the Department of the Environment, Transport and the Regions (DETR 1997a). Reports from the Environment Agency also indicate increased concerns over incinerators. One study estimated that 88 people die, and 168 are hospitalised, each year, for lung-related diseases associated with emissions from the country's twelve furnaces for municipal waste (Hencke 2000a, though see also Hencke 2000b). This is at a time when a massive expansion programme of incineration is proposed as the mountains of waste continue to grow (see Davoudi, Chapter 12, this volume).

And so despite the broader focus adopted at the domestic level, many people are still feeling the effects of unsustainable patterns. Their quality of life has yet to improve. In particular, it is perhaps no coincidence that the most dramatic environmental and social threats – food insecurity, land instability, a lack of sanitation, poor housing, energy availability and abused civil rights – make no appearance onto the negotiating timetables at world summits. Some analysts even argue that the international environmental movement is now so dominated by the concerns of the affluent that the primary environmental concerns of the poor are marginalised (McGranahan *et al.* 1999). Certainly, the relative success stories of recent international negotiation – climate change, ozone depletion, biodiversity depletion – are 'big "global" issues' which appear to threaten richer nations directly (O'Riordan 1995). Intra-generational equity seems to be better represented in rhetoric than in reality.

Even future generations may be no better off. Technological innovation may mean that we replace depleted, non-renewable oil, gas and mineral reserves with solar, wind or thermal energy, yet there may still be limits to human ingenuity, or these changes may come too late. The catastrophic effects many expect to result from global warming or the inevitable misery brought on by increased desertification call for the concerted attention of regulators, manufacturers and consumers alike. Indeed, in the meantime it seems that we are warming the earth's atmosphere. The Inter-governmental Panel on Climate Change now project an increase in global mean surface temperature of 1.5 to 6 degrees centigrade between 1990 and 2100 (IPCC 2000). Whether the estimates are best, medium or high, what is clear is that the average rate of warming is expected to be 'greater than any seen in the last 10,000 years' though the changes expected to occur would include 'considerable natural variability'. Similarly, the *Living Planet 2000 Report* estimates that while the state of the earth's natural ecosystems has declined by about 33 per cent over the past thirty years, the ecological pressure of humanity on the earth has increased by about 50 per cent over the same period. This exceeds the biosphere's regeneration rate (WWF 2000).

And yet, however slippery the idea, and despite the difficulties of implementation, all is not lost. A host of organisations and institutions around the world are attempting to integrate core principles of sustainability into their working practice. Officials, representatives and members of the public all recognise that meeting needs, while minimising the impacts of consumption, providing for people of today and not endangering the generations of tomorrow, are important and worthwhile aims. Even if the concept is, as is perhaps inevitable, misused by some, this is no reason to give up on it altogether. As Wackernagel and Rees conclude, the 'deliberate vagueness of the concept, even as defined by Brundlandt, is a reflection of power politics and political bargaining, not a manifestation of insurmountable intellectual difficulty' (Wackernagel and Rees 1995: 64).

Implications for the Planning System

What, then, does all this mean to planners? One view is that planning in the United Kingdom has long taken environmental and other considerations on board, it is just that the language of sustainability dresses them up in new clothes. Another perception is that it has provided a new 'vision' for the planning system with wide-ranging implications (see Davoudi, Chapter 6, this volume). Sustainable development has added to the range of issues included in the mediation of interests with which the planning system is engaged. It has added new criteria, new ways of thinking about relationships and consequences, and new ideals about the 'good city' and the 'good landscape'. It has also raised significant institutional questions about 'who does what', where responsibility lies for addressing environmental issues, who exercises it and what linkages exist to other policy areas. Some academics go even further, arguing that sustainability 'could be called the post-modern equivalent to a grand narrative, replacing the modernist grand narrative of progress which held sway for much of the twentieth century' (Myerson and Rydin in Buckingham-Hatfield and Evans 1996: 23).

In practice, the answer undoubtedly lies somewhere between these extremes. Of course, it is true that care for the environment has always been acknowledged by the planning system in Britain. But, as outlined below, the meaning given to, and the relative significance of environmental issues as compared to other development priorities, have fluctuated over time. Until the turn of the last century the emphasis was on preservation of a pre-industrial past 'for the nation' but 'from the public' (Newby 1990). Immediately after the Second World War, when the framework of the current planning controls emerged, this preservation from development was combined with regulation of development in order to safeguard communities' 'intangible amenities' such as natural beauty and pleasing landscapes. The 1950s' development plans treated the environment as 'functional resources' to be conserved, and as amenities to be enhanced, yet still for human enjoyment and exploitation. They were dominated by an 'aesthetic utilitarian' approach which saw the environment as backcloth and setting (Healey and Shaw 1993). These conceptions of the environment were echoed in Abercrombie's influential *Greater London Plan* (1944) and in particular in its emphasis on protecting the countryside from urban encroachment.

In the 1960s and early 1970s, when the agenda of the wider environmental movement began to focus on tangible issues such as the scarcity of the earth's natural resources, the planning system remained largely preoccupied with accommodating and managing growth and its associated car-based expansion. Development plans, produced in a culture dominated by architects and engineers, continued to treat the environment as a recreational resource and backcloth. This is evident in many New Town plans of the early 1970s such as *Plan for Milton Keynes* (1970) and *Outline Plan* for Central Lancashire (1974) (Davoudi *et al.* 1996). In fact, it was not until the late 1970s that planners took on board the growing initiatives for the environmental care and management resulting from the 1960s' expansion of urban development across the countryside. Plans began to treat the countryside not just as a setting to be conserved, but in terms of natural systems to be safeguarded for their amenity and economic value (Healey and Shaw 1993). Even then, the environmental care and management approach was short-lived. With the recession and less growth to manage, a rising agenda of economic and social problems faced planners and environmental concerns became particularly vulnerable to the public reordering of priorities.

In the 1980s, the Thatcher Administration launched a major attack on the planning system in order to reduce the scope and scale of the planning regulations. As a result, development plans became marginalised and sidelined as out-of-date (Thornley 1993). There had to be a 'presumption in favour of development' in all development control decision-making (DoE 1985, Circular 14/85: 1). Within this pro-development climate, the quality of environment was treated as a commodity which, along with buildings and sites, could be marketised, packaged and traded. This 'marketised utilitarian' conception of the environment was combined with a narrow conception of conservation focused on the heritage landscapes and wildlife sites (Whatmore and Boucher 1993).

By the 1990s the language of sustainability and the request for sustainable development were, as discussed above, well underway. Attention had begun to focus on global environmental change and on issues related to resource depletion and material constraints on rising living standards. Newby (1990) suggests that at this time, 'ecology' replaced 'amenity' as the focus of public debate. This re-emergence of environmental concerns played an important part in the resurgence of the planning system and in particular the development plans. Here it was an established regulatory system which could be used as an excuse by the Thatcher government to resist the EU requirement to set up separate formal environmental impact assessment procedures for major development projects. Thus, the combination of the rising environmental awareness, the central government's political expediency and the collapse of the property boom gave a new lease of life to the planning system. The introduction of the Planning and Compensation Act, 1991, enhanced the status of the development plan and provided the opportunity for local planning authorities to put plans at the centre of decision-making over land use.

As plans moved to centre stage, the most critical challenge they faced was that of sustainable development. Government policy, outlined in Planning Policy Guidance Note (PPG 12), legitimised the role of land-use planning in sustainable development. It urged planners to 'reflect newer environmental concerns such as global warming and the consumption of new renewable resources in the analysis of policies that form part of plan preparation' (DoE 1992a, para. 6.3). Initially the resulting political pressure on planners to 'turn the plans green, overnight' led to some tokenistic approaches such as putting the environment chapter at the beginning of the plan, or providing a list of environmental objectives without having strategies to implement them. But, gradually planners have made genuine attempts to incorporate some of the principles of the 'new' environmental agenda, albeit with limited success (Davoudi *et al.* 1996; Raemaekers 2000). PPG12 marked the beginning of

15

the government's continuing activities in commissioning research, publishing reports and producing policy guidelines on how to interpret and implement the concept of sustainable development.

Indeed, by the turn of the century it is arguable that in the planning system 'the *concept* of sustainable development has been adopted more extensively, and more firmly on a statutory basis, than in any other field' (Owens 1994: 87). However, this is not to say that any systematic transformation of the planning agenda has yet occurred. Despite the elevated status of development plans, the planning system in Britain is still underpinned by a presumption in favour of development which to some is a sign of inherent contradiction with sustainable development. To others, it is the level of scrutiny to which the system subjects proposals that contributes to sustainable development agenda (Raemaekers 2000). Nevertheless, it remains true that government policy on sustainable development and its implementation through planning mechanisms has failed to move beyond weak sustainability (Merrett 1994). At best, it can be seen as ecological modernisation (see Davoudi, Chapter 6, this volume).

Within this agenda, environmental objectives can always be balanced against other issues and none should be regarded as imperatives. Section 4 of the 1998 Regional Development Agency (RDA) Act, for example, outlines the statutory purposes of the RDAs as follows:

1. to promote the economic development and the regeneration of its area;
2. to promote business efficiency, investment and competitiveness in its area;
3. to promote employment in its area;
4. to enhance the development and application of skills relevant to employment in its area;
5. to contribute to the achievement of sustainable development in the UK where it is relevant to its area to do so.

(Cited in RCEP 1999: 7)

As argued by the Royal Commission on Environmental Pollution (1999), the tensions between the first four purposes and the last one soon surfaced in the debates surrounding the examination in public of the Regional Planning Guidance across the country. By assuming that a balance between these objectives can be found, without clarifying limits, priorities and imperatives, the government and by extension the planning system has been able to avoid politically difficult choices. Planners are expected to 'grow the economy, distribute this growth fairly and in the process not degrade the ecosystem' (Campbell 1999: 252). In other words, planners are expected to strike a *balance* between social, economic and environmental goals every time they make a decision on the use and development of land. As Levett (1999) argues, this balancing principle which underpins most planning decisions has poisoned the whole system and doomed the environment to incremental erosion. It sees planners as non-political experts standing in the middle of the triangle of social, economic and environmental objectives and waving the flag of sustainable development. This of course is an illusion. In practice, planners are often confronted with deep-rooted social, economic and environmental conflicts which cannot be wished away through a simple balancing exercise. As Owens argues, planning is 'not simply a technical means by which sustainability is implemented but an important forum through which it is contested and defined' (1994: 87). It is where conflicts may emerge and solutions *have* to be negotiated.

Indeed, as already discussed, the breadth of issues covered within the sustainable development agenda and its holistic nature can detract from core environmental concerns. Similarly, given the discretionary nature of the planning system and its balancing principle, it would be far too easy for the system to be pushed and pulled in different directions and hence, as has happened before, to experience the sidelining of environmental (and social) interests in favour of economic considerations.

But, this is not inevitable. Whilst the holistic concept of sustainable development remains a powerful long-range goal which links issues and provides a policy bridge, the sustainable society is not going to be reached in a single, holistic leap led by planners or indeed any other 'experts'. It has to be sought through day-to-day contested negotiations over land use, transport, housing, property development, waste management and many other policies. It is the outcome of such negotiations which will constitute the evolutionary progression towards more sustainable practices. As O'Riordan suggests:

The most important point to grasp about sustainable development is the paradoxical observation that it will only succeed by capturing and re-directing social and economic change, yet it also has to act as an accumulative role in the myriad of circumstances.

(O'Riordan 2000: 31)

2 The Politics of Sustainable Development

Sue Batty

Introduction

Sustainable development is generally seen as a 'good' thing. Like democracy, no two people understand it in the same way, but few would argue against it (Lafferty 1996). The most quoted definition was given by the Brundtland Commission in its report *Our Common Future*. The Commission defined it as: 'development that meets the needs of the present without compromising the ability of future generations to meet their own needs' (WCED 1987: 23). The logic of sustainable development appears inescapable. On the one hand, scientific evidence is mounting in support of the notion that there are environmental limits to economic growth, and that we are approaching these limits rapidly. On the other hand, there are political and moral limits that suggest we must maintain global economic growth. The Brundtland Report expressed a widely held view that putting the brakes on global economic development is politically unacceptable. But it also argued that it is morally unacceptable to impose such a slowdown on those nations that depend on global growth to pull themselves out of poverty.

Brundtland's definition does not tell planners or economists how to recognise sustainable development or what its main characteristics might be; rather, it is concerned with identifying the problem. It is technically possible to measure and recognise elements of sustainability or the likely success of sustainable policies (as distinct from sustainable development). We might, for example, compare the rate at which particular urban forms exhaust our forests and countryside or use energy reserves, or assess the impact of

19

pollution taxes on land use and behaviour. But the concept of sustainable development asks us to go much further; it calls for ways to resolve the global political problem of the redistribution of scarce and limited resources.

This chapter, therefore, looks at sustainable development as a political concept, not simply as an analytical one. In other words, it is discussed here as a call for action; a concept that will help us to reach consensus rather than one useful for explaining or looking for causes (Lafferty 1996). We look first at the ethical bases for the concept of sustainable development. This discussion then raises a distinction between two moral positions: one based on the accumulation of scientific evidence and the other based on the accumulation of agreement or popular consensus. This distinction has been at the heart of a long-standing debate about the nature of the planning process and the role of science and technology in planning (see Davoudi, Chapter 6, this volume). In essence, the debate started as a backlash against the rise of the strongly analytical and technical 'systems planning' of the 1960s and 1970s. It was also a response to public demands for more participation in land use and environmental decision-making and to demands for a forum for citizen involvement. Many land use planners began to see themselves answering these demands, moving from the technical to the political, and from an ethical position based on scientific evidence towards one based on public acceptability. Now, at the millennium, the debate has reappeared as some local planners see sustainable development as a renewed validation of their role as local providers of a socially inclusive forum for land use and environmental debate. This is occurring at a time when trust in representative democracy is failing and as government scientific advice offers confused and uncertain messages.

The next part of the chapter goes on to discuss democracy, power and public trust in science. An ethic based on scientific evidence is seen by some as inevitably elitist, in the sense that scientific knowledge bestows power on the holder of such knowledge. Scientific evidence has indeed often been used by governments and business interests as a rationale for regulatory power and top-down control. But increasingly, scientific information can be seen as empowering people not governments. Sources of scientific and tech-nological knowledge are now extremely diverse as an increasing range of non-governmental organisations develop the capacity to undertake their own scientific inquiry.

On the other hand, the consensual basis for sustainable development implies a particular form of social and political organisation, specifically, bottom-up, participatory democracy. Indeed, the output of the Rio Conference and Agenda 21 placed strong emphasis on local participatory and inclusive politics. In reality, those who support the notion of sustainable development cover a wide range of political and ethical beliefs, and while some hold communitarian ideals, many assume that sustainable development is inevitably associated with the process of liberal democracy (Patten *et al.*

2000). Others argue the need for an element of authoritarian government or at least strong central regulatory powers (Rydin 1998), while some, such as the group Earth First, tend towards anarchist views. The chapter finally moves on from this debate about the most appropriate forms of government to the form that sustainable politics and sustainable land use planning are currently taking in the United Kingdom at national and local levels.

An Ethical Basis for Sustainable Development and Land Use Planning

The concept of sustainable development is used in different ways for different purposes. Even the same person might use the idea in different ways under different circumstances. This is obviously a problem. Concepts should be transparent; they should allow us to communicate our ideas and beliefs to one another with clarity and without ambiguity. However, sustainable development is a contested concept with no consensus on its meaning (Redclift 1989; Goodin 1996). In fact, the Brundtland Report's use of the concept has been severely criticised as fudging the analytical and normative issues. Brundtland's privileging of human needs is seen by some writers as flawed, leading to the criticism that the Commission adopted the concept in order to obscure the fact that economic growth and physical sustainability are fundamentally incompatible. Others point to the fact that the inconsistencies are not acknowledged: sustainable development 'pulls together diverse ideas and blends them, often uncritically, into an apparent seamless whole' (Adams 1990, in Backstrand *et al.* 1996: 212).

In order to break through some of this confusion and contradiction, we need to understand that the concept is not purely analytical, for in practice few concepts are. We, therefore, need to evaluate the concept of sustainable development in terms of its overall usefulness in guiding our decisions; in other words we need to identify the ethical basis of the concept. William Lafferty (1996) points to two foundations for sustainability: *realism* and *consensualism*. Realism in this context is an appeal to morality based on natural rather than human law. Under this moral argument, our understanding of how the real world works provides the guide to what is right or wrong. Lafferty (1996) reminds us of the wealth of evidence and argument from natural science that has been the impetus for global environmental concern.

The second basis is quite different. Here the moral rightness of consensualism depends on agreement, not scientific truth. It is quite clear that there is widespread international acceptance of the enterprise of sustainable development, even if the means to its achievement are contested. Despite the range of interpretations of the concept, there is a clear global commitment expressed in the Rio Declaration such as Agenda 21 and the climate change and bio-diversity conventions. Lafferty's analysis clearly has validity in that it strongly reflects the interests of the Brundtland Commission. The Brundtland Report returns frequently to the twin concerns of science and social decision-making, for example in referring to 'The idea of limitations imposed by the state of technology and social organisation on the environment's ability to meet present and future needs' (WCED 1987: 43).

We can now ask the question whether traditional land use planning has a similar foundation. There is little doubt that the land use planners of the 1940s and 1950s would have felt a lot of sympathy for the practice of sustainable development, if not with these ethics. The traditional planner's moral foundation would have been that of public welfare derived from a history of utopian socialism, philanthropic paternalism, and intervention by government to safeguard public health. In the United Kingdom, planning was generated as a professional, but primarily humanitarian, response to the concerns of an emerging discipline of public environmental health. The weight of scientific evidence was limited and the norms were those of a professional elite. The common cause that generated planning as a statutory and political activity in most Western industrialised countries was the unconstrained spread of urban development with its economic and environmental problems. The causes may have been universal but the moral justification varied across the world, from the protection of public amenity and convenience to the protection of individual profits and land development rights. The norms of planning have largely been seen as a national concern, legitimated in different ways for different countries and at different times.

Whatever the moral imperative, the stimuli are identical to those of sustainable development – pollution and the exhaustion of resources through urbanisation and industrialisation, and the inequitable distribution of the burden of living in the resulting degraded environment. The difference between the traditional and the current political and professional responses lies partly in the perception of scale and complexity. Traditionally, governments, planners and people perceived and responded to problems as single issues; single causes with local implications and local solutions. The problems were primarily seen as physical, affecting health, convenience and efficiency. In the United Kingdom, the Town and Country Planning Acts dealing primarily with physical land use were an example, but we can also point to a long history of such piecemeal legislation. Important examples are the 1863 and 1906 Alkali Acts dealing with industrial pollution, the Clean Air Act of 1956 which removed the infamous London smogs, and the Wildlife and Countryside Act of 1982 (see Layard, Chapter 3, this volume).

By contrast, the enterprise of sustainable development is characteristically global in scope and has been driven by the coming together of two rather different moral arguments: the existence of limits to our global natural resources and the problems of unequal human needs and access to these resources. These two understandings are set within an awareness of the complexity of environmental interconnections and the global implications of local policy and activity. Rydin (1999) reminds us that the environmental and land use planning problems that the richer nations now see as traditional or historical, still exist for developing nations. She characterises such problems as occurring in two waves. The richer nations now seek solutions to problems generated by consumption patterns related to lifestyles, which generate diffuse pollution problems. These are seen by Rydin as the second wave of environmental and planning problems. The first wave were problems of production processes – industrial processes, primary and secondary manufacturing processes generating point-source pollution. Clearly, different problems point to different solutions and political processes.

Power and Democracy

We need to ask how these moral arguments of consensualism and evidence-based realism translate into political structures for action and the capacity or power to act. Power can be defined as the ability of one agent to make another do what he or she wants. Power is at the heart of politics, and political responses to environmental crises have traditionally turned to controls, regulations and legislation. Much of the writing and debate in sustainable development has revolved around the redistribution of power and the importance of social and political inclusion in decision-making.

However, power, like sustainable development and democracy, is another contested concept. As well as understanding power as *having power over another*, it can also be understood as capacity or ability; *having the power to act* (Doyle and McEachern 1998). In the case of sustainable development we are particularly concerned about *having the power to act collectively*. The sustainability crisis is generally seen as a crisis of finite limits but the sustainable development response interprets it as a crisis of collective behaviour. Individual demands can compromise the collective good. This is probably best illustrated by Ghandi's often quoted reminder that 'the earth has enough for everyone's needs but not for some people's greed' (quoted in Shiva 2000: 79).

Power as the capacity for collective action

This idea of power as a *capacity for collective action* has a long history in early political writings, for example, those of Jean-Jacques Rousseau. But in more recent years, it is the 1960s era that reminds us most potently of the dangers of individual action and of the power of cooperation. The 1960s and early 1970s are often identified as the first stage of public awareness of the global environmental crisis (Eckersley 1996; Elliot 1998). At this time, the growing scientific evidence of global environmental problems led to mass protests, the rise of environmental groups, the rise of the New Left and the call for more public involvement in policy and decision-making. The publication of articles and books such as Rachel Carson's *Silent Spring* (1962), Garrett Hardin's 'Tragedy of the Commons' (1968), Paul Ehrlich's *Population Bomb* (1972), and the Club of Rome's *Limits to Growth* (Meadows *et al.* 1972) presented powerful arguments about the finite limits of our planet and were an urgent call to action. But although the scientific messages were pessimistic, there were also some ideas that appeared politically optimistic. The notion that political power was necessarily 'zero-sum' – in other words, if you win, I lose – was retreating before the idea of the 'positive sum game', where everyone can win . . . or everyone can lose.[1]

The message of Hardin's 'Tragedy of the Commons' was indeed pessimistic. He argued that land and other resources available for common use, such as public open spaces, common grazing land and commonly held fisheries would inevitably become overused, because there would be no incentive for anyone to limit their use of the property. If, for example, common land is in danger of overgrazing, any individual gets their best outcome from continuing to graze their animals at the same or a greater rate, as long as others limit their grazing. The best overall result would be cooperation such that everyone limits their activities and thus reduces the likelihood of overgrazing. Neither of these outcomes is likely, because each individual argues 'without agreements or regulations, no-one else will stop their activities so why should I lose out completely?'. The most likely outcome is everyone grazing as many animals as possible and a rapid deterioration of the land. In other words, according to Hardin, we are all likely to lose in this positive sum game.[2] The only way to move to the position where 'everyone wins' is to ensure collective action, but Hardin's solution was not cooperation but the privatisation of interests in common goods and properties to provide an incentive to control the use of the property. So, although the problem was clearly identified by Hardin as a lack of agreement and a lack of collective or political will, the solution he suggested was not based on consensus but on private rights and duties. The most appropriate governmental system to implement such a policy was a liberal market-based democracy such as that associated with the United States.

Democracy, scarce resources and authoritarian government

Although many writers assume that sustainable development inevitably means liberal democracy (Patten *et al.* 2000), there are historical and geographical examples of arguments in favour of authoritarian government as an appropriate form of government to deliver a sustainable environmental future. As an example, Eckersley (1996) reminds us that the 1970s were a pessimistic era, both politically and environmentally. Authors such as William Ophuls and Robert Heibroner argued that the environmental emergencies we faced were so extreme as to call for authoritarian political structures.

Survival was at stake and only authoritarian regimes would have the power to compel us to change our consumption patterns. The argument suggested that democratic institutions are vulnerable to situations of scarce resources and need a certain amount of prosperity. This was also a pessimistic view of government as well as of environmental limits (Paehlke 1996). However, the view has been expressed, in less extreme form, in relation to government and land use planning. This view does not go so far as to insist on authoritarian regimes but does suggest that some nations need to retain 'top-down', highly centralised forms of planning.

A good example of such a call for a centralised and technocratic approach is given by Yvonne Rydin (1999) in her report of a United Nations' Economic Commission for Europe (UN-ECE) Congress. Rydin noted that their meeting in Madrid on urban and regional research identified a 'deep split' in the process of achieving a sustainable urban form (Rydin 1999: 61). The best planning outcomes were generally understood and agreed, but the choice of political processes and structures revealed strong disagreements. Delegates from most of the developed and stable countries assumed that their belief in new patterns of 'environmental governance', characterised by public participation and a plurality of agencies, would be generally agreed. They were surprised to find considerable resistance from transitional governments as well as countries such as Spain and Greece. The approach favoured by transitional and developing countries took on the characteristics of traditional planning and government, a process dependent on the technical expertise of the planner, with public involvement only in individual projects (Rydin 1999). Politically and economically, the interests and priorities of these societies are very different from stable economies. Urgent problems of poverty and resources such as housing and energy, push the sustainable development equation towards the priority of economic growth and development through inward investment. Accountability is more likely to be felt towards foreign investors and foreign aid donors, while political stability depends urgently on meeting the needs of the current rather than the future generation.

The second concern is the fact that such transitional and developing economies are still operating within a process of political and institutional learning. The community also is in the process of political learning, rapidly moving towards the democratic maturity needed for participatory democracy. A mature democratic society arguably needs democratic institutions throughout its society; from family and school to the workplace, in order to educate citizens in the processes and expectations of a democratic process. This is the argument of 'congruence' between civil society and government that has long been made by scholars of democracy such as Carole Pateman (1970). The development of these forms throughout a society takes time to mature. The irony of this situation is that new forms of governance prioritise the understanding of the uniqueness of communities as against universal 'one size fits all' policies. This view might need to stretch very widely if it is to allow for the traditional forms of technocratic planning and top-down government that Rydin advocates. In the next section we look at this emerging local form of governance and the way national government is responding, particularly in the United Kingdom. We also look at the impact on environmental programmes and land use planning.

New Forms of Governance

Local governance and Local Agenda 21

Increasingly, the emerging pattern of local level governance is limiting the power of elected local government and the traditional professional and technical role of the land use planner. Elected local government is becoming just one of a plurality of public and private sector agencies, Quasi-Autonomous Non-Governmental Organisations (QUANGOs), private sector companies and Non-Governmental Organisations (NGOs), all involved in land use planning and the local political process. At the same time, there is a commitment towards government accountability, public participation and transparency of decisions, demonstrated in the United Kingdom by central government's programme of local government reform and modernisation. However, the governmental rhetoric of accountability has met with limited response from the public. Trust in government and confidence in institutional science are declining.

This decline in confidence has run parallel to a rise in public sympathy and trust in local interest groups and NGOs. Jim Skea (1999) cites the responses to a MORI Poll in 1998 on public trust. Seventy-five per cent of people questioned on 'who they would trust for information about the environment' selected NGO scientists. Only 46 per cent would trust government scientists and only 43 per cent, industry scientists. Skea attributes much of this loss of faith to food scares such as BSE and food uncertainties such as those surrounding genetically modified (GM) foods. This has certainly had some influence, but the increasing complexity of environmental science often leaves scientists unable to give clear-cut answers. Institutional scientists are unable to satisfy popular expectations for rapid and definitive information. Friends of the Earth or Greenpeace are able to be much more selective about the issues they tackle and the scientific evidence they offer. The presentation of an advocacy case by NGOs can suggest a certainty that is impossible for government scientists to match.

It is clear, however, that some local elected representatives and officers see the sustainable development project as a means of bringing local government in from the cold and reasserting its role as more than a limited service provider, particularly through the Local Agenda 21 programme. Agenda 21 is the comprehensive programme generated after the Rio Earth Summit to guide global activity. Chapter 28 of the Agenda stresses the importance of local participation and social inclusion in decision-making processes. In the United Kingdom much of our response has been in the form of the Local Agenda 21 (LA21) programme. The programme has generated a strong following and appears now to be the principal means of achieving the local environmental agenda and accommodating the environmentalists' pressures towards constitutional reform. However, Selman and Parker (1999: 47) note that this enthusiasm for Local Agenda 21 is matched by a 'degree of scepticism about its ability seriously to influence patterns of production and consumption'.

Even so, some local authority planners view this new initiative as an opportunity to open up the profession to diverse forms of knowledge. Many appear to see it as a means of extending their competence into new areas of unique professional and technical expertise, while others focus on the potential for LA21 processes to improve inter-departmental organisation and working practices. There are a number of different agendas being pursued here. Sustainable development is being used by some groups to add respectability to the NIMBY (Not-In-My-Back-Yard) defence against all forms of local development; by others as a first step to a society no longer based on the perpetual growth of consumption and production.

It is clear from case studies of LA21 experience and from planners' experience that results are not yet matching the enthusiasm and personal commitment generated by local sustainable development programmes. We may acknowledge the argument that: 'Although new political impetus has been given to LA21 and it has generated a remarkable amount of interest, it is still generally run on a shoestring and, objectively, must be seen as a fragile activity within byzantine bureaucracies' (Selman and Parker 1999: 58). Until the organisation of local government catches up with the expectations raised by sustainable development initiatives, the whole enterprise will certainly remain fragile.

National government and the Green agenda

The rise of environmentalism in terms of the plurality of environmental lobbies, interest groups and Green political parties has included an agenda for constitutional reform based on openness in government, minority representation and subsidiarity. Ward (1996: 150) identifies the major element of the Green constitutional agenda in the United Kingdom as a move towards the devolution of power, allowing decisions to be made at the lowest feasible level (the subsidiarity principle). Electoral reform towards proportional representation at all levels of government, elected regional assemblies and the dismantling of official secrecy are also important aspects of their agenda. There is also a very strong ethic in the Green movement arguing not just for this more decentralised and inclusive form of representative government, but the need to move to a more participatory style of democracy.

These demands are clearly aimed at the whole framework of politics in the United Kingdom, and, indeed, some limited progress has occurred under the present Labour administration. While the government has not moved towards proportional representation in national or local authority elections, limited changes have occurred in the elections for the devolved Welsh Assembly and the Scottish Parliament as well as in the European elections. The government has responded to the importance of the environmental agenda by setting up a Cabinet Committee on the Environment to coordinate sustainable development policy. In addition, there is a commitment to include environmental concerns in all areas of government policy through a system of 'Green Ministers' who ensure that environmental concerns are integrated into the work of each department. An inter-departmental group on inter-national development deals with environmental and resource issues relevant to developing countries (Cabinet Office 2000b).

Supra-national and regional government

We are increasingly aware that environmental and planning problems do not respect national boundaries. Historically environmental concerns tended to be single issues such as 'Save the Whales', and the movement for 'clean beaches'. These were issues that could be tackled by a single government agency or at least were confined within a single nation. Increasingly the environmental and sustainability agenda has moved on to global problems of climate change, ozone depletion, bio-diversity and global pollution. No single nation can tackle these global resource problems alone. Equally, trans-boundary pollution and resource depletion squabbles between countries abound, such as fishing quota conflicts, and the conflicts between Britain and Scandinavia on acid rain pollution.

There is no global government to resolve such conflicts, but of course, this does not mean that there are no global politics. Nations enter into treaties and agreements, and sanctions are imposed on those who fail to maintain expected standards. The availability of trade, foreign aid, foreign investment and loans are used both as carrot and stick by nations and multinational firms to enforce conformity. But social and political sanctions can also be effective: from the cutting of formal ambassadorial links between countries to the boycotting of international public events such as the Olympic Games.

Linking the local and the global

Supra-national power in the sense of the capacity to act is increasing. This can be seen formally in the ever-widening authority of supra-national groupings such as the European Union. It can be seen informally through increasing levels of public awareness of global issues and increasing capacity to act globally. The rise of the Internet and international news and communication media has provided a major boost to the organisation of protest at both national and global levels, apparent for example at the anarchist, anti-capitalist protests against the World Trade Organisation meetings at Seattle and Prague.

On the other hand, linking the global and the local through supra-national power has also freed cities and regions to compete globally rather than through the nation. Jim Skea (1999) warns that, while 'Attracting inward investment and promoting economic development are rightly key priorities. . . . If interregional competition results in the driving down of local standards in order to attract cost-conscious investors, then the sustainable development of a specific region may be compromised.' The argument, however, is not an argument against multinational firms but a warning about the potential effect of sub-national competition. Skea points out that many, if not most, large businesses are highly sensitive to the changing demands of their customers and are rapidly enforcing eco-friendly standards in their business and their products. The retail industry in the United Kingdom, for example, has shown an ability to react much more quickly than government to environmental scares such as BSE and GM foods. The real issue is that there is often a conflict between 'the global good' and the priorities of local communities. This can range from the subsistence activities of rain-forest communities to the NIMBY arguments of wealthy estate owners. 'Acting in the global good could attract local resistance leaving agencies caught in the middle' (Skea 1999).

In the United Kingdom, following devolution of authority to the Scottish Parliament, and Assemblies for Wales, London and the Regions, sustainable development has been incorporated as a fundamental principle for these new authorities. While the addition of this regional level of agencies and authorities can, as Skea argues, act as a bridge between national or global and local, it is also clear that such a proliferation of agencies can also lead to shifting bases of power. This, of course, is one of the traditional strengths of liberal, pluralist regimes – the existence of checks and balances against wrongly used power. But, if we interpret power positively, we must also interpret these layers of agencies, with their competing priorities, as a constraint on the ability to develop the capacity to act as a collective. This is especially true of immature democracies or nations moving to democracy where the process of political learning needs effective and stable role models.

Conclusion

The account we have given here suggests a roller coaster ride of good intentions, pessimism and optimism. There are signs that the political will is present to move to a sustainable and equitable future but only if present standards of living are not seriously compromised. The realism of the scientific threat of environmental degradation has been a powerful force towards political rhetoric. However, the *consensualism* of changing public attitudes has probably had most influence on results, through local collective action, the growth of the power of civil society and through protests on the streets.

When this chapter was being written, Britain was faced with the combination of life-threatening floods and the discovery of a dangerous rail infrastructure. The combined effect has led to massive disruption of rail journeys and a consequent substantial percentage increase in private car use. To add to the chaos, the People's Fuel Lobby has shown its anger at rising oil prices and high taxes on petrol, by slow lorry convoys and the barricading of oil depots and petrol stations. In Europe, the United Nations Framework Convention on Climate Change (UNFCCC) meeting in The Hague has just failed to ratify the 1997 Kyoto agreements on reductions in greenhouse gas emissions. Negotiations between Europe and the 'umbrella' group of United States of America, Japan, and Australia floundered on the extent to which these countries could plant forests as 'carbon sinks' instead of reducing their carbon gas emissions.

The science of sustainable development is limited by the contradictions. Nature is a poor teacher offering us confusing and contradictory messages. Unfortunately, as we have seen, responses to natural phenomena such as floods and transport disruptions are too frequently emergency responses, survival responses that threaten the long-run solution. Changing mind-sets through science and observation needs clear and timely evidence, and without this, scientists are discredited and governments distrusted. Scientific evidence as a path towards sustainable development objectives is tortuous at best.

So what of consensus as a basis for action? As we have seen in The Hague, democratic governments know that their best route to re-election is to demonstrate that they can deliver a comfortable life and a thriving economy. Government ministers in international negotiation know that even if they agree a reduction in the use of fuel, and in the emission of polluting gases, they will have to sell the argument at home. They will have to change behaviours. In liberal democracies and mixed economies, this is likely to mean the use of the market as well as consensual politics. It means rationing through price as well as regulatory and redistributive policies. As Garrett Hardin (1968) warned us, there is no incentive for individuals (nations or persons) to limit their use or to limit their pollution, when others cannot be restricted in *their* use. The argument of the 'Tragedy of the Commons', is still compelling, still inequitable and still far from socially just.

Notes

1 Used in this context, a 'game' is a way of describing and analysing a situation where individuals make decisions that affect each other, in other words, strategic decisions. In a positive sum game, if the individuals can communicate and cooperate, they can move to a situation where the overall rewards for all involved

are greater than if they act independently. Mutual cooperation also leads to long-term stability because no individual can then improve their position by taking action on their own. This situation is called in economics 'Pareto Optimality'.

2   The general form of game described here and used by Hardin to model the 'Tragedy of the Commons' was the well-known Prisoners' Dilemma Game. The story of this game involves two prisoners kept in separate cells without communication. They are told that if they inform on the other prisoner, they will be set free, if the other prisoner informs on them they will have a very long sentence, if both inform they get a short sentence and if neither informs there is no evidence to convict and they are both set free. The latter is obviously the best outcome, but the least likely, because failing to inform risks a long sentence if the other prisoner chooses to inform. The most likely outcome is that both will inform and receive short sentences.

Further Reading

For a comprehensive account of political thought and environmental policy read James Connelly and Graham Smith (1999) *Politics and the Environment: From Theory to Practice*. Timothy Doyle and Doug McEachern (1998) *Environment and Politics* provide an interesting comparative account using a range of worldwide examples. The government policy on sustainable development has been set out in a White Paper published 17 May 1999: *A Better Quality of Life: A Strategy for Sustainable Development for the United Kingdom* which can be found on their web site at http://www.detr.gov.uk/sustainable/quality/index.htm.

3 The Legal Framework of Sustainable Development

Antonia Layard

Definitions of sustainable development differ. As the introductory chapter has already suggested, such a lack of uniformity is perhaps welcome: to be effective, the concept must be informed by local context as much as by universal ideals. Inevitably, the practical implementation of sustainable development principles varies as well. Some countries have instituted a system of high profile plans and strategies, others have left core precepts to be developed by local groups; many have undertaken a combination of the two. Few, however, have implemented visionary or demanding laws.

What is clear, however, is that differences in the formalisation of ideas relating to sustainable development cannot hide a core set of shared ideas. Key elements of the principle can be made out. First, comes the recognition that sustainable development must balance differing concerns, particularly economic, social and environmental factors. Second, is a focus on justice both between generations (inter-generational equity) and within generations (intra-generational equity). Third, is the view – in some countries at least – that core principles may have a part to play. In particular, that prevention is better than cure, that the polluter should pay and that damage should best be rectified at source. They also emphasise the importance of adopting a precautionary approach. Finally, there is a new focus on participation, promoted only in part by Local Agenda 21 (see Mittler chapter and Batty chapter). All of these aspects have some form of legal underpinning.

To explain these interlinking systems, this chapter begins by giving an overview of the legal framework for sustainable development in United Kingdom, European Union and public international law. Inevitably, constraints of space render such a discussion illustrative rather than conclusive. Having described these basics, however, the second section then illustrates two important 'structural' issues, crucial to understanding any legislative or judicial regime relating to sustainable development. These are, first, that *legal intervention can occur on a variety of levels and that this is generally determined by principles of legal responsibility and political authority rather than the end to be achieved*. Sovereignty – rather than sustainability – is the key determinant of the legal regime in place. And second, that so far at least, *the legal framework has been concerned with protecting the environment and human health rather than implementing the broad dictates of sustainability*. It is taking some time to adopt a more holistic approach.

Finally, the chapter ends by discussing prospects for the future. It suggests first that one of the most important aspects of sustainable development has yet to be implemented in legal form. The promotion of intra- and inter-generational equity, so central to the Brundlandt Commission's concerns, is the exception rather than the rule. Court cases and rights of intervention stress the rights of humans alive today, acting within their own jurisdiction. The interests of peoples living overseas, in generations to come or even of species at risk, are difficult, though not impossible, to protect. This threatens to undermine a key aspect of thinking on sustainable development. A second question is whether the legal architecture so far established has any value, if, as it so often appears, enforcement is the weak link in the chain. Operators break licensing conditions to little condemnation, while countries can if they wish openly flout rules of international law. Do these limitations confirm what the cynic already suggests; that the promotion of sustainable development is more rhetoric than reality? Or is it a mistake to see legal rules in isolation from their political context, particularly with a movement as slow and ponderous as sustainable development? This will be the chapter's final concern.

Before venturing in, however, it is important to clarify one key set of distinctions at the outset. For the demarcation between national, European Union and public international law is crucial and, if this chapter is to make sense, these differences need to be clarified. Starting then at the national level, the law consists of Acts and Statutory Instruments passed by the Queen in Parliament; these instruments have the approval of the House of Commons, the House of Lords and the Sovereign. Laws are supplemented by cases, decided by judges, in courts, which themselves have law-making capacity in common law countries (such as England and Wales). Indeed, here a further distinction should be made – between the law of England and Wales, Scotland and Northern Ireland. Though substantially similar, differences between these three do continue, maintained on historical and constitutional grounds.

Acting collectively as the United Kingdom, however, the government can, and does, enter into regional arrangements with other countries. The most obvious instance of such legal, economic and political cooperation on a regional level is the European Union. It is here that fifteen 'Member States' make laws (predominantly in the form of Directives and Regulations) and empower judges to decide cases arising under those laws (in the European Court of Justice). The United Kingdom is a committed, if not always enthusiastic, Member State. Finally, all countries in the world can come together to create (or confirm) public international law. When treaties are signed to prevent climate change or encourage world trade, it is public international law that is being made.

Of course these different 'levels' of law subsist and inter-relate. Legislation to prevent climate change, for example, is implemented at the public international, European Union and national level, and in each sphere, inconsistent laws permitting the production of greenhouse gases all still persist. To explain the inter-relationships and differences between these different forms of law, this chapter will now give a brief overview of the legal framework for sustainable development in each sphere.

The Framework of United Kingdom, European Union and Public International Law on Sustainable Development

United Kingdom Law

The legal framework on sustainable development in the United Kingdom is notable for its emphasis on the administrative and institutional framework rather than the introduction of substantive 'sustainability' laws. What this means in practice is that organisations and agencies are often required to have regard to 'sustainable development' but there is no legal control over what they decide.

One early example of this pattern was the National Heritage (Scotland) Act of 1991 which held that the Agency, Scottish Natural Heritage, must have regard to the 'desirability of securing' sustainable development. Such an aim was also imposed on the recently created Environment Agency by the Environment Act of 1995 where section 4 says that the Agency's 'principal aim . . . in discharging its functions' to protect or enhance the environment, is to be the making of a 'contribution towards attaining the objective of achieving sustainable development'. In achieving this end, the Agency is to consider policy guidance rather than binding laws. One such document is the 1999a White Paper *Our Quality of Life*, where the government made a commitment to consider incorporating the sustainable development principle as a legal goal for any newly created body (DETR 1999a). And increasingly, this is a route legislators seem to be keen to take. The Welsh Assembly (discussed further below), Regional Development Agencies and the Greater London Authority, are all, for example, required to take account of sustainable development (s. 121 of the Government of Wales Act, 1998, s.4(e) of the Regional Development Agencies Act, 1998 and s.30(4) of the Greater London Authority Act, 1999, respectively). Indeed, the Local Government Act of 2000 will require each local authority to promote social, economic and environmental well-being. To do this it is to prepare a strategy (referred as a community strategy) to promote or improve these sources of well-being while also 'contributing to the achievement of sustainable development in the United Kingdom' (in sections 2 and 4 respectively).

And so it is evident that when considering the precise legal regime for sustainable development, the emphasis is more on structure than on content. There is no general legislative regime on sustainable development though different aspects of the paradigm – economic, social and environmental regulation – do of course exist. Though this chapter cannot review all these areas, it will briefly discuss environmental and conservation legislation in the United Kingdom. For it is likely that it is from these foundations that more substantive legislation on sustainability will grow.

Indeed despite England's reputation as 'the dirty man of Europe' English environmental laws have existed for many years. As early as the thirteenth century, problems caused by the burning of sea coal required a Commission to investigate the problem in 1285 though it is suspected that this body, together with Royal Commissions banning its use, had little practical effect. Certainly, urban pollution increased, with a series of smogs in cities and towns – culminating in the 'Great Smog' of 1952 and causing an estimated 4,000 deaths. This, finally, was the spur for the Clean Air Act of 1956 (Clapp 1994) which marked a milestone in pollution law and policy by regulating both industry and homes, prohibiting the burning of coal in densely populated areas.

Throughout the subsequent decades, legislation continued to be introduced, albeit in rather an *ad hoc* fashion focusing on one issue at a time – the Rivers (Prevention of Pollution) Acts of 1951 and 1961, for example, and the Deposit of Poisonous Wastes Act in 1972. Vital rejuvenation of the scheme occurred in 1990 with the introduction of the Environmental Protection Act (EPA), and this, together with the Water Resources Act of 1991, went some way to herald in a new era, closing many gaps and loopholes in the existing law. Consolidation continued in the Environment Act of 1995, which also created the Environment Agency, merging the National Rivers Authority with Her Majesty's Inspectorate of Pollution. These were significant initiatives and ones that have brought increasing substantive and institutional coherence to the law. At the turn of the century, government-sponsored Acts now coordinate with policy initiatives, and broad legislative thresholds are fleshed out by detailed statutory guidance.

The present system now focuses on the key environmental media of air, water, waste and soil, and though enforcement practices are not always as strict as might be expected (see below), a legal framework at least is now firmly in place. It includes the 1990 Environmental Protection Act and the Clean Air Act of 1993, implementing the system of air pollution control (APC) as well as the 1989 Water Act and the 1991 Water Resources Act coordinating mechanisms to minimise water pollution. Part I of the 1990 Environmental Protection Act sets out the lynchpin of the regime, the system of integrated pollution control (IPC) being in the process of updating to become Integrated Pollution Prevention and Control (IPPC) under a 1996 European Union Directive and the Pollution Prevention Control Act of 1999. Meanwhile, Part III of the 1990 EPA also sets out a 'cradle to grave' system for waste (Davoudi, Chapter 6, this volume) and the long-awaited Contaminated Land Regulations issued in 2000.

Perhaps inevitably, with the exception of IPC where the movement is reversed, this system is only partly home grown. So much so, for example, that four-fifths of our environmental legislation is estimated to have originated in Brussels (RCEP 1998; Haigh and Lanigan 1995). This is particularly true when it comes to nature conservation – where the key pieces of legislation, particularly the Wildlife and Countryside Act of 1981 and the Conservation (Natural Habitats) Regulations of 1994 have been introduced as a response to Union-wide laws.

Again, however, it is striking that the vast majority of this legislative framework is concerned with environmental protection rather than sustainable development. Broad-based intervention is hard to find. In particular, legislation aimed at controlling pollution has conventionally been rather 'one dimensional' focusing on just one environmental media – air, water or land – at a time. It is left to more recent developments such as IPC and IPPC to adopt a more holistic stance.

One way of developing a more holistic approach is to integrate sustainability into new policies, for example, the Blair government's focus on social exclusion. They define this as 'a shorthand term for what can happen when people or areas suffer from a combination of linked problems such as unemployment, poor skills, low incomes, poor housing, high crime environments, bad health, poverty and family breakdown'. The government claim to be tackling the issue through initiatives on welfare to work, school improvement and strengthening civil rights for disabled people, as well as implementing the national childcare strategy, reviewing pensions, setting up the Low Pay Commission and releasing capital receipts to improve housing stock (Cabinet Office 2000a). And this is certainly one area where sustainability thinking could be applied, as Friends of the Earth have been quick to point out. 'The poorest families,' they report (noting average household incomes below £5,000) 'are twice as likely to have a polluting factor close by than those with average household incomes over £60,000.' This, they conclude, 'is the sharp end of social exclusion' (Friends of the Earth 2000: 1). Such a campaign is assuredly one way to promote a more holistic approach. It might even lead (as in the United States) to legislative intervention to protect such principles of environmental justice (Layard 1999).

European Union Law

As an institution, the European Economic Community (as it then was) was relatively slow in adopting the language of sustainability. It was not until the 1980s that references to the principle were made in even the (legally non-binding) preambles to key agreements. The 1957 Treaty of Rome, for example, establishing the European European Community, as well as Euratom, the European Atomic Energy Treaty, had contained no explicit provisions relating to the environment. This had been rectified in 1986 in the Single European Act when environmental protection became an increasingly important part of the Community's work. Yet it was not until 1992 at Maastricht, that the Union even began to use the language of sustainability, and even then it was strained. Article G, for example, set out the task of promoting 'a harmonious and balanced development of economic activities' and 'sustainable and non-inflationary growth respecting the environment'. Now the 1997 Treaty of Amsterdam has gone even further. The revised Article 2 of the European Community Treaty now makes promoting 'balanced and sustainable development of economic activities' a main goal of Community policy. It states that 'Environmental protection requirements must be integrated into the definition and implementation of Community policies and activities . . . in particular with a view to promoting sustainable development.'

The key innovation in developing a Community policy on environmental (and sustainability issues) was, however, the 1986 Single European Act. For in addition to making it much easier to pass legislation related to harmonisation by enabling qualified majority voting, it first set out a clear constitutional basis for the Community's environmental policy. In particular, Articles 130r, s and t, formally define the goals and procedures of Community environmental policies. They state that Community policy on the environment is to preserve, protect and improve the quality of the environment; protect human health; promote the prudent and rational use of natural resources and promote measures at an international level to deal with regional or worldwide environmental problems. As a result of these changes, the volume of new environmental legislation reached a peak from 1987 to 1992 (Axelrod and Vig 1999), perhaps the Community's 'golden era' (Ward 1997: 178). Certainly, it set in motion a wide range of environmental laws and requirements and in 1990 the European Environment Agency was founded to complement the work of DG XI, the Environment Directorate of the Commission. Largely advisory, its primary role is to gather information and data on the state of the environment within the Community. Nevertheless, it is another tangible link in the Community's environmental (and in future, sustainability) chain.

These institutions supplement legislation – Framework Directives, for example, on air, water and waste or intervention to promote conservation;

in particular the 1979 Birds Directive which combines with the 1994 Habitats Directive to set up a system of protected sites known as Natura 2000. Agriculture is also increasingly under environmental scrutiny, be it concerns over BSE, genetically modified foods or using subsidies to promote sustainable practice. In all these areas, legal instruments formalise the policy compromises politicians reach.

However, once again the European Union has rarely so far implemented its aims and exhortations on sustainability into legislation. In substance its focus remains predominantly environmental. There is certainly potential for such a shift, particularly in the holistic instruments it espouses to promote better practice. For example, the eco-management and audit scheme (EMAS) encourages selected industries to improve their environmental performance by establishing and implementing environmental management systems by companies. These are then systematically, and objectively, evaluated on a regular basis. The system has even been extended to the public sphere by the Local Government Management Board (1998). Their application aims to offer a systematic framework for a local authority to assess and reconsider its environmental impacts. Bodies state their environmental aims, identify their environmental effects, decide what actions to take and monitor and report on progress. The question is whether this can now be extended to include social and economic effects as well.

A similar transition is underway in the context of environmental impact assessment. Here, for example, commentators argue that health (BMA 1998) and other social factors could, and should, be taken into account. This is a route also open to 'strategic' assessment, which will systematically review not only projects but also policies and plans. A forthcoming directive will finally require assessments for plans and programmes likely to have 'significant environmental effects'. There is no reason why this could not be extended to cover other aspects of sustainability as well.

Another striking aspect of the European Union environmental legal framework has been its commitment to increased access to information. This clearly has important implications for the promotion of sustainable development, particularly to the extent that it furthers participation. A 1990 Directive requires public authorities with responsibilities for the environment to make environmental information available (at a reasonable cost) to any person who requests it. Like environmental impact assessment, this was another initiative the United Kingdom government initially opposed arguing that it would not add anything to current procedures (Haigh 1998). Indeed, this legislation has now been supplemented by the 1998 Aarhus Convention negotiated under the auspices of the Council of Europe (a larger organisation than the European Union). This continues to strengthen rights to information, participation and access to justice for individuals and non-governmental organisations. Member States have all signed up and are now in the process of ratification.

All in all then, it is worth noting that in its creation of an integrated environmental regime, the European Union regime has come in for lavish praise. American commentators, for example, conclude that with these and other developments, it 'has created the most comprehensive regional environmental protection regime in the world'. (Axelrod and Vig 1999: 75). The Union certainly goes further than merely promoting free trade having often required States to raise their level of environmental engagement. The most obvious threat to such high standards is now the prospect of enlargement. Twelve countries are on the brink of entry, including ten Eastern European States, Cyprus and Turkey. 'The danger', according to Vig and Axelrod is that 'what is already a "multi-speed" Europe could lose all sense of direction as the potentials for harmonization fade' (ibid.: p. 95). As ever, legal and political factors are inextricably intertwined.

Public international law

What is public international law? And how does it affect sustainable development? Its sources were set out in 1945 in the Statute of the International Court of Justice (ICJ) where the two most important are first, 'international conventions, whether general or particular, establishing rules expressly recognised by the contesting states' and second, 'international custom, as evidence of a general practice accepted as law' (Article 38(1), set out in Brownlie 1995: 448). Conventions are legally binding agreements between States, otherwise known as treaties; custom requires more explanation. It is said to be established when a State or court can point to 'constant and uniform usage, accepted as law' (*Asylum Case* ICJ 1950: 266) and the test entails two elements, the first is consistent State practice, the second, the attitude of the State. To make law, countries must not only act in the same way on each occasion avoiding 'inconsistency and political expediency' but must also demonstrate 'opinio juris' the belief that States are bound to act in a certain way by law. As the Court held in *The North Sea Continental Shelf Cases* in 1969, the countries concerned must 'feel that they are conforming to what amounts to a legal obligation. The frequency or even habitual character of the acts is not in itself enough. There are many international acts e.g. in the field of ceremonial and protocol, which are performed almost invariably, but which are motivated only by considerations of courtesy, convenience or tradition, and not by any sense of legal duty.' (ICJ 1969: 3 at para. 77). What this means is that promoting sustainable development – for example, cutting down emissions of greenhouse gases or reducing overfishing – will only form international binding rules of custom if they have consistency and if countries behave in a certain way because they believe that they are legally required to act in the way they do. Voluntary examples of good practice will not be enough.

This then begs the question: are there any such rules in international environmental or sustainable development law? The best contender is the notion of legal sovereignty and its corollary of non-interference in another State's affairs. This principle was confirmed in the environmental context at both the Conference on the Human Environment at Stockholm in 1972 and the United Nations Conference on Environment and Development at Rio in 1992. Thus Principle 21 of the Stockholm Declaration, read that:

> States have, in accordance with the Charter of the United Nations and the principles of international law, the sovereign right to exploit their own resources pursuant to their own environmental policies, and the responsibility to ensure that activities within their jurisdiction or control do not cause damage to the environment of other States or of areas beyond the limits of national jurisdiction.

What this means is that one country should not pollute another but that as long as they do not do so, they can pursue those environmental policies they wish. Indeed, at the United Nations Conference on Environment and Development in 1992, this central principle was reaffirmed, though this time with two crucial words added. The Rio Conference, reflecting the shift in global politics and the increase in both number and influence of the G77 countries, introduced the words 'and developmental' after 'environmental'. This enshrined the sovereign right of states to pursue both their own 'brown', as well as their 'green', agenda. Nevertheless, the principle still maintained the wording of responsibility – for environmental harm to either the global commons or another State.

Though at first sight these principles are 'soft law', being declarations rather than legally binding treaties, many analysts believe that these pronouncements have subsequently 'hardened', becoming the touchstone for legal rules in this sphere. Sands, for example, writes that Principle 21 'is widely recognised to reflect a rule of customary international law, placing international legal limits on the right of States in respect of activities carried out within their territory or under their jurisdiction' (Sands 1995: 190). Others note that even at the time of the Stockholm Conference several States confirmed that they believed the principle to accord with international customary law (Birnie and Boyle 1992: 90). As such, their central concepts would bind State behaviour unless governments explicitly stated that they did not apply. Nevertheless, even if rules on international responsibility for environmental harm are capable of acquiring status as customary law, in an area as fluid and fast-moving as sustainable development, such binding rules are likely to be rare. Contextual divergences and the hortatory aims of many calls for sustainable development are ill-suited to the precision required to form binding principles of customary international law.

The implication of this point is that the most important way in which international environmental law is made today is by treaty, that is, with each

State's consent. The same would be true for widespread legal commitment to the pursuit of sustainable development. Such treaties may be made either between two parties (bilateral) or between many (multilateral). They will be inescapable if environmental damage or unsustainable activity affects a global resource, be it the atmosphere, the ozone layer or fish stocks on the high seas. Indeed, there are currently over 240 multilateral treaties registered by the United Nations Environment Programme (UNEP 1999), dealing with issues as diverse as trade in endangered species, nuclear accidents and the export of hazardous wastes. Of course, they only say what politicians can be persuaded to agree to; the 1992 Framework Convention on Climate Change and the 1995 Kyoto Protocol did not do nearly as much as many hoped. With no outside authority capable of cracking the whip, countries cannot be forced to implement sustainable measures. Indeed, until the Protocol is ratified – implemented into national law – it has no binding force. And whatever compromises were reached at The Hague, it will be for domestic institutions – in particular the United States Congress and Senate – to decide whether or not ratification will take place.

If high-profile environmental treaties garner little international support when action actually needs to be taken, it might be worthwhile greening existing institutions and legal mechanisms – an indirect way of pursuing sustainable development. One such forum is the World Trade Organisation, the institution established in 1994 to support the post-war General Agreement on Tariffs and Trade. Based in Geneva, its dispute panels have heard arguments on issues ranging from hormones in meat and the fuel-efficiency requirements in cars to the location of growing bananas. In theory this offers a broad-based forum in which to resolve disputes on sustainability. In practice, however, the GATT system's agreements have yet to be greened. Differences in scientific protocol or fundamental disputes over culture or values (Layard 1997) are difficult to translate into the currency of import restrictions and barriers to trade, though progress could and arguably is, being made on this front (Werksman 1996). Still, WTO dispute resolution panels are largely staffed by trade lawyers, making a more holistic approach unlikely. As the protestors at Seattle and Prague, and the unwillingness of many G77 States to sign up to a new Trade Round make clear, these existing agreements do not appear to have sustainable development at their core. There is perhaps still much to be done.

Two Structural Issues

Having reviewed the legal framework for sustainable development at the public international, European Union and national level, this chapter will now analyse two key issues. The first is that laws are made only when legislators have the power to make them – they must have sovereignty. This may sound obvious but in the context of sustainable development this point explains why many issues believed to be deserving of widespread and urgent concern lie languishing in negotiators' files. The second point is that the flexible and subjective nature of sustainability concerns means that these issues are not always capable of translation into precise, binding laws. Hortatory statements and divergent definitions are difficult for legal draughtsmen to deal with.

Jurisdiction

Starting, then, with the concept of jurisdiction, this is of course a familiar idea in the sustainability context. For as Batty *et al.* note in the context of town centres (Thurstain-Goodwin and Batty, chapter 15, this volume), moves towards sustainability can be implemented on a variety of spatial scales. Indeed, environmental policy analysts have long distinguished between global, transboundary and local effects – global warming is a different phenomenon from the pollution of a local lake in terms of both its scientific and its political scale. The danger, however, is that these 'realities' prevent us from taking a truly interconnected and holistic approach. As the Brundlandt Commission noted back in 1987, 'ecological interactions do not respect the boundaries of individual ownership and political jurisdiction'. As a result, 'the enforcement of common interest often suffers because areas of political jurisdiction and areas of impact do not coincide' (World Commission on Environment and Development: 46–7).

Legal authority provides a further reason for differentiation. Here, State jurisdiction 'is the power of a state under international law to govern persons and property by its municipal law. It includes both the power to prescribe rules . . . and the power to enforce them ' (Harris 1998: 264). At its simplest, this means that legislators in Argentina cannot make laws in Zimbabwe any more than judges in Namibia can decide cases from Spain. The most basic reason for this is that public international law works on the premise that nation states make laws by consent. There are few, if any, legal principles they cannot reject. States are sovereign in deciding on the operative legal regime within their own territory and there are almost no legal levers to make them act in a cooperative way outside their borders should they decide on an isolationist stance. As was well established in *The Lotus Case* in 1927, international law 'governs relations between independent States . . . Restrictions upon the independence of States cannot therefore be presumed' (PCIJ Reports 1927).

Even the International Court of Justice does not automatically have jurisdiction. Established by the Charter of the United Nations in 1945, the 'World Court' can resolve disputes only at the behest of nation states. Its intervention in disputes – either settling them or giving an 'advisory opinion' – is only possible if it has jurisdiction to hear the case. In practice only a minority of States have made declarations (many with reservations) recognising as compulsory the jurisdiction of the Court. They exclude the United States, France, Germany, Italy, China, Russia, Israel and Chile, to name just a few.

Indeed, even if the Court can intervene, enforcing its decision may be difficult. If a State breaks the law, with no international army or police force there is very little the Court can do.

What all this means in the context of sustainable development is that when one State's pollution harms another State's territory (or the global commons), no country has the legal authority to legislate alone. Unless it is a rare instance where the matter is taken to court, resolution will depend on the harm – be it acid rain, nuclear pollution or over-fishing – being agreed by the countries concerned. If the offending party does not wish to negotiate, there are almost no legal mechanisms to make them. Indeed, many theorists and countries maintain that 'persistent objectors' can still refuse to be bound by rules of public international law. Some certainly argue that certain principles (*jus cogens*) – relating to the taking of slaves or sanctioning of piracy, for example – are simply too fundamental to contract out of. Anything as relative and fluid as sustainable development, however, is unlikely to command such legal respect. In these cases, objecting States can resist the encroaching effect of international customary law. And if coal-rich and oil-dependent countries wish to emit all the greenhouse gases they can produce, there is no central legal authority that can stop them.

What, then, of human rights? Do they not hold some prospect of success? On occasion, these can work well. In the 1995 case of *Lopez Ostra v. Spain* under the 1950 European Convention on Human Rights, for example, a plant which did not cease to give off 'fumes, smells and noise' made Lopez's environment unbearable. Her daughter suffered from 'dermatological and respiratory problems, diarrhoea and vomiting' (20 *European Human Rights Reports* 277, para. 47) as a result of the exposure to pollutant emissions from the treatment plant near her home. The Spanish government (responsible for the local authority's decisions) was held to have violated the privacy of the applicant's home. Still, these were exceptional facts. Here the local authority had subsidised the construction of the plant and had failed to act against the pollution, tolerating the plant's operation even though the necessary municipal permit had not been issued.

Other instances make more sober reading. When Ken Saro-Wiwa was executed in Nigeria for protesting against the plight of the Ogoni people in the wake of oil extraction sanctioned by his government and undertaken by Shell, no international mechanism lay open to him on human rights grounds. Nigeria had ratified the 1966 International Covenant on Civil and Political Rights (ICCPR) and the 1981 African Charter on Human and Peoples' Rights (ACHPR). Neither regime, however, incorporates a right of individual appeal, implementation of the scheme being left to monitoring committees and the intervention of other States. In Ken Saro-Wiwa's case, widespread condemnation came too late. As a result, he had no available mechanism to seek confirmation that he had had a fair trial, or that the Ogoni people's daily life had not been rendered unsustainable in many ways. Even political action was limited. The European Union, for example, stopped short of applying an oil embargo against Nigeria, opting for a series of visa restrictions, the expulsion of Nigerian military personnel from the European Union and limiting sporting contact instead. As Greenpeace was quick to allege, despite 'its strong condemnation of the executions and the Nigerian dictatorship, the international community has not taken any real action, instead they have said business as usual' (Greenpeace 1995: 1). Certainly, the legal regime could do little to help.

Indeed, explaining the importance of jurisdiction and notion of legal authority demonstrates why the European Union is such an important arrangement. At the heart of its constitutional project is the supremacy of Community law, enshrined in the United Kingdom in Section 2(1) of the European Communities Act of 1972. This overrides the traditional sovereignty of Parliament, holding instead that Community law-making provisions can, and do, take priority. With the introduction of qualified majority voting in 1987, this can even be against the United Kingdom government's consent. There remains, of course, the principle of subsidiarity, now enshrined in Article 5 of the amended Maastricht Treaty of 1992. This determines which areas of policy are to be undertaken at Community level and which are to remain a part of domestic jurisdiction, otherwise known as the question of 'competence'. It is generally thought that there is block of exclusive powers joined by the thread of the internal market over which Community institutions hold sway. These include free movement of goods, persons, services and capital, the Common Commercial Policy, competition, the Common Agricultural Policy, the conservation of fisheries and transport policy. Are sustainable development concerns within this block? Is it individual States or the Commision of the European Union who have power to initiate legislation on these concerns? Certainly, disputes over who has 'competence' to introduce proposals still flare up. Nobody likes to give up control.

Consequently, as this section has explained, legal intervention can occur at a number of levels. Individual countries can make laws either unilaterally (affecting their own citizens) or collaboratively on a regional or international basis. With very few exceptions however (concerning the most crucial of human rights), no body or country can compel another to make or observe laws. Individual States can be as sustainable, or as unsustainable, as they wish.

Legislating for sustainable development

A second point to note at the outset is that legislating for sustainable development is difficult. The concept does not lend itself well to prescriptive requirements and one size does not always 'fit all'. As a result, although policy formulations of the principle abound, legal versions of the principle are rare.

This is striking at all levels. In 1992, for example, when 150-plus nation states met at Rio in 1992 for the United Nation Conference on Environment and Development, they declined to define the concept. The closest they came was in the Rio Declaration, a non-binding instrument emphasising the links between development and environment. Principle 3 noted that the 'right to development' of both present and future generations should be 'fulfilled so as to equitably meet developmental and environmental needs of present and future generations'. Principle 4 stressed that if sustainable development is to be achieved, then environmental protection must 'constitute an integral part of the development process and cannot be considered in isolation from it'. The phrase was also included in the preamble to the 1994 Agreement to set up the World Trade Organisation. This exhorted signatory States to recognise 'that their relations in the field of trade and economic endeavour should be conducted with a view to raising standards of living . . . while allowing for the optimal use of the world's resources in accordance with the objective of sustainable development'. None of these fine words, however, are binding.

Indeed, perhaps inevitably, when they are binding, pronouncements advocating sustainable development are watered down. The 1992 Convention on Biological Diversity, for example, talks extensively about 'sustainable use' of biodiversity and its components, but does not mention sustainable development. The phrase *is* included in Article 3(4) of the 1992 Framework Convention on Climate Change, which sets out as a principle that parties 'have a right to, and should, promote sustainable development'. The remainder of this paragraph, however, implies that this would be a reason for delay rather than action. 'Policies and measures to protect the climate system against human-induced change should be appropriate for the specific conditions of each Party and should be integrated with national development programmes, taking into account that economic development is essential for adopting measures to address climate change.'

Even at the European Union level, it took until 1997 for the language of sustainability to enter even the preamble of key agreements, as earlier discussed. Even now, European Union legislation relating to sustainability is almost exclusively environmental. Land use planning, for example, is barely regulated by the Community. The initiatives that do emerge – work on European Spatial Planning or initiatives to promote Sustainable Cities, for example – are limited to policy proposals and have no legal framework as yet. Conversely, related strategies with a spatial element which do have legislative underpinning – Structural Funds or Trans-European networks, for instance – are only indirectly linked to planning (Marshall 1996). So far, though the European Union's good intentions are clear, set out in the Forewords to the Treaties of both Maastricht and Amsterdam, concrete legislative implementation appears to be lacking.

However, all is not lost. For perhaps the way forward for sustainable development is not to legislate content – but to enshrine procedures, providing for access to information and participation, giving individuals 'standing' to challenge decisions. Though developments are undoubtedly at the beginning of a long, hard road, the early signs of progress are there. Agenda 21, for example, the 600-plus page 'blueprint for sustainability' that sets out the agenda for the twenty-first century, pays particular attention to action at the local level. Chapter 4, for instance, makes a number of (non-binding) recommendations on how to improve citizen participation in environmental decision making. As discussed above, the European Union has also implemented legislation on Access to Information, and policy initiatives on Local Agenda 21 abound (see also Mittler, Chapter 4 this volume).

Even at the domestic level, changes are underway. In 1991, for example, the Czech Environment Act proclaimed simply that it 'follows the principle of permanently sustainable development' (Kiss and Shelton 1997) and recently emerging constitutions have often taken environmental and sustainability concerns on board. Indeed, by 1998 over seventy countries had constitutional environmental provisions of some kind, with thirty of these taking the form of environmental rights (Hayward 2000).

Certainly, as already mentioned, devolution in Wales has followed this lead. Here Section 121 of the 1998 Government of Wales Act requires the Assembly to 'make a scheme setting out how it proposes, in the exercise of its functions, to promote sustainable development'. Such a scheme is to be revisited on a regular basis and 'the function of making, or remaking or revising, the scheme' may not be delegated. The Assembly is to publish a report at the end of each financial year setting out how its proposals as set out in the scheme were implemented in that financial year. It must also report after each set of elections assessing how effective its proposals have been in promoting sustainable development. Many Welsh politicians embrace these principles (for example, Dafis 1998). Indeed, Wales is the first country in the European Union to be guided by a statutory duty to promote sustainable development (ENDS 2000).

In any case, it is true that in practice the distinction between regulating for environmental protection and promoting sustainable development should not be overstated. On many occasions, the two are inextricably intertwined. Climate change has fundamental implications for economic, social and cultural well-being as well as for the atmospheric environment. Protecting biological diversity from unscrupulous foreign prospectors anxious to make a profit, or from local operators intent on slashing and burning precious natural sites, has impacts on indigenous lifestyles, local economic viability and even the availability of medicines. Environmental effects rarely occur in isolation. It is also important, however, to maintain efforts on integration. Fundamental to the concept of sustainable development is that economic, environmental and social concerns should be 'married'. Legislative instruments implementing such a union are so far the exception rather than the rule. All they require to succeed is political will. Indeed, this last section will now consider what future developments we might expect to see.

Prospects for the Future

Future generations and other species

It is clear that entities other than current legal actors can be protected by existing legal regimes. Whales are to be safeguarded by the 1946 International Convention on Whaling, birds and habitats are to be preserved by the Natura 2000 regime. The principle of 'common but differentiated responsibility' enshrined in the 1992 Rio Declaration acknowledges that more industrialised countries must take the lead in tackling unsustainable patterns, assisting poorer and less developed countries in reaching these ends. Key conventions including the 1987 Montreal Protocol concerned with ozone-depleting emissions, or the 1992 Framework Convention on Climate Change impose fewer obligations on less developed States, allowing grace periods and requiring technology transfers, financial aid and scientific assistance. Future generations are referred to, for example, in Article 4 of the 1972 World Heritage Convention, which requires the parties to protect, conserve, present and transmit cultural and natural heritage to 'future generations'. The 1991 Environmental Protection Act of Malta proclaims that 'it shall be the duty of the Government for and on behalf of the present and future generations to take all measures . . . necessary for the protection of the environment of Malta . . . [and to] safeguard the common heritage of mankind' (Kiss and Shelton 1997: 38).

Yet this begs the question. Do these initiatives adequately incorporate principles of inter- and intra-generational equity into legal edicts? As one sympathetic commentator concludes in the context of future generations, it is 'unclear what practical legal consequences might flow from these undertakings' (Sands 1995: 200). To many the real question is whether rather than just being the recipients of regulatory measures of protection, future generations and other species could bring actions in their own right. They might complain, for example, about global warming due to flood their shores, or pollution affecting the viability of their species. This revolves around the concept of 'standing', legal shorthand for saying that interested parties have a right to bring a claim to court.

The principle of jurisdiction, explored earlier (see p. 41), is relevant here as well, for it entails that citizens of one State cannot bring a claim against another, even if the latter has breached public international law. They can bring an action against another individual resident or citizen in another State (under private international law), they may even be able to bring a claim against their own State if they are enforcing observance of their human rights.

Only States, however, can bring a claim against other States. The International Court of Justice can entertain contentious claims only from States. Very occasionally other organisations, for example, the Red Cross or the United Nations, may be granted standing, yet such events are rare. Individuals have no legal 'personality' outside their country's borders (Harris 1998). Perhaps inevitably, neither future generations nor non-human species can come to court and bring a claim.

In a seminal paper in 1972, however, Stone questioned this basic premise, asking whether trees could not after all 'have standing'. Ospreys, newts and tigers might be so threatened by development-destroying habitat – could they too not be said to have an interest at stake worthy of protection? One way to achieve this would be to have court-appointed guardians to protect their interests, arguing their case directly before the judge. 'Presented with possible invasions of the interests of certain persons who are unable to speak for themselves, such as otherwise unrepresented infants, the insane, and senile, courts are empowered to appoint a legal guardian to speak for them. So, too, guardians can be designated to be the legal voice for the otherwise voiceless environment: the whales, the dolphins, important habitats and so on. The guardians could either be drawn from existing international agencies that have the appropriate focus, such as the World Meteorological Organization for the atmosphere, or from the many nongovernmental organizations (NGOs) that might be willing to serve' (Stone 1993: 84).

This is an attractive proposition. It is far more difficult to sanction building on protected wetlands if papers are shuffled behind a regulator's desk or suited expert witnesses squabble over methodologies and projections in court, than if a fully-suited albatross is sitting in the front row. Stone even notes that with his encouragement and advice, a group of German environmental lawyers put this technique into practice. In *Seehunde v. Bundesrepublik Deutschland* the seals were the applicants, even though their case was quickly dismissed by the administrative law court (Stone 1993). Despite being in its infancy, the technique is intuitively attractive. It could be extended to cover respondents overseas and generations still to come as well.

A second option is to permit NGOs rights to proceed directly. One early instance of such a provision was included in the Council of Europe 1993 Lugano Convention on Environmental Liability which would also have made funds available for groups meeting the treaty's requirements. For a number of reasons, however, of which this controversial measure was one, this agreement has never received sufficient ratifications to come into force. The 1998 Aarhuus Convention has again picked up this theme, requiring in Article 3(4) that each Party 'shall provide for appropriate recognition of and support to associations, organizations or groups promoting environmental protection and ensure that its national legal system is consistent with this obligation'. Most recently, the 2000 European Commission White Paper on Environmental Liability has included a suggestion that non-governmental organisations (NGOs) might be able to bring a claim for the cost of cleaning up a contaminated site or obtain an injunction preventing damage to areas containing protected biodiversity. This would enable NGOs to highlight any government inactivity, bringing attention and action to damaged areas. It is another way of giving a legal 'voice' to habitats or species. It would be harder, however, than the concept of guardianship to translate into use for generations distant in either space or time.

In any case, a decision to enact such legislation is of course dependent on the legislature in any given jurisdiction. The proposal is most likely to succeed under national laws where governments are truly concerned about the interests of other species and believe that conventional anticipatory protective regimes (for example, the Natura 2000 system) are ineffective for any given reason. Seals in court are provocative and attention grabbing. They focus attention onto the interests of other species, giving non-governmental organisations and the like ample opportunity for effective and innovative campaigning. Still, granting guardianship would be a resource-intensive, time-consuming practice, ensnared with problematic legal minutiae. It is perhaps unsurprising that so far such techniques have been slow to make their way into binding laws despite their obvious appeal.

Enforcement – the weak link in the chain?

A second factor to bear in mind when looking to the future is that making laws is one thing, enforcing them another. Flexibility in enforcement is a particular characteristic of British regulators, who conventionally keep an eye on long-term cooperation rather than short-term prosecution. Now, however, even regulators are bemused. One survey at the Environment Agency found that they 'relate poorly to the concept of industry as their "customer", and have been left unsure whether their job is to police compliance with legislation or "be nice to industry"' (ENDS 1999b). Even more innovative sticks, notably the threat of media attention or considering withdrawing Eco-Management Scheme (EMAS) approval, have not, it appears, affected the policy of constructive dialogue (Mehta and Hawkins 1998). The result of all these factors is that the prosecution rate is strikingly low. In 1997/98, for example, of the 1,311 substantiated pollution incidents noted by regulators inspecting the 1,992 processes regulated under the system of integrated pollution control, only a tiny minority of 'substantiated pollution incidents' were prosecuted. Just fifty enforcement notices were served and twelve prosecutions taken. Fines totalled a miserly £220,500. Indeed, these are trends replicated in Scotland and at the local level as well (ENDS 1998, 1999a).

These *ad hoc* reports of sporadic enforcement are borne out by academic research as well. In their analysis of IPC enforcement from 1993 to 1997, Mehta and Hawkins found that 'HMIP still operated in a largely conciliatory fashion, albeit under more formal procedures than the regime it replaced. An enforcement game was still played out between HMIP and firms with a rising hierarchy of regulatory demands and enforcement pressure applied incrementally. Pollution officers took into account their perceptions of the polluter and pollution and used a cooperative approach. Accordingly, bargaining and negotiation remained a central part of HMIP's law enforcement' (Mehta and Hawkins 1998). As Smith found, HMIP officers are unlikely to issue enforcement notices against operators generally thought to be co-operative. 'Confrontation hardens operators and tends to solicit unhelpful "yes" or "no" answers to questions' (Smith 1997: 197). Though this flexibility and an eye on the long-term cooperation are a peculiarly British phenomenon (Hawkins 1989), regulators around the world frequently have discretion when it comes to enforcement.

These findings make depressing reading, especially for those who had believed new legislation in 1995 would alter enforcement practices (Rowan-Robinson and Ross, 1994). They seem to indicate that many of the legislative requirements are failing to have the required effect. 'Normal' pollution seems to be inescapable. To a large extent this is true. Extreme events will still be prosecuted but many 'everyday' breaches are let through. Yet this is not necessarily as dreadful as it sounds. It may make good organizational sense to work with operators on improving procedures, aiming ultimately to prevent pollution from occurring in the first place rather than cleaning it up after the fact. Command and control policies may simply be out of date.

Whether or not this is true, it is certainly true that enforcement remains a problem at the international level as well. The problem of enforcing decisions reached by the World Court has already been discussed. And the corollary of requiring each State's consent to enter into binding treaties, of course, is that a country's refusal to sign up to international agreements can stultify action on promoting more sustainable ways forward. Indeed, even if heads of States sign, and negotiators agree, domestic politicians must still consent. Treaties signed in triumph still need to be ratified at home. Even though the Kyoto Protocol to the 1992 Framework Convention on Climate Change was finalised in 1995 it has yet to be ratified by a single 'developed' State. Inevitably some signatories are more important than others. Many States see no point in signing up until it is clear that the United States at least is on board. Political realities have a significant impact on the effectiveness of legal provisions.

This raises the final point. Are legal mechanisms simply incapable of providing a sufficiently rigorous and demanding framework to implement sustainable development? If compliance is half-hearted and politicians only agree to what they think is electorally viable, does the law have anything to contribute to the pursuit of sustainable development? The answer, it is suggested here, is yes. Laws cannot work in isolation. Their formulation and their effectiveness are inextricably intertwined with politics. They can, however, at either the international, regional or domestic level, promote transparency. It is only because the Kyoto Protocol has been agreed that it becomes clear that States are not signing up to its requirements. When the seals were denied the ability to pursue their case in court, 'the very filing of the case and attendant publicity was considerable and favourable . . . When the time came for the government to renew the ocean-dumping permit, the authorities who initially gave their permission were forced by a kindled public opinion to revoke it . . . The seals lost the battle in court, but even so gained an advantage in ultimately winning the war in the public and political forums' (Stone 1993: 84). The legal framework can be improved, of that there is no doubt. Introducing stricter requirements on pollution, appointing guardians for future generations and enforcing breaches more strictly, are all worthwhile and effective reforms. Even so, the chances of promoting sustainability would be a great deal less if the current legal framework were not in place.

Further Reading

The best book on environmental law in the United Kingdom is undoubtedly the 5th edition of *Environmental Law* (Blackstone Press, 2000) now written by Stuart Bell and Donald McGillivray. This provides a wealth of further information on all aspects of the legal agenda in the United Kingdom. At the European Union level, Kiss, A., and Shelton, D., 1997, *Manual of European Environmental Law*, Cambridge: Cambridge University Press is extremely useful as is Nigel Haigh, *Manual of Environmental Policy: The EC and Britain*, Longman, London which is consistenly up-dated. At the international level, two good texts are Patricia W. Birnie and Alan E. Boyle, 1992, *International Law and the Environment*, Oxford: OUP, though this is rather out-of-date in some respects (it predates the bulk of the Rio Conference, for example) it remains a great place to start. More recent and also good (but still rather out-of-date) is Philippe Sands *Principles of International Environmental Law*, Manchester: Manchester University Press, published in 1995.

4 Hijacking Sustainability? Planners and the Promise and Failure of Local Agenda 21

Daniel Mittler

Most sustainability literature chooses to be blissfully ignorant of the history of the concept. Many commentators talk as if sustainability was invented sometime in the late 1980s – and has only been an issue since the Brundtland Commission's report *Our Common Future* was published in 1987 (WCED, 1987). Of course, the concept is much older. Earlier versions can be found in medieval thought, seventeenth-century forest practices, colonial land management and most of the alternative thinking of the 1960s (e.g. Cobb and Daly, 1989; Pepper, 1984; Reid, 1995). The planning pioneers, Geddes, Howard and Osborne, can also be credited with having provided early visions for sustainable cities (Leonard, 1992; Hall and Ward, 1998; Hall, this volume)

However, it is true that sustainability suddenly became 'sexy' in the late 1980s. There has been a growing avalanche of political pronouncements and scholarly studies on the subject ever since. Planners, especially in the United Kingdom, have played a significant part in fuelling and sustaining this boom. 'Virtually every planning policy document now emerging . . . makes a ritual nod in the direction of the Brundtland definition of sustainable development' (Evans and Rydin, 1997: 55). This chapter examines why and evaluates some of the results in planning practice by looking at Local Agenda 21 – a participative planning process developed in response to political demands for sustainable development.[1]

Battling Irrelevance

Planners have not been a popular species for quite some time. They have been blamed for everything that went wrong with the 1960s' and 1970s' housing projects and were a prime target for the Thatcherite attack on inefficient public servants during the 1980s (Evans and Rydin, 1997). Local planners in particular were hit hard by the centralisation of planning functions and policies during the 1980s. They lost most of their political power – and with it much of their (self-)esteem (Rydin, 1998). In this context, the sustainability agenda came to be seen as an exciting opportunity to reclaim lost authority. Here was an international agreement, Agenda 21, Chapter 28 of which said what Whitehall decidedly didn't: *Local Authorities matter*. Here was an (allegedly) new, internationally significant concept – sustainable development – and local authorities were acknowledged as *the* key players in its implementation. Two-thirds of the recommendations that the 130 heads of state signed up to at the Earth Summit in Rio de Janeiro in 1992 are addressed primarily to local authorities (Grubb *et al.*, 1993).

Local Agenda 21 in particular seemed like the perfect opportunity to put the generalist knowledge that is the hallmark of planners (Evans, 1997) to use once more. Its definition sounds much like definitions of progressive planning of a bygone age: Local Agenda 21 calls on local authorities to, in consultation with their local citizens, draw up a *consensual* plan for the future development and resource use of their locality (Robinson, 1993; Mittler, 1997). There is a great emphasis on consultation and local democracy. This allowed British local authorities to dream of reconnecting with a populace that is no longer interested in turning out for local elections. Planners, therefore, dusted off 1970s' planning tools such as planning cells, future visioning and neighbourhood discussions and sold them as 'new and improved' sustainability tools (O'Riordan and Voisey, 1998). It has become popular once more to allow citizens (especially children) to design hypo-thetical cities, using these as an indicator for citizens' demands and desires in their urban environment. Planners were back in business. They, at long last, again had something to contribute to the development of their locality (Buckingham-Hatfield and Percy, 1999). They were at the centre of a process, which promised to once again make planning matter.

Local Agenda 21: The Promise

Many of the participation exercises that Local Agenda 21 initiatives spurred were (and are) impressive. In Edinburgh, for example, children 'planned' a new housing development known as the South East Wedge. Their ideas have been passed to the developers. The City Council, meanwhile, instigated a high-powered Commission on Sustainable Development which gauged the public's attitudes on sustainable development. It made no less than 132

Figure 4.1 Local Agenda 21 in action

recommendations on how Edinburgh could move towards a more sustainable path of development. More than one-third of these recommendations require action by local authority planners (Mittler, 1999a). In Reading 'neighbour-hood agendas' set out detailed visions for change and in some areas helped recreate a sense of community. Locals once again felt that their planners listened and that their suggestions would not just linger in an over-worked planner's in-tray (Webster, 1999). Lancashire County Council developed an impressive state of the environment report and drew up specific sustainability indicators for the County in collaboration with the public.

Every Local Agenda 21 is different; its local specificity is, after all, one of the key attractions and hallmarks of the Local Agenda 21 process. Even the more humble Agendas, however, amount to more in *direct* citizen involvement than most of Britain has seen in decades (Buckingham-Hatfield and Percy, 1999). The Hounslow Local Agenda 21 in West London, for example, may not have attracted thousands or changed local policies overnight. But the Local Agenda process brought together many dozens of citizens over months in order to discuss specialised fields such as transport and planning policy in considerable detail (Buckingham-Hatfield and Matthews, 1999). That alone, is a considerable achievement.

Local Agenda 21: The Limits

Ultimately, however, Local Agenda 21s have not reversed the planners' professional marginalisation or turned around the decline in local community power in Britain. Despite all the hype, the international commitment to sustainability proved less substantial than may have appeared possible in the aftermath of Rio (Sachs, 1995). Local authorities were not given any resources to implement Local Agenda 21s which, to this day, remain a non-statutory process that local authorities can leave by the wayside if they so wish. National policies were and are often directly contradictory to the aims of the Local Agenda 21 process. While many local authorities, for example, try to reduce energy use as part of their Local Agenda 21 programmes, energy market liberalisation leads to constantly declining energy prices. Of course, lower prices tend to generate higher demand (CAG Consultants, 1998). As long as energy prices are low, the public is unlikely to heed local authority calls to switch lights off or even be interested in subsidies for housing insulation programmes. Local authorities trying to implement sustainable transport policies encounter similar problems. With national tax and investment policies still in favour of the car, local initiatives face an uphill struggle (ibid.). Even the best public awareness programme will not attract people onto buses if the marginal cost of driving remains artificially low.

All was (and is) not well at a local level either. For all their original enthusiasm, planners have often found it hard to engage with the local population and abandon their jargonated discourse. They still prefer to be 'on top' rather than 'on tap'; a new professional ethic in which planners are community service providers rather than technical experts has so far proved elusive (Carley and Spapens, 1998). However, planners were also understandably weary of creating public expectations, which they knew local authorities – be it through a lack of resources or political will (or both) – would or could not fulfil. They thus tended to spoil the fun of Local Agenda visioning exercises, by pointing to brute and unfortunate facts such as finite budgets or limits in planners' ability to tell developers what to do. Furthermore, the planners' 'new and improved' participation tools routinely failed to attract anybody apart from the 'traditional meeting junkies' (Parker and Selman, 1999: 21) and the already articulate middle classes (Mittler, 1998a). Women and ethnic minorities in particular remained painfully underrepresented (Buckingham-Hatfield and Percy, 1999; Mittler, 1999a). These groups often grew very disillusioned with the Local Agenda process as it proved yet another arena in which groups of white men discussed and decided upon *their* future.

Not that that much is actually being decided! Another key problem from early on was the move from the 'drawing up nice plans' phase of a Local Agenda 21 to that of concrete political implementation. Some Councils managed to implement quite a few Local Agenda 21 initiatives very quickly. But on closer inspection it turned out that what had in fact been 'achieved' was little more than a rebranding exercise. Councils' existing environmental and social services suddenly were *talked* of as Local Agenda 21 initiatives. But few of these were actually new (Parker and Selman, 1999). The more innovative and radical ideas more often than not remained locked inside the Local Agenda 21 action plans, which quickly gathered dust on local authority's shelves (Mittler, 1999a). Worse, some of these plans were badly written and excessively vague. They failed to 'engage the public intellectually, emotionally or practically' and thus did not achieve 'significant changes in individual, agency and institutional behaviour.' (Smith *et al.*, 1998: 225). Action plans were often written only because the Council – and planners in particular – needed and wanted to be seen as 'doing something'. The Local Agenda process failed to be linked to the mainstream politics of the local authority. The planners and environment department employees charged with drafting Local Agenda 21 documents often led frustrated lives in the 'portacabin'. They were smiled upon rather than revered by their colleagues (Mittler, 1998a). Instead of acting as intermediaries between departments and breaking down barriers between them, Local Agenda 21 employees themselves became embroiled in departmental conflicts and turf wars. For planners, the hoped for regaining of initiative and (self-)esteem has therefore proved elusive – at least to date.

Local Agenda 21: The Future

But it is too easy to dismiss Local Agenda 21 as a whole because of these multiple shortcomings. There were and are plenty of worthy local initiatives both in Britain and abroad (Mittler, 1998b). Local authorities *did* gain a higher profile through their promotion of Local Agenda 21. At the 'Rio-Plus-Five' Summit in New York in 1997, for example, Tony Blair talked proudly and at considerable length about how British local authorities (allegedly) lead the world in Local Agenda 21. The government is still expecting *all* local authorities to have had Local Agenda 21 processes in place by the end of 2000 (DETR, 1998a). It has supported the process with many worthy statements (if not yet with hard cash). Planners, meanwhile, often continue to feel that Local Agenda 21 gives a new air of legitimacy to their profession, and in particular to more innovative planning tools such as future visioning or planning cells (Oels, 1997). That these tools are now back on the agenda is, indeed, good news. For it is not these tools that are deficient but the political context in which they are being employed. They only become counter-productive when the ideas expressed in Local Agenda 21 consultation exercises cannot be implemented due to legislative, financial or political restraints. Indeed, the greatest value of the continuing Local Agenda 21 efforts lies precisely in having made these limits on local action painfully obvious. When Local Agenda 21s started to be developed in the early 1990s, there was a considerable amount of naivete among planners and politicians alike. It was thought that if everyone worked together in 'partnership', if education was improved and citizens 'enlightened', local authorities could achieve wonders and save the planet in no time. That naivete has now gone. Instead,

Local Agenda 21s are starting to feed into calls for meaningful local empowerment (Smith *et al.*, 1998) and for the relocalisation of the economy. Local Agenda 21, at least in some local authorities, is starting to mean not just the drawing up of worthy plans: the process is beginning to lead to direct support for formerly fringe activities such as Local Exchange Trading Systems (LETS) (Croall, 1999). It is starting to make people rethink their relationship to their own locality and the wider world. Local Agenda 21, in other words, has started to grow up as a process. It is beginning to respond to the challenges of an increasingly globalised market place rather than simply being a straw that planners (and other local authority employees) hold onto in order to counter the centralising instincts of Whitehall.

However, for Local Agenda 21s to succeed in their more mature phase, many things need to be changed in the way they are being implemented. Most importantly, Local Agenda 21s need to be directly linked with local policy making. Local Agenda 21 documents need to feed directly into the local legislative process. The details may be left to the planners, but when, for example, a Local Agenda 21 transport group says: 'We want to reduce road traffic by x per cent', this must oblige the Council to draw up a plan to achieve this aim. Local Agenda 21 groups could also act as local sustainability watchdogs. They should look at a Council's environmental performance on a yearly basis and ascertain whether the Council has, at the very least, implemented all the projects it promised (Mittler, 1999a).

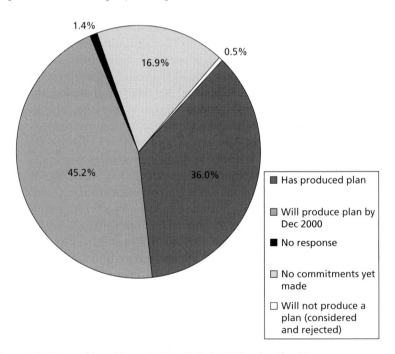

Figure 4.2 Status of Local Agenda 21 activity in UK local authorities

Local Agenda 21 departments must also receive greater clout within the local authority structure. Rather than being mere adjuncts to the Environment and or Planning Departments, they must get a truly cross-cutting remit and be allowed to advise and even cajole officers in other departments. City of Edinburgh Council, for example, has now set up a Sustainable Development Unit in order to take Local Agenda 21 forward as a holistic process. Early evidence suggests that this is proving successful. 'A variety of departments have already requested help and information from the Unit, which was unprecedented in Environment Department days' (Child, personal communication, 2000).

Local authorities, furthermore, should work together and highlight the areas where achieving the aims of Local Agenda 21 has so far been impossible due to national policies or legislation (CAG Consultants, 1998). They should formulate a catalogue of necessary national policy changes and, with their new-found clout, lobby central government to implement these demands. The 2000 target date set by the government for all local authorities to have a Local Agenda 21 in place, may provide an opportunity for such collective lobbying. Throughout 2001, local authorities should get together and say to central government: 'We have done our bit. Now it is time for you to make life easier for us, too.' Key required policy changes will, for example, be higher taxes on non-renewable resources and a further tightening of planning rules governing out-of-town shopping and housing developments as well as major infrastructure investments (CAG Consultants, 1998). Local authorities should also, predictably but rightly, call for more and *more regular* funding for Local Agenda 21. Otherwise many worthy initiatives started during the early enthusiastic phase of the process will themselves not be sustainable in the long run.

Only if these parameters for implementation are put into place will Local Agenda 21 have a future (Mittler, 1998a). Otherwise, the process, much like consultative planning exercises of past decades, will simply fade. In a decade's time, it will be seen as a possibly worthy but ultimately futile attempt at responsive, community planning.

Conclusion

After a long and varied history, sustainable development reached the British planning profession in the late 1980s and early 1990s. The concept promised recognition and a guiding vision at a time of crisis. The concept was thus embraced speedily and with delight. Planners up and down the country set about implementing sustainable development through Local Agenda 21 processes. After decades of 'planning by the book' they once again got out of their offices to consult the public on their future visions for their locality. However, after an initial honeymoon, reality set in. When Local Agenda 21s moved from the planning to the implementation phase many hit a brick wall.

Others slowed in speed and determination or proved less inclusive and radical than had initially been thought possible. Nonetheless, Local Agenda 21 spurred numerous worthy initiatives and has brought many planners once again closer to the populations that they are employed to serve. The limits of Local Agenda 21 are, in fact, not so much limits of the process itself but of the unsustainable political, legislative and economic climate in which Local Agenda 21 is trying to flourish.

Planners must therefore now work towards changing the national parameters for sustainable development. They must engage in the messy business of, for example, persuading central government to implement not immediately popular policies such as eco-taxes. Planning students, meanwhile, should study a number of Local Agenda 21s in detail. Through these case studies they can learn about the professional aims to which they should aspire as well the multitude of constraints with which they will be faced once they qualify. If Local Agenda 21 does not succeed in coming years, planners will not only have to face the environmental consequences (like everybody else). They will have missed another opportunity to show the relevance and value of their discipline. Another decade in the wilderness then beckons.

Note

1   In this chapter I talk of Local Agenda 21 as a planning process and focus on how planners have used and developed Local Agenda 21. This is not to say that planners are the only people with an interest in Local Agenda 21. Many Local Agenda 21 coordinators are not (professional) planners. There are, in fact, often differences between Local Agenda 21 officers and professional planners of a specific local authority. These differences cannot be addressed without looking at local case studies, however (e.g. Mittler 1998a and Mittler 1999a). They are thus ignored in this chapter. Local Agenda 21, in any case, is *always* a planning process. It involves devising strategies for the future of a locality. And professional planners *did* push the Local Agenda 21 process especially in its early phase (see main text). Bearing in mind that 'planning seems to be all things to all men' (and women!; Hall, 1992: 1), this chapter's focus on planning is thus deliberate but (hopefully) not too limiting.

Further Reading

The key texts for further reading on Local Agenda 21 are Buckingham-Hatfield, S. and Percy, S. (1999) *Constructing Local Environmental Agendas, People, Places and Participation*, London: Routledge; and O'Riordan, T. and Voisey, H. (1998) *The Transition to Sustainability: The Politics of Agenda 21 in Europe*, London: Earthscan. As a policy text, DETR (1998a) *Sustainable Local Communities for the 21st Century, Why and How to Prepare an Effective Local Agenda 21 Strategy*, London: DETR, is useful.

5 The Planning of Sustainable Urban Development: The Institutional Dimension

Harry T. Dimitriou and
Robin Thompson

Introduction

It is self-evident that the principles of sustainable development affect urban and rural areas. Both can contribute to sustainable economic, social and physical development, at global and local levels alike. Cities are important because they provide much of the capital for the expansion of national and regional economies, the production and consumption of goods and services, and the institutional structures for governance, trade and community development. Rural areas matter because it is here that ecosystems are often better protected, cultural traditions are longer-standing and influential. They produce food and resources, absorb waste and provide leisure and recreational opportunities. In both instances, however, institutions are key to the development of such areas – and are the focus of this chapter. For it is often argued that ineffective institutions explain why both urban and rural development efforts too often under-perform and fail to benefit adequately those who were initially targeted. Yet research in the rural sector of the so-called Developing World has shown that strong effective institutions can make a difference in promoting sustainability (see Brinkerhoff and Goldsmith 1990). This chapter now applies these arguments in an urban context. It suggests that the importance of institutional effectiveness is as salient here as elsewhere.

The discussion that ensues is in two parts. The first is a conceptual discussion based on Brinkerhoff and Goldsmith's generic framework for understanding institutional sustainability. This was outlined in *World Development* (1992) and derived from work conducted by the authors in the agricultural and health sectors of development studies. The second part of the chapter attempts to apply this conceptual framework to an urban regeneration strategy for the Thames Gateway area of London where the issues of institutional sustainability have proven (and continue to prove) to be of paramount importance to its success. The premise examined here is that while the Thames Gateway has already attracted considerable investment and potentially offers much to London's future overall development, the effectiveness of the Thames Gateway's regeneration efforts is constrained by the present unsustainable nature of its institutional support framework(s). These limitations have fundamental implications for the pursuit of sustainable development in this context.

The belief that sustainable development is conditional on the development of sustainable institutional frameworks is supported by evidence from the field of development studies (see World Bank 1990: 32; Kean *et al.* 1988).[1] The growing evidence in the Developing World has steadily led development assistance donors to make institutional sustainability *itself* a goal of the projects they support. Despite the very different contextual circumstances, it is argued here that the goal of institutional sustainability *must* be incorporated into regeneration goals of sustainable urban development from the outset, irrespective of context – with recent developments in the regeneration of the Thames Gateway offered as evidence of this need.

Concept of Sustainable Institutions

Acknowledging need to strengthen institutions

International development agencies and investors such as the World Bank have long encouraged local institutions to train up and develop agencies involved in the delivery of projects in the Developing World, recognising the need for institutions to be strengthened for the duration of project investment and construction. These efforts, however, have typically taken place without paying too much attention to the long-run requirements of institutional development. This is despite growing evidence (see Dimitriou 1988 and Paul 1990) which suggests a strong, positive association exists between the strengthening of indigenous organisations and the continuation of benefits beyond the project period (Brinkerhoff and Goldsmith 1990: 370). The focused concern with project institutions has in more enlightened circumstances led certain international development agencies to support the development of institutions other than project-specific agencies that can contribute to long-term development beyond the lifetime of the project.

Notwithstanding the better resourced situations of the *so-called* Developed Economies, the premise of this chapter is that stakeholders of urban sustainable development in this part of the world would be well advised to imitate (with, of course, the appropriate adaptations) these more recent developments in the Developing World. The case for this is strong as the discussion about the Thames Gateway below suggests.

The importance of institutional sustainainability is an aspect that is inadequately appraised even among the main infrastructure investors of Europe. The European Investment Bank (EIB), for example, which has a larger portfolio of investments than the World Bank, does not at present significantly incorporate institutional capacity concerns into its investment appraisal procedures. This is on the grounds that their lending is typically with 'mature, reliable European (often, governmental) institutions, well versed in project development'.[2] What this description of mature and reliable institutions masks is the fact that many such organisations are well versed in the appraisal of narrow conventional project deliverables as opposed to broader sustainable development goals. This was confirmed by recent research on the institutional contexts for the planning of large-scale transport infrastructure projects in five such countries. This revealed that many government agencies and consultancy firms involved in the planning and appraising of such projects largely confined themselves to operational performance concerns rather than their environmental and social impacts (Dimitriou 1998). The same research also suggested that the unsustainable nature and uncertain future of many of the institutional arrangements for the planning, construction and maintenance of these projects markedly increased the investment risks associated with their delivery.

Clarifying the use of terms

An important feature of the concept of sustainable institutions cited by Brinkerhoff and Goldsmith that needs to be taken into account in *any* transfer of its application to more developed contexts, is that sustainable development and sustainable institutions need to be kept analytically distinct. The former entails 'choices of strategies, policies, tactics and actions that will reliably produce long-term, self-renewing development' of which an important aspect is how these relate to institutions. (The critical question here is 'which institutions at which levels can best fulfil the functions required for sustainable development?') The latter is concerned with 'the making of these institutions effective and sustainable, given the identification of appropriate institutions'. This distinction is discussed further below in the context of the Thames Gateway case study.

As in the case of all complex problem-analysis exercises, defining the use of terms clearly is critical. Relying upon the same definitional sources as Brinkerhoff and Goldsmith, this chapter considers sustainable institutions as organisations that offer 'stable, valued, recurring patterns of behaviour' (after Huntington 1968: 12). These include rules and procedures that shape how people (and institutions) act, and the roles of organisations that have obtained special status or legitimacy.[3] When urban planning practitioners and/or academics advocate the introduction of enhanced institutions they typically have this role-orientated definition in mind (see the following case study discussion).

The call for more attention to be paid to sustainable institutions in urban development is in fact a call to incorporate the vision of sustainable urban development (and its follow-through actions) into the institutions that are designed to deliver *and* support this vision. Honadle and Van Sant (1985) characterise institutions that are consciously designed to do this as organisations that:

- survive over time as identifiable units,
- recover some or all of their costs, and
- supply a continuing stream of benefits.

Taken alone, however, these criteria do not define institutional sustainability. As Brinkerhoff and Goldsmith point out, longevity in itself is a dubious measure of institutional sustainability; the very fact that an organisation persists does not necessarily mean it produces anything of use/value. They emphasise that cost recovery alone is also a questionable criteria of institutional sustainability, particularly where communities are so poor that they cannot sustain themselves without subsidised assistance from central or local government. This is important because institutions that fail to service their 'target group(s)' adequately are also not sustainable. Pointing out that sustainable institutions are *not* an end-state but 'an on-going input-output process', Brinkerhoff and Goldsmith (1992: 371) argue that in certain cases the concept of a sustainable institution may accept that maintaining existing institutions can be undesirable. In other cases, however, the enhancement of an existing institution can offer a critical focal point of sustainable development efforts, depending on their functions and who benefits. These diverse outcomes reflect the need for an on-going review/monitoring of agencies set against the goals they were set to achieve and criteria of sustainable development as measures of performance.

Framework for Interpreting the Sustainability of Institutions

Underlying hypotheses

Two hypotheses underlie the conceptual framework offered by Brinkerhoff and Goldsmith to promote sustainable development institutions. The first is that 'the survival of an organisation over the long-run is affected by its internal capabilities *and* its external environment'. The second is that 'to remain viable in a changing world, an organisation *must* develop and stick to a strategy or game plan with a strong fit among its own internal strengths and weaknesses, and the external threats and opportunities' (Brinkerhoff and Goldsmith 1992: 372–7). In the event of a mismatch between the two, institutional decline/demise is predicted.

Looking inward

Looking inward, the principal internal variables of the framework proposed above for understanding institutional sustainability are twofold:

- an institution's production and decision-making processes (referred to as its 'technology'); and
- an institution's distribution of tasks among the people it employs (referred to as its 'structure').

In both cases, complexity is seen as a key issue.

Typically, complexity (e.g. the use of intricate technologies and elaborate structures) is inversely related to sustainability. In other words, the more complex the organisational structure, the more prone it is to being unsustainable. Putting it another way, the more simple the structure, the better, on condition that it reflects the concerns of sustainability. This conclusion in part led in the 1980s and 1990s, in the United Kingdom and elsewhere, to the introduction of reforms and restructuring in the private sector and the pruning of unwieldy organisations in the public sector. Sadly, it also led to the unwarranted dismantling of certain other public institutions and their replacement by less efficient private organisations, as in the case of the United Kingdom's national railway system; a case strongly made by many political commentators and journalists in the context of the current chaos in the operation of the country's national railway network.

Looking outward

Perhaps more important than the internal variables are those that are external to the institutions. In terms used by Brinkerhoff and Goldsmith, these can range from 'hostile to helpful'. As in the case of complexity, the 'environmental hostility' encountered by an institution has an inverse relationship with its sustainability. To help better understand the environmental conditions of institutions they can be seen to have both indirect and direct features (see Table 5.1). Of the direct characteristics, the demand for goods and services is typically the most critical. It is widely recognised that problems are often encountered in generating support for institutions that principally

Table 5.1 Indirect and direct features of environmental conditions affecting institutions

Indirect features include:
• stability (the rate of external change)
• flexibility (the degree of openness to change)
• extent of environmental artificiality (in the economic sense of not reflecting market prices or in the political sense of lacking widespread legitimacy)
Direct features include:
• level of demand for the institution's goods and services
• whether these goods and services are private or public (or a product of a partnership of both)
• economic characteristics of the institution's stakeholders

Source: Derived from Brinkerhoff and Goldsmith (1992)

supply public goods/services (particularly community services) rather than commodified services. This too can significantly affect the sustainability of such institutions and the services they provide.

According to Brinkerhoff and Goldsmith (1992: 374), for institutional sustainability to occur there needs to be a 'critical mass' of stakeholders who hold the institution's product/services in 'sufficiently high regard that they are willing to continue to exchange other resources for the product/services' on offer. It is clear that 'the poorer, less empowered, or more factionalised these stakeholders are, the greater the challenge to the institution' in delivering its product/services. They explain that 'elites are, therefore, especially influential stakeholders as their support can make or break an institution's sustainability'. Their support can also account for 'why some institutions prevail though they contribute little or nothing to development'. Albeit in a rural context of developing economies, Bates (1981) claims that elite stakeholders in government often prefer to retain control of key sectors of development, such as transport and utilities infrastructure. They thus see the status quo as best serving their interests, even if there is a heavy cost to the public purse; a conclusion that can be shared with many urban development situations in the *so-called* Developed World.

Institutional strategy formulation

For an institution to perform effectively and sustainably, the above discussion implies that there is a need for it to adapt and match its internal capacity with that of its external environment. The task of setting an institution's goals to achieve this, and providing sustained follow-up action with the necessary committed resources, can be seen to represent the strategy to attain sustainable institutions. A strategy of this kind ultimately specifies:

- *how* an institution plans to adapt itself in the face of change;
- *how* it plans to achieve the goals it has set; and
- *how* it plans to manage this change.

Of critical importance in the strategy-formulation process is the scanning of the environment in which the concerned institution operates and the institution's awareness of the special skills and resources it has to offer. It is important here to appreciate that 'Sustainable institutions are ones whose strategies enable them to make the best of their capabilities and to capitalise on their surroundings', whereas, unsustainable institutions lack such strategies. Finally, in presenting the above case, it should be understood that there is no such thing as an 'optimum strategy' that suits all circumstances equally as well. Rather, each strategy needs to be organisation-specific whereby (employing earlier terminology) 'different combinations of internal complexity and external hostility call upon institutions to find different ways to obtain inputs and generate outputs' (Brinkerhoff and Goldsmith, 1992: 375–6).

Strategies typically differ according to their emphasis on action versus learning,[4] and whether their focus of attention is mainly internal or external. In the former case, strategies may emphasise the optimum use of resources as opposed to novel ways that change the institution's capacity for action based on newly acquired knowledge. In the latter case, strategies may take on an internal orientation where the external environment is taken for granted as rather stable. Alternatively, an external orientation can be adopted which favours an institution positively engaging with the external changing variables, monitoring developments and attempting to influence the sources of change.

Whichever of these approaches is adopted, it is important to appreciate that the most appropriate fit for a strategy can change over time, as new challenges are encountered. Learning-based strategies tend to favour a participatory management style rather than a top-down management approach. Brinkerhoff and Goldsmith (1992: 376–7) note that 'Studies consistently find advantage in having people participate in planning, in taking implementation one step at a time, and in tapping the energy and knowledge of local organizations . . . when the clientele sees an institution as alien or imposed from the outside, it is unlikely to contribute to resources to making the institution last.'

Drawing from the above discussion one can highlight two related universal observations. First, the lack of community involvement in *any context* is a significant constraint on sustainability and attracting greater stakeholder participation. Second, the prevalence of passive stakeholders, particularly in the lower income levels, poses significant problems in achieving the same end.[5]

Implications for Urban Development Institutions

Value of demonstration projects

Good institutional performance is important to the promotion of the concept of urban sustainability and sustainable urban institution building. Poor institutional performance has the converse impact. It lowers the expectation of stakeholders and may even permanently destroy the basis of the demand for the institutions' services/deliverables. The fear of poor performance can lead to some urban institutions taking on limited high-priority goals first. This is often done in the interest of demonstrating success early on in the strategy and used as a lever to raise more resources so as to sustain further action. Advocates of a more comprehensive approach, however, argue that this selective approach is itself not sustainable as it steers attention away from the long-run tasks of institution building.

In the case of the most problematic urban development challenges, however, institutions are probably best advised to tackle these tasks in incremental steps, and only speed up action as the institutions gain experience and confidence after first addressing the more 'easy' problems. Increasingly in urban regeneration efforts 'to build on the lesson that success sells, involves looking at mixes of public and private sector service delivery'. Associated with this is the fact that the private sector has the advantage of being able to more easily measure success through charging mechanisms it employs for services/sales (Brinkerhoff and Goldsmith, 1992: 378).

As already indicated, there is a general consensus in urban institutional development for organisations to commence with 'doable' tasks first. Successful demonstration projects, however, do not mean that complexity can automatically be avoided. The reality of urban development is that many institutions require inter-disciplinary, inter-sectoral and inter-agency teamwork as well as 'the fine tuning of service production in the light of contextual factors' (Anderson 1985). However, 'complex activities are frequently difficult to sustain without special sources'. Increasingly, 'distant stakeholders' provide these resources from the international community as investment money becomes more global and mobile. As a result, it is imperative to keep such parties informed of developments as they progress, since 'tapping resources from such sources . . . can sorely test the entrepreneurial skills of an organisation . . . with the only remaining option being to lower the organisation's sights and/or retrench, seeking sustainability at a reduced level of activity' (Brinkerhoff and Goldsmith 1992: 378–9).

Deteriorating institutions

The notion that 'institutions (urban development institutions included) are automatically apt to become less sustainable over time' (Brinkerhoff and

Goldsmith 1992: 379) is difficult to dismiss, especially if they have not been made adaptive in the first place. This is despite the fact that the personnel of such institutions typically become more competent as they gain experience. Where urban development agencies are technology-based and/or dependent, 'staff must consciously expend effort just to keep up with their fields'. The failure to sustain this rejuvenation inevitably leads to the deterioration of the institution, its performance and its sustainability.

Also contributing to institutional deterioration is what Brinkerhoff and Goldsmith (1992: 379) call 'organisational ossification'. This can result from:

- the neglect of plant and equipment investment;
- a retention of outdated procedures and practices; and
- a growing alienation from the environment in which it operates.

All three concerns are commonly found in urban areas in need of regeneration/redevelopment and constitute major obstacles to the attainment of sustainable development goals.

Prerequisite qualities of sustainable urban development institutions

To make institutions in support of urban development sustainable, one can conclude from the above that there is a need to:

- secure internal commitment to this notion;
- select feasible objectives for the institutions/agencies involved;
- choose the right moment for strategy formulation and its implementation;
- build alliances among stakeholders;
- differentiate between perceived and actual payoffs of the strategy;
- offer long-term training for institutional development; and
- set common planning horizons for all institutional activities.

The following review of the experience of institutional developments associated with the regeneration efforts of the Thames Gateway investigates the extent to which many of these qualities are present.

Examining Institutional Sustainability in Practice: The Case Study of the Thames Gateway

Background

The Thames Gateway at present is the most ambitious of the United

Kingdom's urban regeneration initiatives. It addresses a corridor of land inhabited by 1.6 million people on both sides of the River Thames from London Bridge through to Swale along the Kent coast (see Figure 5.1). In theory the institutional arrangements in place for the regeneration strategy of this area represent a model of stability and sustainability in which an explicitly stated strategy is carried forward by a set of powerfully entrenched institutions. In practice, however, the initiative has been characterised by institutional instability with many of the failing features described in the preceding theoretical discussion about unsustainable institutions. In recognition of these failings, new attempts are currently underway to restructure the organisational systems for the redevelopment of the Gateway to restore that stability and more efficiently deliver the proposed strategy.

The proposed urban regeneration strategy was prepared for the Thames Gateway initially by the Llewelyn David study of 1993 and then as Regional Guidance in 1995. It can be seen to represent an explicit commitment to sustained urban development. First, it seeks to make more effective use of the skills and resources of a sector of London and South-east England which is performing at a lower level than the prosperous area to the west and south of the region. Second, it focuses on the redevelopment of brownfield land left by the contraction of traditional dockland, manufacturing and cement quarrying industries. Third, it links the regeneration of under-used land with improvements in transport systems, including the Channel Tunnel Rail Link (CTRL) which was re-routed through the Gateway in order to serve as a catalyst for redevelopment. Fourth, the initiative is pitched to promote

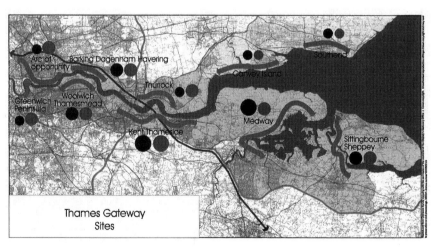

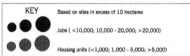

Figure 5.1 Map of the Thames gateway area

sustainable mixed-use communities, generating up to 200,000 jobs and accommodating some 60,000 houses all by the year 2006.

These objectives have been given potency by their incorporation into the government's Regional Planning Guidance (RPG) through the exceptional form of a special 'supplement' to the statutory guidance (DoE 1995a). This provides central government backing and a firm legal basis for a long-term strategy. It also satisfies some pre-conditions of institutional stability in that it contains a clear and long-term strategy as well as an authoritative platform of decision-making for the whole Thames Gateway area.

Institutional structures of the Thames Gateway area

The regeneration initiative for the Thames Gateway was initially promoted by the local authorities in the sub-region in the late 1980s and endorsed by the regional planning authority. Subsequently, it was adopted with great initial enthusiasm by central government and launched in 1991. In Michael Heseltine the regeneration strategy found a very enthusiastic champion. In his capacity as Secretary of State for the Environment during the early 1990s he met on a regular basis with the leaders of all the local authorities in the Gateway Area, providing political momentum for change from the centre, thereby fulfilling an important condition of sustainable institutional development. Indeed, the option of an Urban Development Corporation was considered and rejected in favour of a more pluralist and accountable model. This represented a departure from the tradition of establishing dedicated institutions for strategic development established by the new town development corporations. Instead, the elected representatives (at both national and local levels) collaborated closely and jointly endorsed the strategy. This collaboration was underpinned by the establishment of a small, dedicated unit within Heseltine's own department charged with producing and then facilitating the implementation of the strategy. Another criterion of sustainable institutional development was met by the creation of an organisational structure that carried specific responsibility for the Thames Gateway as a whole (see Figure 5.2). The Gateway also benefited from significant injections of resources that delivered some tangible benefits. These tended to be in the form of very large-scale generators of investment, the most spectacular examples of which are the re-routed Channel Tunnel Rail Link with the designation of stations at Stratford and Ebbsfleet (see Figure 5.1) and the Millennium Dome at Greenwich.

Lack of institutional sustainability in practice

Despite these promising preliminary conditions for institutional sustainability, the experience of the past few years in regenerating the Thames Gateway area has been one of institutional instability. While there has been some progress

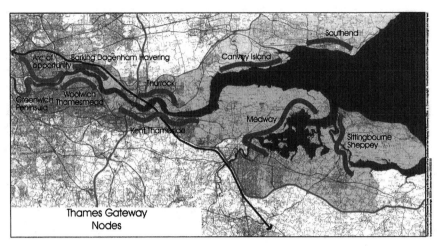

Figure 5.2 Nodes of the Thames Gateway

in the development of the Gateway, the institutional arrangements described above have generally not proved durable:

- Although the RPG strategy remains in place, a recent confidential consultant's report to government suggests that its implementation has been erratic and limited, and that the Gateway is still under-performing.
- The Thames Gateway special unit in the Department of the Environment was dismantled by the previous administration following the publication of Regional Guidance in 1995 and not reinstated by the present government. A new unit with a similar remit is now being established.
- Regular meetings between central and local authorities in the Gateway stopped following the change of government in 1997.
- Despite the spectacular funding 'one-off' major projects such as the CTRL and the Dome, there is little evidence of a significant re-direction of mainstream central government resources into the regeneration of the Gateway area. Even the current new Government Spending Review has identified no new dedicated funding specifically for the Gateway round.
- Infrastructure developments central to the strategy, such as the East London River Crossing, were not always followed through and the CTRL itself has been greatly delayed.

Reasons for lack of institutional sustainability

There has been, first, a lack of clear and durable organisational capacity matched with the regeneration tasks of the Thames Gateway as a whole. Second, there is an absence of a sustained identification by the various stakeholders with the objectives and decision-making processes of the

Gateway regeneration strategy, including the public authorities (at national, regional and local levels) and, crucially, developers, local business interests and the local communities. These problems appear to have been mutually reinforcing. and point to deteriorating institutional developments.

During its existence, the central government's special Thames Gateway unit performed an excellent job under its committed leader, Mike Ash. By working closely with stakeholders during its lifetime and by, for example, secondments of local expertise, it bridged the national–local span of the regeneration initiative. However, as a 'special' unit it was always vulnerable to closure and found constant difficulty in fully engaging the support of the mainstream Whitehall government machine, including the Treasury. When its powerful patron, Heseltine, moved on, the unit's life expectancy declined until eventually it was prematurely closed before the last election in 1997. Despite its sound work on strategy-making and facilitation, the unit did not have sufficient life span to allow it to put in place an implementation process on a sufficiently robust basis to ensure that the process could continue after its demise. Using Brinkerhoff and Goldsmith's terms, the core 'institutional technology' of the Gateway disappeared with the unit.

Stakeholder commitment and territorial identity

The structure of the Thames Gateway area is highly complex. It comprises a large number of distinctive communities each with their own ambitions and priorities and divides into two geographical and historic 'sets' – east London and Thurrock (in west Essex), and North Kent. The wider South Essex area has now been added. These communities do not identify with the Gateway whose name and boundaries have no historic echoes. They identify rather with their own neighbourhoods which have more immediate and accessible institutions. These neighbourhoods have cultures of competition rather than collaboration with each other.

Although all the authorities and major local stakeholders endorsed the broad brush regeneration strategy as expressed by RPG 9a, the conflicting agendas of these groupings emerged and became obstacles. So that as the guiding and co-ordinating role of central government became emaciated, cracks began to show. For example, the issue of where to locate stations on the CTRL became highly competitive and a source of hostility between the London and Kent areas. The former (through the London Planning Advisory Committee) made a formal objection to the Kent Structure Plan on the station issue.

As the commitment of local authorities to the overall Gateway regeneration strategy wavered under these pressures, so the involvement of other sectors and communities inevitably weakened. Given it took some time to successfully recruit business and other interests to the regeneration cause, the weakening represented a significant retrogression. This was damaging because the regeneration of the Thames Gateway area had insufficient time and opportunity to establish its own identity. It was, for example, marketed at more than one exhibition for investors with promotional maps showing *only* the London part of the Gateway! This identity problem is aggravated by the fact that few in the local communities were unable to identify with the name given to the area. The Thames Gateway area made sense to regeneration planners but few lay people understood a redevelopment concept that spanned community boundaries in ways never seen before. The private sector also found difficulty in identifying with the Thames Gateway as a whole and had little locus in the institutions which were established to promote it. Their commitment tended to be to local and sectoral issues rather than the wider regeneration agenda. As a result, the community ownership of the wider Gateway concept has been relatively weak and the identification with the more local institutions has been much stronger than with the Gateway-wide institutions. This has had the effect of reducing the stakeholder ownership of the local community groups of the stated sustainable development goals of the sub-region.

Restoring institutional sustainability in the Thames Gateway area

The sustainability of the Thames Gateway strategy has in large part been demonstrated by its enduring and recently enhanced status as a national regeneration priority. While substantial progress has been made, it is clear that achievement of the strategy has been inhibited by the lack of institutional coherence.

The recent establishment of the Regional Development Agencies (RDAs) as champions of economic regeneration was intended to provide a new opportunity to reinforce the institutional framework of the Gateway. However, no fewer than three RDAs were set up in the Gateway area: namely, the South East England Development Agency (SEEDA), the East of England Development Agency (EEDA), and the London Development Agency (LDA). The opportunity to create a single powerful development agency for the Thames Gateway area was thus lost.

There are now, however, potent signs that the instability of the institutional planning framework for the regeneration of the Gateway area is being addressed by government. In its new draft Regional Guidance for the South East published in 2000 the government has reasserted the importance of the Gateway as a national priority (DETR 2000b). This may be largely a response to the need to find a growth point in which to absorb development pressures in the south-east but it is very welcome. In addition to this, a number of moves are underway to provide greater organisational capacity to support this renewed aspiration. These moves include:

- the establishment by government of a 'Strategic Partnership' for the area to be chaired by a Minister; this body met for the first time in October 2000 and includes Ministers from several Departments, the three RDAs, and representatives of the local authorities and partnerships in the Gateway;
- the setting up of a new unit in government to 'join up' central government action in efforts to regenerate the Gateway area, involving key actors such as the Department of Education;
- the preparation by the Strategic Partnership of an 'implementation framework' to co-ordinate development and give greater coherence to the delivery of proposed regeneration strategy;
- initiatives by the new Partnership to re-establish the Thames Gateway area as a single marketing brand and to co-ordinate the inward investment effort on the basis of this;
- beneath the Gateway-wide Strategic Partnership are more local partnerships bringing together local government, Development Agency, business and other interests: these include the Thames Gateway London Partnership and the Thames Gateway Kent Partnership;
- the promotion by government of the idea of new 'development companies' or 'regeneration companies' as a means of channelling and co-ordinating public and private sector funding.

It remains to be seen whether these efforts will create the institutional sustainability required to implement the planning framework for Thames Gateway. One question these developments raise is whether the effort to restore unity of purpose among the various stakeholders is being made at the cost of excessive centralisation. Powers do appear to be shifting back into central government, especially with the involvement of the RDAs whose accountability is to Ministers. This reflects both the centralised context tendencies of the current government and its frustration with the apparent lack of satisfactory progress by local institutions particularly. The participation of other stakeholders, most especially of local communities, appears to be at risk of being made marginal, thereby reducing their perception of a shared strategy being pursued in the formulation of a sustainable development strategy for the area. There will need to be strong communication mechanisms between the Strategic Partnership and local interests if this is to be avoided. A more convincing institutional arrangement would be one that straddled the space between the national and the local institutions in the form of a core Gateway institution. An institution of this kind would ideally be located visibly in the area (rather than hidden in Whitehall), be guided by elected repre-sentatives of the local community as well as national and regional agencies, and draw in stakeholders from all quarters. It would, as Sir Peter Hall has advocated, have at least a 20-year lifespan with strong connections.

Conclusion

Notwithstanding recent developments (including the strengthening of government commitment), it is clear from the case study that the implementation of the sustainable urban development strategy for the Thames Gateway has been highly jeopardised by the instability of the institutional planning mechanisms framework charged with its delivery. In Brinkerhoff and Goldsmith's terms, the current institutional framework lacks stable, valued, recurring patterns of operations, as well as effective rules and procedures that shape how institutions act. Some agencies involved in the regeneration efforts of the Gateway have not survived over time as identifiable units. Others have under-performed by failing to recover enough of their costs to sustain themselves or by failing to supply a sufficient continuous stream of benefits. The Millennium Dome is the most dramatic example of a project which was imposed by central institutions and which found insufficient resource in its area.

The internal capabilities of many of the agencies assigned a role in the regeneration of the Thames Gateway (see Table 5.2) clearly require additional investment and restructuring if they are to avoid further deterioration. This is particularly important, as they have been unable to match their internal capabilities to the external environment in which they have had to perform. They have been obliged to operate within an external changing policy environment and with a declining central government commitment to which they have been unable to adapt. In hindsight, this suggests that under these circumstances a greater level of achievement of institutional sustainability might have been achieved had an early successful demonstration project been implemented. The Dome was intended to fulfil this role but proved to be counter-productive. As already pointed out, a successful demonstration project can prove useful as a lever to raise more resources so as to sustain further action as part of the overall regeneration strategy. More effective sustained dialoguing with key stakeholders – both international and (particularly) local – may also have strengthened the institutions, though the identified absence of a common identity and shared set of interests by the various local stakeholders of the different parts of the Thames Gateway have inevitably made this task much more difficult than expected. This is an aspect likely to be made worse by the involvement of three (as opposed to one) RDAs in the future redevelopment of the area.

In light of the above, new institutional initiatives currently under consideration need to address a number of issues if they are to promote sustainability. First, action needs to be taken to consolidate and urgently re-galvanise central government's renewed commitment to the regeneration of Thames Gateway. Action also needs to be taken to arrest the deterioration of any existing organisations seen as key players in the delivery of the strategy. This will require the pursuit of a more action-orientated strategy, focusing

Table 5.2 Current partnership – roles and remits

Thames Gateway Ministerial Strategic Partnership	
Members	**Remit**
• Ministers (& other government reps) • Chairs of SEEDA / EEDA / LDA • Chairs of Sub-regional Partnerships (anticipate from the private sector) • Sub-regional Chamber representatives (anticipate from Local Authorities)	• Formulate / Agree overarching TG Strategy and key issues / initiatives • Agree Delivery Route • Set objectives / Review progress • Ensure complementarity in policy at national and regional level
Thames Gateway Strategic 'Executive'	
To be discussed	
Sub-regional 'multi-sector' Partnerships	
Typical Members	**Remit**
• Local Authorities • Private Sector / Business Community • Community / Voluntary • RDA & GO • LSCs / SBS etc.	• Formulate / sign-up to sub-regional strategies and establish / agree delivery mechanisms • Prioritise actions / initiatives • Monitor & (where necessary) co-ordinate sub-regional actions • 'Umbrella' group to lever in public funding streams • Report to ministerial group
'Nodal' Delivery Teams	
Typical Members	**Remit**
• Key landowners • Local authority – planning and economic development teams • Transport authorities • Other 'focused' Public & Private Sector contributions • Community	• Development Framework / Area specific strategy • Delivery & Implementation (where no 'strategic' public intervention needed above local level) • Community participation • Procuring employment opportunities and skill needs • Relationships with 'Regeneration' company & Private Sector developers
Sub-regional 'Regeneration' / Development Companies (Ltd)	
Potential Members	**Remit**
• RDA • Key / strategic LAs • Private sector • Funders	• Responding to delivery requirements of Sub-regional Partnerships • Delivery of key strategic infrastructure components • Delivery of key sites to the market (incl. Site-specific infrastructure) • Commercial arrangements with developers / funders etc.

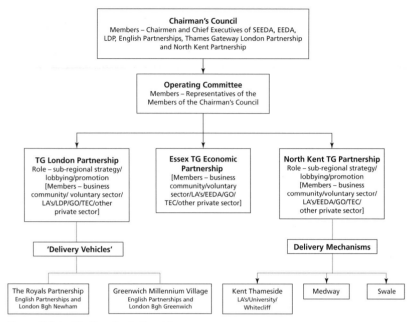

Figure 5.3 Institutional relationships

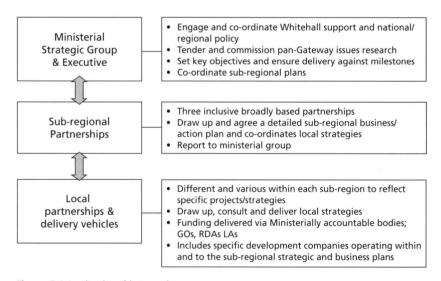

Figure 5.4 Institutional interaction

strategically on demonstration projects that provide levers for further action and pay more attention to the timing of project deliveries. Such efforts (together with the implementation of the overall strategy) would particularly benefit from the building of strong alliances of stakeholders, focusing on common interests and shared benefits. There is also a need to ensure that all organisations work to common planning horizons, avoid unnecessary complexity and invest further in skilled manpower and long-term training; such training is particularly welcome in dialogue enhancement among stakeholders, community development, resources management, public administration and marketing.

Notes

1 The World Bank study evaluated some 550 projects of which only 52 per cent were deemed to have successfully achieved sustainability goals. The USAID study was more extensive. It evaluated 212 projects and concluded that only 11 per cent of the projects had 'strong prospects for being sustained' (Brinkerhoff and Goldsmith 1990: 360–1).

2 This view was expressed in discussion with the author by the head of the bank's infrastructure division in 1996 and is reflected in the institution's appraisal methodologies employed which do not incorporate any significant appraisal of the institutional capacity and longevity of support for project development.

3 An example of a rule-orientated institution is a system of land tenure. A role-orientated institution, on the other hand, is the legal authority established to adjudicate disputes arising out of the land tenure system.

4 The private sector has long valued market research (i.e., learning what is new and what the changing needs of clients are) to remain viable.

5 Select groups tend to dominate institutions by controlling their agenda, and keeping down the opposition by the use of veiled threats and spreading misleading negative impressions of options not supported by the elite.

Further Reading

As this is an area of negligible research, there is little in the way of further reading for this topic. Readers should, however, refer to D.W. Brinkerhoff, and A.A. Goldsmith, (eds) (1990), *Institutional Sustainability in Agriculture and Rural Development: A Global Perspective*, New York: Praeger; and D.W. Brinkerhoff and A. Goldsmith, (1992), 'Promoting the sustainability of development institutions: a framework for strategy', *World Development*, Volume 20, No. 3: 369–83 for the theoretical framework. S. Paul, (1982), *Managing Development Programmes: The Lessons of Success*, Boulder, Colorado: Westview, is also useful on the development experience. For further reading on the Thames Gateway area, see Sir P. Hall, (2000), 'Thames Gateway – nine years on'. London: Thames Gateway London Partnership – Occasional Paper No. 1.

6 Planning and the Twin Discourses of Sustainability

Simin Davoudi

Introduction

'The world has changed: can planning change?'

(Castells, 1996)

If sustainable development does require new iterations, then planning does appear to have a changing role. This question embraces the growing concerns about the role of planning in rapidly changing societies. Debate on the future of the planning system and its role in shaping the trajectory of spatial change is now widespread, engaging the whole spectrum from public and private sector organisations to academic and professional institutions (Davoudi and Cadman, 1997). In addition to the growing focus on sustainable development, the late 1990s marked the celebration of two significant events in Britain, the 50th anniversary of the 1947 Town and Country Planning Act and the beginning of the Town and Country Planning Association's Centenary. This, added to an approaching dawn of a new millennium, provided a strong stimulus for planners to take stock. Many academics and practitioners began to reflect on planning, its past, present and future development. Discussions on the future of the planning system have since become regular features of the professional journals and academic literature in Britain (*Planning*, 1997; Blowers and Evans, 1997; Hall, 1997). A similar preoccupation can be observed in Europe and the United States (Dagenhart and Sawicki, 1992; Baum, 1997; Healey *et al.*, 1997; Kunzman, 1997).

By contributing to this ongoing debate, this chapter provides a contextual framework on the changing role of the planners and the potential new directions in the planning system in the light of emerging concerns over sustainable development issues. A review of the evolution of planning in Britain will be followed by an account of the different interpretations of the concept of sustainability. The two parts will be linked together in an attempt to examine the potential pathways for the planning system under a specific concept of sustainability.

The Changing Paradigm of Planning

Town planning in Britain emerged from a series of radical, reformist ideas about changing and improving the city. Its impetus came from concerns over the late nineteenth-century industrialisation and rapid urbanisation and the associated problems with public health and sanitation, housing and settlement and fear of social unrest. These social concerns combined with physical and architectural appreciation formed the major thrust of the celebrated works of the 'founding fathers' of the planning 'movement'. Their socially concerned yet physically deterministic ideas characterised planning for the first half of the twentieth century. A functionally appropriate and aesthetically pleasing environment for work and leisure was believed to provide 'a peaceful path to real reform'.[1] The planners' expertise was envisaged to be 'town design'. Influenced by the discourses of architects, engineers and surveyors along with the emerging theories of the modern movement, the planners' role was to imagine and create the Utopia, the 'social city' (Ward, 1994). Their task was to produce 'blueprints' of their imagined places which could be used by an interventionist state as a basis either for public sector development projects or for regulation of the private investment in the interests of 'the community' as a whole.

As the interventionist state of the post-war period gave way to the enabling state of the 1970s, the 'classical town planning' ran out of steam. On the one hand, the state's power, resources and political commitment to turn the planners' imagined places into spatial reality were substantially reduced. On the other hand, the planning profession's theoretical knowledge and expertise to tackle the rapidly changing and complex society of the 1960s proved narrow and inadequate. 'The golden age of planning', when planners free from political interference and confident of their technical capacity were left to get on with the job, came to an end (Hall, 1994). The sudden acceleration of urban change coupled with a shift in political ideology based on a market-dominated economy overwhelmed the 'classical town planning' that was geared to a static world. The changing context came along with the introduction of systems theory.

The consequence for planning was what Thomas Kuhn (1962) called 'a paradigm shift'. 'The discipline of planning changed more in the 10 years from 1960 to 1970, than in the previous 100, possibly 1000 years' (Batty, 1979). Instead of the old master plan approach which assumed that the objectives were fixed from the beginning, the systems theory see planning as a continuous process aimed at controlling and monitoring the complex urban and regional 'systems'. The decision-making process shifted from a single shot, Geddesian approach of survey-analysis-plan to a constantly recycled series of logical steps. These included goal setting, forecasting changes, assessing alternatives, appraising costs and benefits, and monitoring (McLoughlin, 1969; Chadwick, 1971; Faludi, 1973). This 'rational comprehensive' planning method with its extensive use of computer modelling became the new stock-in-trade of the planner. The planning profession focused on new expertise, that of managerial competence – the ability to oversee and co-ordinate the activities of a multi-disciplinary team of professionals – and that of strategic competence – the ability to develop plans, policies and strategies for the future to meet specified goals (Evans and Rydin, 1997).

This technical rationality which assumed that complex political and socio-economic processes could be technicised, commanded and controlled, soon proved ambitious and naive. Systems planning came under attack from both the right and the left. The right criticised it on the grounds that it did not match the incremental, partial and experimental reality of planning in practice (Meyerson and Banfield, 1955; Altshuler, 1965). The reaction from the left was to call on planners to become advocate planners and to promote bottom-up planning (Davidoff, 1965, Webber, 1968–69). The theoretical debates focused so much on distinguishing planning process as something separate from what is planned that the latter became neglected. By the mid-1970s, planning reached the stage of a 'paradigm crisis' (Hall, 1994).

The Thatcher years of the 1980s which were characterised by further rolling-back of the state's activities witnessed various attempts by the government to modify, by-pass and simplify the planning system (Thornley, 1993). The dominant New Right ideology saw physical planners as obstructive bureaucrats who would stifle wealth-creating private enterprise by unnecessary rules on development projects. The notion of comprehensive approach to planning became fragmented into a series of disjointed and piecemeal initiatives. Planners were expected to mediate between the competing interests on a project-by-project basis. The capacity to manage conflict by mediating and negotiating became the new stock-in-trade of the planner.

However, the early 1990s' recession indicated that the deregulation of planning had failed to facilitate economic miracles. As property booms bust, developers began to press the government to inject some stability and confidence into the property markets, suggesting more interventionist planning. At the same time, the 'green movements' of the 1970s began to achieve a new political salience in the late 1980s. The two forces led to a dramatic swing in government's attitude towards both planning and environmental issues. Town planning survived the intensive scrutiny of the 1980s. New legislation, the Planning and Compensation Act 1991, restored the status of the plans. Some argue that planning emerged 'leaner but fitter' (Stroud, 1995).

The failure of the neo-liberal agenda in the 1980s to undermine planning regulations has led to the suggestion that 'if British planning system survived Thatcher, Ridley, and Heseltine, it's pretty solid and is going to remain in place for a very long time' (Personal comment, January 1997). This may be the case; 'there will be planning but (perhaps) not as we know it' (Morphet, 1997).

Despite these developments, the planners' role in the 1990s, within both public and private sectors, remained largely the same as it was in the 1980s, overseeing the legislative process and mediating between competing interests. The difference, however, was that, with the introduction of the plan-led planning and a resurgence of plan-making activity, the arena of conflict mediation increasingly moved away from individual development control cases towards the plan preparation stage. The plans themselves, however, became development control manuals, stuffed with central government's regulatory norms and criteria for land use development (Colenutt, 1997). They often got entangled in vociferous public opposition and caught up in never-ending public inquiries. As the arena of conflict management was moving to the earlier stages of the regulatory system, the 'planning-by-appeal' approach of the 1980s gave way to the 'planning-by-public inquiry' of the 1990s. Many argue that an era of *accusation* against planning system has been succeeded by one characterised by *expectation* particularly with regards to environmental issues (Stroud, 1995). However, the planning profession, faced with long-term and exhaustive criticism, has retreated to the status of managing the semi-judicial process of planning legislation (Evans and Rydin, 1997). But, this is only one face of planning, the one which is most visible today. There is, however, another face of planning, that of its pro-active role in pursuing 'public interest' objectives. This face of planning has been largely undermined particularly in the last two decades.

The Twin Faces of Planning

The twin faces of the planning system have existed side by side though not always closely inter-linked and certainly not always with equal significance in influencing the process of urban change. One of these two faces is the purposive, ideological face of planning, the other is the regulatory function of the system. The former has its roots in social purposes and reformist ideas of the early twentieth century, the latter is the outcome of the insti-tutionalisation and professionalisation of the planning movement. One portrays planning as an independent and radical thought, the other represents it as a technical and politically neutral activity. One is visionary, capable of imagining the kind of places in which people want to live and work, the other is regulatory, focused on reconciling conflict of interests on the use and development of land. One aims to enhance and promote spatial strategies which combine multiple objectives, the other involves addressing the impacts of development. One is to do with strategic place-making, the other with tactical conflict mediation (Figure 6.1).

The post-war history of the British planning system has seen periodic resurgence of the two purposes shown in Figure 6.1. Until the mid-1960s the social and ideological face of planning was the dominant purpose of the system, manifested in either the radical design ideas or the 'rational' steering of the urban systems to achieve a specified goal. The reason was twofold. On the one hand, the focus on place-making activities was encouraged by the existence of a strong and resourceful state which was capable of implementing the planners' visions and putting them into physical context. On the other hand, the regulatory function of the system was of little significance since the public sector was almost the sole player in carrying out major development projects.

As the state's activities gave way to market forces, the imaginative and pro-active face of planning was increasingly marginalised, whilst at the same time its regulatory actions gained strength. Since the 1970s there has been little room for 'visionary planners' in the activities of a public sector which is being denied resources and roles in carrying out development schemes. Instead, the mounting activities of the private sector have shifted the focus of the system towards its regulatory mode of action. The demand for site-specific conflict management has succeeded the need for strategic vision.

The changing face of planning in the last few decades has been so profound that it is difficult to imagine the depth and breadth of planning as a tradition of thought, policy and action. The social purposes that once shaped its original foundation seem to have been entirely renounced. The way planning is practised today represents it as a bureaucratic routine and a technical exercise which has little in common with its long-term affiliation with some notion of

Ideological face	Regulatory face
• rooted in social purposes and reformist ideas of the early twentieth century	• outcome of the process of institutionalisation and professionalisation
• independent and radical thought	• technical and bureaucratic
• visionary	• short-termist
• promotes spatial strategies	• assesses development impact
• integrated	• sectoral
• concerned with strategic place-making	• engaged in conflict mediation
• dominated planning until mid-1960s	• dominated planning since the 1970s

Figure 6.1 The twin faces of the British planning system

reform. Some suggest that, 'planning thought has become a prisoner of policy process' (Ward, 1994). 'British planners have once again let themselves get caught in a policy/legal culture which restricts their ability to integrate around spatial issues and which emphasises a vertical power relation inside the public sector' (Interview, January 1997). Whilst the policy roles of the planners are now more diverse than ever before, their ability to shape or even influence the process of urban change has been largely atrophied (Ward, 1994). Some interpret these as the consequences of 'imagination deficit' in the current planning practice (Hague, 1996). Planners seem to 'have lost [their] capacity to think strategically and [they] need to recover that capacity' (Hall, 1997).

In Search of a New 'Vision' for Planning

In order to regain such strategic capacity many commentators believe that there is a need for a new vision, one which can 'reach out to society as whole, addressing its wants, needs and insecurities' (Ward, 1994), a 'vision to rank those of Ebenezer Howard a century ago' (Hall, 1997). There is a consensus that such a vision can now emerge from what has come to be called sustainability (Ward, 1994; Hague, 1996; Hall, 1997). However, the discourses of sustainability offer a variety of interpretations, each leading to a distinctively different development path. Despite the variation, it is possible to categorise the sustainability discourses into two major groups. One discourse draws on the ideology of 'ecological modernisation', the other is based on 'risk society' theory. They reflect the underlying conflicts between those who believe that society can achieve sustainability without seriously impeding economic growth, and those who argue that society cannot achieve sustainability unless alternative modes of production with their compatible social forms are pursued (Blowers, 1997).

The concept of ecological modernisation was first introduced in the mid-1980s by the German political scientists, Joseph Huber and Martin Janicke (Hajer, 1997). It has its roots in two influential but fundamentally different strands of environmental discourses which dominated the debate in the early 1970s. These were the radical environmental movements represented in *Blueprint for Survival* (*The Ecologist*, 1972) and the technocratic approach of environmental scientists reflected in the Club of Rome's *Limits to Growth* study (Meadows *et al.*, 1972). Ecological modernisation, the product of a coalition of forces, provides a common language and a common way of framing the environmental problems for a range of actors who initially held converging ideas (Hajer, 1997). It can therefore be seen as the political accommodation of the radical environmental movements of the 1970s. This partly explains its legitimacy and dominance in the environmental discourses since the mid-1980s.

The risk society theory was introduced by the German sociologist, Ulrich Beck (Beck 1992; Beck *et al.*, 1994; Beck, 1998). For Beck, the present ecological crisis, along with other social transformations, signifies the emergence of a new form of societal arrangement which he describes as risk society. Risk society represents a new phase in the process of modernisation in which environmental issues should be seen as a 'providential gift for the universal self-reformation of a so far fatalistic industrial modernity' (Beck, 1998: 160). In his recent work, Beck defines this process as the 'modernisation of modern society' or the 'reflexive modernisation'. Beck argues that, 'the more modern a society becomes, the more unintended consequences it produces, and as these become known and acknowledged, they call the foundations of industrial modernisation into question' (Beck, 1998: 91). In other words, modernity becomes political, that is to say 'the foundations and basic norms in business, science, politics and the family must be re-negotiated and re-established' (ibid.). In the context of industrial society, modernisation has been seen as a renouncement of traditions and liberation from the constraints of nature. In the context of risk society the objective of modernisation is the management of risks which are inherent by-products of industrial society itself. Beck argues that today people are 'discharged from the security of industrial society into the turbulence of global risk society . . . Their lives are burdened with most varied and contradictory global and personal risks' (1998: 32). The emphasis of the politics has, therefore, been forced to shift from conflict over distribution of welfare to conflicts over social and environmental risks which are the 'unwanted consequences' of industrial society itself. The central problem and a key characteristic of the risk society, or the reflexive phase of modernity, is decision-making in the context of uncertainty on all sides, experts and non-experts.

The Twin Discourses of Sustainability

The ecological modernisation theory suggests that the economy and the environment are not in conflict and indeed economic prosperity is essential for achieving environmental improvements. It represents environmental politics as a 'positive sum game' in which the concern for environmental degradation no longer endangers the profit margins of the businesses and the industry (Weal, 1993; Hajer 1992, 1997). Risk society, on the other hand, suggests that there is an irreconcilable conflict between the contemporary mode of production and the ecological needs. It suggests that, 'environmental risks are produced industrially, externalised economically, individualised judicially, legitimised scientifically and minimised politically' (Beck, 1998: 26).

Within ecological modernisation, environmental degradation is not conceptualised as an anomaly of modernity. In fact, the ecological modern-isation approach relies on science and technology to 'refine production' in order to achieve better environmental performance. It is a strategy based on 'fundamental belief in progress and the problem solving capacity of modern techniques and skills of social engineering' (Hajer, 1997: 33). Risk society, on the other hand, sees the development of modern technologies as the cause of risk to ecosystems. The consequences and devastations caused by the chemical and nuclear industries can no longer be limited spatially, temporally or socially. Thus, Beck (1998) argues that in the face of such hazardous side effects, all the fundamental concepts of risk management in business, law and politics fail.

Ecological modernisation draws on modernist policy instruments such as expert systems and science to mitigate and control environmental side effects of economic dynamisms. Risk society, on the other hand, highlights the conflict of rationality and knowledge where the claims of different expert groups collide with one another and with those of 'ordinary knowledge', the latter often being discredited and falsified in the key institutions of state, business and politics (Beck, 1998: 93).

Within ecological modernisation theory, the conception of sustainability is a marketised, utilitarian one which perceives the environment as a stock of assets that can be quantified, priced and traded in a quasi-monetary terms (Whatmore and Boucher, 1993). It is understood that this can be most efficiently achieved if left to market forces (Pearce *et al.*, 1989). Within risk society, the conception of sustainability is a radical and moral one. Here, the protection of ecosystems has priority over any other demands. This approach emphasises the need to constrain human activity within the carrying capacity of ecological systems (Jacobs and Stott, 1993).

As regards the process of policy-making, given the high degree of risk and uncertainty associated with decision-making processes, risk society emphasises the need for greater democracy and participation (Harrison and Burgess, 1994) whilst ecological modernisation theory relies mainly on elitist, techno-corporatist approach to decision-making (Hajer, 1992). According to ecological modernisation the state has an enabling role, facilitating the market operation. It provides a technocratic regulatory framework within which environmental standards and criteria can be set up to mitigate development impacts. Risk society, on the other hand, promotes an interventionist state but one which is based on the power of collective action. Politicisation of environmental issues can lead to contrasting social structures ranging from democratic to dictatorial ones. Thus, risk society emphasises the necessity and indeed urgency of environmental democracy and the significance of deliberative processes to achieve that. Whilst ecological modernisation accepts the status quo, risk society calls for fundamental social transformation (Figure 6.2). Beck argues that, 'a key to combating destruction of the environment is not found in the environment itself, nor in a different individual morality or in different research or business ethics; by nature it lies in the regulatory systems of the institutions that are historically questionable' (Beck, 1998: 26). Risk society theory, therefore, calls for a new social relationship between the individual and society and, closer to the discussion of this chapter, between the state and society. In this context, ecological crisis is conceived as a liberating process that leads to the collapse of bureaucracy and the rigidity of roles that industrial society and its functionalism asserts.

Blowers (1997) argues that risk society is a 'utopian and idealistic' approach which highlights the social consequences of technological changes but offers little solution beyond the quest for a 'new Enlightenment'. Ecological modernisation, on the other hand, is a pragmatic and seemingly 'rational and realistic' approach which provides a fairly clear direction. However, if the scientists' predictions regarding, for example, the global environmental changes are to be believed, ecological modernisation will fail to provide a solution beyond its mitigating attempts or, as Beck put it, beyond 'indulgence in cosmetic ecology on a grand scale' (Beck, 1998: 26).

The Future Directions for the Planning System

Given the inherent flexibility of the British planning system and its diverse policy roles throughout the twentieth century, the system can play a part in each of these approaches (Figure 6.3) albeit under very different definitions and conditions in each case (Blowers, 1997).

The 'professional' definition of planning as conceptualised by government and adopted in practice, fits neatly into the ecological modernisation approach. Within this approach, planning is seen as a legitimate arm of the state's regulatory regime. Its purpose is, first, to correct the land and property market imperfections, i.e. economic regulation; and, second, to facilitate economic

Ecological modernisation	Risk society
• optimistic approach	• sceptical approach
• sees no conflict between economy and environment	• sees irreconcilable conflict between current mode of production and environment
• relies on science and technology to 'refine production' for improving environmental performance	• sees modern technology as the cause of risk to ecological system and survival
• sustainability concept is marketised and utilitarian, can be priced and traded off with other goods	• sustainability concept is radical and moral with protection of ecosystems having the highest priority
• relies on elitist, techno-corporatist approach to policy-making	• calls for greater participation in policy-making at the local level
• state as enabler, facilitating market forces within a regulatory framework	• interventionist state based on power of collective action asserting its will on private interest
• accepts the status quo	• calls for social transformation

Figure 6.2 The twin discourses of sustainability

growth whilst protecting amenity and resources, i.e. environmental regulation. In the trade-offs between the economy and the environment, the planners' role is to draw on judgemental nature of the British planning system and to strike a balance between economic imperatives and environmental concerns. Their role is to set the terms of the trade-offs by drawing on a series of state-formulated non-spatial policy criteria for environmental regulations.

Here, as in other areas of public policy, the planning process is a techno-cratic and sometimes elitist one. The 'public interest' objectives of planning, often interpreted as being the same as the government's policies, are articulated through a hierarchical, issue-based approach with little inte-gration, reflecting the highly centralised and sectoralised institutional relations in British public policy. This regulatory, non-spatial and apolitical face of planning whose purpose is to facilitate economic processes whilst making them environmentally benign has little to offer in the context of risk society approach to sustainability. However, following Blowers (1997), planning, in its broader definition, as was conceptualised by its 'founding fathers' and to some extent practised in the 1940s and 1950s, can play a significant role here.

Within risk society, planning has a pro-active dimension. It is ideological, socially responsive and interventionist. Here, planning is seen as an activity which is leading rather than following the state's policies. The planners' role is to defend the environment and the local identities against the risk associated with contemporary economic processes. Their role is to reveal the uncertainties surrounding the expert knowledge and the 'technical fix' solutions to the environmental problems. Thus, rather than ignoring and hushing things up, which intensifies the 'actual dynamic of routine self-endangerment in industrial modernity' (Beck, 1998: 98), planners should acknowledge the 'unintended consequences' of development options and avoid those alternatives whose long-term consequences remain illusive.

Planning in ecological modernisation	Planning in risk society
• regulatory face of planning	• radical and ideological face of planning
• legitimate arm of the state's regulatory regime	• pro-active arm of an interventionist state
• facilitates economic processes while making them environmentally benign	• defends the environment against risks associated with economic processes
• focus on centrally-formulated, non-spatial, apolitical regulatory criteria	• focus on strategic and holistic approach to place-making
• elitist, hierarchical	• participative, collaborative
• issue-based and fragmented	• territorial-based and integrated

Figure 6.3 Potential future directions for the planning system

According to risk society, the uncertainty of knowledge requires a precautionary approach, one which gives priority to long-term views on ecological processes and takes a strategic stance to decision-making. Planning institutions, therefore, need to be re-constructed in a way that requires the actors to reflect on the distant effects of their action. Uncertainty in decision-making requires drawing on all forms of knowledge, expert and non-expert, as well as sharing of the risks with a wide range of stakeholders. The emphasis on moral argumentation in risk society approach, as opposed to the significance of scientific knowledge (Owens, 1997), requires the planning processes to be inclusionary and participative. The task of planning is seen as providing the strategic sites where the vested 'experts/scientific' interests are prevented from dominating the creative debate.

The multiplicity of the sustainable development goal also demands a holistic and coherent approach to policy-making, one which combines the objectives of environmental sustainability with that of social equality and economic well-being (Figure 6.4).

For planners, these are all familiar principles though mostly forgotten or unfashionable today. The new environmental agenda has provided an opportunity for planners to assert much from their traditional conceptual repertoire (Ward, 1994). There is therefore a strong argument suggesting that incorporating sustainability and social responsiveness as the central feature of planning agenda can articulate a new direction for the future of planning.

However, the current climate of British government's public policy is dominated by the discourse of ecological modernisation and its interpretation of the planner's role. This is reflected in a whole series of planning policy documents ranging from *This Common Inheritance* (DoE, 1992b) to the planning policy guidance notes and the development plans. Despite the rhetoric of sustainable development, the planning system has remained deeply preoccupied with short-term economic priorities against the interests of long-term environmental concerns (Davoudi *et al.*, 1996). It is therefore difficult

- strategic thinking

- holistic approach

- expert and non-expert knowledge

- political commitment

- social responsiveness

- ethical guideline

- participative processes

- reflexive institutions

Figure 6.4 A sustainable development agenda

not to conclude that the future of planning will be one of continuation of status quo with some changes in its quasi-technical role in development impact assessment and in its negotiative role in conflict mediation.

However, there are increasing pressures, particularly at the local level, for the development of the kind of policy agendas and processes that have a strong resonance with the risk society perspective (Vigar *et al.*, 2000). These can be best observed in two interconnected trends. One is the rising social and environmental concerns about the 'unintended consequences' of scientific and technological development (such as genetically modified food). The other is the cultural and environmental concerns about the erosion of local identities by the globalisation processes and the degradation of local environment justified by the techno-economic necessity of development (such as in the case of open cast mining and waste disposal activity). Both of these trends are enveloped with the crisis of democracy (Giddens, 1998) and an increasing distrust of the capacity of expert systems and government institutions in managing the risks involved. The beef crisis was becoming a classic example of this.

What concerns planning more directly is the latter, i.e. the significance of *local*, or as Beck put it, the magic of place in a world society. What is often maliciously called NIMBYism (Not In My Back Yard) can be in fact interpreted as the defence of local identity and environment as well as a sign of emerging civil spheres in the face of diminishing trust in politicians and authorities (Castells, 1997). Responding to the demand for strengthening and enhancing the specificity of localities is a role that planning in a risk society can fulfil. As Castells put it, 'planning can contribute to the new world by making new spaces and meaningful places' (1996: 8). Strengthening local identity also plays a major role in fostering an active civil society. Here again, planning can draw on its traditional roles. Some eighty years ago, when the town planning movement began to grow as a wider public concern with the trajectory of urban change, Patrick Geddes described town planning as 'the development of a local life, a regional character, a civic spirit, a unique individuality, capable of course of growth and expansion, of improvement and development in many ways . . .' (1915). The world has changed dramatically since then but describing planning as a place-making activity is as good a definition today as ever.

However, fostering and creating local identities may no longer be defined by specific geographical position, given the intensity of mobility and communication, but may well be achieved through, for example, imaginative planning solutions to urban problems, solutions which have been arrived at not behind the closed doors of planning offices but in a continuous dialogue with all the stakeholders and above all with the inclusion of civil society. New forms of social associations are replacing the traditional ones.

(Giddens, 1998)

Harnessing these to wider societal ends in ways that benefit local communities as well as the society as a whole is what planners can contribute to, given their traditional affiliation with 'public interest' objectives.

Concluding Remarks

As Friedmann argues, 'planning is less and less about technical matters' and more and more about the 'critical appreciation and appropriation of ideas' (1998: 250). Planners' unique competence is in their knowledge of 'socio-spatial processes that, in interaction with each other, *produce* the urban habitat' (ibid.: 251). However, if we agree that there is a rising demand for the planning system to play a role in a risk society approach to sustainability, the knowledge of city-forming processes constitutes only one part, although a critical one, of the planners' competence. The other dimensions relate to knowledge of how to interact with and be socially responsive to the rising civil society, and, more importantly, how to intervene and influence the decision-making processes. In addressing the RTPI Summer School of 1996, Cliff Hague suggested that, 'as planners, we must presume that intelligent action by institutions and agencies can make a difference, and if planning means anything it must be that the outcomes of these momentous social changes are not pre-determined' (1996: 10). It is the conscious intervention of collective actors in the production of urban space that constitutes planning in the context of risk society approach. This in turn requires a more daring and less codified, as well as a more collaborative and less corporatist planning (Healey, 1997).

Acknowledgement

A slightly longer version of this chapter has been published in Davoudi, S. (2000), 'Sustainability: a new vision for the British planning system', *Planning Perspectives*, 15: 123–37.

Note

1   This was the title of the Ebenezer Howard's book as published in 1898. It was later republished under the more commonly known title of *Garden Cities of Tomorrow* (1902).

Further Reading

You can find out more about the risk society theory in U. Beck (1992), *Risk Society: Towards a New modernity*, London: Sage; or U. Beck (1998), *Democracy Without Enemies*, Cambridge: Polity Press.

For a full discussion on ecological modernisation theory see: M. Hajer (1997), *The Politics of Environmental Discourse*, Oxford: Oxford University Press

PART II

The Challenge of Sustainable Development: Exploring the Complexities

Simin Davoudi

In Chapter 1 we stated that there is now extensive evidence, provided in hundred of books and reports (see for e.g. the Report of the United Nation Environment Programme, UNEP, 2000), which points to the growing environmental degradation of our planet. There are also numerous assessments of social and ecological 'footprints' of specific activities and consumption patterns. At the same time, substantial progress has been made in offering innovative solutions for better management of resources (see for e.g. Club of Rome's recent report, Weisacker *et al.*, 1997). Nevertheless, there remains major disagreement, often coloured by political motivations, on the exact passage of transition to sustainable development. What is evident is that the pathway from current non-sustainable development to an environmentally sustainable one is unlikely to be travelled by a single giant leap towards a 'misty-eyed vision of a peaceful ecotopia' (Campbell, 1999: 252). A more realistic scenario is that of a complex and contested journey which involves making difficult choices by individuals and by society as a whole, often in a climate of deep uncertainty.

Take for example one of the most serious and life-threatening global environmental problems of the twenty-first century, climate change. Until recently the scientific community was divided on the causes of climate change and more importantly whether human actions were to be blamed. That division was finally overcome and scientists became convinced that human-made greenhouse gases are the main culprits for the earth's recent warming (*The Economist*, 18 November 2000a: 133–6). However, reaching political consensus proved to be an even bigger obstacle in finding solutions. So far, it has been notoriously difficult to bridge the ideological and political gulf which has emerged between the developing and the developed countries on the one hand and amongst the developed countries themselves on the other. The political disagreement led to the breakdown of negotiations in The Hague meeting in November 2000, the latest in a series of United Nations' summits on global warming. The ongoing scientific debates and political bargaining, or indeed horse-trading, about the climate change problem typify the unpaved nature of the path to sustainable development. It raises a number of crucial issues, including the link between local actions and global impacts, the tension between economic growth and environmental concerns, the rights of the developing countries to modernisation versus their responsibilities for environmental protection, the limitations in existing regulatory systems, the inadequacies of public policy responses and the thorny issue of individual lifestyle and life choices versus the need for collective responsibilities and actions.

Reflecting on this contested nature of the sustainable development agenda is what links together the contributions to this part. The common thread in all chapters is their attempt to make sense of what 'sustainability' means in various areas of policy and practice. It is about exploring the complexities, identifying the barriers and opportunities and reflecting on potential solutions in the passage to more sustainable practices in a variety of policy areas including urban growth, housing, transport, property development, urban design and waste management. The contributions show how the sustainable development agenda has become one of the most prominent cross-cutting themes threading through all areas of government policy.

In Chapter 7, *Peter Hall* deals with one of the most heated debates in planning circles since the publication of the 1992-based household projections by the Department of the Environment in 1995 (DoE, 1995b), what is the most sustainable way of accommodating the growing number of households in the next quarter century? Drawing on a number of empirical studies carried out in the UK and internationally, the chapter demonstrates the inconsistencies in the research findings on the relationships between urban density, travel pattern and energy consumption. Given the existing confusion over these relationships, Hall settles for the insight offered by Rasmussen (1937) and his admiration for English suburban way of life which is most clearly manifested in early London suburbs such as Bedford Park and Bloomsbury. The chapter concludes that it is possible to achieve high density, even as high as 100 dwellings per hectare, on the basis of single-family homes with private open space particularly in areas with a buoyant housing market such as inner London. However, he reminds us that in order to make these attractive to affluent middle classes a combination of good urban design ideas, architectural talents and experienced private developers is essential. Hall argues that 'the easiest way to repopulate our depopulated cities would be to develop extensive new suburbs in town . . .'.

The pathway from current non-sustainable housing policy to a more sustainable one becomes more contested and complex if the goal is to make the journey less painful and more acceptable in social as well environmental terms. In Chapter 8, *Nick Gallent* explores the concept of the sustainable 'home' and extends what is meant by sustainable housing beyond physical development to cover its social dimension. He argues that this can be achieved through 'focusing on consumption and prioritising the individual and the home'. He then examines how both housing delivery at the local level and nationally formulated housing policy can affect the realisation of a sustainable housing system understood in broader social terms. Gallent emphasises that the concept of sustainability is understood differently depending on the weightings given to its dimensions, characteristics and objectives at the levels of housing consumption, delivery and policy. Looking at it in this way, the chapter highlights the weaknesses of the current housing policy in the UK and, most importantly, reveals the complexities of developing sustainable strategies in this policy area, and indeed in any other.

When it comes to sustainable transport policy, however, the solution might be seen as a simple one: reduction in cars. Yet, as *Stephen Marshall*'s contribution in Chapter 9 shows, the reality is far more complex. Transport has moved away from being part of the urban solution in the Modernist era to being seen as part of the urban problem. It consumes a high proportion of land and energy and contributes significantly to air and noise pollution. It impacts on almost every aspect of environmental resources and plays a direct role in human mortality and health. The first part of Chapter 9 describes the growing problems associated with the current pattern of transport: it shows how the increasing number of journeys we make, at greater speeds over longer distances is accelerating environmental problem. The second part examines three main groups of policy responses to these problems including policies focusing on changing travel modes, land use policies and policies for reducing the need to travel. As Marshall points out, whilst each of these policies presents a potential contribution to sustainability, they all have limitations and can lead to undesirable social and economic consequences. The protests against increased fuel taxes which brought Britain to a halt in the autumn of 2000 are an example of the failure of such policy considerations. It is, therefore, not surprising that Marshall, along with other contributors to this book, calls for complementary 'policy packaging' as a way of moving towards more sustainable practices.

If a more integrated approach to policy-making is to be adopted, it is crucial to examine the entire development process. Chapter 10 by *Michael Edwards and Christopher Marsh* is a move in that direction. In looking at the contribution of property development to the sustainable development agenda, they adopt a hierarchical approach moving from the scale of individual building through neighbourhoods and localities to the whole settlement pattern. They pay particular attention to the rules and regulations which govern the development process. In conclusion, Edwards and Marsh highlight a number of 'problems' and 'solutions' associated with some of the key relationships influencing the operation of the property development sector. They put particular emphasis on the power of 'green consumerism' to force the property market to produce more environmentally friendly buildings, and hence to transform the built environment into a more sustainable one. However, as mentioned in their last remark, the 'green movement' is still far from presenting a clear direction for changing unsustainable practices.

An important aspect of development process is urban design. In Chapter 11, *Matthew Carmona* explores the conception of a sustainable development agenda for urban design. The chapter traces the scope and nature of the agenda and the application of its principles across various spatial scales. Carmona argues that to achieve sustainable urban design the life-time environmental impact of any development should be reduced; making it as self-sufficient as possible whilst addressing the needs of all sections of society. By reviewing and combining a number of contributions to the debate on sustainable urban design, ten principles are identified which are then linked to the 'key tenets of sustainable development' at different spatial scales. In conclusion, Carmona reminds us of the complexity and the formidable barriers to delivering a sustainable urban design; a view shared by all contributors to this book who explore and analyse other policy and implementation issues.

The final chapter in Part II focuses on waste, an area of public policy which has gone under sea changes since the last decade of the twentieth century and is likely to face further challenges in the coming years. The ability to achieve sustainability in this politically contentious and environmentally critical area has become one of the touchstones of progress towards sustainable development. However, as *Simin Davoudi* in Chapter 12 shows, surrounded by information deficiencies, political and institutional tensions and technical and procedural complexities, management of waste in the UK is still far from being sustainable. Her review of the past policies and processes reveals that decades of unsustainable practices and inadequate regulatory systems coupled with a persistent 'throw away' culture continue to build barriers to more prudent use of resources and better management of conflicting interests. Davoudi concludes by reminding us that the pressures to divert waste from landfill are irreversible particularly after the UK agreement to implement the EU Landfill Directive. The critical question is whether these pressures would lead to more recycling and reuse of waste or to an increase in the level of incineration with energy recovery; the latter option will undoubtedly set the planning system on course for a tough ride.

The overall aim of Part II is to move beyond the conceptual principles of sustainable development and explore their application in the day-to-day policies and practices of the different sectors. Although the contributions are heterogeneous in their analyses as well as their subject areas, together they point to a number of key common themes. The first one is the inconsistency in research findings and the lack of reliable information, an indication of the limited knowledge available in many areas of public policy on what constitutes a more sustainable path. The other key theme emerging from the contributions is the difficulties of tackling undesirable social and economic consequences of environmental polices. The pathway from current non-sustainable development to a sustainable one becomes more contested and composite if the goal is to make the journey as painless as possible to the deprived communities.

Finally, what underlines most of the contributions to this part, although sometimes implicitly, is the question of choice. Should we, as a society, focus on improving the quality of urban living or should we continue to 'escape' and spread out to the countryside? Should we invest in public transports or should we continue to add more cars and build more roads? Should we invest in waste reduction and recycling or should we continue to produce more waste and to bury and burn them? Should we invest in more energy-efficient and affordable 'homes' or should we carry on building more new houses, fit for single affluent households, and demolish those in the 'unpopular' areas? We know, not least from the contributions to this book, that there are no simple answers to these questions but in our search for better understanding of the complexities it is important to distinguish between our *needs* and our *wants*. As Michael Redclift put it:

Environmental problems . . . are the outcome of a series of choices, many of which we make collectively as a society. The epicentre of these choices is the developed world, and most of these choices are so culturally grounded that few people recognise them as choices at all; they are routinely depicted as 'needs' rather than wants.

(Redclift 1992: 40)

7 Sustainable Cities or Town Cramming?

Peter Hall

The question is: at what densities can we (and should we) reconstruct our cities to help meet the challenge of the 3.8 million new households, projected to form in England between 1996 and 2021? This chapter will avoid the question of numbers, debated endlessly both before publication of the Urban Task Force report (Urban Task Force 1999), and since. But the question of urban density is very relevant to the final answer, and is the central point of this contribution.

It might be regarded as a frivolous and vexatious question: everyone knows we must save land. I have questioned that assumption; I have argued that we were making a fetish of land without asking why (Hall and Ward 1998: 107–8). There is a bad reason and a good reason for more compact urban development. The bad one is to save rural land. It is bad because there is no reason to do so, either now or in the foreseeable future. About 10 per cent of the land of South East England, in 1995, was in EU set-aside, growing nothing but weeds. EU farm policies are undergoing the most fundamental shake-up in their forty-year history, and the outcome is still undecided, but it is certain that agricultural subsidies will be slashed, so if anything the problem of surplus agricultural land will rapidly get worse. The main problem for the government, who delivered a rural as well as an urban White Paper during 2000, will be how to find new land uses and new activities to replace farming in large areas of the country. One of these might just be urban development.

The good reason, or possibly good reason, has to do with sustainability. A lot of evidence, starting with the much-quoted study of Newman and Kenworthy, in 1989, and continuing with the analysis in the ECOTEC report of 1993 (Newman and Kenworthy 1989; DoE/DoT 1993), has suggested that denser cities use less energy for travel, perhaps appreciably so. ECOTEC showed that inner London and the big provincial cities were the most energy-frugal parts of Britain in terms of energy used for transport, while rural areas were the most profligate; in between, there was a steady rise in energy consumption as settlements became smaller in size and lower in density. Michael Breheny has used the ECOTEC figures to calculate that by the start of the 1990s we were using perhaps 3 per cent more energy for travel than we would have done if we had all remained stuck in the geographical patterns of 1961 (Breheny 1990: 9.1–9.28).

However, the research results are not consistent; indeed they are confusing. A paper from the Bartlett School of Planning argues that higher population densities widen the range of opportunities to develop local personal contacts and activities that can be maintained without resort to motorised travel. They also widen the range of services that can be supported in the local area and reduce the need to travel long distances. They also tend to reduce average distances between homes, services, employment and other opportunities, and that in turn will reduce travel distance. And finally, higher densities may be more amenable to public transport operation and use and less amenable to car ownership and use, which have implications on modal choice (Stead *et al.* 2000).

Empirical studies, they say, largely confirm these hypotheses. Average journey distance by car, bus and rail does decrease with increasing population density, while the average journey distance by foot is more or less constant, regardless of population density. These findings are supported by the most recent data from National Travel Surveys. But total journey frequency does not show a clear gradation with population density, and there is little variation in trip frequency according to population density. True, the highest trip frequency is in areas where population density is low, while the lowest trip frequency is in areas where population density is high, as ECOTEC found. But a study by Ewing *et al.* (1996) finds no significant statistical link between trip frequency and population density.

Similarly, a recent DETR study on density concluded that total distance travelled was lowest in areas with a density of over 50 persons per hectare; the total distance by all modes was lowest in towns with 250,000 and more people; and the distance travelled by all modes increased as density decreased. Earlier, the ECOTEC study showed that with increasing population density, the proportion of trips by car decreases, while the proportion of trips by both public transport and foot increases (DETR 1998b).

Comparing very low density areas and very high density areas, David Banister has found a fourfold difference in public transport trips and almost a twofold difference in walk trips. Car trips, he finds, account for as much as 72 per cent of journeys in low density areas (less than 1 person per hectare) but only 51 per cent of trips in high density areas (more than 50 persons per hectare). The proportion of shopping trips by public transport and the proportion of commuting trips by foot are both positively linked with population density, even after accounting for socio-economic differences. However, it is important to notice in Banister's work that he is talking about very low density areas. His highest density range, 50 persons per hectare and above, equates to about 20 dwellings per hectare, not even as dense as Unwin's recommended standard (Banister 1999a). (This is probably because 50 is the highest density recorded in the National Travel Survey.) We can conclude again that there is no evidence here for taking densities above 30 dwellings per hectare.

Newman and Kenworthy find a correlation between urban population density and transport energy consumption. However, much of this variation comes from the extremes of the distribution. Crudely, it is very clear that in transport terms American low-density cities are energy-profligate and that Hong Kong is very energy-efficient. But it is less clear what happens in the critical middle part of the range.

Significant work by Michael Breheny, Ian Gordon and Suzanne Archer of the University of Reading analysed three data sets – Newman and Kenworthy, the United Kingdom National Travel Survey (which has also been used by David Banister and others), and commuting data from the 1991 Census, all of which relate travel behaviour and densities, and they found a relatively weak link between densities and energy use (Breheny *et al.* 1998). Both here and internationally, travel is much more strongly linked to fuel prices and incomes. About one-third of individual variations in fuel use from transport comes from socio-economic factors, while another third is due to location: the size and building density of the town they live in, and the accessibility of features. More compact cities, they conclude, will not necessarily have the effect of reducing traffic volumes. This is far more likely to come from concentrating employment, which will make it easier to use public transport to get to work.

Specifically, they found that the Newman–Kenworthy results were distorted by three very high-density cities – Hong Kong, Singapore and Moscow. When these were removed, the results showed that the effect of building density is very much less: on average, cities with double the density cut the energy demand by only 15 per cent. The same figures showed that doubling petrol prices would have a far bigger effect, cutting fuel use for transport by 40 per cent. Similarly, the National Travel data figures showed that only about one-third of the variations in individual travel patterns were attributable to size and density and accessibility effects, with about one-third due to socio-economic effects.

Rather predictably, people living in small compact cities tended to travel shorter distances and to use environmentally friendly modes of transport. Those in London and the other major conurbations also used green transport modes, but travelled longer distances. The census data showed that the effect of density was less clear than that of the location of jobs and housing, and a regional effect. There was a link between density and distance travelled but no clear relationship between compaction and distances.

The Reading researchers concluded: 'This project casts doubt on the orthodoxy that increasing building densities will necessarily reduce travel in towns and cities' (Breheny *et al.* 1998: 4). High-density areas do have lower rates of car use, but the differences are small. Overall, they concluded, making cities more compact should not be used as a general prescription for cutting fuel use; concentrating employment is likely to be a better strategy, though it could be counter-productive if it led to longer trips.

However, there are yet other complications. Density is associated with certain other features, particularly availability of residential parking. If this is poor, it may discourage car ownership and use, particularly if finding a parking space close to home is difficult. It may also have the effect of encouraging trip chaining, rather than several journeys starting or ending at home and encouraging local journeys by non-motorised modes especially where there is the prospect of a long search for parking. Empirical evidence does indeed show that the availability of residential car parking is linked to both trip frequency and modal choice. However, there is also a counter-intuitive result: as the availability of residential car parking increases, the average number of trips per person actually decreases. The researchers think that maybe residents with more parking spaces make fewer, longer journeys, while residents with fewer parking spaces make more journeys but they tend to be shorter. It also emerges that as available residential car parking increases, so does the proportion of car journeys. In other words, residents with more parking spaces not only make fewer, longer journeys but also more of these journeys are by car. Another piece of research, which the Reading group quote, suggests that where parking is limited, people make more trips on foot, in order not to lose their parking spaces (Breheny *et al.* 1998).

But we now have to come to the major complication, which is that density and other land use characteristics tend to be associated with socio-economic factors, which may themselves affect travel patterns. The most obvious is that trip frequency is linked to household income: richer household members make more journeys than poorer household members. Studies from a number of countries show this fairly obvious relationship, and it is related to transport energy consumption. In most western cities, including British ones, average incomes increase with increasing distance from the city centre, with the exception of residents in very central locations in cities like London and Paris (within approximately 4 kilometres of the city centre). And this is related to another very obvious relationship, which is that trip frequency and trip distance increase with car ownership (although not all the evidence is consistent on frequency). Higher density areas tend to have lower levels of car ownership, but it is not always clear as to whether density or income is the real causal factor.

Crudely put, the problem may be that London and Birmingham and Manchester use less energy not only because they are built at higher densities, but also because they contain quite high proportions of poorer people who cannot afford cars. There are doubtless some hairshirt environmentalists who would wish that everyone were as poor, but it is not an argument likely to appeal to many people, or to the politicians who represent them.

However, the DETR research study concludes, 'There is little research on the relationship between urban form, density and energy consumption' (DETR 1998b: 47). The latter is influenced by a number of factors including layout, topography and aspect. Compact higher-density layouts use less energy than low-density areas with a similar population; they also facilitate thermal exchanges between buildings, helping to retain warmth. Buildings account for 42 per cent of energy consumed and 47 per cent of CO^2 remissions in the United Kingdom, and housing consumes over 28 per cent of energy supplied to end-users in the United Kingdom (DETR 1998b: 47).

Many of our basic assumptions about density derive from the world of fifty years ago, before the sexual and cultural revolution that changed so many things, not least living patterns.. The assumption was that we were building homes for households which had a mother, father, two or three children (Frederic Osborn, writing to Lewis Mumford in 1971, assumed an average household size of 4.7; Whittick 1987: 145), and minimal space. But for the next twenty years, as the household projections have shown us, we will be building new homes principally for households that typically have one or at most two professional people, no children (or maybe some children who are in the custody of the divorced partner, but come back to the other one at weekends) and some friends and quite a lot of need for workspace. Ironically, these two very different households may want the same kind of space in quantitative terms, though it is going to be used very differently.

These changes upset our basic assumptions, in two ways. First, they alter all the relationships between dwellings per unit of area, bedspaces per unit of area, and people per unit of area. The number of bedspaces per unit comes down, but not so much as one might think, because of the need to provide for those separated children or friends, and because the concept of 'bedspaces' completely ignores the other kinds of space that a home is now increasingly required to provide, especially home offices. The resulting equation is anyone's guess.

In fact – and this is the next critical point – it is no longer set, because these relationships derive from a completely different world in which benevolent public providers provided units of accommodation for a subservient public; now, the market provides for the 75 or 80 per cent of the population that has choice, and no one – whether politicians or planners or the Council for the Protection of Rural England or the Town and Country Planning Association – is going to tell them how they should live. These relationships are interesting only as market research, for what people are going to demand.

And we hardly know anything about them. What little we do know is that people have much more possessions, and much more complex needs for space, than forty or fifty years ago. I invite the reader, doubtless a typical middle-class professional, to consider his or her own use of domestic space. It is likely to be complex and also space-consuming. Mine, which may or may not be representative (and perhaps nothing is), consists of an Edwardian detached villa in London middle-ring suburbia with a kitchen-diner, three reception rooms, four bedrooms and a loft space. It is occupied by a two-person household. Two of the four bedrooms and the entire loft space are 100 per cent used as offices. A third is used as a guest bedroom but is full of books and will soon become another office. This may be an academic eccentricity. But the number of working academics has expanded exponentially since 1950, and so has the number of all other professionals who need home workspace.

The third complication, though it may be less difficult, is difficult enough: it is the relationship between net and gross density. The strange fact here is that again no one knows: even the best recent work is derived directly from figures that are half a century old. An important DETR research report, *The Use of Density in Urban Planning*, from the Bartlett School of Planning and Llewelyn Davies, has two graphs of these relationships (DETR 1998b). It shows that as we move from low to medium densities we save a lot of land, but as we go even higher the density bonus drops rapidly, and that this is complicated by the need to provide community and social facilities like schools, open space, health centres and local shopping. The report rightly points out that sustainable urban development demands that as far as possible such facilities are provided close to home. The point, which the report emphasises, is that the demand for such facilities, and the area needed to accommodate them, arises more from population and age and social structure than from the density of the housing. In fact, as can be seen, it is almost like a constant figure at the bottom of the diagram.

The report does not give the actual figures, but Llewelyn Davies has kindly provided them, and the results are shown in Table 7.1. They are surely very significant.

If the pattern of provision depends on demography – if for instance there is no longer a demand for schools and playing fields – then it may be possible to make do with fewer facilities. If people are going to fulfil more of their demand for shopping and entertainment in big centres outside the neighbourhood, then it may be possible to drop that element too, although there will have to be compensating provision somewhere else, and it will be less sustainable, of course. This makes the entire equation more complex than it was when most people met their demands inside the local neighbourhoods.

On this, the DETR research report concludes that 'the relationship between changes in net residential density and the overall demand for urban land will be variable' (DETR 1998b: 62). In some cases new residential development will be driven by population growth, and here the additional demands created by the increased population will lead to increased demands for other non-residential uses, so that the residential component of the total urban

Table 7.1 Land needed to accommodate 400 dwellings

Density dws/ha	Net				Area required, ha gross (with local facilities)			
	Land needed	Land saved	% Total saving	% Cumulative	Land needed	Land saved	% Total saving	% Cumulative
10	40.0				46.3			
20	20.0	20.0	50.0	50.0	25.3	21.0	45.4	45.4
30	13.3	6.7	16.7	66.7	17.9	7.4	15.9	61.3
40	10.0	3.3	8.3	75.0	14.3	3.6	7.8	69.1
50	8.0	2.0	5.0	80.0	12.1	2.2	4.8	73.9
60	6.6	1.4	3.5	83.5	10.6	1.5	3.2	77.1

Source: DETR 1998b, based on charts, 61; original figures supplied by Llewelyn Davies Planning

development would be smaller and the impact of changes in net residential densities on the total area would be much reduced. But in other cases new residential development will reflect household rather than population growth, and existing urban services – schools, shops, leisure and entertainment facilities – will be able to absorb much of any increased demand, so that the residential component of the new urban development will be larger and the impact of changes in net residential density on the overall urban area more significant.

Notwithstanding all this, the overwhelmingly important conclusion that comes out of the study is that there are big gains in going from 10 to 20 dwellings per hectare, and substantial gains in going from 20 to 30. A density of 30 yields three-fifths of all potential gains, and a density of 40 yields 70 per cent. Thus the greatest potential land savings, the DETR research concludes, come from minimising the amount of development below about 20 dws/ha, rather than from increasing densities of 40 dws/ha and higher. The reason is that at the local level residential areas require community and social facilities, such as schools, open space, health centres and local shopping, which are especially important if sustainability is the aim. The demand for such facilities and the area required to accommodate them arises more from population, age and social structure than from density of development. This is relevant both for large and small developments, because all have equal need of facilities.

The message could hardly be clearer: it is that it would be worthwhile designing urban areas somewhere about the 30–40 range. We probably should go higher than this in some places that are very accessible to shops and services and transport, with a high proportion of flats, which will allow us to go less in areas that are a little more peripheral. This should allow us to redevelop the majority of our urban areas at the Unwin density of 30 units per hectare or a little above, approaching the maximum suggested long ago by Frederic Osborn (Whittick 1987: 145).

These conclusions, very significantly, confirm Susan Owens' work of some years ago (Owens 1984: 215–24). She suggested that a sustainable urban form would have the following features. First, at a regional scale, it would contain many relatively small settlements; but some of these would cluster, to form larger settlements of 200,000 and more people. Second, at a sub-regional scale, it would feature compact settlements, probably linear or rectangular in form, and with employment and commercial opportunities dispersed to give a 'heterogeneous', i.e. mixed, land use pattern. Third, at the local scale, it would consist of sub-units developed at pedestrian/bicycle scale; at a medium to high residential density, possibly with high linear density, and with local employment, commercial and service opportunities clustered to permit multi-purpose trips. Her work strongly suggests that a cluster of small settlements may be more energy-efficient than one large one; that the optimum upper limit would be 150,000–250,000; that linear or at least rectangular forms will be the most efficient; and that though densities should be moderately high, they need not be very high to be energy-efficient. Thus, a density of 25 dwellings per hectare (10 per acre), which in terms of household composition might translate into about 50–60 people per hectare, would allow facilities with a catchment area of 8000 people to be within 600 metres of all homes, and a pedestrian scale cluster of 20–30,000 people would provide a sufficient threshold for many facilities without resort to high densities, which actually might be energy-inefficient. She also pointed out that district heating systems are viable at moderate densities of 30/37 dwellings per hectare.

It is interesting, though also frustrating, to compare these figures with a study from URBED (Rudlin and Falk 1999). Its analysis of densities and housing yields (Table 7.2) seems to assume a linear relationship between net and gross densities, quite contrary to the results of the DETR research. It is important to relate these densities to indices of sustainability. URBED quote the Local Government Management Board rule of thumb: 100 persons per hectare to support a good bus service. But when these are measured gross, it is easy to fall below. Also distances must be walkable: the maximum distance people are prepared to walk is taken at around 2000 metres but the optimum is 800 metres, a comfortable ten-minute walk; shopping developers use 400 metres as the maximum with shopping.

So we seem constantly to return to some kind of magic density of between 30 and 40 dwelling units per hectare, or between Unwin's norm of 30 and Osborn's maximum of 37.5. But we should realise, to come back to the other part of the paradox, that these dwelling densities will not yield anything like the person densities that we could achieve forty or fifty years ago. URBED's study assumes four bedspaces per dwelling. They do say that this will only translate into population density if all of the properties are fully occupied – a very unlikely supposition. So they also use a measure of people to the hectare based upon an average household size of 2.4 people – the average household size across the country in the 1991 Census, though maybe a little high in view of the growth in single-person households. I think this must be right: the best that we can achieve is probably about 2.4 people per unit, and even this may be too high for many parts of our urban areas, where the figure may well fall to between 1.5 and 2.0 – a far cry from the assumptions Osborn was making thirty years ago, admittedly in relation to the new towns.

A very interesting – indeed central – piece of evidence on this point also comes from URBED's work for Friends of the Earth, reproduced in their new book (Rulkin and Falk 1999: 26). Their diagram of comparative densities (which appears to be based on net densities) puts Howard's Garden City of 1898 in the middle, at 45 units/ha, Raymond Unwin's 12 houses to the acre of 1912, reproduced in the 1918 Tudor Walters report, are lower at 30. Friends of the Earth suggest 69 as a sustainable urban density; Victorian/ Edwardian terraces in Hertfordshire achieve 80. The working assumption, however, is that all dwellings have an average of four bed-spaces. That may be a good working assumption, but it certainly does not mean four beds and four people anymore.

Here, we need to take heed of two significant pieces of research. One comes from Alan Hooper and colleagues from Nottingham Trent University for

Table 7.2 Analysis of densities and housing yields

Basic data	Acres	ha	
Neighbourhood area	112	45	
Developed area	69	28	
Area developed for housing	49	20	
Densities:	Low	Medium 'Unwin'	High
Units			
Net/acre	12	25	50
Net/ha	30	62	124
Gross/ha	13	27	54
Bed-spaces			
Net/ha	119	247	494
Gross/ha	52	108	216
Persons			
Net/ha	71	148	296
Gross/ha	31	65	130
Housing yield	588	1225	2450

Source: Rudlin and Falk 1999

the Housing Research Foundation (HRF 1998). Called *Home Alone*, it focuses on the housing needs and preferences of those one-person households who will make up nearly 80 per cent of the total growth in household numbers. It finds that 53 per cent of these will be never-married people living alone, and that the fastest growth will be in both male and female one-person households in the 35–54 age groups. Most will be home-owners and they will be discerning purchasers. They are very conscious of their residential environment. Most importantly, most want two bedrooms and some want three or more. Only 10 per cent would prefer a flat to a house, and fully one-third would not even consider a flat. They want parking for their cars and they also want private open space: not a large garden, but a small garden or patio. Town and mews type houses are popular, but with better quality and more spacious product than the average 'starter home'.

The other study is for CPRE by Tony Champion and colleagues of the University of Newcastle (Champion *et al*. 1998). Most of it deals with the numbers moving between the towns and the countryside, and there is an important finding: that there are big moves in both directions, so that a fairly small change in either flow could reverse the direction of change. However, there is also a very useful chapter which reviews the available evidence on people's motives for moving. And there are no surprises here: the authors conclude 'The English are, by and large, a nation committed to living in the countryside or as near as they can get to it . . . the main reason for leaving cities is that the latter fall short in social and environmental terms, but given that most newcomers to the shire counties and their rural areas are moving from the more attractive and less deprived parts of metropolitan England, the "push" factors associated with city life would appear to be of less importance than the "rural idyll". 'Their places are taken, so Champion and his colleagues conclude, by people moving from the less salubrious parts of the cities. To parody it, people move from high-quality suburbs to the country, and are followed by people moving from the low-quality parts of cities into the high-quality suburbs. This might be thought hardly surprising; research may demonstrate the obvious, but nevertheless reach conclusions that are profoundly true.

This, in turn, finds support from another piece of work by Hedges and Clemens, quoted by Michael Breheny (Breheny 1997: 209–18). It shows that 76 per cent of city dwellers were 'very satisfied' or 'fairly satisfied' with their area of residence, compared with 86 per cent in suburbs and 91 per cent in rural areas. But if we consider only the 'very satisfied' category, only 36 per cent of people living in urban/city centre locations came into that group, compared with 51 per cent in suburbs and 68 per cent of rural residents. These results are all perfectly consistent: they show that those who have the choice aspire to a rural lifestyle but will be satisfied in the suburbs; they are quite averse to city living. The *Containment of Urban England* study, over a quarter century ago, reached the same conclusion (Hall *et al*. 1973: Chapter 5); this is far from a new phenomenon.

That brings us back to the basic question: what kind of urban or rural living do people want? The answer to that has to be that different people, different kinds of households, want different qualities (which they cannot always afford, of course). Here, we can usefully go back to a very old source: the best book ever written on London, by the Danish modernist architect Steen Eiler Rasmussen. It was called *London: The Unique City*, and that indeed was its thesis: unlike most cities on the European mainland, London (and by extension other British cities) had never had to grow up tight and dense, because they had no need of defensive walls. He concluded his book with some amazing prophetic words. He wrote:

My object has been to show my compatriots that we have a great deal to learn from that form of civilisation in which London has taken the lead. I wished to call attention to the fact that there are two ways of organising large towns, the English and the Continental. According to my experience, he who learns to know the English way cannot fail to admire it. But it is dangerous to copy a single detached feature. It must be clearly understood that all conditions of life in English towns which evoke admiration on the Continent today, belong to a special English world that is utterly different from the Continental.

(Rasmussen 1937: 386)

We had gained a great deal from our 'utter ignorance of what was being said and done in other European countries'. But by the 1930s, when he wrote, 'an unfortunate mania for imitating foreign nations has appeared in England' (Rasmussen 1937: 386). There was a 'fashion to agitate for smaller homes; this is one of the results of the romance of engineering, the admiration of the sleeping-car on the railway and the cabin of the aeroplane' (ibid.: 401). He says in italics that 'plenty of room in the home is an absolute necessity for health and human dignity . . . It is not a question of how many bodies can be kept in a dry and quiet place, but of living beings, who need an opportunity of satisfying their need of exercise, of meat and drink, of a healthy sexual life and of sleep'. And, he emphasises, 'You English who come over to the Continent and see big residential quarters with miles and miles of tall houses in which the people live in dwellings piled one on top of the other, should try to realise that this unfortunate system is not the result of the need for good homes or the improvement of the conditions of traffic. The only reason for its existence is this: the landlord gets a higher return on his investment' (ibid.: 403).

That of course was an attack on Le Corbusier. He underlined his point, if it needed underlining:

You English must know that in all towns, in your own as well as others, there is a strong tendency to de-populate the most thickly populated areas. And this tendency is a right and wholesome one. But when replacing poor little houses by big blocks of flats, large sums are tied up in quarters which should normally de-populate, and wholesome evolution is thus hindered by the building of these large blocks. We on the Continent know something of this, for we have learnt it at our cost. To build flats in slums will not stem the current, London will continue to be a town of one-family houses, and it is tragic to see the enormous sums of money spent in this way and employed to a wrong purpose, for instead of planning the moving out of factories, business premises and private houses in connection with each other, living houses are being built with a quite un-English standard and according to types which are everywhere regarded as inadequate.

(ibid.: 404)

Rasmussen ended his book with a prophetic warning:

And now London, the capital of English civilisation, has caught the infection of Continental experiments which are variance with the whole character and tendency of the city! Thus the foolish mistakes of other countries are imported everywhere, and at the end of a few years all cities will be equally ugly and equally devoid of individuality.
This is the bitter END.

(ibid.: 404)

Of course, it really was the bitter end. We failed to listen to Rasmussen. We got the tower blocks and the slab blocks, and they proved a disaster, against which Frederic Osborn lambasted in vain.

But Rasmussen had another and a more subtle point. This was that London had grown up as a suburban city. Every place in it, except the square mile, grew up as a suburb and has suburban features: Bloomsbury and Chelsea as much as Ealing and Richmond after them and Raynes Park and Ruislip after them. But there were good suburbs and bad suburbs, and it was vital to distinguish between them. He makes a remarkable point in discussing Bedford Park, the first and still justifiably the most famous of the planned garden suburbs:

From a technical standpoint the whole layout was exactly as in the other quarters of London. It was as a sensible scheme of dwelling houses necessarily must be: long parallel streets with rather narrow and deep sites and comparatively few cross-roads. Still it was a little less stiff than a plan by a common surveyor.

(Rasmussen 1937: 266)

Rasmussen clearly was puzzled by Bedford Park. He said:

For those who have learned to appreciate the Georgian architecture and who have understood how modern it really is, it seems a little strange that the 'eighties considered it necessary to go back to a more primitive, somewhat rustic phase in order to create something good. But in any case the result is creditable. Norman Shaw's red brick houses are as a matter of fact no better than those refined oil-painted buildings to which he was strongly opposed, but they were just as good, in a different way. There are no means of proving that the aesthetic effect of one building material is better or more correct than another. It is the way the things are carried out that matters, and Norman Shaw's garden suburb has just as much unity of style as we find in the old Regent Street or the best parts of Bloomsbury.

(Rasmussen 1937: 267)

And he says something equally remarkable about Ebenezer Howard's Three Magnets diagram:

There is nothing surprising in this manner of thinking, for was this not the very thing those Englishmen of our day had in their minds when they built Bloomsbury, with one-family houses round the squares leading out into the open country? And was not that the idea of the Regent's Park quarter? And of Norman Shaw's Bedford Park villas?

(ibid.: 366)

Rasmussen got it exactly right. The genius of the English, the genius of London, is in its suburbs. And that is the conclusion we need to draw in forging our twenty-first-century urban renaissance. It is paradoxical: the easiest way to repopulate our depopulated cities would be to develop extensive new suburbs intown, places like Ealing or Edgbaston or Jesmond, complete with their own schools and their own community life.

But this still leaves open a question about density. Many of Rasmussen's preferred examples, like Bloomsbury and Regent's Park and even Bedford Park, were built at high densities, as high as 100 dwellings per hectare. This demonstrates that it is quite possible to achieve relatively high densities on the basis of single-family homes with private open space, as URBED's work reminds us. The clue is substantial ground coverage with big units and more than two floors. Two leading American urban designers, Allan Jacobs and the late Donald Appleyard, have contributed a definitive statement on creating urban quality (Jacobs and Appleyard 1987: 112–20). They conclude that a good urban area needs a certain minimum density, which they say is about 15 dwellings per acre (37 units per hectare) which translates to 30–60 people per acre (74–148/ha), typified by generous town houses. That is uncannily close to Osborn's maximum, so we might be inclined to leave it there, as a kind of historic compromise. But they do point out that San Francisco achieves superb urban quality with three-storey row houses above garages at densities as high as 48 units per acre (119/ha), translating to 96–192 people per acre (237–474/ha), yet offering separate entrances with direct access to the ground, and either private or public open space at hand.

Such densities, they point out, are also characteristic of much of inner London, which also achieves great urban quality and liveability. (Donald Appleyard was born and grew up in north London, Allan Jacobs is a great Londonophile, and the best parts of San Francisco represent as good an urban ambience as one can hope to find.) But, they warn, at densities much more than 200 people per net residential acre (500 persons per hectare) – the highest planned density in Abercrombie's famous London plan – 'the concessions to less desirable living environments mount rapidly'.

That might seem to contradict much of the argument of this chapter, but it can be resolved. If there is buoyant market demand for urban space, as in inner London where desirable Georgian and Victorian terrace houses go for anything between half a million and a million pounds, or in San Francisco, then we can take the densities up to Islington or Chelsea levels, which means the levels of Russian Hill or Pacific Heights in San Francisco. But if such demand is lacking, which means much of our midland and northern cities, then we should work to bring people back in by giving them the kinds of densities they understand and like.

They are just beginning to do this in the United States. Peter Calthorpe, one of the seminal figures of the New Urbanism, has designed the Jackson-Taylor Revitalization area in San Jose: it combines higher-density residential blocks at 40–50 per acre (100–125/ha) above a parking podium one-half level above grade, necessary to achieve the area's parking requirement of 2.2 spaces per unit, with lower-density residential areas at between 12 and 25 units per acre (30–62/ha); each lot can include up to three residential units plus parking (Katz 1994: 194–7). In a newly developed greenfield area which has become almost the icon of the New Urbanism, Laguna West south of Sacramento, he has produced a design based on detached residences ranging from two to three bedrooms at 14 units per acre (35/ha). These figures tell us what will sell to the more adventurous and pace-setting, but also highly discriminating and highly affluent, Californian middle class; they can serve as a useful model for what will sell here, in our cities, in a decade or more.

We can do it too. But it will require new mechanisms to bring together the best ideas in urban design, the best architectural talents, with the experience of the private developers who will have the job of building and selling these homes. We can do it. We can return the suburbs to the place they began and the place they still belong, in the hearts of our great cities.

8 Housing, Homes and Social Sustainability

Nick Gallent

Introduction

This chapter presents an interpretation of the term '*sustainable housing*' and considers the variety of meanings attached to sustainability in the context of housing policy, delivery and consumption. Recent debates in the area of housing policy and production have tended to focus on future development patterns and the way particular strategies may limit the consumption of green-field land whilst reducing the need to travel (Breheny, 1999; Banister, 1999b; Hall, this volume). In this discussion, it will be argued that underlying what is now seen as the 'great debate' in housing, are numerous additional issues, which together, determine the overall sustainability of the United Kingdom's housing system. Some of these have been highlighted by Williams (1997: 1) who has argued that:

For the last seventy years or more the UK has been struggling to identify and put into practice a coherent set of housing policies (and housing practices) which might be sustained through the life of governments of different political persuasions and a range of social and economic conditions.

It is hoped that a broad focus on different levels of meaning will provide at least an introduction to what is meant by the term *sustainable housing*. With this goal in mind, the chapter traverses a number of disparate, but related, topic areas. Very basic concerns centring on material usage and the energy efficiency of new dwellings are considered briefly. But in a rather different dimension, socio-cultural questions – linked to the segregation of different groups and the type of society that housing and planning policy is contributing towards – are explored in greater depth. Whilst great importance should be attached to issues of resource usage and the appropriateness of different residential development strategies (the products of policy and delivery), it is equally important to gauge sustainability in terms of broader social objectives, and to understand what is meant by sustainable 'homes'. This last point provides the main rationale for this chapter.

Following a brief conceptual review outlining the different levels/ perspectives that will be brought into focus, the main discussion begins by considering individuals and the way that policy contributes to different experiences of housing and views of sustainability.

Sustainable Housing – A Framework

In the introduction above, it was suggested that conceptions of sustainability are scale-dependent, often because particular aspects of this 'universal' principle are prioritised at different levels. The individual (consumer) or local planners (deliverers), for instance, may have priorities that differ markedly from those of central government (policy-makers). That said, it cannot be satisfactory merely to assert that sustainability is an amorphous concept that defies definition. It is perhaps more useful to argue that specific definitions are variations on a standard theme and that the notion of *sustainable housing* can be disaggregated into components that exist at all levels, but are prioritised in various ways by particular groups. This provides the opportunity to define these components and therefore build a framework on which to peg this discussion. A breakdown of both the components (which recur as themes in subsequent sections), alongside the three levels of focus, is provided in Figure 8.1.

Put simply, it can be argued that views of sustainability (at the different levels) draw on various *characteristics*: these include policy durability, flexibility and choice. They also place sustainability within various *dimensions*: environmental, economic, ecological, social, political and cultural. And finally, they would appear to aim towards particular *objectives*: policy *compromise*, community *balance*, environmental *protection* and so forth. Again, these characteristics, dimensions and objectives have weightings that vary at different levels, though a broad conception of sustainable housing demands a focus across all levels in order to understand how sustainable strategies and polices might be designed.

The remainder of this chapter focuses on these levels, beginning with consumption, and outlines the preoccupations which contribute to particular views on sustainable housing.

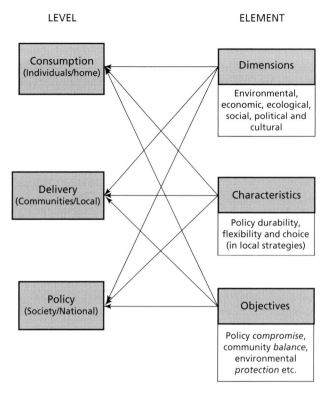

LEVEL   ELEMENT

Figure 8.1 Sustainable housing – dimensions, characteristics and objectives

Sustainable Housing and Homes – Alternative Scales and Meanings

Consumption

Individuals and homes

In recent years, a great deal of intellectual effort has been directed towards attaching meaning to, as well as exploring, the physical, social and psychological aspects of, the notion of 'home'. Numerous researchers have sought to identify the various complexities by focusing on the myriad dimensions and levels of home, first, within its physical parameters and, second, across different 'user' or 'consumer' groups. The first of these endeavours has resulted in the separation of home's various aspects. First, home in the simplest sense is viewed as a physical structure. Second, it provides territory in which both self and possessions enjoy a degree of protection (Hill, 1991) and freedom. Third, home provides a locus in space, which feeds, fourth, into the notion of home as self and self-identity.

The second major endeavour identified above has been to explore the dimensional meanings of home as they pertain to different user groups. Thus, work has focused on older people's experiences of home (e.g. Dupuis and Thorns, 1996) or the particular experiences of women faced with housing difficulties (Hill, 1991; Thomas and Dittmar, 1995; Gurney, 1997). Added to these are those studies which have concentrated on meanings attached by specific property classes, including studies of the homeless (Somerville, 1992), nursing-home residents (Katz, 1989), emerging or established homeowners (Mandic and Clapham, 1996; Saunders, 1990) and even the owners of second homes (Salletmaier, 1993). In short, academic effort has been driven by a desire to constantly refine our understanding and conceptualisation of home as a physical, social and psychological construct.

The idea of home as both social and cultural unit is central to the discussion presented in this chapter if the notion of sustainable housing is seen to extend across both social and cultural dimensions. Homes provide more than shelter and cannot be viewed as dead structures or, worse still, units of residential space to be allocated in development plans. Society is underpinned by its housing system and access to housing for different groups – often differentiated in terms of income – is essential if communities are to be balanced and inclusive. Consequently, this discussion rests on two principles – that a *home* is more than just a place of shelter and that sustainability encapsulates the notion of *balanced communities*. Sustainable strategies are inclusive rather that exclusive and therefore, the 'right' housing policies are those that prevent rather than promote social division. This idea is considered in the next section.

Balanced communities versus the erosion of choice

The problems that have faced individuals in their search for inclusion (or acceptance) and decent housing can be exemplified via a review of some recent housing policy which, it can be argued, contributed little to social sustainability and resulted in both the division and polarisation of communities and households. Since the early 1950s, for instance, local authorities in the United Kingdom have been able to sell council-owned houses to sitting tenants. After 1980, this process was accelerated by the Conservative government's decision to transform this right to sell into an obligation and authorities were forced to off-load significant proportions of their housing stock, often with significant discount, to tenants. The pattern of sales, nationally, reflected market processes and as Forrest and Murie (1990) point out, the best housing in the desirable areas sold rapidly whilst the worst units, often in the inner cities, were left in public ownership. By the 1990s, the most desirable housing was gone and the councils – and housing associations – were left to manage numerous 'problem' estates. But their duty to house those in need of a home remained unchanged. These were frequently the people who, despite government efforts during the 1980s and into the 1990s, could still not afford home ownership or higher rents in the private sector. As a result, they ended up in the poorest housing, in the worst locations and suffered the least opportunities. By sharpening the spatial divisions between richer and poorer households, policy was actively promoting social fragmentation. The Right to Buy rested on a philosophy of *individual* choice, causing a fragmentation of communities along income lines, and did little to foster sustainable (i.e. inclusive) *community* building.

The policy promoted a short-term view of housing consumption, as opposed to a long-term perspective on social sustainability. The name of the game was to cut public expenditure, give people (or, at least certain people) what they wanted and, as a result, win votes. Indeed, housing policy has been governments' favourite political football for more than a hundred years, with periodic shifts between private and public provision depending on party biases. The political process has militated against any long-term vision of where policy is eventually leading. Indeed, the products of short-term policy decisions include a rising level of homelessness and a failure to sustain the social balance of communities as residential areas become defined in terms of wealth rather than racial or social equality. Policies that place too great an emphasis on market processes tend towards both exclusion and polarisation; and can certainly not be viewed as socially sustainable.

The problems of home ownership

If the Right to Buy can be held up as a policy which has contributed little to social sustainability (for the reasons noted above[1]), then so too can the broader promotion of home ownership during the 1980s and into the 1990s. Indeed, the desire to push people into the private sector was grounded in an economic policy (based on huge subsidy, in the form of mortgage interest tax relief) that was visibly unsustainable. Mortgage interest tax relief acted to heighten the market boom of the late 1980s and its reduction in 1988[2] led to a rush in home purchases, a spiralling number of over-stretched buyers, and to a slump in the early 1990s of unparalleled depth (for a full discussion of market changes see Muellbauer and Murphy, 1997). The Conservative governments promoted their single-tenure policy to the point of collapse and beyond. By the late 1980s, the sale of council properties was bottoming out and the cost of subsidy support for mortgaged households had increased to £6.75 billion per annum in 1990 (Drabble, 1990: 4). At this point, many additional commentators began to question how far the policy of increasing the national proportion of homeowners should be pursued. Any answer, however, was pre-empted by a catastrophic market collapse which saw thousands of buyers having their homes repossessed and many more falling into the 'negative equity' trap (that is, where the value of their property falls below the amount they have left to repay on their mortgage). The answer

119

then, came of its own accord: the dogmatic promotion of a single tenure to serve all needs was, at that time, unsustainable both economically and socially.

Boléat (1997: 65) has argued that the present situation, with almost 70 per cent of households owning their homes, *is* sustainable given 'radical changes in the economics of the housing market'. But political or economic sustainability does not always equate with social sustainability. A great many homeowners enjoy relatively modest incomes and may not be able to afford all the long-term costs (including maintenance and renovation) associated with home ownership. Similarly, great play has been made of evidence that the labour market is becoming increasingly flexible and associated with casual employment and fixed-term contracts. In particular, job instability (e.g. a new emphasis on fixed-term employment contracts), rising unemployment and low pay all appear to diminish the ability to meet the long-term responsibilities associated with mortgage costs or the costs of maintaining private property. Ford and Wilcox (1998) argue that the particular relationship between housing and the labour market is contributing to deteriorating physical conditions in the private stock and reshaping attitudes towards home ownership. Moreover, this relationship continues to push people into financial difficulty, leading to additional mortgage arrears and repossessions. Indeed, as labour market conditions change, can it be safely assumed that all of those households making up Boléat's 70 per cent will *always* be able to sustain their current tenure? Meen (1998) points out that the market dictates what is sustainable and that market cycles will influence the degree to which home ownership can satisfy housing needs. In other words, policy-makers should plan for the unexpected, for the worst-case scenarios and for the long term. A housing system which is sustainable into the future and across social groups is one that possesses inherent variety and where switches are possible, between tenures, as needs and market conditions change.

Consumption: final remarks

A home is more than a physical structure. Rather, it is a fundamental need that helps shape an individual's place in society. In this context, problems of homelessness or poor housing become critical as they contribute to a breakdown in social relations. These problems have been accentuated by short-term housing policies, which fail to produce a sustainable housing system that will continue to meet changing needs and adapt to new market conditions into the future. A socially sustainable strategy is, in these terms, one that responds to future needs and offers choice.

Broader social concerns, then, may be seen to dominate notions of sustainability at the level of consumption and from the point of view of individual households and there is, by inference, less explicit concern for the environmental dimension (depicted in Figure 8.1) which may, as later discussion reveals, be prioritised at other levels. However, that is not to say that environmental concerns are unimportant from an individual perspective or that environmental considerations do no heavily influence patterns of social sustainability. But whilst the environmental dimension *impinges* on the individual experience of housing, its impacts are not as immediate (from the point of view of the household) as homelessness, overcrowding or any of the housing difficulties which affect the daily lives of households. Yet the environmental dimension often translates into a social cost or impact, which belies the fact that the different dimensions of sustainability, whether prioritised or not, are interdependent. This is illustrated by the work of Bhatti (1996) who has argued that the increased unit costs of environmentally benign homes are a cause for particular social concern – causing new fractures between higher and lower income consumers.[3]

The different dimensions of sustainability – economic, social, environmental and political – are, of course, inter-dependent. But because housing has a great deal of social importance, what is meant by *sustainable housing* must be understood in terms that extend beyond physical development. By focusing on consumption, and prioritising the individual and the home, it is possible to secure some deeper understanding of the different meanings that may be attached. But having gained such an understanding, it is then necessary to consider how housing delivery (at the local level) and housing policy (formulated nationally) can affect both this understanding and the realisation of a sustainable housing system.

Delivery

Local housing strategies

In this section, the intention is to focus on the way the goal of social (as well as environmental) sustainability is interpreted within local housing and planning strategies. It will again be argued that particular elements of sustainability (i.e. those outlined in Figure 8.1) are prioritised locally, and that an *official* view of sustainability is developed. This view may be neither *social* nor *cultural* in tone, although government sees the goal of social sustainability as an integral part of local housing strategies and subsequent housing delivery. New guidance was issued on the development of such strategies in 1998 (DETR, 1998) in which clear references to social sustainability were made. The first of these emphasised that a local authority's housing strategy will

ensure that spending on housing supports improvements in other areas of people's lives such as health and personal security and contributes to achieving balanced sustainable communities.

(DETR, 1998c, *see web reference*)

This, according to the government, should be the broad aim of any strategy and is achievable if the plans laid down by authorities are 'comprehensive', 'forward looking' and encompass a 'vision for the future'. There is a recognition that the nature of spending on housing provision should contribute, first, to individual health and security and, second, to a broader community well-being. Despite the preoccupations of past housing policy discussed earlier, it is now recognised that community balance (and therefore inclusion) is a key element of social sustainability.

A second reference in the 1998 document refers to a sustainable strategy as one which is 'endurable'. It will have a clear time dimension and will be able to negotiate and manage social and economic change impacting on the local area. In other words, such a strategy will have inherent flexibility and a capacity to respond to changing housing requirements (e.g. sudden upsurges in need or a slackening of demand) and manage future uncertainty. The ability of any strategy to survive social and economic uncertainty is, as Williams (1997) has noted, a key element of sustainable policy. Similarly, a location-based approach will also be important in any sustainable local strategy. The government calls upon authorities to 'consider the effects of decisions taken in other service areas such as education and transport to ensure sustainability of housing [provision]' (DETR, 1998c, *see web reference*). So, an overall sustainable housing strategy combines social balance with flexible management and policy integration.

Local strategies and problem housing

Goss and Blackaby (1998: 9) consider the ways in which these aspects of sustainability should permeate local strategies, beginning with the assertion that 'sustainability involves a frame of mind that thinks long term rather than short term [and] imagines how homes and localities will be to live in over time'. This strategic long-termism should, they argue, take account of the way individual dwellings may need to adapt to the changing needs of occupants – perhaps, with the onset of illness or as individuals age. But at the same time, management responses must also be fixed within a wider strategic framework. Homes must be located within a safe environment, where residents can be free from the fear of crime. Past research has revealed that 'even minor crimes and forms of public disorder' are potentially cumulative phenomena, with particular areas becoming increasingly blighted by the incidence of criminal activity (Giddens, 1998: 86). The spiral of decline which causes housing areas to become 'sink' or problem estates is well documented (Merrett, 1979: 225–6) and the swathes of empty and abandoned dwellings across a number of inner city areas bear testimony to the fact that these communities were never sustainable (Power, 1997).

Some public sector estates were not simply blighted by crime, however, and it was also a sense of isolation and abandonment, which contributed to their decline.[4] Government is increasingly concerned that housing development should be related to transport infrastructure, service provision and job opportunities (DETR, 1998d). Its concern, in this context, is focused on environmental sustainability with an emphasis on reducing individual travel and energy consumption. But this same strategy should also ensure that communities do not find themselves isolated and excluded from essential services or from sources of employment or training opportunities. In relation to this particular issue, Taylor (1998) focuses on the remedial impact of the Labour government's New Deal, whilst Evans (1998) explores the prospect of better integrating homes and services via 'housing plus' approaches.

At the heart of many housing strategies is a recognition that *desirable* residential environments must be created. The only way to achieve long-term viability (and hence sustainability) is to ensure that housing areas meet with the preferences, aspirations and changing needs of existing and future residents. The abject failings of a great many past housing schemes (which suffered the added burden of poor design) were rooted in a failure to provide people with the types of housing or the types of communities that they actually wanted to live in (Power, 1993).[5] For this reason, local housing authorities (in partnership with other departments and agencies) are now attaching greater importance to the means by which their strategies for managing housing change more closely reflect both needs and aspirations (in both new build and renewal: Power, 1999).

For instance, recent work by Karn *et al.* (1999) for Bolton Metropolitan Borough Council emphasises the importance of focusing on resident aspirations and housing preferences, investigating those qualities that contribute towards a pleasant and liveable residential environment. The ability of authorities, in partnership with other agencies and groups, to make areas safe, accessible and healthy will determine whether, in time, a particular strategy is judged sustainable.

Finally, the work of Karn *et al.*, along with a great many other studies across the north of England, raises one of the most pressing questions to face housing professionals and planners at the present time: how can sustainable housing strategies be developed in the face of economic decline? Across the United Kingdom, numerous authorities are grappling with this issue, manifest in a falling number of employment opportunities and a sharp downturn in local and regional housing demand (see DETR, 2000c). Clearly, housing and the provision of good quality homes are only one aspect of sustainable community building: and communities will only thrive where the right economic conditions bring adequate services, jobs and the prospect of financial security and prosperity.

The cornerstones of sustainable delivery?

The cornerstones of a sustainable local strategy might be defined in two ways – in 'mechanical' and in 'managerial' terms (though these are heavily inter-dependent). Mechanically, there may well be a concern to pursue policies aimed at maximising land recycling, building conversion, mixed use development or offering a sufficient variety of tenure and housing choice. Similarly, through a corporate (management) approach, authorities should ensure a proper integration of policy planning (bringing together, where possible, homes, jobs and services). These are the obvious criteria against which degrees of sustainability might be judged. In the same mechanical terms, there might also be a concern with the aesthetic qualities of the residential environments being created or the design standards affecting homes (see Carmona, this volume) – together these should be tailored to housing aspirations. But all these mechanical attributes are underpinned by a need for flexible management approaches that acknowledge the changing fortunes of local areas. Local policy must be responsive and see housing as just one part of a wider suite of local needs, which will also include, amongst other things, the provision of support services and job opportunities. Williams (1997) emphasises that sustainable policies are those that endure through shifting political, social and economic conditions and this means that sustainable policies are likely to be flexible rather than dogmatic or fixed. The same is true of local housing strategies, which seek to offer sustainable housing at the grass roots. These need to recognise the complex and changeable relationships between housing, the labour market and service provision as well as the complexities of the wider geographical and social context in which social needs arise and policy implementation occurs. Choice, flexibility and integration in service delivery (characteristics emphasised in Figure 8.1) are central to an understanding of the term sustainable housing.

Policy

The two previous sections have tried to develop a more nuanced understanding of the term *sustainable housing* and began by offering definitions that have a clear social (and economic) dimension. This was followed, in the last section, by an examination of the characteristics constituting a *sustainable housing strategy*, designed and delivered by local housing authorities. At the level of policy, conceptions of sustainable housing are commonly (but not exclusively) subsumed under the broader banner of sustainable development. In this context, it is crucial to provide some overview of broad debates before focusing on what is meant by *sustainable housing* at the policy design level as well as the central ideas driving forward housing development patterns and processes nationally.

From projections to land recycling

It is important to place the current housing development debate within the context of the 1992-based growth projections (DoE, 1995b). The suggestion that 4.4 million additional households would form in England up to 2016 was perhaps less important than the fact that much of this growth would stem from fundamental social changes, and the much-publicised rise in the number of single person households. The global figure has recently been reduced to 3.8 million by 2021 (DETR, 1999b) though the make-up of this increase in households will reflect the trends identified in 1995. Government's vision for the planning system has been shaped by the apparent challenge thrown down by the projections and these remain at the forefront of strategic thinking. In particular, there has been a primary concern for the way in which new households will be accommodated. Harking back to questions raised by Howard (1898) at the turn of the century, the TCPA has been first amongst many to consider where these new households are likely to live (Breheny and Hall, 1996). According to the last Conservative government, at least half of those requiring new homes would find themselves housed on 're-cycled' land sites (DoE, 1995c). In 1997, the incoming Labour government was keen to demonstrate its own environmental credentials and there was soon talk of 60 or even 75 per cent of all new development being guided onto brownfield sites (*Planning 1245*, 1997: 3).

This move towards greater levels of recycling was largely motivated by a concern for the environmental impacts of large-scale housebuilding and based on an implicit acceptance that land recycling, as opposed to the use of green sites, was inherently more sustainable. This assertion sparked a range of debates centring on a need to prevent town cramming (e.g. through improvements in building design) whilst ensuring sustainable countryside quality. At the policy level, calls for the sequential phasing of new development (i.e. a presumption against building on greenfield sites if suitable brownfield options were available) were matched by muffled talk of a possible 'greenfield tax' used to discourage development of such sites and, in turn, make brownfields more appealing. In short, more housing *would* be needed and a greater proportion of it would have to be built at higher densities in already urbanised areas – for the sake of the nation's principal asset, namely its countryside (Countryside Commission, 1998).

From 'sustainable development' to 'sustainable housing'

It might be argued that at the level of broad policy, the notion of sustainable housing has a somewhat implicit definition in that a general view of *sustainable development* is seen to reflect directly on what is meant by sustainable housing. This idea was challenged at the beginning of this chapter. Movement towards these implicitly *more sustainable* development patterns have been driven within the general policy framework – outlined in *Planning for Communities of the Future* (DETR, 1998d) – and, it is hoped, will be operationalised via revamped planning tools. These are detailed in both *Modernising Planning* (DETR, 1998e) and in the recently re-issued Planning Policy Guidance Note 3 (DETR,

2000c). The former includes a new emphasis on urban extensions, higher densities and, in some instances, the creation of sustainable new settlements. The latter relates to the rationale behind planning processes (including a move from the highly prescriptive 'predict and provide' to one of 'plan, monitor and manage') and the tools with which particular objectives are sought (e.g. compulsory purchase orders for land assembly, capacity assessment, parking standards and so forth). This wider agenda, and particularly the revision of tools and approaches, suggests that those charged with policy implementation may be able to work with a greater degree of flexibility, giving them the capacity to offer better integrated and choice-based strategies.

As an interim conclusion, it might be noted that conceptions of sustainable housing, at the broad policy level, have a dominantly environmental and ecological tone: many sections of society see housing as simply another threat facing green sites or, more specifically, the English countryside. In this context, the notion of sustainability becomes a convenient shield with which to ward off unpalatable development pressures. But on a more positive note, there is some evidence that future policies, based on a revised rationale within the planning process, might prove more endurable and better able to meet the varying future needs of particular areas and groups. In other words, the context may be changing and this is to be welcomed; yet, this change may not come quickly enough, and a misuse of the sustainable label may have unfortunate social consequences. These might include, for instance, excessive development restraint in the countryside – and the stagnation of some communities – or town cramming, with an associated reduction in quality of life (see Hall, this volume).

There are numerous other concerns stemming from the current emphasis on land recycling and many of these relate back to the arguments forwarded earlier concerned with sustainable local strategies. For example, in the case of urban development, will higher densities result in fewer green-spaces (i.e. *social* spaces), a fall-off in opportunities for urban tourism, or a reversal of the successes achieved by recent regeneration programmes? Indeed, many of the brownfield sites targeted, far from detracting from environmental quality, are in many cases valued community assets and unique pockets of bio-diversity (DoE, 1996a). In this rush to implement sustainable *development* strategies, it is all too easy to neglect the needs and aspirations of those who will live in higher density developments, new settlements or in village extensions. It would be wrong to suggest that these models lack appeal, but any development which fails to retain population and create opportunity, however environmentally benign, will not, in the final judgement, be seen as sustainable.

Quality environments and healthy communities

At the broad policy level, there is an acceptance that notions of sustainable housing cannot be solely development-led. At the individual level, it is apparent that housing is more than a physical resource; recognition of this fact at the community level is essential to understanding how needs are differentiated and how strategies should seek to promote balanced and enduring communities (where feasible). Nationally (and regionally), the issue of new housing provision should be considered in the context of both minimised environmental impact (which itself has a social cost) and social sustainability. Sustainable solutions often represent a compromise between the needs of individuals, community interests and environmental objectives – they are flexibly designed and delivered. Work by Karn *et al.* (1999) for instance, has suggested that Bolton's population values its urban green space, its low residential densities, the fact that many homes have gardens and the great variety of housing choice that is on offer within the borough. The best way to ensure that these positive attributes are not stifled by overbearing environmental objectives is to improve design standards whilst also emphasising, in local strategies, a need for compromise policies which properly balance social and environmental priorities. These are perhaps obvious points, yet conceptions of sustainability at the policy level suggest that some social concerns are frequently relegated beneath environmental issues and the protection of land may supersede the promotion of healthy communities.

Conclusion

Although this chapter has not been specifically concerned with problem solving, the discussion has said something about what a sustainable approach to housing is, and is not. It is, for example, about individual choice rather than prescription, flexibility rather than dogma and, durability rather than short-termism. It also draws on ideas which are beyond the protocol of physical development. For instance, whilst it is clearly unsustainable to commute over long distances or concrete over swathes of countryside, it is equally unsustainable to push lower-income households into long-term mortgage commitments or force households into dwellings that are unsuited to their long-term needs.

It was noted at the beginning of this chapter that conceptions of sustainability at particular levels are grounded in the changing weightings given to different *characteristics*, *dimensions* and *objectives*. At the various levels of consumption, delivery and policy, relative emphasis on these elements shifts and a partial view of sustainability is gained. It was also suggested that a complete picture might be conceived as the sum of these elements along with the interrelationships between each. However, neither the dimensions nor the levels, which are shown again in Table 8.1, are discrete. The impossibility of separating, for example, society from the individual, or the national from the local is patently obvious. This framework has merely served to highlight key concerns whilst providing some pointers for this discussion.

That said, an assessment of the way in which different elements are

Table 8.1 Levels of focus (and prioritised elements)

	Characteristics	Dimensions	Objectives
Consumption Individuals/Home	• Access • Affordability • Move away from dogmatic policy	• Notions of 'home' rather than housing • Sense of belonging • Social/Cultural emphasis	• Choice • Affordability • Security (of *any* tenure)
Delivery Communities/ Local	• Flexibility (local strategies) • Meeting needs & aspirations • Integration (local strategies)	• Multi-dimensional • Reconcile national policy with local needs	• Community balance • Access • Opportunities • Affordability
Policy Society/National	• Policy durability • Environmental priorities (via land recycling, travel reduction etc.)	• Political (across changing govts) • Economic (control expenditure) • Environmental	• Environmental protection • Compromise (between levels) • Consistency

prioritised – from the point of view of consumers, local practice and policy makers – helps us understand the translation of paradigm into practice and, indeed, the way in which the United Kingdom's housing strategy might be refined. On a more sober endnote, it also reveals the complexities of designing and delivering a comprehensive and sustainable housing strategy for the United Kingdom.

Notes

1 It could be argued, however, that the selective nature of RTB has, in some instances, created mixed tenure estates. In areas of high house prices (such as parts of London) this *may* have contributed to greater social balance. However, more recent evidence has suggested that re-sale in areas of high house prices results in gentrification rather than social balance (Chaney and Sherwood, 2000).

2 Multiple mortgage tax relief on a single property was abolished on 1 August 1988.

3 Bhatti subscribes to the notion of an 'environmentally sustainable housing system', but questions the UK government's emphasis on market mechanisms as means of achieving environmental goals. In particular, he focuses on energy conservation and argues that market mechanisms – aimed at enhancing energy conservation in house building – are largely ineffectual and uncoordinated. Moreover, they tend to accentuate social inequalities, with additional housing costs hitting lower-income households the hardest. If housing is to be more energy efficient – with triple glazing, better wall and roof insulation, etc. – then this will have a price and this price may be affordable to some households, but not to others. Indeed, environmental objectives, at many different levels, shape individual experiences

of housing and these may range from the economic costs of double glazing to the psychological costs of higher density living (see also Hall, in this volume).

4 Discussions of specific examples can be found in Power (1997), Taylor (1998) or Evans (1998).

5 Power was specifically concerned with high-rise living and has recently refocused on this issue, exploring whether a focus on 'people-centred' remedies and better design could herald a brighter future for such estates (Power, 1999).

9 The Challenge of Sustainable Transport

Stephen Marshall

In visions of idealised societies, transport is often a prominent component. Le Corbusier's *Contemporary City* famously depicts futuristic superhighways, but also features a railway interchange and airport at its heart. While strikingly different in terms of urban form, Frank Lloyd Wright's *Broadacre City* is also based on modern transport, enabled by the ubiquity of the automobile. Similarly, Ebenezer Howard's cluster of *Garden Cities* was based on railway accessibility, while Arturo Soria y Mata's *Ciudad Lineal* – a city extendable from Brussels to Peking – was more or less defined by its public transport spine (Houghton-Evans, 1975). Even Utopian literature takes care with its transport plans: Etienne Cabet's *Icaria* envisaged urban 'streetcars' running at two-minute intervals as far back as 1840, while Thomas More's original *Utopia* features cities set apart by a day's walking distance (Berneri, 1982).

Today, transport is no less important to planners and society in general, in an age when sustainability has become the key paradigm for long-term planning and development (see Davoudi and Layard, Chapter 1 this volume). This chapter explores the challenge of transport in the context of sustainable planning and development. While the modernist visions described earlier clearly saw transport as part of the urban solution, today transport is often seen as part of the problem. In fact, cities are now as likely to be designed explicitly to minimise travel, as to expedite it.

In this chapter, then, we shall first investigate the transport problem, and then go on to explore how understanding the environmental impact of different transport modes can translate into policies that may lead to more sustainable solutions. While all forms of mechanised transport can be seen to contribute to the environmental problem, the policy solutions considered in this chapter are principally directed to land transport, since this is the main area of concern for urban planners.

Stephen Marshall

The Transport Share of the Environmental Problem

Transport is clearly and visibly a significant land use in its own right. According to one estimate:

Worldwide, at least one third of all developed urban land is devoted to roads, parking lots, and other motor vehicle infrastructure. In the urban United States, the automobile consumes close to half the land area of cities; in Los Angeles the figure approaches two thirds.

(Southworth and Ben Joseph, 1997)

In fact, the exact proportion of urban land used by transport will be dependent on the definition of urban boundaries, and on the definition of transport land uses. Transport land can be taken to include not only the surfaces used for movement – roads, railways and runways – but any surface used by vehicles – off street parking areas, airport aprons, other hardstandings and marshalling yards. To this we might add areas for vehicle storage and maintenance, and sites of vehicle disposal. If we also add in all kinds of pedestrian space and navigable waterways, then the total potential significance of transport is considerable.

Moreover, from an environmental perspective, the transport impact on land can be enlarged further than the immediate land surface occupied, if the materials and energy consumed in the construction of infrastructure and the propulsion of vehicles are factored into the equation. In fact, this kind of calculation is made explicitly in concepts such as environmental space and ecological footprinting (Mittler, 1999b; Wackernagel and Rees, 1995). In attempting to estimate the full impact of human activities on the environment, these approaches point to the finite nature of land and energy resources, and the implications for sustainability in all its dimensions.

Just as transport consumes a considerable proportion of land, it also plays a significant and increasing role in terms of overall energy consumption. The transport sector is now the largest and fastest increasing consumer of energy. For example, in 1970, the transport sector accounted for 14 per cent of Europe's energy consumption; by 1995, it was over 21 per cent (Banister *et al.*, 2000). In Great Britain, the energy used by transport is a third of all energy used in 1997 (DETR, 1998f).

Transport is also a significant contributor to pollution. Transport's share of carbon dioxide emissions has increased from a fifth to a quarter in the last ten years. Across a variety of pollutants, the transport contribution is significant (Figure 9.1).

Transport's impact on the environment is of course not limited to land, energy and pollutants, but extends to include noise and vibration, disturbance to the natural and built environment, the consumption of mineral and water resources and impacts on biodiversity. Finally, transport directly impacts on human mortality and health; in Great Britain, transport is estimated to

Pollutants

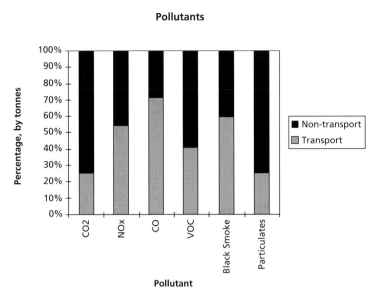

Figure 9.1 Percentages are by tonne of pollutant, by end user
Note: Figures are for Great Britain, 1996. *Source*: DETR (1998f)

account for 3,500 deaths every year, and several thousands more die prematurely due to air pollution (Banister *et al.*, 2000).

The evidence of a transport problem is clear. Added to this, the extent of the problem is growing, as can be shown with reference to historic trends in mobility. It has been estimated that in 1700 the average Briton travelled just nine kilometres a year, in terms of interurban travel (Wells, 1970). This annual figure increased to 140 km by 1850, and 1,000 km by 1900 (Wells, 1970). By the end of the twentieth century, the average annual travel exceeded 10,000 km per person – for domestic travel alone (Banister, 1999c).

These figures are per capita; once population growth is factored in, the absolute magnitude of travel growth is even more remarkable. For the most immediate implications for sustainability, it is useful to look in more detail at the last half century or so. As an example, Figure 9.2 shows figures for passenger travel in Great Britain.

We can see that the amount of travel has been increasing more or less steadily over the last four decades. What is more, the most significant growth is in the least environmentally friendly transport sectors. The lion's share of growth has been in the car travel category, which now accounts for some 86 per cent of all passenger kilometres travelled in Great Britain. In relative terms, passenger car travel has increased tenfold since 1952, while air passenger travel has increased thirtyfold, including a trebling between 1977 and 1997 (DETR, 1998f). From a simple comparison of travel growth and energy consumption by mode (Table 9.1), the consequences for sustainability are apparent.

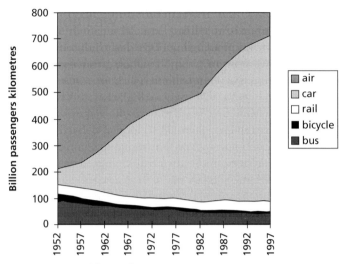

Figure 9.2 Passenger travel by mode
Notes: Figures are for Great Britain. Car includes van and taxi. Bus includes coach.
Motorcycle omitted for clarity.
Source: DETR (1998f)

In order to understand what is happening, it is necessary to consider more closely how this travel growth is manifested. Clearly, the increasing total amount of travel is fuelled partly by population growth. But per capita travel is also increasing, so individually we are travelling more than before. This increase is not so much due to more trips being made, but due to longer trips being made. For example, in Great Britain the number of trips increased by only 3 per cent between 1985/86 and 1994/96, while total distance increased by 23 per cent (Banister, 1999c).

The growth in passenger transport is mirrored by growth in freight transport. Materials and products are travelling further than ever; this is stimulated not only by economic growth and low costs, but by liberalisation of markets. To use just one graphic example: it has been calculated that the ingredients of an average pot of German yoghurt travel some 3,500 km –

Table 9.1 Travel growth and energy consumption by mode

Great Britain	Growth factor for passenger km, 1967-97	Energy: Megajoules per passenger km
Air (domestic)	3.57	5.00
Car	2.31	2.10
Rail	1.21	1.60
Bus	0.65	0.92

Source: DETR (1998a); Banister (1999a)

even before leaving the factory. A reported 3 billion pots of yoghurt are consumed annually in Germany (Weisacker *et al.*, 1997).

If we are making longer journeys, does this mean that travel has somehow become a more attractive pastime? Not necessarily; these longer journeys do not always imply more time spent travelling since travel speeds are faster: within the same 'time budget' a greater distance can be gained.

The increasing speeds are partly enabled by technological advances. But this is only part of the story. We have more or less the same transport modes available as there were from the early part of the twentieth century (Hall, 1988). In particular, the operational speeds of trains, buses and planes are not much different from what they were twenty or thirty years ago, due to congestion in urban areas and in the skies around major airports.

Seen this way, the increase in average speeds is not so much because transport modes are faster than they were, but because people are 'trading up' to faster modes. Up until the start of the twentieth century, the majority of travel was not by motorised transport (Wells, 1970). By the mid-twentieth century, most travel was motorised in Great Britain, though the majority of this was by public transport. Now, private road transport accounts for most travel.

To sum up, on average we are now travelling more, faster and further than ever before. The environmental consequences of this combination are considerable. The faster modes tend to consume more energy. Moreover, faster modes also consume more space. The space requirements of pedestrians are almost negligible compared to those by motorised modes. For motorised modes, vehicle occupancy evidently influences per capita use of space, but speed also plays a role: the space required by a car moving at 80 km/h is double that required of the same car travelling at 40 km/h (Roberts, 1990).

This increased use of faster modes is enabled by the fact that travel is less expensive in real terms than in the past. Gross domestic product per capita has increased while the cost of private travel has decreased (Banister *et al.*, 2000). On top of this, the need or occasion for travelling further must also be to do with the wider geographical distribution of interests, activities and destinations.

It so happens that those travel modes showing most growth (car, air) are not only relatively inexpensive, but are also particularly flexible. The car combines long-distance range with door-to-door accessibility. The plane hardly requires any route-specific infrastructure, and new routes can be opened up, according to demand, without new infrastructure investment. This flexibility accommodates and stimulates decentralisation and dispersal, from the urban to the international scales.

Energy Budgets

Speed, time, energy and cost are all linked. Where inexpensive high speed travel is available, longer journeys will be encouraged. From London, it is possible to travel to Barcelona in about the same time as it takes to get to Bridlington (a traditional holiday resort in the north-east of England), for less than twice the cost. From the leisure traveller's point of view, the trip to Barcelona is a good deal. But the environmental cost is high: the trip to Barcelona consumes five times as much energy (see Box 9.1).

In fact, it is possible to link travel with energy budgets as well as time and financial budgets. It has been estimated that the average total annual travel by land modes in Great Britain is 20,000 MJ per capita. This 'energy budget' equates with one return air flight from London to Athens (Banister, 1999c). This has importance for transport policy, since much of current policy is directed towards curbing car use in urban areas. Yet, even modest use of air travel may overwhelm any savings made by greener travel on the ground. In addition to the need to consider air travel, these figures also highlight the importance of considering travel across political boundaries (i.e. beyond the jurisdiction of many travel reduction policies), especially as the liberalisation of markets tends to encourage longer-distance cross-border travel.

Taking this kind of argument to the scale of the urban region, we can see that the energy budget of 20,000 MJ supports a daily commute (say, 240

Box 9.1 Time, money and energy

	London to Bridlington	London (Luton) to Barcelona
Mode	Rail	Air
Distance	350 km	1150 km
Typical journey time	$4^1/_4$ hours[1]	$2^1/_2$ hours[2]
Average speed	82 km/h	460 km/h (air leg)
Cost of return travel	Apex fare £46	Economy fare £78
	(Open return £117)	
Assumed energy consumption	1.6 MJ/pass km (GB rail)	2.42 MJ/pass km (EC air)[3]
Total energy for return trip	$2 \times 350 \times 1.6 =$ 1120 MJ	$2 \times 1150 \times 2.42 =$ 5566 MJ

Notes
1. Assumes changing at Doncaster and Hull.
2. Up to $4^1/_2$ hours city centre to city centre, including access time by rail.
3. Energy consumption for air is an estimate based on EC figures (Banister, 1999c). This is less than the GB air figure given in Table 9.1 since domestic trips are shorter while still consuming much energy during take-off, etc. The precise energy value will depend on aircraft type and passenger load factors, and the total environmental cost will include pollutants, noise, etc. (Schipper, 1999).

return trips per year) of 20 km by car, or 26 km by train, or 45 km by bus (using the generalised energy consumption figures given in Table 9.1).

However, commuters are more likely to travel according to time budgets or financial budgets, rather than energy budgets. The notional annual energy budget 'allows' a daily commute of 26 km by rail, roughly equivalent to the 47-minute journey from Uxbridge to London (King's Cross) by underground railway. Yet, by fast train, it is possible to commute all the way from Cambridge to London in 49 minutes, over three times the distance (93 km). Hence, there is a 'distance deficit' of 67 km – that is, a deficit in environmental terms between the distance a commuter is prepared to travel (for a given time budget) and that notionally allowed by the energy budget. Yet this distance may be seen as a *surplus* by the commuter, since it effectively represents the additional distance – into a possibly more attractive hinterland – over which it is feasible to travel, due to the availability of (relatively affordable) high speed transport.

A similar situation is seen for the car, where the time and cost of travel may be much less than that via public transport. This is especially the case for rural and non-radial suburban travel, and for travel in off-peak periods. Overall, the result is a pattern of travel which increases energy consumption.

Considerations for Sustainable Transport Modes

Given the differential effects of different transport modes on the environment, it makes sense for a sustainable transport policy to discriminate by mode. Indeed, there is often assumed to be a working 'hierarchy' of modes prioritised according to their sustainability. Typically, pedestrians and cyclists come first, followed by public transport, and private motorised transport comes last in priority – at least in principle. The approach is encapsulated in slogans such as 'feet first' and 'two wheels good, four wheels bad'.

Walking and cycling have in their favour a number of advantages which mark them out as the most favourable modes in terms of sustainability. Unlike motorised travel, walking and cycling are non-polluting; indeed, they can be healthy activities in their own right, as a form of exercise (Hillman, 1997). Almost everyone can walk, so this is a mode that is available to the widest cross-section of society: 'humans using their feet for transport are inherently equal' (Tolley, 1997). For those who cycle, the energy benefits are appreciable; the human–bicycle combination is more efficient than any animal or machine (Tolley, 1997).

Although walking and cycling represent a small proportion of overall travel in passenger kilometres, they become significant in terms of trips: for example, in the United Kingdom walking accounts for over 80 per cent of trips of under a mile in length (IHT, 1997). Walking in particular is complementary to other, non-transport activities, allowing social interaction and enhancing the vitality of urban areas. In this sense, walking is a favoured mode of travel not just from the point of view of energy and the environment, but the potential contribution to social and economic sustainability.

Public transport can be regarded as being complementary to these 'greenest' modes. Together, public transport with walking or cycling can offer the range and speed of motorised transport with the door-to-door penetration of individual transport.

Public transport on its own is not necessarily a panacea to transport problems (Pickrell, 1992; Richmond, 1998). Increasing public tranpsort use *per se* is not environmentally benign unless it is replacing a more harmful alternative. Major public transport schemes can cause much disruption to the environment, urban or rural, just as much as major road schemes. That said, many public transport measures may be effective even at a small scale. Bus gates, bus lanes and bus priority at junctions can all achieve impressive improvements in journey times at relatively small cost (DANTE Consortium, 1998; Mathers, 1999).

Effectively, there is a trade-off to be had. On the one hand, the high cost of a single light rail scheme might be put to better use funding a multitude of small-scale bus improvements. On the other hand, if these improvements are insufficient to attract cars users, then there may be little or no net environmental gain; in the end, the expensive, high profile light rail system may be necessary to tempt people out of their cars.

Finally, it is worth noting that although the kind of 'hierarchy' promoting of pedestrians, cyclists and public transport may seem natural and commendable, it is a relatively recent innovation. Previously, the private motor vehicle car was implicitly or explicitly given the greatest attention and priority. It is only the contemporary drive for sustainability that has accompanied and justified a significant turnaround in approaches to the planning of transport systems. This turnaround can be represented by a series of shifts from 'conventional approaches' to more recent 'sustainability- oriented' approaches (Table 9.2). The general shift may perhaps be epitomised by the contrasting titles *Traffic in Towns* (MoT, 1963) and *Transport in the Urban Environment* (IHT, 1997).

Some of the changes are simply methodological improvements, for example better modelling, which now take into account the greenest modes, or the wider context of mobility (Ettema and Timmermans, 1997; Stopher and Lee-Gosselin, 1997). Others are more explicitly aiming to address the concerns of a sustainable society (Roberts, 1989; Pharoah and Apel, 1995; Tolley, 1997; Newman and Kenworthy, 1999). Measures such as reducing road capacity are clearly seen as radical departures from conventional approaches. Traffic engineers trained to squeeze the maximum vehicular flows out of the available street width now find themselves deliberately slowing traffic and handing back roadspace to pedestrians.

Table 9.2 Contrasting approaches to transport provision

Conventional approaches (Traffic and Transport)	Sustainability-oriented approaches
Transport planning and traffic engineering specialism	More holistic, involving urban planning and environmental disciplines as well as transport professionals
'Traffic oriented' – and especially car oriented	'People oriented' – whether towards people in (or on) a vehicle or on foot
Concern for large-scale movements, often ignoring local trips (e.g. within zones)	Concern for local movements, and small-scale accessibility
Concern for motorised transport, especially road transport, often ignoring bicycles and pedestrians (e.g. in traffic surveys)	Concern for all modes, often arranged in a 'hierarchy', with pedestrians and cyclists at the top and car users at the bottom
Focus on the street as a movement artery	Wider concern for the street as a public space, used for activities and purposes other than movement.
Evaluation focused on economic criteria	Evaluation takes greater account of environmental and social criteria
Evaluation directed at road user costs and benefits (e.g. time saved by drivers or their passengers)	Evaluation acknowledges non-user costs and benefits (e.g. pedestrians; residents relieved of traffic; road users benefiting from rail improvements)
Concern for transport and tripmaking in isolation	Concern for transport in context of overall accessibility and tripmaking in context of wider activities and purposes
'Predict and provide' – capacity provision based on forecast demand	Demand management – attempt to moderate demand for travel
Design based on traffic efficiency and facilitating the flow of traffic	Design based on traffic calming, slowing traffic where necessary
Segregation of pedestrians and vehicles (use of walkways, underpasses, barriers to prevent pedestrians crossing the road)	Integration of pedestrian and vehicular space where appropriate (traffic calming, shared surfaces, woonerven etc.)

Policies Towards Sustainable Mobility

We have seen that the professional approaches seem to be moving in the right direction as far as sustainable travel is concerned. The question is then one of what specific policies may be taken. These will not merely be technical measures, but must take account of political feasibility and consumer choice, acknowledging the realities of the desire for continued mobility and economic growth, which tend to run counter to the sustainable path.

In this section, policies are arranged in three groups. Broadly speaking, we can change the mode of travel, we can change the spatial pattern of travel, or change the need to travel in the first place. These approaches are discussed in the next three sub-sections.

Promotion of greener modes

The promotion of greener modes can include making more use of the greenest modes; making less use of the less green modes; and finally, making modes 'greener'. The first approach implies making use of walking and cycling whenever possible, and where necessary complementing this with public transport. The second implies making less use of car and air travel. Together, these imply a 'cascading down', replacing car travel with public transport for medium to long distance journeys, and replacing motorised modes (whether private or public transport) with walking or cycling for shorter trips.

The third approach implies making the individual modes cleaner and greener. For example, today's cars are much more efficient and emit fewer pollutants than even ten years ago. However, clean technology cannot be more than a partial solution. As Wackernagel and Rees have pointed out, even zero emission vehicles pollute and consume resources in their construction, operation and disposal (Wackernagel and Rees, 1995). If there were to be no restraint on use of even the cleanest car, much environmental harm would still be done.

To consider how modes can be greened, a selection of policies is now given in Table 9.3. This notes how policies can contribute to sustainable travel, but also points out the potential complexities involved. These complexities give an indication of how implementation and realisation of sustainable transport policies are not necessarily achieved – even when there are good intentions from the outset.

The list of policies in Table 9.3 is not exhaustive, but shows a range of typical policies available. Often these will be combined with each other: for example, a 'green commuter plan' may combine restraint on car use with the promotion of cycling or car sharing. Similarly, the reallocation of roadspace normally involves a combination of taking roadspace away from cars and general traffic and redistributing it to buses, cycles and pedestrians.

The measures in Table 9.3 are mainly those conventionally implemented by transport authorities. They comprise the familiar 'carrot' and 'stick' approaches of incentives to travel by greener modes, and disincentives to using the car. The above transport policies go some way towards achieving more environmentally friendly travel, but only tackle part of the problem.

Another part of the problem is the spatial separation of activities and the distribution of land uses, which give rise to the need to travel in the first place. These issues are typically considered by urban planners, and are grouped for discussion in the following sub-section.

Table 9.3 Transport policy measures promoting greener modes

Transport policy	Potential contribution to sustainability	Complexities
Promoting walking e.g. pedestrianisation, pedestrian crossings and footpaths	Can reduce motorised travel, energy use, etc.	Not ideal for all users, purposes, distances, locations, times of day, climate, etc.
Promoting cycling e.g. cycle lanes, traffic signals, parking, signage, company cycle subsidy, etc.	Can reduce motorised travel, energy use, etc.	Not ideal for all users, purposes, distances, locations, times of day, climate.
Promoting public transport e.g. public transport priority, bus lanes, park and ride, subsidies, etc.	Can accommodate more passenger trips using fewer vehicles, less energy and less space, etc.	Not ideal for all users, purposes, locations, times of day. Must attract existing car users, not existing walkers or cyclists
Parking charges and parking capacity reduction	Can reduce demand for car travel	May result in more trips of shorter duration, or lengthen car trips
Road capacity reduction, road closures	Can reduce demand for travel; encourage switch away from car use	May shift traffic problem elsewhere
Road pricing	Can reduce demand for travel; encourage switch away from car use	May shift traffic elsewhere. Possible implications for equity and economic vitality
Fuel tax	Can reduce vehicle use and promote cleaner or more efficient vehicles	Scale of tax increase required to achieve significant change may be politically unacceptable. Possible implications for equity and economic vitality
Clean vehicle technology (promoting fuel efficiency)	Can reduce emissions and energy consumption	May stimulate more travel (now cheaper since using less fuel), while other environmental impacts remain
Clean fuel technology (electric, hydrogen fuel cell)	Can reduce emissions and energy consumption	Other environmental impacts (i.e. not relating to direct emissions or energy) remain

Urban planning policies contributing to sustainable transport

A number of urban planning measures which may be used to influence travel demand indirectly are listed in Table 9.4. This selection of policies is particularly important in the context of an integrated approach to transport, planning and sustainable development. The idea is to build sustainable travel patterns into the patterns of urban form and layout (Hall, this volume). Tackling these can assist towards more sustainable travel mainly by reducing distances, but also, where distances are sufficiently reduced, by triggering a switch to non-motorised modes.

As before, some of the complexities are pointed out in Table 9.4. With land use policies, the relations of cause and effect are not always clear, and travel patterns may be more influenced by the socio-economic characteristics of particular neighbourhoods than their physical form. That said, the spatial layout can help support more environmentally friendly choices. At least, a compact city allows the choice of walking to facilities within a short range, even if not everyone actually does so (for further discussion of the compact city idea, see Hall, this volume).

It should also be borne in mind that changes to the built environment take place at a relatively slow pace. Measures introduced now may take a long time to take effect and these effects may be swamped by general growth in travel in the meantime. However, this is not an argument to do nothing. Rather, it draws attention to urgency of acting now, as we will still be feeling the consequences of previous decades' car-oriented development for years to come.

Unlike some of the transport policies in Table 9.3, which often appear to be in competition (for share of roadspace, or investment) the land use planning measures in Table 9.4 tend to be complementary. Many may overlap, often at different spatial scales, and reinforce each other towards the objectives of sustainable mobility.

Well-known examples which combine various aspects include urban villages in the United Kingdom (compact, mixed use), the ABC policy in the Netherlands (location of businesses relative to public transport nodes) and transit-oriented developments in the United States (Urban Villages Group, 1992; Calthorpe, 1993). Evidently, there are many other examples where dense urban form and high pedestrian and public transport use occur anyway, for pragmatic reasons of efficiency or spatial constraint, as is typical in many Asian cities.

Reducing the need to travel

A third broad approach towards sustainable transport is to reduce the need for travel in the first place. While the policy measures in the preceding tables

Table 9.4 Land use measures contributing to sustainable transport

Land use planning policy	Potential contribution to sustainable transport policy	Complexities
Compact cities (overall densification and concentration of activities and facilities in limited area)	Can reduce travel distances; if these are sufficiently reduced, then cycling and walking become feasible alternatives to the car	Individuals may still prefer car use; alternatively, inhabitants may be predisposed to not using car
Mixed use development	Can enable travel distances to be reduced (e.g. journey to work) and support public transport over longer period of day	People may not actually live next to their work, but in- and out-commuting may persist
Location of homes near facilities, and vice versa	Can be located to minimise overall travel	Individuals may not choose to use closest facilities
Walk- and cycle-friendly development (design of buildings, spaces, route layout)	Can encourage walking and cycling	Individuals may still prefer car use
Public transport-oriented development	Locating homes and businesses near to public transport nodes or corridors can encourage switch from car use	Individuals may still prefer car use; shops and offices may still prefer to locate at car-oriented sites
Car-free developments, car-free areas and 'clear zones'	Can restrict car use and encourage alternatives to the car	May simply shift traffic problem elsewhere. Individual 'car-free' participants may already be predisposed to not using car
Settlement size	A large enough settlement can provide the critical mass for a viable public transport system. (Banister, 1999b)	The car may still be the preferred mode, especially for cross-town and interurban travel, and travel at off-peak times

might also reduce travel to some extent (e.g. reducing distances or motorised trips), the policies grouped in Table 9.5 represent those more directly aimed at substituting for travel, or otherwise reducing travel by switching journey type or journey time. Note that these measures are often taken by private organisations and individuals (e.g. employers or employees) rather than being implemented by transport or planning authorities.

Many of these policies are innovative, and their contribution to sustainability has not been fully evaluated. Broadly speaking, there has been

Table 9.5 Other policies for reducing the need to travel

Travel-reducing policies	Potential contribution to sustainable transport policy	Complexities
Home shopping	Can replace several individual shoppers' trips with a single delivery round	People may move further from shopping facilities, and make longer non-shopping trips
Teleworking	Can cut out commute trips	Employees may move further from place of employment; may still need to make non-work trips; may make car available to other household members
Off-peak travel (time switching)	Can cut congestion, travel time; spread demand for public transport	May encourage more car travel (both peak and off-peak)
Logistics	Can be used to minimise overall need for vehicles and vehicle trips (passenger or freight)	May free up vehicles for further use
Informatics	Can provide information on nearest parking facilities shortest routes, or routes to avoid congestion	May make car use more attractive
Car pooling/lift sharing	Can reduce number of vehicle trips by boosting vehicle occupancy	Compatibility of matching people and destinations may be difficult. Restricts flexibility for time switching
Car clubs/shared ownership	Can restrict car ownership and moderate demand for car trips	Not ideal for commuting at times of peak demand

less data collected on the travel effects of these kinds of policies in comparison with, say, patronage data for public transport schemes or journey to work data for different settlement patterns. The policies in this group may therefore seem to represent the greatest new opportunities for travel reduction, if only because the upper limit of their potential effectiveness is not fully evaluated.

Discussion on Policies

Achieving sustainable mobility is not straightforward, but remains a major challenge. Even where some progress is seen to be made – a documented case of telecommuting here, or a shift from car to bus there – it is often difficult to be sure that a more sustainable result has been achieved overall. Traffic growth may simply be diverted to alternative corridors; wherever one person reduces their own travel, it is always possible that someone else will make use of the freed-up roadspace, or someone else will make use of the freed-up vehicle (Banister and Marshall, 2000). This explains why there is a need to package the policies together in a complementary way such that they reinforce each other towards more sustainable mobility.

Looking at all the policies in Tables 9.3, 9.4 and 9.5, many of the measures can be seen to increase choice and encourage the use of alternatives to the car. However, those restricting car use or air travel are less prevalent. In fact, a study of European cities has demonstrated that restrictive measures tend to be applied mainly to the inner areas of cities, while travel growth – and the use of the most 'unsustainable' modes – continues in the outer city and the interurban hinterland (Marshall, 1999).

Politically, it may be difficult to implement the more restrictive anti-car measures. While there may be broad consensus that the environment is important, the individual motorist will still wish to maintain his or her own mobility. Authorities may not wish to risk being seen as being too anti-car. In any case, measures such as road pricing face opposition not only on grounds of mobility, but for their potential effects on equity and the competitiveness of cities: who is being priced out of their car, and which localities gain or lose. These issues bring social and economic dimensions to the fore in the sustainability equation.

As well as technological, operational and political feasibility, the challenge of sustainable transport must acknowledge the reality of the public response. Where people's aspirations and lifestyles happen to coincide with historic sustainable patterns – such as compact walkable cities – then sustainable travel patterns may be achieved. But if people's lifestyles are irrevocably 'suburban', based on dispersed activities, separation of home and work *by choice*, and car use *by preference*, then the provision of physical solutions such as urban villages may not work – they may simply not be used in a sustainable way. This is why a final type of measure is required, which relates to public information and education. Only when the public appreciate the need for change will policy measures be accepted more positively, and more sustainable patterns be realised.

What Prospects for Sustainable Transport?

It is clear that practices are becoming more sensitive to sustainability (Table 9.2), and some progress has been achieved in boosting green travel, in making vehicles cleaner and in containing growth in car use in some conditions. However, many of the gains may be local and rather small relative to the overall magnitude of growth in travel, and the consequential scale of land and energy consumption and environmental degradation. The continued momentum towards travel growth, especially when factored to the global scale, must continue to give cause for concern.

Much will depend on whether it is possible to decouple travel growth from economic growth (Banister *et al.*, 2000). If this can be achieved, then it might be possible to continue to sustain enonomic growth without perpetuating current rates of travel growth. One way that might be possible is through substitution of electronic communication for physical mobility. However, the grounds for optimism on this front are not certain. First, there appears to be a symbiotic relationship where travel is complementary to electronic communication, and may even be stimulated by it. Second, there will be continuing need for the physical transport of material goods. Third, there may be an innate human desire for mobility, requiring to be satisfied even when other reasons for travel are nullified. Finally, the effects of telecommunications on patterns of urbanity are yet to be felt. These may restructure cities and settlements in ways which give rise to more conventional travel.

The technological advancement in telecommunications in the twentieth century has eclipsed developments in transport technology.[1] Just as urbanity has progressively been reshaped by mechanised travel and rail travel in the nineteenth century and the car in the twentieth, so telecommunications become increasingly important in the twenty-first. Whether the spatial patterns stimulated or accommodated by telecommunications technologies will give rise to more or less sustainable patterns of physical mobility remains to be seen. In an optimistic scenario, long-distance travel could be increasingly replaced by telecommunication, while walking and cycling meet the needs of local face-to-face interactions and leisure mobility.

In the end, the kind of sustainable city that we might see in the future will depend on what kind of city we aspire to. It is likely that a range of solutions might be possible, which are equally sustainable in environmental terms. One can imagine, for example, one scenario where the information-rich 'digiterati' telecommute between physically forbidding disurban enclaves (Graham and Marvin, 1996); on the other hand, another scenario where liveable, walkable urbanity is maintained and enhanced. Each might use the same amount of energy, but the implications for society and quality of life would be quite different.

Either way, the heavy emphasis of conventional mechanised transport would be less marked than in previously envisioned 'futures'. Overall, taking account of trends in the built environment in general, it looks as if the sustainable city will not be some grand vision of futuristic transport after all, but perhaps a more human-scale, intelligent, recyclable extension of the present. At the same time, if global warming continues unabated, and predictions for sea level rises are realised, perhaps the model on which to base the city of the future will turn out to be Venice.

Note

1 According to Karniadakis and Orszag, for example, 'Electronic component speeds and densities have improved by a factor of more than 10^5 in the last half-century . . . if automobiles had undergone similar improvements, today a Cadillac would sell for less than a penny, or it would be capable of a peak speed in excess of 1% of the speed of light' (quoted in Coveney and Highfield, 1995).

Further Reading

For a comprehensive overview of transport issues seen from the point of view of the transport planning and traffic engineering profession in the United Kingdom, see *Transport in the Urban Environment* (IHT, 1997). Specific guidance on how planning can reduce the need to travel is given in *PPG13: Guide to Better Practice – Reducing the Need to Travel through Planning* (DoE/DoT, 1995). General United Kingdom government policy is given in the Transport White Paper (DETR, 1998g); *Planning for Sustainable Development* (DETR, 1998h); *Places, Streets and Movement* (DETR, 1998i).

More detailed discussion of travel trends is given in *A Billion Trips a Day* (Salomon *et al.*, 1993). Further discussion of relationships between transport and sustainability is given in *Sustainability and Cities*: *Overcoming Automobile Dependence* (Newman and Kenworthy, 1999). The *Greening of Urban Transport* brings together a diversity of material, mainly on walking and cycling but also public transport (Tolley, 1997).

The discussion on sustainable transport policy measures and their complexities was based on a series of case studies and analyses which have not been attributed individually here, but are explored explicitly in *Encouraging Travel Alternatives* (Banister and Marshall, 2000).

10 Sustainable Property Development

Michael Edwards and Christopher Marsh

Introduction

The endless transformation of land and buildings in modern societies mobilises financial and production capital, professional skills, construction labour and material inputs. Taken together, these activities make up a large part of most economies and loosely comprise the development sector, though they are not identified as such in any statistics. They contribute powerfully to the 'sustainability' or 'unsustainability' of the individual building, of the locality and of the settlement system as a whole.

The effects of the development process are not distinct from (or additional to) the effects of design, of planning, of law or of transport but represent the concrete process which crystallises these forces in actual urbanisation. Since the immediate purpose of all this activity is to produce or improve buildings and settlements, the analysis of the development process is a valuable way of integrating our separate studies of distinct sectors and functions which are the subject of other chapters in this book – housing, transport, shopping, and so on. The focus of this chapter on the process which delivers all this production casts light on the motives, the driving forces and the constraints which regulate the transformation of settlements.

Forms of ownership and development of land and buildings vary a lot through time and between countries. In pre-enclosure Britain much land was owned in essentially feudal forms with extensive 'common' rights which regulated community use of space. In modern capitalist countries land and property *markets* have been constituted to enable buildings and land to be traded as *private property* alongside collective (public) provision of infrastructure and open spaces (Massey and Catalano 1978; Offer 1981; McMahon 1985). The driving force in most modern development is thus to secure returns for property owners and most development can thus be called *property development*.

Many of the changes in the role of the *state* since the 1970s are reflected in the increased importance of property development in shaping our settlements. The cuts in direct state provision of social welfare and infrastructure in the USA and Europe have been promoted by neo-liberal conservative regimes and by trans-national bodies like the International Monetary Fund and the World Bank. These ideologies seem to be unchallenged so far by most of the centre-left parties now governing in Europe. The role of the state – including local government – is thus increasingly to commission or persuade private bodies to build and provide what had – in the early post-war decades – been considered as public facilities in these countries, even though they were mostly financed by public borrowing from private investors.

The state and the sectors it directly regulates (transport, utilities and so on) still account for nearly half of the demand for construction in western Europe (Winch 2000) but more and more of it is now to some degree property development. Social housing is now produced on a shrinking scale and at arm's length from government in most of Europe. Universities, health buildings, leisure facilities, prisons and a host of other necessities of life are now treated as property development projects, as investment opportunities and as financial assets. So too is infrastructure, either through the privatisation of whole sectors (gas, electricity, telecomms) or through Private Finance Initiative (PFI) schemes for specific projects like the Birmingham Northern Relief Road or the Channel Tunnel Rail Link (CTRL). The role of the state in our urban development is thus drawing closer to what it has been in Latin America (Smolka 1984) and the rest of the capitalist world which never went through the full Fordist experience in which the state was the major provider.

This chapter outlines how the development process can succeed or fail in contributing to environmental, economic, social and cultural sustainability – though all those concepts are ill-defined and controversial. The discussion moves from the scale of the individual building, through local ensembles of buildings (neighbourhoods and localities) to the development of the whole settlement pattern. Much of the substance of the chapter is developed through reflecting on current research (Sustainable Property Consultants 1999; Marsh *et al.* 2000) and on the positive and negative features of recent developments. Throughout attention is necessarily paid to public regulation and policy since this is what sets the rules and constraints within which the property markets largely operate.

The chapter concludes by looking at the instruments through which sustainability in the development process might be fostered, ranging from changes in attitudes, better building regulations, through taxes and subsidies to new organisational forms for developing, planning and managing the built environment at various scales.

A Dream in a Nutshell: Where Should Today's System be Going?

It may help to start with a an explicit sketch of what is implicitly required. Here is an optimistic retrospective — looking back from the year 2020.

The building

We live and work in buildings which use very little non-renewable energy for heating or cooling and are produced with materials which have a low energy content in their production, transport and use. Often these are local materials and incorporate the re-cycling of structures or materials from previous buildings nearby. Many wastes – organic material, water, unwanted heat – are re-cycled within the plot or in the neighbourhood. The buildings themselves embody a long-term structural flexibility, adaptable to rapidly changing social preferences and patterns of activity. This reduces the rate at which buildings need to be torn down to make way for new ones; on the other hand, some replacement has been necessary where the old structures were performing really badly or where land could be used much more intensively.

The locality

Configurations of buildings provide for a variety of activities close enough together to reduce the need for motorised travel, to produce safe pedestrian and cycle environments and good local conditions for people with limited mobility – young, old and those with disabilities. Telecommunications obviates a lot of the trips people used to make, but by no means all. Most people living in towns and cities are now able to find schools, some shopping, primary medical care, cafes, pubs, recreation and public offices within easy reach. Innovations in local service provision – by businesses, collective action and non-profit bodies proliferate. For example Adams (1997) initiated local car-hire pools in each city street, operating from an office which also served as a conciergerie, taking in parcels and deliveries. In London, corner shops gained a new lease of life as they became order-points and pick-up points for internet deliveries – one of the early strategic successes of the Greater London Authority (Hall *et al.* 1999). Similar transformations of the village shop have arrested the rundown of services in many rural areas too, stabilising a new balance between small producers and multinational chains. Many low-density suburbs and new towns have been modified as well to improve their sustainability (Edwards 2000a).

The city

The configuration of whole towns and city regions has been adapted to reduce the energy and ecological impacts of modern life and to reduce the economic and social inequalities which were growing fast in most countries as the century turned. The energy-efficient city is configured so that we can achieve better balances between access (to work, to cultural and educational sites, to shops, to sport, health and so on) and travel, especially private car travel. This means we have some centralised services, but also many diffused service centres, with efficient, cheap and thoroughly pleasurable public transport and telecommunication networks linking them.

The effects of city structure on economic and social sustainability often used to be disregarded. Large and dynamic cities used to generate high rents and huge variations in land and property prices. Where this was reinforced by restrictive planning regimes prices were higher still – in 'rural' as well as 'urban' areas (Edwards 2000b; Edwards 2000c; Cheshire 2000). While we were subject to increasing income inequality early in the twenty-first century, housing and premises needed to be available cheaply to sustain low- and mixed-income communities and small and new businesses. Steady growth in the supply of housing and other buildings was necessary to bring prices down in the interests of equality and to avoid forcing urban residents out to ex-urban places where they were trapped in their motor cars and/or costly long-haul commuter trains. This is essentially why we have settled the London green belt so intensely, producing hundreds of new settlements at nodes on the transit networks, knitting Hertfordshire, Buckinghamshire, Surrey and Sussex together with London and bringing housing costs down to the national average level (Edwards 2000d).

Cities and regions were not able to achieve all this by themselves and it proved necessary in the first decade of the twenty-first century to transform the European Community into a mechanism for reducing geographical disparities, but that is another story.

This picture of urban structure is far from what we actually have at the turn of the century and in many respects the gap is widening. Even if oil prices (or tax on energy) rise dramatically, we are unlikely to move in this direction on current trends and the impoverishment effects would not be reversed even by a reduced use of cars.

Radical Alternatives

The scenarios just sketched above are essentially modest and reformist: they imply that some modifications to present social forces could suffice to produce a sustainable society and built environment. Even the achievement of this modest 'ecological modernisation' presupposes a major shift in power relations in the United Kingdom. Those changes may not be feasible. It could well be that the global, European and local systems of production, consumption, exploitation and use of resources will hurtle us towards social breakdown or into worse ecological catastrophes than we already have. The future could and should be radically different from the past, as the historian Eric Hobsbawm puts it:

> We do not know where we are going. We only know that history has brought us to this point and . . . why. However, one thing is plain. If humanity is to have a recognisable future, it cannot be by prolonging the past or present. If we try to build the third millennium on that basis, we shall fail. And the price of failure, that is to say, the alternative to a changed society, is darkness.
>
> (Hobsbawm 1994: 585)

Essentially this chapter (and most of this book) is about tinkering with present arrangements to produce a more humane and environmentally friendly capitalism. It may not be a feasible project and we should also be planning for other eventualities – some quite radical changes in the pattern of world trade, growth of local self-sufficiency and of proliferating egalitarian and non-exploitative enclaves and initiatives. Agenda 21 constitutes a tentative commitment in this direction and the world is generating a lot of instances (INURA 1998). Providing space for social and ecological movements outside the mainstream should be a high priority in modern society but tends to conflict with the elaborate and rather authoritarian regulations used to contain capitalism. Some interesting work is being done on how the British statutory planning system could accommodate the initiatives of permaculture and low-impact development (Fairlie and This Land is Ours 1996), but there will continue to be conflicts between radical movements and the institutions of regulated capitalism.

Urban Development Projects: Actors and Functions

Property development is essentially a matter of projects. The city grows and changes through the cumulative effect of thousands of individual development projects. With only rare exceptions, developers have to take the market, the infrastructure and the planning system as they find it: individual developers cannot change their customers' preferences, the structure of the city or the land market. The understanding of our current problems thus depends on analysing how development projects take place.

It is very common to read about the 'agents' or about the 'players' in urban development: land owners, banks, tenants, builders and so on. They are easy to identify in any project. It is common for critics of architecture and urbanism to 'blame' particular agents for faults in what gets built: 'greedy developers', 'short-sighted investors', 'bureaucratic planners' and so on. However, for two reasons we are writing instead about *'functions'* – for example, credit and investment, building production, consumption and use – because:

- the main functions in urban development *always* have to be performed, while particular kinds of agents may be absent in a particular case – for example, we don't always find banks; we often now don't find a distinctive class of land owners;
- the functions may be performed by a single agent or by a lot of separate ones and it is useful to look at these different organisational forms as important in themselves – for example, we may find vertical integration where one organisation combines all functions and the sustainability implications may be very different.

The basic approach here is to think of the social relationships in the whole long life of buildings and the land they stand on in a capitalist economy. This approach draws principally upon research by Topalov (1985), Harvey (1996), Ball (1983), Chambert (1997) and participants in the Bartlett International Summer Schools on the Production of the Built Environment (1979–99). Also very valuable in this context is the work of Healey and Barrett (1990), Madanipour (1996), Guy (1998) and Pratt (1998).

Think of the sequence in the course of a development project (in this case rental housing being built on farm land): land starts in one sort of previous use (in this case a farm). The conception of change requires a transitional or mediating stage which can involve the land changing hands, design, legal and political work about permissions, the arrangement of grants, subsidies, investments and loans: everything necessary for the project then to go ahead. Actual production can then begin: engineering, building and other processes which will have economic and social impacts (the generation of direct and indirect employment and incomes) and environmental effects (through the resources used, waste produced and so on).

When the work is done it is still not economically complete: until it is sold and the money received, those already involved cannot be paid and the accumulation of capital stops. New owners, financiers or users must therefore be found. Thus begins a stage of use – the life of the finished project, but still with a stream of costs in maintenance, heating, repair and adaptation. It is in this long life of the development that most of the social, economic and environmental impacts will arise – and because they stretch into the future they will not be precisely foreseeable.

Finance

All four stages of our simple model may involve finance, i.e. there may be people who have invested money capital either as shareholders or partners, or as interest-bearing loans. In principle this role is simple to describe but in practice it can be very complex, and the forms which investment in real estate take are becoming endlessly more elaborate.

Finance phase by phase

Since we are interested in the development process we may not need to know much about the financing of pre-development activity. But it can be important in triggering development: the farmer, in debt to the bank, paying rising interest rates from a falling income, may be forced to sell or to develop. The industrial company may consider its property asset better used by selling it for development than by carrying on production – and will be influenced by the likely price it could receive on sale. This in turn will be influenced by what the planning system would permit on the site and by the costs of any decontamination for which it might be liable.

The transitional phase of getting development projects ready is often carried on with the owner's or developer's own money. It is risky (because of uncertainty about permission and/or about market demand). The attitude and involvement of the state can be very important here in determining the level of risk, creating general conditions such as the supply of infrastructure, limiting competition.

Actual production is always very costly and is hardly ever feasible without borrowing or equity finance coming from outside the organisation. (The exception is in self-build housing where the household builds a bit each year – just what it can afford from its income.) The financing of urban development is a very important kind of asset for the world's banks and investors. It can be very risky, depending principally on whether the project is commissioned, pre-let or speculative and, if it is speculative, what the demand conditions are likely to be.

When a building is finished the developer may simply sell it, using the money to pay off any debts and ending up with a profit or a loss. But that can only happen if a buyer can be found who has (or can borrow) the money to finance the purchase. So the credit problem is a continuing one. We find in many countries that particular kinds of financial institutions (e.g. pension funds, insurance companies) specialise in the long-term ownership of real estate as investments; other institutions may specialise in long-term finance for housing or for particular industries. In some places there are strong regional banks which can be very important – e.g. in Italy. In the United Kingdom the specialised and localised banks have almost disappeared now though there is no sign that the huge general-purpose banks are particularly good at making decisions and using their huge market power in anyone's interests.

The degree of power and influence of the lenders and investors can vary enormously from case to case, and can change fast. Often we see that property development or investment companies have debts to the bank which seem quite modest and the interest can easily be paid out of rental income or building sales. But then if building rents fall or if interest rates rise (or both) the company can quickly be weakened or destroyed and the banks and creditors end up owning a lot of (devalued) buildings. This is what happened to Olympia and York, the world's biggest promoter, and to many others in 1990–92. The power relations can shift. Thus banks in the United Kingdom have become quite influential on the property development process.

In a world where money capital can flow increasingly freely – not just in Europe but globally – the capital markets can channel very large sums in to and out of the real estate sector, as we have seen. A sudden rush of money can drive prices up. Investors confront special problems when they try rapidly to withdraw from real estate: real estate assets quickly become rather illiquid when everyone is trying to sell and a dramatic fall of values can easily be precipitated. It is fair to say that today's international markets in real estate assets are very volatile and not at all self-regulated. However, one advantage of cross-border flows into property is that foreign investors may have different priorities, likes and dislikes, knowledge and skill compared with the national financial fraternity. In London foreign investors seem to have been to the fore in some important innovations – in the Docklands, in the conversion of surplus offices to housing and in mixed-use developments (Sustainable Property Consultants 1999).

Land Ownership, Promotion (= Development)

Historically the ownership of land has been an enormous problem for the development of capitalist economies – often presenting great barriers to modernisation, inhibiting investment and enabling local monopoly powers to suck income out of local economies which could otherwise have been used for productive investment, enjoyed as personal income or enabling wages to settle at lower levels. Sometimes the mere structure of ownership (small plots, complicated tenure) can prevent owners from developing easily, even when they want to. Occasionally there have been cases where forms of large-scale private land ownership have enormously simplified and helped development (as in the great leasehold estates of London, like Bloomsbury, or in the early evolution of the coal mining industry) but the general rule is that land ownership is a barrier.

In modern Europe we have seen changes which – to varying degrees – have removed some of these barriers, usually by giving the state powers to acquire land and to service it for development, or to re-parcel sites, or to acquire land if the existing owners do not develop it in the way (and at the time) required by some plan. The British government's current policies of encouraging development on 'brownfield' (previously developed) land can often be impeded by problems in assembling profitable development sites and compulsory purchase powers need to be used.

Property development can be a demanding and complex function, including:

- conceiving of the possibility;
- finding a location;
- market research (for speculative projects) or consultations with future users, and feasibility studies;
- specifying the product, commissioning designers;
- obtaining permissions;
- finding investors, credit, state subsidies;
- contracting with, and controlling, builders;
- marketing the finished product in advance;

and often doing all these things fast – to minimise interest charges and to complete and sell on to an investor before a rising market passes its peak.

The agents which perform these development functions vary enormously. Some industrial firms do it for themselves. Some banks and insurance companies have their own development divisions. Sometimes there are integrated firms which combine construction, promotion (and often finance too) as in France and Japan for example. Sometimes developers become also property investment companies, holding on to their completed projects and becoming large-scale managers as well as producers. And then there are the pure promoters, sometimes called 'merchant developers' – often very small firms with few staff and little capital – who specialise in getting projects together, completing them, selling and going on to the next. This could be the small speculator who builds one house a year or a large-scale operator like some development companies in the United Kingdom. The time horizon of these operators is very short.

Perhaps the most important distinction to make here is between development which is speculative or not. Speculative production is where, when construction starts, there is no particular user of the building contracted to use it. In some places speculative development is the dominant form; in others most building is done by or for clearly identified users.

Speculative developers will tend to produce buildings of the type and location which *they think* will sell. They may be wrong, so some buildings are under-used while people seeking buildings of some types or in some places may not get them. Also developers and those who finance them tend (with a few brave exceptions) to play safe – to converge on the types, designs and locations for which they think there will be a steady mass of demand — what are called 'prime' properties. In this case marginal locations will be under-supplied and unusual kinds of building will not be built (Henneberry 1995). So investment is over-concentrated in prime locations (e.g. London and the South East, in central and west areas within London) with adverse effects on the economic sustainability of more peripheral regions (e.g. the North, and, within London, eastern districts). Simon Guy has examined the distinctive relationships in British and French office development in this spirit, identifying how each configuration tends to have its own positive and negative features in terms of sustainability (Guy 1998).

In a detailed survey of British developers, Marsh *et al.* (2000) conclude that developers will adopt 'sustainability' criteria in their developments when the market gives them a positive motive for doing so – when occupiers, buyers and users show that they will pay the best rents and prices for more sustainable buildings. The other key influence to which developers will respond is the attitude of lenders and investors – those who finance development or buy completed schemes as investments or who (especially in the housing market) lend to owner-occupiers to finance purchase.

The developers reported that they were reluctant to respond to cajoling from central government or to pressures – often inconsistently applied – coming from local authorities (Marsh *et al.* 2000).

Production Itself

The construction process seems familiar: we all know what it is. However, there are some important changes in the division of labour within the production process. For decades, the model in the United Kingdom and elsewhere used to be that the developer or construction client commissioned an architect (or engineer) who designed. Then builders were found to build. It was the tradition of the liberal professional.

Imagine Nissan or Sony working this way! They want to integrate design and production for speed, for effective learning and feedback and for cost control. Nowadays in construction (especially for offices) we are beginning to see in the United Kingdom the arrival of American and Japanese approaches in which the building contractor or a construction manager takes control of the whole design-and-build process. The architect becomes a servant of the builder. If there is a distinct design firm it may only be involved at the early stage of getting permission and later as a sub-contractor to the main contractor (Ive 1995). Thus the architectural and other professions are being placed under great pressure in a new social division of labour. Even where architects and engineers work in the conventional way with clients, the United Kingdom differs from other European countries in that long-term relationships tend to be developed, so the cooperation is much closer in Britain than it might appear (Winch 2000). It does seem likely that the integration of design with the management of actual production could assist the adoption of more sustainable construction practices. Guy is also optimistic about the impact of the new 'facilities management' profession, committed to the management of long-term costs-in-use of buildings and likely to be resistant to the excessively lavish specification of many prime United Kingdom office buildings (Guy 1998).

Another distinctive feature of United Kingdom construction, however, probably works the other way: the fact that our planning system is quite separate from our system of building control. Here developers have to negotiate and argue the merits of their projects to secure planning permission. But the environmental performance of the proposed building is not yet a factor in this process: instead the environmental performance of a building is considered in a quite distinct process of gaining approval under the Building Regulations. That process essentially just checks *conformity* with the rules. Although rising standards (especially for thermal efficiency) have raised the level of performance of new buildings over the years, it is the view of many experts that developers would be much more highly motivated if they had to demonstrate the 'greenness' of their projects at planning application stage and could make an environmental case as part of their bid for planning permission (DETR Property Advisory Group 1998; Marsh *et al.*, 2000).

As local planning authorities increasingly write environmental, accessibility and related policies into their development plans this situation should improve. It should be noted, though, that the government and the courts have tended not to let local authorities use development plans as vehicles for progressive social or economic policies. The requirement upon the new Mayor of London to prepare an Economic Strategy (and to integrate it with his Spatial Development Strategy) is thus a most welcome U-turn in policy.

Consumption and Use

The simple form of consumption and use is owner-occupation. For housing this is the dominant form in many countries and (with elaborate credit arrangements) is becoming widespread in many more parts of Europe. For industrial and commercial buildings it is also very common for firms to own their own buildings – either getting them built to their requirement or buying them from others. Often – in Germany for example – it seems that this form of tenure is attractive to businesses: they can borrow against the security of their land and buildings to raise capital for any business purpose, not only to buy the real estate itself. A second advantage may be that the firm can get exactly the building it requires – rather than having to buy what the market offers. A third advantage may be that the firm is insulated from the effect of changing rents. Owner-occupation of factories, offices and shops has been dominant in Germany, Holland and many other parts of Europe.

Alternatively there are many forms of tenancy. This means that a landlord or investor retains some of the rights of ownership in the land or in the land+buildings and collects a rent in exchange for giving a tenant the rights of occupation. The details vary enormously from country to country and there is absolutely no European harmonisation yet. This rental system has been dominant in the United States of America and United Kingdom and there are those who believe that it will spread through Europe.

When a rental system exists we get two distinct markets: (a) a user market in which users compete with each other to rent the available space. This supply–demand interaction determines the level of rent in each place and rents can be very volatile since demand changes much more rapidly than supply. If users have a preference for 'green' buildings they can express these preferences in the user market and clearly there is scope for 'green consumers' to become influential in property markets; (b) an investment market in which investors compete with each other to buy the available buildings (occupied or empty) to use as investments in order to gain the flow of rent from them and the hope of capital gain. In these markets capital values are determined. Capital values depend of course on levels of rent (more rent, more value), but also on expectations of future rental growth, the quality of the tenants, on expectations about future lettability and on the returns available in other kinds of investment. (Investors will not buy buildings which yield less than bank deposits or government bonds unless there are strong compensations like the prospect of future growth.)

In the kind of dual market we have in the United Kingdom it is investors' demands which mainly determine the quantity and character of commercial building (Luithlen 1994). We can and do get enormous fluctuations in building production and these are only influenced by fluctuation in the actual demand (from users for buildings) in a very indirect and inefficient way, and with some years of delay. It seems very inefficient and it is certainly very damaging to the development of skills and capacities in the construction sector.

The dual market also weakens the relationship between producers and consumers. If there are 'green consumers' anxious to occupy more sustainable buildings, their preferences will only work through indirectly to the developers who produce buildings when they come to be reflected in the rents or prices and (with some delay) in the expectations of capital value growth which investors form in the investment markets.

On the other hand, the existence of big rental markets can be good for the efficiency of firms which use space and thus for growth in the rest of the economy. Firms have a choice of where to locate and about the quality and quantity of space they occupy: it is very flexible for them providing that their leases are flexible. During the 1990s we have seen the balance of power shift in favour of occupiers and away from investors so that these benefits of a rental market do now seem to be coming available. Marsh *et al.* (2000) point out that shorter and more flexible leases may encourage developers to increase the sustainability of their buildings to retain their best tenants. But they also fear that owners of secondary property – who already tend to take a very short-term view – may be even less inclined to invest in long-term sustainability as leases get shorter.

Another damaging feature of investment markets is that a limited number of building types emerge because investment markets are best at handling standardised commodities. This may reduce the diversity of what gets built and seems to have militated against the production of more mixed-use developments (and especially of mixed-use buildings) in the United Kingdom. It is hard to say to what extent this resistance to mixed-use flows from:

- specialisation among development companies, each of which becomes highly expert in shopping, housing, offices or business parks;
- the practices of portfolio managers, and the valuers advising them, who tend to think in single-use categories and be rather ill-informed about the attributes and performance of mixed-use schemes; or
- the long tradition in the planning system of using planning to separate, rather than to integrate, uses.

Recent research has explored these questions, concluding that the growth of consumer demand for more sustainable buildings and locations will be crucial in pushing investors and the development industry (Sustainable Property Consultants 1999; Marsh *et al.* 2000). Changes in consumer preferences could come purely from heightened awareness, but could also reflect material self-interest in response to the taxes, costs and risks which consumers face. Thus carbon tax or rising energy prices would be expected (indeed intended) to influence households and firms in their demand for buildings. Corporate preferences would be influenced by the need to prepare Green Transport Plans or if they had to carry some of the direct or indirect costs of their employees' travel. The proposed taxation of workplace parking is a start in this direction (Marshall, Chapter 9 this volume). On a broader scale, Cox and Cadman envisage that occupier firms and investment firms will increasingly adopt 'triple bottom line' accounting in which they report on their activities in terms of social and environmental, as well as narrowly financial, criteria (Cox and Cadman 2000).

Problems and Solutions

In this chapter we have analysed some of the key relationships which can influence how the property development sector operates as it delivers our new buildings. Could it be expected to transform our built environment into a much more sustainable one?

On the face of it *no*, and for a number of reasons:

1 Most buildings are old ones. We add only 1–2 per cent per year to the stock. Thus changing the character, location or price of what gets built each year is, at best, a very slow way of changing the whole built environment.

2 Like any business sector, the property development industry and those who invest in it are operating in a competitive context and pursue profits and capital growth. Firms cannot safely sacrifice short-term profitability

for the long-term imperatives of sustainability and it is unrealistic to expect them to do so: those who fail to make profits go bankrupt or are taken over by others. Today's economic conditions, with quite high real interest and profit rates, means firms have to take a short-term view, especially in the United Kingdom (Hutton 1995). It would take very strong pressure from 'ethical investors' and green consumers to produce a longer-term perspective in the development industry.

3　Many of the negative effects of an 'unsustainable' built environment are not experienced by the property developers' immediate consumers so self-interest is unlikely to produce strong consumer demand for more sustainable developments. Future generations have no voice among today's consumers; congestion and pollution effects are diffused across wide local, or even global, communities, not just among the customers for new buildings. And the social exclusion, displacement, homelessness and segregation resulting from high rents and house prices are experienced by low-income people who by definition have no market power at all.

4　Even if we could design (as we certainly can) futures which are both more sustainable and potentially profitable, there is no market mechanism to orchestrate individual actors to get there. Attempts to do so often fail (Edwards 2000c). Markets, in general, are not good at coordination of multiple small agents to move in radically new directions. In particular the development process could only be expected to lead us to a radically different regional settlement structure – for example the green belt development sketched above – in the context of a profound shift in political power and planning policy.

On the other hand there are grounds for hope:

1　Although the building stock is renewed only slowly, the use we make of it can change relatively fast. Premises can switch fairly freely from one use to another (with or without official sanction – and much of the recent blurring of the distinction between 'home' and 'workplace' has been un-authorised). People can switch the destinations of their trips, especially for shopping and leisure, or switch their mode of travel (Marshall, Chapter 9, this volume). Telecommunications offers many new ways of using space and economising on transport. If the problems of transforming the city through new building production seem intractable, the study of the rest of the stock may generate more optimism (Hebbert 1998). William Morris's environmental utopia, after all, consisted of a transformed way of using the familiar building stock of nineteenth-century London (Morris 1912 edn).

2　Changes in the way British public buildings are commissioned through the government's new 'best value' policy should lead to the choice of buildings and locations which are good value (in terms of explicit criteria) – not just the cheapest in capital cost, which was always the problem in public procurement in the past. Closer partnerships between users and providers of buildings, and a stronger voice for users, could lead to more appropriate technologies and a longer-term approach to costs-in-use in the private sector (Guy 1998).

3   There is some scope for ensuring that the users of buildings do have to bear (at least more of) the environmental and social costs they generate. Fuel or carbon taxes are clearly the most direct and efficient way of giving everyone a material motive to behave in a more environmentally sustainable way – much better in many respects than rules and regulations (Evans 1998). Politicians, however, are unlikely to impose such burdens on drivers, on pensioners' heating and on the 'countryside' so it probably will not be fully implemented. But there are many other ways in which environmental damage can be charged to perpetrators, such as the tax on private parking spaces, the tax on landfill (Davoudi, Chapter 12, this volume) or the reallocation of road space to buses. In a messy way we shall probably see quite a lot of these measures implemented and then we'll see significant shifts in 'consumer demand' as a result. In the jargon of economics, we shall have internalised some externalities.

4   There are ways to orchestrate individuals so they pursue their collective self-interest instead of a mutually destructive individual interest. The classic example in the past has been government encouragement of housing improvement and conservation areas which have radically upgraded and improved great tracts of United Kingdom cities. The same philosophy could be applied to the strategic planning of London by the Mayor's office (Edwards 2000b) or to a wide variety of environmental problems. At the level of development plans and development control, the adoption of social, economic and environmental policies should encourage developers to prepare more 'sustainable' schemes in the quest for permissions.

None of these grounds for hope, however, does very much for social or cultural sustainability: they just may help with the ecological problems. Moves towards a less exploitative, less unequal, society remain a distant hope. While the green movement and the 'sustainability' debate offer an invaluable way to re-discover the crisis of modern society, they do not yet offer a solution.

11 Sustainable Urban Design – A Possible Agenda

Matthew Carmona

Introduction

In the United Kingdom the sustainable dimension of urban design has steadily emerged. Many ideas about the interpenetration of town and country, for example, can be traced back to the pioneers of the planning movement like Howard, Geddes and Unwin, as can notions of local social and economic sustainability. Nevertheless, the recent proliferation of writing on concepts of sustainable development has firmly shifted the urban design agenda towards broader environmental concerns. As with planning, the sustainability agenda is giving the discipline a new and broadly accepted legitimacy.

Most conceptualisations of urban design now include reference to a sustainable dimension, so that sustainable urban design now fits four-square within a theoretical framework for urban design that already embraces well-established visual, morphological, social, perceptual and functional concerns. In the United Kingdom, for example, the ten general design principles for creating more liveable places identified by the Urban Task Force (1999: 71) demonstrate a clear emphasis on environmental concerns. Meant as a basis for assessing plans and proposals, rather than as a prescriptive set of commandments on urban design, the Task Force identified:

- site and setting;
- context, scale and character;
- public realm;
- access and permeability;

- optimising land use and density;
- mixing activities;
- mixing tenures;
- building to last;
- sustainable buildings;
- environmental responsibility.

Parts of this agenda have already been recognised in United Kingdom government policy, although nothing is straightforward in this fast-developing field and arguments can be made both for and against many of the new policy directions (Carmona, 1996: 19). Nevertheless, a glimmer of consensus amongst writers on many aspects of a sustainable design agenda has been emerging to give added legitimacy to the United Kingdom government's – so far – still tentative advice in this area. This chapter aims to unpick this agenda and unscramble some of the confusing and overlapping language used to describe sustainable urban design. It traces the scope and nature of this agenda, the application of the principles across different spatial scales, and concludes by briefly postulating on the difficulties of delivering more sustainable urban design.

The Environmental Impact of Design

Some argue that planning and to a lesser degree urban design have always pursued notions of sustainability and that their public interest *raison d'être* implies that concerns for environment, economy and society should be balanced (see Davoudi and Layard, Chapter 1, this volume). The reality is that even if such notions have existed in theory, more often than not they are largely absent in practice, being compromised by the need to deliver outcomes largely through market processes, by public political agendas that prioritise economic growth coupled to social (rather than environmental) well-being, and by private agendas that too often see the environment as of little concern. Nevertheless, as the damage being wreaked on the environment both locally and globally has become more apparent, notions of sustainability have moved up the public and political agenda and have led to a renewed questioning and refocusing of most professional remits; amongst them urban design.

Therefore, although an explicit sustainable goal is a relatively recent concern in urban design practice, it is arguably also the most important amongst design objectives. Unfortunately, urban designers have been primarily concerned with changing the physical world so that it better fits a set of human needs. Hence, like all built environment professionals (at least those operating in the private sector), the urban designer's primary responsibility has tended to be first to his/her client and only second to the wider community and natural environment.

Consequently, when the design process operating within most Western economies is considered, the major effort goes first to achieving the functional requirements of the client – within the economic constraints set by the budget. Second, to a concern for the visual, contextual and social impact of the development – to the extent that it is either financially prudent or a requirement brought about by public intervention in the design process. And – usually – last to broader environmental concerns, which feature poorly in both private and public agendas and responsibility for which is frequently highly fragmented.

The problem stems from the failure of Western development processes to fully reflect the environmental impact (and therefore cost) of development within the development process (see Edwards and Marsh, Chapter 10, this volume). This is because any one development has a much larger environmental impact than is immediately apparent. At first sight the imprint may appear small, just the impact on the site on which the development sits. But, when the environmental capital inherent in the construction of that development is considered – the energy and resources expended in the manufacture and transport of materials, the energy required to prepare the site and construct the development, the energy required to expand the above and below ground infrastructure to service the site, and so forth – a hidden, but much larger environmental impact is apparent.

Subsequently, when the development is in occupation, the ongoing energy and resources expended to sustain the development – the maintenance requirements, the energy requirements of the development (heat, light, electricity, etc.), the waste disposal requirements, and the travel requirements of the occupants – the impact extends even further. Thus, even in a 'very' efficient building, ongoing energy use over the lifetime of a building will represent four times that of the embodied energy used in the construction process (Barton *et al.*, 1995: 27). Finally, when the development reaches the end of its life, the energy required to alter or demolish the development and to deal with the resulting site and materials completes the lifetime environmental costs of that development, so extending the environmental impact further and far beyond the original perceived impact. In all of this, the original developer is often only concerned with the direct development and construction costs – costs which directly impact on the project's economic viability – but rarely with the subsequent environmental impacts over time.

Therefore, to achieve sustainable urban design, the aim should be to reduce the lifetime environmental impact of any development by reducing the energy and resources used and waste produced at each stage of the development lifecycle – construction, occupation and if necessary demolition. This can be achieved through reducing dependence on the wider environment for resources and reducing pollution of the wider environment by waste products – in other words by making any development both in its original construction, and throughout its lifetime, as self-sufficient as possible.

In this context, self-sufficiency is relevant at a range of scales from the individual building to the city region, and although most urban design interventions are relatively minor, the succession of minor changes can add up to major modifications to the overall natural systems of the neighbourhood, town, city-region and eventually to the earth's biosphere. Therefore, if each scale is visualised as a sphere of influence (Barton *et al.*, 1995), then at each level the designer should attempt to maximise the degree of autonomy by reducing the impact of the inner spheres on the outer spheres. Alongside architects and planners, urban designers and the design process will have an important direct role to play in the first three of the spheres identified in Figure 11.1. Therefore, at whatever scale they are working, built environment professionals – architects, urban designers, planners, property managers, surveyors, engineers, and developers – all have an important role to play in building and managing sustainable urban forms.

Towards Agreed Sustainable Design Principles

A number of key tenets underpin general notions of sustainable development. These include:

- futurity – because we owe future generations an environment at least as rich and opportunities at least as good as those available today;

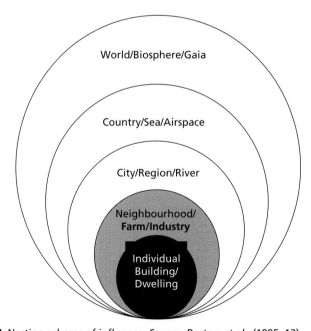

Figure 11.1 Nesting spheres of influence. *Source*: Barton *et al.*, (1995: 12)

- environmental diversity – because maintenance and enhancement of various forms of natural capital underpin notions of sustainability;
- carrying capacity – because by remaining within the carrying capacity of environments, activities can be accommodated in perpetuity;
- the precautionary principle – because environmental impacts are by their nature uncertain and because prevention is better than cure;
- equity/quality of life – because sustainability extends to the needs of people in that environments which fail to meet human needs and in which resources are poorly shared are unlikely ever to be sustainable;
- participation – because sustainability is a process as much as an objective, requiring the acquiescence and preferably involvement of communities;
- the polluter pays – because those responsible should pay for the consequences of their actions.

But how do such general principles relate to urban design? Lang (1994) has argued that sustainable approaches to urban design should first avoid the misconception that dealing with the environment is merely 'an engineering problem' to be overcome by technology; and second, that designing to meet people's social needs is appropriate at the expense of the natural environment. Unfortunately, in the presence of cheap energy, theorists have long argued that the urban environment is being shaped by a technology whose goals are economic rather than environmental or even social. The result has been the alienation of city from the country through a misuse of urban and rural resources and an alienation of urban dwellers from the natural processes which in earlier times dictated so much of the flux of life. In the 1960s McHarg (1969) argued that towns and cities were still part of a wider, functioning ecosystem – no matter how distorted – and that decision makers should understand the altered but nevertheless functioning natural processes still operating within the city.

Thus settlements can be viewed as natural ecosystems. In this regard, a settlement is like a living organism which has the capacity to reproduce or renew itself (in part through urban design); which ingests quantities of food, fuel, water, oxygen and other raw materials and which ejects waste fuels, solids and atmospheric emissions. Therefore, just 'as ecology has now become the indispensable basis for environmental planning of larger landscape . . . an understanding and application of the altered but none the less functioning natural processes within cities becomes central to urban design'.

(Hough, 1984: 25)

Lang (1994: 348) has written of a 'pragmatic principle' for urban design: '[t]he pragmatic approach for urban designers to take in dealing with the biogenic environment is to ask what is the human self interest in the long run. The urban design objective is then to avoid creating patterns of built form that might ultimately harm people by leading to a deterioration in the quality of life'. Given this position and the fact that future needs are unpredictable, Lang argues that the wise position for urban designers to take is an environmentally benign one and not to assume that humans will always find technological ways out of any bind. He suggests '[n]ecessity may be the mother of invention, but the invention that may well be necessary is for urban designers to have a conservation ethic'.

If only for selfish reasons therefore, the human race has an interest in reducing its collective impact on the planet. A number of theorists have identified design principles to help achieve this. Hough (1984), for example, has identified five ecologically sound design principles which seek the integration of human with natural processes at their most fundamental level:

- the concepts of process and change – in that natural processes are unstoppable and change is inevitable and not always for the worse;
- economy of means – that derives the most from the least effort and energy;
- diversity – as the basis for environmental and social health;
- an environmental literacy – that begins at home and forms the basis for a wider understanding of ecological issues;
- a goal that stresses the enhancement of the environment as a consequence of change – and not just damage limitation.

Others have simplified the philosophical argument for sustainable urban design. For example, Bentley amended and extended the principles from *Responsive Environments* (Bentley *et al.*, 1985), to take on board one of the omissions of the earlier work – sustainability. He termed this 'ecological urban design' and argued that at the cultural heart of modern industrial societies lie the values of freedom and consumer choice. These, he suggested, find expression through consumerist lifestyles, but that the urban expression of such lifestyles is essentially ecologically destructive. In an extension to the 'pragmatic principle' he reasoned that urban designers cannot ignore these values but must seek to balance human desires with their ecological effects.

Bentley (1990) defined eight qualities which together cover the key issues for designing places which are both 'sustainable' and 'responsive'. At the same time the EC's *Green Paper on the Urban Environment* (CEC, 1990) emphasised the concept of 'green urban design' and with it a set of broader concerns emphasising the link between green urban design and green planning processes to secure sustainable design across the different spheres of influence (see Table 11.1).

Subsequently, research has focused upon the environmental stock as regards the global ecology (air quality, climate, bio-diversity), regional resources (air, water, land, minerals, energy resources) and the local human environment (buildings, infrastructure, open space, aesthetics, cultural heritage), with Blowers (1993) arguing that sustainability should focus on the satisfaction of basic human needs (shelter, health, food, employment) and the retention of self-sufficient ecosystems. Other work has attempted to define now commonly accepted principles of sustainable development (Breheny, 1992a) and relate these specifically to urban design (Haughton and Hunter, 1994), although perhaps the most comprehensive analysis of sustainable design principles to date has come from Barton *et al.* (1995; Barton, 1996) in their work for the Local Government Management Board. The authors identify seven clear principles for the creation of more sustainable urban design (see Table 11.1).

More recent contributions develop many of the themes of the earlier work and to some degree reflect the consensus emerging around a number of principles. At the local scale, Rudlin and Falk (1999); URBED (1997) have through detailed analysis attempted to understand how to design the sustainable urban neighbourhood as an alternative to ecologically destructive suburban sprawl. At the spatial scale Richard Rogers (1997) in his 1995 Reith Lectures outlined his vision for the sustainable city; analysis which culminated in a series of sustainable city principles. Relating the sustainable agenda to the design of new settlements, Evans (1997) identified a further range of sustainable criteria (see Table 11.1), whilst in one of the few empirically based studies of sustainable urban form across macro and micro scales, Frey (1999: 32–3) has broken desirable sustainable characteristics into their constituent parts:

- physical properties of the city: containment, densities to support services, mixed use, adaptability;
- provisions of the city: readily available public transport, reduced and dispersed traffic volumes, a hierarchy of services and facilities, access to green space;
- environmental and ecological conditions: low pollution, noise, congestion, accidents and crime, available private outdoor space, symbiotic town and country;
- socio-economic conditions: social mix to reduce stratification, a degree of local autonomy, a degree of self-sufficiency;
- visual-formal quality: imageability of the city and its constituent parts, a sense of centrality and a sense of place.

Individually, all these contributions represent valuable conceptualisations of sustainable urban design/form. Nevertheless, by placing them together it is possible to identify a combined set of sustainable urban design principles (see Table 11.2).

Returning therefore to the key tenets of sustainable development discussed at the start of the section and to the question 'how do these relate to urban

Table 11.1 Strategies for sustainable development/design

Breheny	CEC	Evans	URBED
1. Urban containment policies should be adopted and decentralisation slowed down.	1. Appropriate open and civic space to improve health and quality of life.	1. Freedom from pollution – minimising waste.	1. Quality space – attractive, human and urban.
2. Extreme compact city proposals are unreasonable.	2. The importance of planting and landscape in ameliorating pollution.	2. Biotic support – by maintaining biodiversity.	2. A framework of streets and squares – well observed routes and spaces.
3. Town centres and inner cities should be rejuvenated.	3. Compact and mixed forms of development.	3. Resource conservation – air, water, topsoils, minerals and energy.	3. A rich mix of uses and tenures.
4. Urban greening should be encouraged.	4. Reducing travel.	4. Resilience – a long life for development.	4. A critical mass of activity – to sustain facilities and animate the streets.
5. Public transport needs to be improved.	5. Recycling and energy reduction initiatives.	5. Permeability – providing a choice of routes.	5. Minimal environmental harm – during development and in the ability to adapt and change over time.
6. Intensification should be supported around transport nodes.	6. The maintenance of regional identity.	6. Vitality – making places as safe as possible.	6. Integration and permeability.
7. Mixed use schemes are to be encouraged.	7. Integrated planning across disciplines and bureaucracies.	7. Variety – providing a choice of uses.	7. A sense of place mixing new with old.
8. CHP systems should be used more widely.		8. Legibility – enabling people to understand the layout and activities of a place.	8. A feeling of stewardship and responsibility.
		9. Distinctiveness – in landscape and culture.	

Bentley	Barton	Haughton & Hunter	Rogers
1. Energy efficiency – minimising the external energy needed to construct and use a place, and maximising the use of ambient, particularly, solar energy.	1. Increasing local self-sufficiency - seeing each development as an organism or a mini eco-system in its own right. 2. Human needs – matching a	1. Variety – multifunctional districts with varied building styles, ages and conditions. 2. Concentration – sufficient density to maintain variety	1. A just city – where justice, food, shelter, education, health and hope are fairly distributed and where all people participate in government.

2. Resilience – building to adapt to different uses over time, rather than wastefully tearing down and rebuilding each time human aspirations change (an extension of the earlier robustness principle). 3. Cleanliness – designing places to minimise pollution output, and where a degree of pollution is unavoidable designing as far as possible to be self-cleansing. 4. Wildlife Support – designing places to support and increase the variety of species. 5. Permeability – increasing choice by making places accessible through a variety of alternative routes. 6. Vitality – the presence of other people and 'eyes on the street'. 7. Variety – the choice of experiences. 8. Legibility – understanding the potential for choice.	and activity including people who are resident. 3. Democracy – offering choice where activities are conducted. 4. Permeability – connecting people with each other and to facilities. 5. Security – through the design of spaces to enhance personal safety. 6. Appropriate scale – developments building on local context and reflecting local conditions. 7. Organic design – respecting historic narrative and local distinctiveness. 8. Economy of means – designing with nature and using local resources. 9. Creative relationships – between buildings, routeways and open spaces. 10. Flexibility – adaptability over time. 11. Consultation – to meet local needs, respect traditions and tap resources. 12. Participation – in the design, maintenance and running of projects. concern for sustainable development with the satisfaction of basic human needs. 3. Structure development around energy-efficient movement networks – taking circulation of the people on foot and bike and effectiveness of public transport as a starting point. 4. The open space network – to manage pollution, wildlife, energy, water, and sewage as well as enhancing the local provision of greenspace. 5. Linear concentration – around movement networks whilst avoiding town cramming. 6. An energy strategy – for every new development to save money; reduce fuel poverty; and reduce resource exploitation and emissions. 7. A water strategy – to decrease water run-off and increase infiltration into the ground.	2. A beautiful city – where art, architecture and landscape spark the imagination and move the spirit. 3. A creative city – where open-mindedness and experimentation mobilise the full potential of its human resources and allow a fast response to change. 4. An ecological city – which minimises its ecological impact, where landscape and built form are balanced and buildings and infrastructures are safe/resource-efficient. 5. A city of easy contact – where the public realm encourages community and mobility and information is exchanged both face-to-face and electronically. 6. A compact and polycentric city, which protects the countryside, focuses and integrates communities within neighbourhoods and maximises proximity. 7. A diverse city, where a broad range of activities creates animation, inspiration and fosters a vital public life.

Table 11.2 Sustainable design principles combined

	Hough	Bentley	CEC	Breheny	Blowers	Haughton	Barton	URBED	Rogers	Evans	Frey
1. Stewardship	enhancement through change		integrated planning	town centre rejuvenation				a feeling of stewardship	a creative city		
2. Resource efficiency	economy of means	energy efficiency	reducing travel/energy reduction, recycling	public transport, CHP systems	land/minerals/energy resources, infrastructure & buildings	economy of means	energy-efficient movement, energy strategy	minimal environmental harm	an ecological city	resource conservation	public transport, reduce traffic volumes
3. Diversity and choice	diversity	variety, permeability	mixed development	mixed use		variety, permeability		integration & permeability, a rich mix of uses	a city of easy contact, a diverse city	permeability, variety	mixed use, hierarchy of services and facilities,
4. Human needs		legibility			aesthetics, human needs	security, appropriate scale	human needs	quality space, a framework of scale/legible space	a just city, a beautiful city	legibility	low crime, social mix, imageability
5. Resilience	process and change	resilience				flexibility		ability to adapt and change		resilience	adaptability
6. Pollution reduction		cleanliness	ameliorating pollution through planting		climate/water/air quality		water strategy			freedom from pollution	low pollution and noise

7. Concentration	vitality development	compact intensification	containment/		concentration, linear concentration of activity	a critical mass polycentric city	a compact, vitality densities to	containment, support services
8. Distinctiveness		regional identity		heritage	creative relationships, organic design	sense of place	distinctive-ness	sense of centrality, sense of place
9. Biotic support		open space	urban greening	open space, bio-diversity	open space networks		biotic support	green space – public/private, symbiotic town/country
10. Self-sufficiency	environmental literacy			self-sufficiency	democracy, consultation, participation / self-sufficiency		self-sufficiency	some local autonomy, some self-sufficiency

design?', the answer is found in a complex web of inter-relationships where each tenet relates in turn to a range of sustainable design principles (see Figure 11.2). So, for example, the need to plan ahead and consider the impact of urban design today on the experience of future generations (futurity) concerns the careful stewardship of the environment through the ability of projects to enhance established environments and create manageable places that people will want to look after. It relates to the need to design for energy efficiency because energy and resources are finite. It concerns human needs because sustainable environments are those that cater for human requirements alongside other sustainable objectives. It requires that environments are resilient because future needs remain unpredictable. It concerns attempts to reduce pollution because irreversible changes to the environment will most likely undermine future inheritance. It encompasses notions of local distinctiveness because what is special about place can easily be undermined by insensitive development. And it requires biotic (ecological) support, in that bio-diversity is often the first casualty of the over-intensive human occupation of the environment.

From Theory to Practice

In theory therefore, urban design has a direct and potentially important role to play in realising the fundamental aims of sustainable development. Moving, however, from theory to practice, what do sustainable urban design principles imply? Rowley (1994: 186) has argued that 'Urban design considerations arise over a spectrum of spatial scales extending from the very local to the metropolitan scale of urban form and city image.'

City urban design strategies often provide the best illustrations of this multi-levelled nature of the discipline. In the United Kingdom, the best known design strategy – the 'City of Birmingham, City Centre Design Strategy' (Tibbalds *et al.*, 1990) – provides a case-in-point. The strategy develops a 'spatial framework' for the city centre within which a set of urban design objectives is outlined. This recognises the distinct character of individual areas in the form of a number of 'city quarters' (areas of character). Large-scale city-wide 'spatial' qualities are then defined to develop and protect existing and potential views across the city and to reinforce the city's topography. Medium-scale principles are next established at the level of individual urban spaces or groups of spaces, aiming to help people find their way around the city by redefining a network of barrier-free streets with well articulated public and private realms and activities at street level, and by softening and enhancing the city's open spaces. Finally, small-scale architectural and urban management issues are discussed focusing on sweeping away the clutter and the enhancement of prominent facades.

In the remainder of the chapter, it is worth therefore considering just what the ten identified sustainable principles of urban design (from Table 11.2)

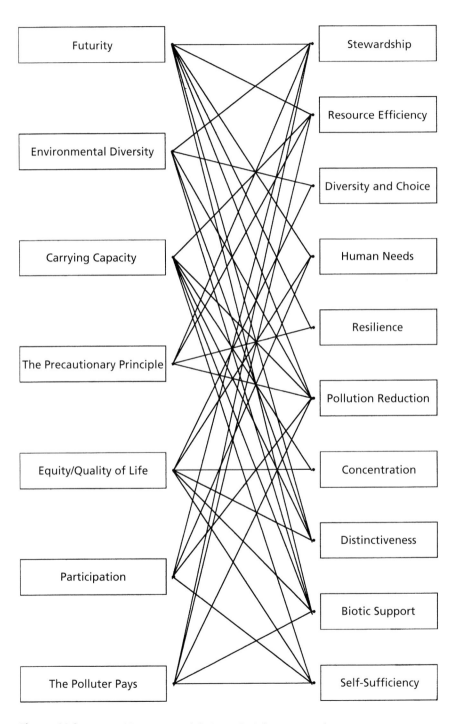

Figure 11.2 Sustainable tenets and design principles compared

imply by considering their impact across the range of different spatial scales, in this case at the building, space, quarter and settlement-wide scales (summarised in Table 11.3). The chapter concludes by briefly examining how more sustainable patterns of design might be delivered and by whom.

Stewardship Urban design, like architecture and planning, represents a process, as well as a series of end products, and an ongoing process through time that begins long before a development is conceived and continues long after it is completed. Indeed, urban design is concerned above all with the careful and ongoing stewardship of the built environment through a myriad of contributions – public and private – only some of which concern the actual development of new buildings and spaces. Thus, processes of urban maintenance, traffic management, town centre management, regeneration, planning and conservation, and individuals personalising their own properties, all impact on the quality and therefore collective public perceptions of particular places. In this regard, sustainable places are those where at all scales of development, these ongoing processes of adaptation and change are positively channelled in an integrated manner towards achieving a better quality built environment. Typically, this will need to respond to any positive contextual characteristics of the building, space, quarter or settlement and address any negative aspects. Sustainability implies recognising quality, achieving quality and maintaining quality which in turn requires 'taking a broad and long-term view of the cost and benefits of any change, and understanding what makes towns and cities sustainable' (Urban Design Group, 1998: 45).

Resource efficiency underpins all notions of environmental sustainability, implying as it does care in the use of energy and care in the use of non-renewable or environmentally destructive materials. For urban design this implies a concern for the use of both energy and resources in and by the fabric of the built environment, and on the larger scale, an increasing concern for energy use through preventing unsustainable spatial patterns of building and their implications on energy consumption through travel demands. It is clear that mainstream technological means exist to reduce much of the current resource profligacy – in the use of more sustainable building materials, in designing for natural light, sun and air and for solar gain, in more efficient heating and power systems, and in more efficient use of existing infrastructure (Mandix, 1996). It is also clear that many of these technologies can be applied immediately across the various design scales to retrofit established environments as well as in building more resource efficient new environments (Terence O'Rourke plc, 1998). Unfortunately, until the economic imperative reflects the sustainable one, either by market, fiscal or regulatory means, the fact that it is cheaper over the short term to build and live unsustainably with destructive use of resources – particularly high energy consumption –

Table 11.3 Sustainable design by spatial scale

	Buildings	Spaces	Quarters	Settlements
Stewardship	Responding to and enhancing context Design for easy maintenance	Responding to and enhancing context Managing the public realm Allowing personalisation of public space Traffic calming	Design for revitalisation Developing a long-term vision Investing necessary resources	'Joining-up' contributions to quality-design, planning, transport, urban management Governance that supports stakeholder involvement
Resource efficiency	Using passive (and active) solar gain technologies Design for energy retention Reduce embodied energy – local materials and low energy materials Use recycled and renewable materials Design for natural light and ventilation	Layouts to allow sun penetration Spaces that reduce vehicle speeds and restrict vehicle circulation Design spaces that reduce wind speeds and enhance microclimate Using local, natural materials	Reduced parking standards Urban block depths that allow sun and natural light penetration and which encourage natural ventilation Using combined heat and power systems Local access to public transport	Investing in public transport infrastructure Utilise more efficiently before extending the established capital web (infrastructure)
Diversity and choice	Provide opportunity to mix uses within buildings Mix building types, ages and tenures Build accessible, lifetime homes and buildings	Mix uses along streets and in blocks Design for walking and cycling Combat privatisation of the public realm Remove barriers to local accessibility	Mix uses within quarters Design a fine-grained street and space network (micro scale) Support diversity in neighbour-hood character Localise facilities and services	Integrate travel modes Connect route networks (macro scale) Centre hierarchy to boost choice Variety in services and facilities between centres Remove barriers to accessibility

Table 11.3 Continued

	Buildings	Spaces	Quarters	Settlements
Human needs	Support innovation and artistic expression in design Design to a human scale Design visually interesting buildings	Provide high quality, imageable, public spaces Combat crime through space design and management Enhance safety by reducing pedestrian/vehicle conflict Design for social contact and for safe children's play	Design visually interesting networks of space Enhance legibility through landmark and space disposition Socially mix communities	Enhance legibility through quarter identity and disposition Promote equity through land use disposition Build settlement image to foster sense of belonging
Resilience	Build extendable buildings Build adaptable buildings Build to last Use resilient materials	Design robust spaces, usable for many functions Design spaces able to accommodate above and below ground infrastructure requirements Design of serviceable space	Design to allow fine-grained changes of use across districts Robust urban block layouts	Build a robust capital web – infrastructure to last and adapt Recognise changing patterns of living and work
Pollution reduction	Reuse and recycle waste water Insulate for reduced noise transmission – vertically and horizontally On-site foul water treatment	Reduce hard surfaces and run-off Design in recycling facilities Design well-ventilated space to prevent pollution build-up Give public transport priority	Match projected CO_2 emissions with tree planting Plant trees to reduce pollution Tackle light pollution	Question 'end-of-pipe' solutions to water/sewerage disposal Control private motorised transport Clean and constantly maintain the city
Concentration	Design compact building forms to reduce heat loss i.e. terraces Bring derelict buildings back into use	Reduce space given over to roads Reduce space given over to parking Increase vitality through	Intensify around transport intersections Raise density standards and avoid low density building Build at densities able to	Enforce urban containment and reduce expansion Intensify along transport corridors Link centres of high activity

	Buildings	Spaces	Quarters	Settlements
	Consider high buildings where appropriate	activity concentration	support a viable range of uses and facilities Respect privacy and security needs	
Distinctiveness	Reflect surrounding architectural character in design Enhance locally distinctive building settings Retain important buildings	Reflect urban form, townscape and site character in design Retain distinctive site features Design for sense of place – local distinctiveness Retain important building groups and spaces	Reflect morphological patterns and history - incremental or planned Identify and reflect significant public associations Consider quarter uses and qualities	Protect any positive regional identity and landscape character Utilise topographical setting Preserve archaeological inheritance
Biotic support	Provide opportunities for greening buildings Consider buildings as habitats	Design in robust soft landscaping Plant and renew street trees Encourage greening and display of private gardens	Provide minimum public open space standards Provide private open space Create new or enhancing existing habitats Respect natural features	Link public (and private) open space into a network Green urban fringe locations Integrate town and country Support indigenous species
Self-sufficiency	Demonstrate a sense of public sector civic responsibility Encourage private sector civic responsibility Provide bicycle storage Connecting to the Internet	Encourage self-policing through design Providing space for small-scale trading Provide bicycle parking facilities	Build a sense of community Involving communities in decision-making Encourage local food production – allotments, gardens, urban farms Paying locally for any harm	Encourage environmental literacy through example and promotion Consultation and participation in vision making and design

ensures that the incentive to look long term and to reduce resource consumption is all too weak. Even where efforts are made, contradictions are often readily apparent (see Figure 11.3).

Diversity and choice Environmental diversity is a key tenet of sustainable development (see Figure 11.2). In a natural context this implies bio-diversity (see below), and in the built context diversity and choice. Choice is also frequently cited as a key tenet of urban design, which in that regard seeks a freedom of choice in movement, in the facilities and amenities available to people and in how they use the public environment (Bentley *et al.*, 1985: 9). In sustainable terms this implies the need to tackle processes in the built environment which in the post-war period have acted to undermine choice. These include the increasing domination of urban areas by cars at the expense of pedestrians and those without cars (see Marshall, Chapter 9, this volume), the increasing zoning of the environment into mono-use areas with an associated reduction in diversity of use, and the increasing 'privatisation' of parts of the public realm leading to the effective exclusion from these areas of significant portions of society. These patterns are compounded by the ongoing ignorance of the design needs of certain sections of society such as the elderly and disabled. At the various scales across which urban design acts, the reintroduction and designing-in of diversity and choice in the built environment therefore represent a key aim: through mixing uses and tenures; by removing barriers to access and designing for walking; by connecting up the different spaces and networks that constitute the public realm; and by supporting diversity in the character of what results.

Figure 11.3 'Energy Efficient Supermarket' in Greenwich, London

Human needs Hand-in-hand with choice comes a concern for human needs. Indeed, on the grounds that environmental needs are never likely to be met if human needs are ignored, many conceptualisations of sustainability are underpinned by notions of social sustainability – equity, opportunity, quality of life and participation (CAG Consultants, 1997: 7–8). Drawing from Maslow's (1943) well-used hierarchy of human needs, sustainable environments should cater for physiological, safety and security, affiliation (belonging and acceptance), esteem (status) and self-actualisation (expression and fulfilment) needs in that order, although the most civilised societies will cater equally for each. Relating such broad concerns to the sustainable urban design agenda, human needs encompass the creation of comfortable environments that are of a human scale and visually interesting, that allow safe and crime-free human contact, movement and navigation (legibility), that are socially mixed, and that through their design and the disposition of uses are available to all. At the larger scale of settlement and quarter design, human needs can increasingly be met through positive image building to foster the identification with place so necessary to build commitment to, and sense of ownership of, the environment.

Resilience relates to the need for resource efficiency, in that built form once constructed represents a considerable investment in energy and resources. Furthermore, if all the embodied energy in an established town or city is added up – of the buildings, roads, landscape, and above and below ground infrastructure – that investment will represent many times more energy than the ongoing processes of adaptation and change consume over many decades. Studies of conventional new houses indicate that the accumulated energy costs in use exceed the embodied energy of the actual basic construction within five years (Barton *et al.*, 1995: 133), but as more energy-efficient construction techniques are adopted, so the energy and resources invested in the construction process become more and more significant. Building to last also reduces the pressure on sources of construction materials, reduces the waste from, and energy used in, demolition, and encourages the construction of more adaptable buildings, spaces, urban forms and infrastructure. This last concern is significant because to be long-lasting, patterns of development need also to be adaptable, in the case of buildings to be able to adapt to different functions and to be extendable if required; in the case of spaces, to cater for the many overlapping and sometimes contradictory functions required of urban space; and in the case of quarters and settlement patterns to be able to adapt over time to changing technologies and patterns of life and movement.

Pollution reduction If settlements are viewed as living organisms which ingest resources and eject waste products, then reducing waste emissions represents a key role of sustainable urban design – to use resources more efficiently, to reduce the impact of development on its surroundings and to reduce the energy expended in waste removal and disposal. Pollution reduction potentially also has an important role to play in improving quality of life in urban areas. This is because some of the most negative collective perceptions about urban areas and a major factor driving migration out of cities to more suburban and rural areas concerns the pollution, dirt and noise characteristic of many such areas (Mulholland Research Associates Ltd, 1995). The key objective across all spatial scales is to tackle pollution by reducing it in the first place – insulating against noise, ventilating against fumes, designing-out light pollution, designing-in filtration by trees, and investing in public transport whilst (as far as possible) controlling private car-borne travel. Following reduction efforts, the reuse and recycling of waste products (energy, water, materials, etc.) – where possible on site such as the filtration of foul water – should form a second objective. Removal of waste from sites should be a last resort, although investment in cleaning and maintenance is a necessary dimension of good urban management as well as a necessary component of urban renewal.

Concentration is perhaps the least straightforward of the design principles (see Hall, Chapter 7, this volume). Therefore, concentration across spatial scales is widely held to be a desirable strategy to reduce travel demand, energy use and land-take and to increase the vitality and viability of established centres. Nevertheless, in a challenge to those advocating higher density living it has been argued that a renewed emphasis on higher density development could mean more congestion and pollution and probably the demolition of at least part of the historic heritage (Hall, 1995). Furthermore, that higher-density living, although technically sustainable in the short term, may be individually unacceptable and perhaps unsustainable in the long term as working at home becomes more the norm, as non-polluting motorised transport is developed and as the reduced supply of greenfield sites drives up densities at the expense of open space in established areas (Davison, 1995). Research, sponsored (predictably) by Safeways, has even shown that in some circumstances new out-of-town shopping development can result in a reduction in car journeys over town centre alternatives on the basis that customers will travel to such developments come-what-may, and therefore that the more such developments there are, and the closer they are to each other, the less individuals will need to travel to reach them (JMP Consultants, 1995).

Nevertheless, Breheny (see Table 11.1) has reflected a broad consensus on these issues by arguing that urban containment policies should continue to be adopted and decentralisation slowed down and that this should go hand-in-hand with the rejuvenation of existing urban areas, with intensification prioritised around transport nodes, but with extreme 'compact city' proposals rejected as unreasonable. More recent work has confirmed this advice, arguing that if nothing else intensification can support urban living and reduce land-take, although the case for widespread compaction has yet to be convincingly made (Jenks *et al.*, 1996: 342). Furthermore, concentration can help to reduce space given over to the car and increase pedestrian movement and the viability of public transport, therefore helping to support other sustainable urban design objectives. At the building scale, compact building forms such as terraces are clearly more energy efficient than, for example, detached ones.

Distinctiveness Supporting local distinctiveness as an objective is intimately tied to achieving other sustainable objectives: to careful stewardship, in that conservation of the built fabric is a process of management and maintenance through time; to the delivery of human needs, because perceptions of place are intimately tied to the familiar and cherished local scene; and to resilience, because distinctiveness inevitably requires the long-term valuing of built and natural assets. It also represents a key objective of most planning systems through conservation legislation covering buildings, townscapes and natural landscapes (English Heritage, 1997). Fundamentally, however, distinctiveness is concerned with the preservation and enhancement of what is special about places (Clifford and King, 1993), in that places can be viewed as constructs of often unique geographic, physical and environmental characteristics, combined with unique cultural circumstances manifest in a settlement's original form and purpose and subsequent human interventions over time. The result is environments of distinctive character in building design, space composition, mix of uses and spatial layouts, which once altered can rarely be repaired. This should not imply that change is inappropriate and should be resisted, merely that to be sustainable the precautionary principle should be applied and careful consideration given to identifying what is special, to resisting ubiquitous pressures for homogenisation, and to ensuring that new development across all scales respects and enhances the best of what already exists.

Biotic support is fundamental across the different design scales in meeting the challenge of maintaining environmental diversity. Landscape design is often the forgotten dimension of the urban environment, too often being treated as an afterthought or as a purely visual concern, for example, to reduce the impact of ugly buildings or acres of parking. However, more fundamental approaches to landscape have long been advocated (McHarg, 1969) in which urban areas are seen as just one part of a wider functioning ecosystem, and in which the biotic environment (fauna and flora and space for it to flourish) exist side-by-side, and even dictate the form of the human-made environment. Therefore, like the associated need to reduce pollution and the use of natural resources, the need for biotic support equates to support for the ongoing natural processes in and around human settlements. At the level of buildings and spaces, this might include the integration of soft landscaping in new and established developments – particularly trees. At the scale of the urban quarter, the concern extends to respect for existing and provision of new open spaces within settlements and to their nurturing as natural habitats. Finally, at the settlement-wide scale, the concern relates to the integration of town and country through the design of open space networks and the careful transition between town and country at the urban fringe.

Self-sufficiency relates back to human needs, but also encompasses issues of resource management. Pre-twentieth century, development of the built environment was in the main slow and incremental with most lives centred on local areas and utilising local resources – both human and natural. With increasing internationalisation and greater ease of communications and travel, patterns of living and development processes take place in the Western world on an ever widening stage. The implications are unsustainable because of the loss of identification with place in development processes, because of the homogenisation of building types, forms and styles, and because of the increasing distances that populations and resources need to travel to cater for everyday needs. Although patterns of life will be difficult to change over the short term, design has a potentially important role to play in providing choice for more self-sufficient modes of living in the future. This may include physical measures such as providing for cyclists to encourage greater self-sufficiency in travel, connecting to the internet to allow home working, or simply allowing space for local food production in less dense urban areas. More fundamentally, it will require key stakeholders and local populations to have a greater active involvement in developing a vision for their locality (see Mittler, Chapter 4, this volume). Participation (going beyond consultation) therefore represents a key tenet of self-sufficiency as it does to sustainable development (New Economics Foundation, 1998: 3). It extends to the notion that in a democratic society the actions of the few should not impact adversely on the amenities enjoyed by the many. This implies that development through its design should be environmentally benign, or that recompense be made locally to redress the balance.

Delivering Sustainable Design

Discussion of the ten sustainable design principles at their different scales has revealed the complexities inherent in developing – let alone delivering – a sustainable urban design strategy. It also reveals the aspirational nature of much of the agenda. Clearly, however, a conceptualisation of sustainable design is of little value unless it can be implemented. The drivers encouraging more active approaches to delivering sustainable design are well accepted and relate to the potential for lasting damage wreaked by increasingly unsustainable patterns of life and development and to a recognition that mankind holds both the potential to irreversibly damage the natural environment or to repair and enhance it. The decisions are essentially moral ones to be debated through international, national and local political processes for delivery through associated processes of development and governance.

The barriers to delivery are, however, formidable and may sometimes seem impossible to overcome. Some have already been mentioned, but together encompass:

- established patterns of living – which are frequently ingrained and difficult to change, for example, the reliance on car-borne modes of travel and the layout of the urban environment based on that premise;
- public aspirations – which often aspire to unsustainable, high consumption modes of living, including aspirations in the Anglo-Saxon world for low-density housing and to own a car (and sometimes two or three);
- economic systems – which rarely reflect the true costs of development (particularly the environmental and social costs) and which tend towards decisions based on short-term economic gain rather than long-term investment;
- lack of political will – to influence development processes because of the over-riding pressures to deliver, first, economic goals, second, social ones, but only a poor third, environmental objectives;
- lack of vision – in either the public sector or the private sector to innovate new solutions and think beyond tried and tested – but often unsustainable – development processes;
- selfishness – because too many stakeholders see the environment as 'someone else's problem' and therefore fail to consider (and sometimes actively dismiss) the potential role they might play;
- lack of choice – because many individuals have little or no choice in the way they lead their lives because of cultural, economic, educational and physical constraints;
- the scale of the problem – in that turning around unsustainable patterns of living and development is a massive long-term process dependent on fundamental changes to attitudes and to co-operation between many different stakeholders across spatial scales. In such a context, it is easy to think that individual contributions will have little impact and that positive action can be put off for another day.

This last point is significant and helps to illustrate the complexity of the task. Thus, even to deliver just one part of the wider sustainable development agenda – better urban design – a whole series of stakeholders are required to support a shared vision of a more sustainable future.

Table 11.4 reveals the diversity of stakeholders needed to deliver more sustainable design, as well as the diversity of means across spatial scales

Table 11.4 Delivering sustainable design – stakeholders and influences

	Buildings	Spaces	Quarters	Settlements
	Private Sector			
Design professionals	Building design Urban design Design vision	Urban design Landscape design Design vision	Urban design Landscape design Design vision	Urban design Design vision
Developers	Building developments	Urban developments Public/private partnerships	Urban developments Public/private partnerships	New settlements Public/private partnerships
Investors	Project financing Long-term investment	Project financing Long-term investment	Project financing Long-term investment	Project financing
	Public Sector			
Planning authorities	Local plan policy Design guidance Design briefs Development control	Local plan policy Design guidance Design briefs Development control Planning gain	Local plan policy Design guidance Design frameworks Development control Planning gain	Strategic planning policy Local plan policy Design strategies
Highways authorities		Road construction standards Road adoption procedure	Highways layout standards Road adoption procedure	Transport plans Traffic management
Building control	Building controls			
Fire authorities	Fire spread standards	Fire spread standards	Fire prevention access standards	
Environmental health	Noise control	Refuse disposal/ control	Vehicle emissions control	Pollution control

	Buildings	Spaces	Quarters	Settlements
Housing authorities/ Providers	Social housing provision/ subsidy Design standards	Design standards/quality indices		Housing strategies
Parks & Recreation Departments		Open space maintenance	Open space provision/ preservation	Landscape/open space strategiea
Police authorities	Architectural liaison	Architectural liaison Public order Traffic control	Public order bylaws	
Regeneration Agencies/ Authorities	Design guidelines	Design guidelines Gap-funding/grants Public/private partnerships	Land reclamation Gap-funding/grants Public/private partnerships	Public/private partnerships
Conservation agencies	Gap-funding/grants Listed building designations/controls	Enhancement schemes/ funds Conservation area designations/controls	Enhancement schemes/ funds Conservation area designations/controls	
Urban managers		Urban promotion/ management/ co-ordination	Urban promotion/ management/ co-ordination	

Table 11.4 Continued

	Buildings	Spaces	Quarters	Settlements
		Public/Private		
Utility providers		Road/pavement repair standards		Infrastructure provision
Public transport providers		Public transport management	Public transport provision	Public transport integration
Educational institutions/sector			Local engagement	Raising environmental awareness
		Community based		
Voluntary groups/ communities	Consultation response	Actively engaging (participation, urban management)	Campaigning Actively engaging (design, appraisal, participation)	Campaigning
Local politicians	Statutory powers	Statutory powers Spending priorities	Statutory powers Spending priorities Lobbying	Statutory powers Spending priorities Lobbying
Individuals/Companies	Home/building maintenance	Lifestyle choices Civic responsibility	Civic responsibility	

through which to influence its delivery. The table identifies – in particular – the wide range of public sector agencies and potential influences on sustainable design, as well as the diverse interests across the four spatial scales of public, private and community sectors. It confirms the need for 'joined-up' approaches to governance in this area – perhaps above all others – where responsibility is spread so thinly. It also confirms the important role of agencies with plan-making and grant-making powers – planning authorities, highways authorities and regeneration agencies – in a central co-ordinating role to co-ordinate public sector contributions and deliver public/private partnerships.

However, of greatest importance to deliver more sustainable urban design, is the need to first establish an impetus for change. In delivering this objective not all is doom and gloom as increasingly, international, national and local government agendas are recognising that change is not only desirable, but is both necessary and inevitable. In the United Kingdom, for example, the work of the Urban Task Force (1999: 71) in outlining the need for an 'urban renaissance' has linked future development patterns firmly to a vision of a more sustainable future. In this (as outlined at the start of the chapter), it is suggested that sustainable urban design across all scales has a central role to play.

Conclusion

Fundamentally, good urban design is sustainable, but as the chapter has shown this implies much more than simply facing buildings south and insulating them well. It also implies a much more profound basis on which to make decisions which impact on the design of the environment. In assessing whether proposals are sustainable, Table 11.3 might be used to indicate the range of relevant issues applicable at different spatial scales. To summarise, however, planners, designers, developers and other stakeholders might usefully ask:

1 Do proposals enhance their context, effectively join up the range of contributions and therefore help to carefully steward in change over time?

2 Are proposals efficient in their consumption and long-term use of energy and natural resources?

3 Do proposals support diversity and choice in movement, access and land use mix?

4 Do proposals support human needs for security, social contact, comfort and artistic fulfilment?

5 Are proposals resilient enough to withstand and adapt to changes over time?

6   Do proposals minimise pollution of the wider environment both in their construction and long-term management?

7   Are proposals concentrated to reduce land take and energy use and increase urban vitality and viability?

8   Do proposals respect what is distinctive about their environment and help to build or preserve local sense of place?

9   Do proposals support the biotic environment through the careful integration of built and natural resources?

10 Are proposals likely to support the establishment of more self-sufficient, involved local communities?

Further Reading

Perhaps the most comprehensive discussion of the full sustainable design agenda to date can be found in Barton, H., Davis, G., and Guise, R. (1995) *Sustainable Settlements: A Guide for Planners, Designers, and Developers*, Luton, Local Government Management Board. This looks at the full range of issues, from architecture to settlement-wide. Another good text is Frey, H. (1999) *Designing the City: Towards a More Sustainable Urban Form*, London, E&FN Spon, which offers one of the few empirical attempts to apply sustainable urban design principles to an existing city, in this case Glasgow.

Hough, M. (1984) *City Form and Natural Process*, London, Routledge, is a classic urban design text, making the case for a more fundamental view of natural processes in the strategic design of settlements. On compact cities, Jenks, M., Burton, E. and Williams, K. (1996) *The Compact City: A Sustainable Urban Form?*, London, E&FN Spon provides a wide ranging and comprehensive discussion of sustainable urban form drawing together papers from a wide range of authors. This volume is now also complemented by its sister publication from the same team – *Achieving Sustainable Urban Form*.

Two final further readings are, first, Lang, J. (1994) *Urban Design: The American Experience*, New York, Van Nostrand Reinhold, a wide-ranging and deeply theoretical review of urban design in America, including a new functional rationale for urban design which takes sustainability as one of its key tenets. The second is Rudlin, D. and Falk, N. (1999) *Building the 21st Century Home: The Sustainable Urban Neighbourhood*, Oxford, Architectural Press. This is an excellent and very accessible introduction to sustainable design issues, drawing from a long-term research programme.

12 Planning and Sustainable Waste Management

Simin Davoudi

Introduction

Sustainable waste management means using material resources efficiently, to cut down on the amount of waste we produce. And where waste is produced, dealing with it in a way that actively contributes to the economic, social and environmental goals of sustainable development.

(DETR, 1999c: 9)

At its face value, the above quote from the most recent government document on waste management strategy represents a simple, straightforward, and in fact common-sense approach to achieving sustainability in waste management. However, beyond this simplistic facade lies a complex picture of data and information deficiency, the development of technical solutions, changing institutional landscapes, rising public concerns and pressures, spatial variability in facility capacity and increasing disposal costs. These complexities combine to present significant decision-making challenges over the management of waste and the allocation of sites for the required facilities. As a result, managing waste has become a highly contentious area of public policy with increasing tensions between industry and regulators and between citizens and the state over regulatory policy.

This chapter aims to unpack some of the complexities surrounding waste issues by reviewing the profound changes which took place in the last decade of the twentieth century in waste policy discourses and its institutional relationships. It will particularly focus on the changing role of the planning system in the management of waste.

The Problem

Where does the waste come from?

Every year, we produce over 400 million tonnes of waste in England and Wales (DoE, 1995d; DETR, 1999c). This is enough to bury an area four times the size of Bristol under one metre of waste. About half of this is '*controlled waste*', comprising household, industrial and commercial waste. The remainder is '*non-controlled waste*' and includes agricultural, mining and quarrying waste (EPA, 1990: 83), (Figure 12.1). Municipal solid waste, which is the focus of the discussions in this chapter includes all waste collected by or on behalf of the local authority. Some 27 million tonnes of municipal waste are produced every year and this is growing by around 3 per cent annually. Over 90 per cent of the municipal waste comes from household sources. It is estimated that each household produces over a tonne of waste per year on average (DETR, 1999d, 2000e).

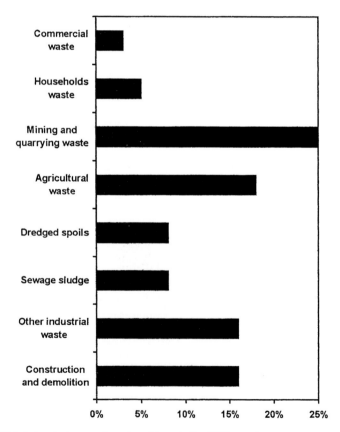

Figure 12.1 Estimated annual waste arisings in the UK by sector.
Source: Adapted from DETR, 2000

Where does the waste go?

By far the greatest proportion of the controlled waste, including 85 per cent of household waste (Figure 12.2) is disposed of to landfills (DETR, 1999d, 2000). Across the country the number of landfill sites has mushroomed in the past 20 years (CPRE, 1997). Former landfill sites make up the largest percentage of the different types of contaminated sites In 1989, it was estimated that up to 1,400 closed or active landfill sites were capable of exploding or causing fire (RCEP, 1996).

Since the late 1980s, this alarming situation has led to a shift in public policy agenda away from total reliance on disposal of waste to landfill towards the adoption of a variety of waste management options. This has taken place in the context of rapidly changing institutional relationships which govern waste management and planning. At the same time, various developments, particularly since the 1990s, have moved waste management issues and the allocation of sites for waste facilities from being a relatively new discourse in land use planning system, to one at the forefront of national and local planning policy agendas. What follows is an account of these dramatic changes with a view to unpacking some of the discursive and institutional complexities involved in pursuing a sustainable waste management strategy.

The Changing Waste Policy Discourses

The early municipal solution to handling waste particularly in large cities was to burn it in incinerator plants, of which some produced electricity. Later, the rising amount and the changing nature of the waste stream created a rationale for centralised sorting and recycling of waste, yet, as a marginal activity associated with operational efficiency of incinerators. In the early

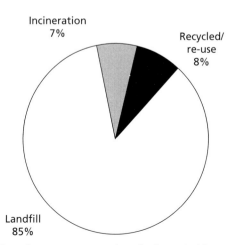

Figure 12.2 Proportion of management options for household waste in England and Wales. *Source*: Adapted from DETR, 2000e

1930s the use of incineration began to decline sharply as the cheaper method of tipping of waste often at sites on outskirts of urban areas proved to be a more economical option. The increasing post-war affluence and consumption, the rising amount of packaging, and the escalating costs of waste collection re-introduced the recycling activities and led to the establishment of many kerbside schemes in large urban areas (Gandy, 1994). However, given the predominant concerns over the emerging 'energy crisis' of the 1970s and the predicted shortage of raw materials, the underlying concept of recycling was a utilitarian one with a focus on the economic recovery from waste. This was echoed in the 1974 Green Paper, *War on Waste*, which promoted the 'local salvage schemes' and urged people to 'learn, or relearn, the habit of regarding waste material as potentially valuable resources' (DoE, 1974: 2). This was accompanied by the statutory provisions in the form of the Control of Pollution Act in 1974 which, for the first time, required local authorities to examine ways of promoting recycling. Despite these provisions, the increasing labour costs of kerbside collection and the effects of economic slowdown of the 1970s on the waste material markets resulted in the collapse of many established recycling schemes (Gandy 1994). Moreover, the cut back in local authority expenditure reduced the ability of the public sector to maintain such activities without major private sector finance. By the mid-1970s, therefore, the discourse of recycling slipped down the public policy agenda. At the same time, the economic disadvantage of incineration coupled with criticism of its associated air pollution reduced the use of incinerators in the UK to one of the lowest in the developed countries. Since then, the disposal of waste through landfill continued, almost unchallenged, to dominate the waste management policy and practices throughout the country. This shift of emphasis towards landfill was reinforced in the 1980s when the intensification of the privatisation processes introduced market mechanisms into local authorities' arrangements for collection and disposal of waste. This further curbed the discourses of waste management to those dominated by economic efficiency. The existence of an active minerals industry and the availability of geologically suitable sites meant that landfilling remained the most economically viable option.

The predominance of landfill in current waste management practices reflects the fact that landfill is the most adaptive and least expensive waste management option in most areas of England and Wales.

(DoE, 1995d: 4)

Although the introduction of the Landfill Tax in 1996 and the rising land value have pushed the cost of landfill up, this method of waste disposal has remained cheaper than other waste management options in most parts of the country (DoE, 1995d). Since the late 1980s, however, the discourse of recycling has found a new salience as part of a wider environmental sustainability agenda. Following the European Union's increased attention to promotion of sustainable waste management (CEC, 1989) and in particular the requirements of the EC Framework Directive on Waste,[1] the British government adopted a waste strategy based on a hierarchy of options (Figure 12.3). This urged the local authorities to increasingly focus their activities towards the top of the waste hierarchy (DoE, 1992c, 1995d). The strategy also introduced two new interconnected concepts of regional *self-sufficiency* and *proximity* to encourage management of waste as close to place of production as possible.

By the late 1990s, the discourse of the '*waste hierarchy*' had already made its way on to the waste policy agenda. However, the fundamental tension between recycling and disposal of waste has continued to shape the discursive conflict within the waste management debate. But, given the difficulties of finding suitable large landfill sites, attention has now moved to the use of incineration with energy recovery. Whilst the rhetoric of the waste hierarchy conceals these conflicts, the tensions are increasingly manifested in the polarisation of debate around recycling versus incineration. At one end of the spectrum are the environmental groups who are in favour of a moratorium on new incinerators (see for example LPAC, 1997) in order to get the recycling activities established. At the other end are the influential packaging lobby and the fast-growing private sector waste management industry who are promoting the profitable, capital intensive option of incineration with energy recovery (*New Scientist*, 1998). Despite such tensions the waste hierarchy puts energy recovery through incineration on a par with material recovery through recycling, on the ground that both options reduce the amount of waste being

Reduction

Re-use

Recovery*

Disposal

Figure 12.3 The waste hierarchy
*Material recovery (recycling and composting) and energy recovery (incineration)

landfilled. This has left the way in which the discourse of the waste hierarchy is adopted and operationalised open to interpretation of different stakeholders in different localities (Davoudi, 2000).

Moreover, the new discourse regards waste policy-making as a series of simple descending steps down the ladder of the waste hierarchy. In practice, however, there are fundamental cost barriers in adopting the options at the top of the ladder in a market-dominated economy. There are also tensions between the various options, such as the impact of incineration on the level of recycling and vice versa, or the implications of the local authorities' long-term contractual commitments to waste disposal companies. The two 1998 national guidance documents, draft Planning Policy Guidance Note (PPG) 10 and *Less Waste More Value*, caused further confusion by giving contra-dictory advice to local authorities. While the former stated that, '*no automatic preference should be given to any options within the recovery category*' (DETR, 1998j, para.12), the latter suggested that, '*incineration with energy recovery should not be undertaken without consideration first being given to the possibility of composting and material recycling*' (DETR, 1998k: 10). It is interesting to note that the two guidelines were produced by separate divisions within the Department of the Environment, Transport and the Regions reflecting a lack of policy integration at the national level.

Four years after the publication of the 1995 draft waste strategy, *Making Waste Work*, the Labour Administration produced another draft waste strategy for England and Wales: *A Way With Waste* (DETR, 1999c, d). This indicates a clear, though subtle, shift of emphasis in the policy agenda. The 'waste hierarchy' is no longer seen as the ultimate goal of a sustainable waste management strategy but as a 'conceptual framework which acts a guide to the options which should be considered . . . [and] a useful presentational tool for delivering a complex message in a comparatively simple way' (DETR, 1999c: 17).

The reasons for such a setback in policy discourse, include first, as discussed above, the realisation of the simplistic view presented in the discourse of the waste hierarchy and the difficulties of operationalising it in a market-oriented economy. Second, the failure of local authorities to meet the recycling and reduction targets set out by the 1995 draft strategy. The 1995 strategy set a target of 25 per cent recycling for household waste by 2001. As the 1999 draft strategy points out 'progress has been disappointing' (DETR, 1999d: 55). In 1997/8, only 8 per cent of household waste was recycled. Third, the growing market interests, helped by financial incentives through Non-Fossil Fuel Obligation scheme, in energy from waste incineration and the slow take-up of the options at the top of the hierarchy. In 1998 (the latest available statistics) thirteen energy-from-waste incinerators (compared with 4–5 in 1995/6) handled 7 per cent of household waste in the United Kingdom. At the same time, there were three approved and two proposed incinerators in the pipeline (DETR, 2000e: 160). Fourth, the urgency of complying with the

1999 EU Landfill Directive[2] which requires a stepped reduction in the land-filling of biodegradable municipal waste in all member states to 35 per cent of 1995 levels by 2020. The Directive also requires an end to the traditional United Kingdom practice of co-disposing hazardous with non-hazardous waste by 2004.

These pressures are forcing the government to divert waste from landfills yet increasingly towards the technically and economically more 'attractive' option of incineration with energy recovery. The 1999 draft strategy was quite explicit about the implications of meeting the EU-driven targets in terms of waste facility provision. It envisaged a dramatic growth in incinerators (Waste Planning, 1999). This could be in the order of 33 million tonnes of incineration capacity, in other words some 130 new incinerators plus 200 new material recovery facilities (DETR, 1999c: 25). However, following an unprecedented coverage on national newspapers (see for example *The Guardian*, 2000) and the ongoing opposition of local communities to incinerators across the country, the final version of the strategy, *Waste Strategy 2000*, had to drop all the references to the required incinerator capacity and other waste facilities for meeting the EU targets (DETR, 2000e). Nevertheless, the pressures for moving away from landfill and developing incinerators are there to remain, with or without explicit reference in the government's waste strategy. Identifying sites in development plans and determining planning applications for these facilities will be one of the greatest environmental and political challenges for the planning system at the beginning of a new century.

The Fragmented Institutional Relationships

The 1990s' developments which began to shift the waste management discourses and practices took place within a constantly shaping and re-shaping institutional context characterised by the increasing confusion over roles, responsibilities and relationships, the continuing process of privatisation, the formation of the new regulatory mechanisms, the rise and fall of established arenas and networks, the mounting profile of the planners' roles, and more recently the emerging regional mechanisms.

A complex web of regulatory system

In England, responsibilities for managing waste lie with different tiers and departments of the local authorities. In general, the districts are responsible for collection and recycling of waste as well as preparation of waste recycling plans, whilst the counties are responsible for arranging the disposal of waste through contracts, preparation of waste local plans, and determination of waste planning applications. The unitary authorities are responsible for all these functions (Table 12.1).

Table 12.1 Who does what for managing waste in England and Wales?

Boundaries	Authority	Main responsibilities
District Councils Unitary Authorities London Boroughs	Waste Collection Authority (WCA)	Collection of municipal waste Recycling Preparation of statutory Waste Recycling Plans
County Councils Unitary Authorities London Joint Waste Disposal Authorities	Waste Disposal Authority (WDA)	Arrangement for disposal of waste collected by WCA either through private companies or arm's length Local Authority Waste Disposal Company Recycling for Civic Amenity Sites Preparation of non-statutory waste strategies
County Councils Unitary Authorities London Boroughs	Waste Planning Authority (WPA)	Land use planning control Preparation of statutory Waste Local Plans Determination of waste planning applications
Environment Agency (EA)	Waste Regulation Authority (WRA)	Pollution regulation and waste management licensing Provision of information Advising the SoS on national waste strategy
Regional networks of waste disposal and planning officers, waste industry, government regional offices and the EA	Regional Technical Advisory Bodies (RTAB)	Assembling data, providing technical advice on waste issues to regional planning bodies

Additional confusion and often overlapping efforts are caused by the division of the regulatory responsibilities between the land use planning and the pollution control systems, each operating under a different set of legislative frameworks. The environmental impacts of the landfill sites are partly monitored and regulated by the land use planning system under the provisions of Town and Country Planning Acts and partly by the licensing system under the Environment Act 1995.

Until the formation of the Environment Agency (EA) in April 1996, this regulatory responsibility was carried out primarily by the counties in consultation with other regulatory bodies. Within this regulatory framework, the role of the land use planning system was relatively marginal. Its role in the mitigation of the environmental impacts of waste activities was limited mainly to the questions of amenities, leaving the more tangible environmental issues to be tackled through the regulatory mechanisms governed by the pollution control system. One of the cornerstones of this system since the Alkali Act of 1874 has been the concept of *best practicable means* (BPM) which focuses on achieving means which meet desirable standards for dealing with pollution without restraining the polluters' resources too far. Today, the BPM has been replaced with the concept of the BPEO: *Best Practicable Environmental Option* (RCEP, 1988) which, although it incorporates wider environmental dimensions, still strongly holds onto 'a system of comfortable negotiation between government technicians and industry' (Cullingworth and Nadin, 1994: 138). This informal and relatively secretive system which has been traditionally based on voluntary compliance, avoiding confrontation and legalistic procedures, has been a characteristic feature of the waste management practices. These have predominantly taken place within a narrow and closed policy community, dominated by the regulators and the industry with the environmental group playing a marginal reactionary role. As McCormick (1991: 12) states, the 1974 Control of Pollution Act, for example, 'was essentially shaped by industry and local government'. The subsequent implementation of the Act was heavily criticised by the House of Commons Environment Committee (HCEC, 1989) who pointed to extremely low standards in many waste disposal authorities who have 'encouraged contractors who had no regards for the potential dangers to the environment'. They concluded that, 'the cheapest tolerable option was too often deployed instead of the best practicable environmental option' (EPA, 1990: Part II). Thus, the combination of a dominant economic imperative and a negotiated regulatory system resulted in a growing number of landfill sites operating at low environmental standards. Similarly, out of thirty-two waste incinerators, only a few were capable of meeting the EU standards on emissions, the rest had to be closed by the mid-1990s (DETR, 1999d, 2000e).

Meanwhile, the location of waste disposal sites has been determined by the planning system largely in the context of a national policy-vacuum. Until 1994, when the first national Planning Policy Guidance, PPG23, *Planning and Pollution Control*, was issued (DoE, 1994b), government's legislation and guidelines had solely concentrated on waste licensing and pollution regulation with the role of the planning system in management of waste being largely neglected. PPG23 was later revised (DoE, 1996b), but faced mounting criticisms from industry and local authorities regarding its lack of clarity and effectiveness (Adams, 1996). In 1998, the Labour Administration abandoned its revision and instead published a draft PPG10 (DETR, 1998j) which reiterated the waste hierarchy and proposed a regional co-ordinating mechanism. This was eventually adopted in September 1999 (DETR, 1999e). However, despite the lack of consistent national policy, for planners the siting of landfills was a relatively easy task because these were often made available through the process of mineral workings. The 'holes in the ground' created by quarrying were often used as tipping sites. Thus, the waste disposal activities were regarded by both the regulators and the regulated as temporary, logical and even useful extensions to minerals development. This is clearly reflected in the following quote from a district planner who in 1996 in an interview with the author stated that:

At the time, landfill seemed quite an attractive way of getting these holes in the ground dealt with. Fill them up, put grass and trees on the top and presto! But then you have tricky things like landfill gas to deal with.

(Pers. Comm., 1996)

For a long time, this seemingly beneficial association of mineral extraction and waste disposal, coupled with the general availability of 'technically' suitable sites for landfill made the challenge of land allocation through the planning process relatively problem-free. The strongly held and persistent discourse of 'filling holes in the ground' pre-empted the system from any attempt to search for other spatial-ordering concepts and limited its task to the formulation or indeed reiteration of a series of often standard site-specific regulatory criteria. Planning policies for waste, often no more than two or three policies tacked on at the back of the development plan, were therefore primarily confined to a set of 'bad neighbour impacts' criteria to be drawn upon when development control decisions on specific sites were to be made.

The 1990s, however, witnessed a major change both in the planning system and in the approach to environmental and subsequently the waste management issues. In 1991, the provisions of the Planning and Compensation Act introduced two changes. First, the Act made the preparation of specific development plans for waste mandatory. These were to complement the waste disposal plans which prior to the formation of the EA were produced by the counties' waste regulation department under the pollution control system.[3] Second, the Act enhanced, at least in theory, the status of development plans in the decision-making processes. Thus, on the one hand, the process of making a waste local plan itself introduced the potential for long-term strategic spatial planning for waste and began to tentatively challenge site-specific approach. On the other hand, the plans themselves found a higher status and were taken more seriously by the developers and the local authorities. These twin processes gave the discussion on waste a higher profile within the planning community (Davoudi, 1999). Handling waste issues, which had traditionally been a marginal activity for the planners, became an increasingly significant area of local authorities' planning policy agenda. The discourses of waste management entered the arenas of the planning system and through the statutory consultation processes embedded in the system reached the public domain.

Yet, this happened at a time when the seemingly unproblematic task of landfill sites allocation through the process of mineral workings had become increasingly contentious. The reasons for this were multifaceted. First, the stricter regulatory criteria particularly for protection of the underground waters began to challenge the geological suitability of 'holes in the ground'. Second, the task of site identification became more and more politically contentious as people who had already had their lives affected by the mineral extraction activities and did not want a further phase of disturbance caused by using the holes for waste disposal began to raise their concerns more actively.

Parallel to these changes, the 1990s also witnessed rising development pressures by the waste disposal companies who began to build up their supply of landbanks for disposal facilities in an unprecedented way. Their main objective was to maintain their competitive position in a rapidly restructuring waste management market. This is reflected in the increasing number of planning applications after the introduction of the plan-led system. The number of waste planning decisions taken by English planning authorities increased from 684 in 1989/90 to 1,315 in 1992/93 with landfill being the most common category of development involving 720 planning decisions (*Waste Planning*, 1993). Further, the changing spatial pattern of disposal sites towards a smaller number but much larger sites meant that the environmental and political pressures became more geographically concentrated in fewer localities. This strategy, which was stimulated by the cost saving practices of large international companies in order to cope with increasing costs of Landfill Tax and the tighter EU regulatory standards, has led to an increase in the haulage of municipal waste, rise in demand for development of waste transfer stations,[4] growth in waste haulage companies, and a major restructuring of waste disposal industry as smaller firms are squeezed out of the market by larger and often international competitors.

Thus, for a planning system which was relatively new to the challenges of waste management at a strategic level, the allocation of sites for waste disposal became not only an environmental challenge but also a political nightmare. The oppositions to the siting of waste facilities (Petts, 1995), often maliciously labelled as NIMBYism,[5] the long list of objections to the waste local plans and the never-ending public inquiries (see Lancashire experience in Davoudi, forthcoming) are clear illustrations of the scale and scope of this new challenge. In cases where public reactions have been particularly vociferous some local authorities have decided to cut the debate short by avoiding site identification in the development plans, altogether. This has often been justified by clinging on to the rhetoric of the waste hierarchy and/or the principle of self-sufficiency. The resultant inconsistencies in the regulatory criteria for site allocation throughout the country and the uncertainty for the waste disposal market mobilised the industry to lobby the government for a change in what they called 'the planning gridlock' (Adams, 1996: 3). In 2000, these difficulties are still on the rise. Given the growing public opposition to large-scale waste facilities, an application for an incinerator is likely to take eight to ten years (Planning, 1999).

The impact of privatisation

In the past, it had been widely perceived that the private sector would not handle the municipal waste management in a cost-effective and environmentally safe manner. However, this perception began to change during the mid-1970s when the high and increasing costs of waste collection and disposal provided the ground for criticism of the structure of municipal waste management in public sector. As a result, competitive tendering was introduced into the area of municipal waste collection. In the 1980s, the intensification of the political shift towards a market-based ideology and the re-configuration of pubic sector role in service provision added to the political pressures for the privatisation of waste management. Therefore, the privatisation of the waste collection function of the local authorities was extended to the privatisation of their waste disposal responsibility. An 'arm's length' local authority waste disposal company (LAWDC) was to be established in order to separate the dual operational and regulatory role of local authorities which did not seem to be in the best interests of high environmental standards. However, on the one hand, the structure of the LAWDCs, which were operating within the constraints of the public sector's financial and legislative rules, has made it difficult for them to raise the necessary capital to improve their waste disposal facilities and their environmental standards and hence successfully compete with larger private sector disposal companies. On the other hand, the local authorities' desperate budget situation has led to the sell-off of their assets (i.e. land and facilities) to private companies rather than the formation of the LAWDCs. Given these two processes, the creation of LAWDC can be viewed as a phased privatisation of waste management in the United Kingdom. By the late 1995, about three-quarters of local authorities had already passed on responsibility for disposal operations to private companies or to LAWDCs (DoE, 1995d). Consequently, the spatial distribution of sites and the patterns of waste movement around the country are now profoundly affected by the market processes.

The new regulatory mechanism

The removal of decision-making processes away from the public sector arenas to the private sector was followed by the transfer of the regulatory aspects of waste management from local authorities to a centrally appointed body, the Environment Agency (EA). In the past, the recovery and disposal of waste in England and Wales were regulated primarily by local authorities in consultation with other regulatory bodies notably the National Rivers Authority (NRA). The EA was set up in 1996 in an attempt to 'ensure effective co-ordination between all the key waste regulatory functions' (DoE 1995d). It took over the waste regulation responsibility of local authorities and combined it with the functions of the NRA, and the regulatory functions of Her Majesty Inspectorate of Pollution (HMIP) for large incinerators.

Although the introduction of the EA contributed to co-ordination of the regulatory functions, it weakened the links between the waste licensing and the land use planning systems. The two functions which used to be carried out by a single local authority, although in different departments, were split between two organisations: one accountable to its local constituency, the other to the central government. The legislative division between the planning and pollution control systems was complemented by the organisational split, adding a new layer to an existing complex web of regulatory networks, and to the confusion over 'who does what' (see Table 12.1). Despite various governmental guidance which urges local authorities to avoid duplication of regulatory controls (DoE, 1996b, DETR, 1998j), in practice there are several grey areas where the boundaries of the planning and pollution regimes are blurred and the responsibilities overlap. Moreover, the removal of the regulatory functions from local democratic arenas seems to have increased rather than diminished such duplications. Having lost their licensing controls, local authorities have stretched their planning powers to ensure that local political and environmental concerns are not overlooked. The siting of waste facilities with their associated environmental implications is a contentious political process, one which the locally elected politicians are unlikely to leave unchecked in the hands of a centrally appointed and technically minded quango whose agendas as well as administrative boundaries differ from those of local authorities. In fact, the ambiguities surrounding the regulatory responsibilities can be interpreted by the local authorities as a welcome opportunity which provides them with room for manoeuvre in a centrally structured regulatory system which is slipping further away from their direct control.

The disruption of the established networks and arenas

The formation of the EA led to another re-configuration of institutional relationships by breaking the networks of local authorities' waste regulation officers which had been established either on a statutory or voluntary basis at the regional level. The disruption of these regional advisory mechanisms not only led to the collapse of waste planning co-ordination among the local authorities, it also broke the existing, albeit *ad hoc*, links between the regulatory and the planning functions. Despite various link-making initiatives by the EA, building up effective co-operation and integration with the local authorities proved difficult, particularly at the initial stages, given the differences in the mentalities and discourses of the two organisations and their different constituencies and policy agendas. As one of the EA officers, who had been transferred from a local authority's environment department, put it:

Everything is quantified in the Agency . . . It is either regulation or scientific, the social side of it and how they integrate with people is very badly serviced. Because they have never had a remit to do that. . . . A lot of our people are so professionally qualified in their technical / scientific field that they are afraid to be social animals.

(Personal Communication, 1996)

The formation of the EA also marked the end of an embryonic arena, that of the waste disposal plan preparation. These plans were introduced under the 1990 Environmental Protection Act in order to provide information on the amount and type of waste production, treatment and disposal as well as directions for the future waste management options. Therefore, the abandonment of these plans created an information gap at the time when the planners were facing the challenges of formulating long-term land use policies in the emerging waste local plans.

Faced with these pressures and given the ambiguity of the discourses of waste hierarchy and the elasticity of the Best Practicable Environmental Option principles as well as the lack of appropriate delivery mechanisms, the planners began to interpret the government's 'sustainable waste strategy' in different ways depending on the local circumstances (Davoudi, 2000). As mentioned above, these inconsistencies have created a lot of frustration for the waste industry. In 1998, the House of Commons Environment, Transport and Regional Affairs Committee reported its 'profound disappointment . . . that waste management in this country is still characterised by inertia, careless administration and ad hoc, rather than science based decisions' (HC, 1998).

The Regionalisation of Waste Planning

The most recent addition to the existing array of institutional arrangements is the Regional Technical Advisory Bodies (RTABs) (DETR, 1998k, 1999e). These comprise officers from the waste planning authorities, Environment Agency and representatives from the industry and the Government Office in each region. Their task is to provide technical advice to the Regional Planning Conferences on waste management options. These will then inform the Regional Planning Guidance (RPG) which has to be taken into account by the waste planning authorities in formulating policies and proposals for waste. The structure and the remit of the RTAB strongly resemble the much contested Regional Aggregate Working Parties (RAWP) established in the 1970s (Davoudi, 1997). As with the RAWPs, the RATBs consists of a narrow range of participants, excluding for example the environmental groups. And, again, as with the RAWPs, the emphasis is on the technical–advisory role. However, waste management and the identification of sites for waste facilities are highly political processes. Although the new-style RPGs have to go through a public hearing before formal adoption, as with the public examination of structure plans, this is a selective, topic-based probing discussion open only to a limited number of invited participants and closed to the wider range of stakeholders, including those who are going to be landed by waste disposal sites nearby. Such a process will inevitably postpone the conflicts of interests to end-of-pipe adversarial debates in public inquiries and appeals (Davoudi and Petts, 2000).

The setting up of the RTABs by the government was partly a response to the issues of regional self-sufficiency. The greater move towards regional-isation of waste planning has also been encouraged by the waste management industry. As mentioned above, under pressures from stricter environmental standards and competition from large international companies the waste industry is moving towards fewer but larger and hence economically more viable facilities capable of handling waste from areas often larger than a single district or even county. Development of such facilities, however, has often triggered strong opposition from the public who perceive larger facilities as presenting greater environmental risks, and as raising significant locational and social inequalities (Wolsink, 1994; Petts, 1995).

The combination of economic imperatives, declining void space and regulatory principles is likely to lead to further cross-boundary movements of regional waste and may mean that one administrative area will have to treat or dispose of the waste produced in another. This will be highly contentious for the host community. Previous research has shown that the tensions arising from the cross-boundary movements of waste are already evident particularly between the waste-exporting metropolitan districts and the waste-importing shire counties in regions such as the North West, the West Midlands (Davoudi, 2000) and the South East. The establishment of the RTAB is seen by the government as a way of allaying these conflicts and preventing parochial approaches to strategic waste management. However, first, the technocratic nature of the RTABs is likely to reduce their ability to seek consensus, and, second, their task of parcelling out of a projected level of waste which has to be managed in their constituent local authorities will be strongly contested. As experienced in aggregate planning processes or the housing land allocation debates, such a predict-and provide-approach will turn the planning arenas into battlegrounds.

Conclusion

The emerging EU waste policy in the late 1980s generated a wave of change which in a relatively short period of time reached all areas of waste management debates in the United Kingdom, unsettling the established policy and practices and bringing to the fore the political and environmental tensions. The evolution of the waste policy discourse has been manifested in a move away from 'filling holes in the ground' towards adopting the 'waste hierarchy'. However, the failure of effective implementation of the options at the top of the hierarchy and the urgency of meeting the EU targets set in the Landfill Directive are increasingly driving the government and the local authorities towards incineration.

Meanwhile, the discursive shift took place at the time when the institutional landscape surrounding waste management was also undergoing major transitions leading to further fragmentation of waste management responsibilities. This has often deprived the stakeholders of coherent discussion on and dissemination of the new discourse. With little national and regional guidelines, the local planners have had to take the strains of the contentious process of site identification for waste facilities. Whilst the consultation processes embedded in the system have widened the traditionally closed waste policy community to include a more diverse range of stakeholders, this has often taken place at the 'end-of-pipe', adversarial planning fora, provoking polarised debates rather than building up consensus.

However, given the absence of public participation mechanisms in other areas of waste policy-making and the removal of the regulatory function from locally accountable authorities, the potential role of the planning system in providing inclusionary arenas capable of levering in the local political and environmental concerns should not be underestimated. Such potentials would substantially increase if the system were capable of linking the economic, environmental and social aspects of waste policies. However, development of such 'joined-up' thinking in planning system has still a long way to go. The sectoral nature of the system and the marginal place traditionally given to the discussion on waste in the mainstream planning fora have hindered the development of a place-based integrated approach to waste. The long-held practice of filling holes in the ground has pre-empted the planning system from pursuing other spatial-ordering concepts. The location of quarries often dictated the location of landfill sites. This is changing under the pressures to move away from landfill, and to develop the twin principles of self-sufficiency and proximity. However, the adoption of these new concepts does not necessarily mean that the debate on quality of those places where the waste facility sites are to be landed will penetrate the decision-making processes. Nor does the technical remit of the RTAB and its composition provide an effective regional arena for such debates and in particular for alleviating the inevitable tensions of site identification. These tensions are bound to get more intensive with the growing number of proposed large-scale incinerators. The planning system is set to face one of its greatest environmental and political challenges in the coming years of the twenty-first century.

Notes

1 75/442/EEC as amended by 91/156/EEC and 91/962/EEC.
2 1999/31/EC.
3 Whilst waste local plans deal with the land use planning issues and the siting of

the waste facilities, the waste disposal/management plans provided the data on waste production and identified the amount and type of future disposal options.

4   The number of planning applications for these rose from 96 in 1990/91 in England to 226 in 1994/95 (Waste Planning, 1996).

5   Not-in-my-backyard is a concept used to describe the kind of planning politics where discussions are polarised into for and against with NIMBYs fighting any form of developments which affect their localities (Healey and Davoudi, 1998).

Further Reading

For an overview of various waste streams and the advantages and disadvantages of different waste management options see: DoE, 1995d, *Making Waste Work: The UK Strategy for Sustainable Waste Management*, London: HMSO. The most recent government policy on waste is set out in DETR, Department of the Environment, Transport and the Regions, 2000e, *Waste Strategy 2000: England and Wales Parts One and Two*, London: HMSO. For a case study-based discussion of changing waste policy and its institutional arrangements, see S. Davoudi, 2000 'Planning for waste: changing discourses and institutional relationships', *Progress in Planning*, 53, 3: 165–216; and for a discussion of public participation in waste planning and examples of current participatory practices see S. Davoudi and J. Petts 2000, 'How to involve the public in waste planning', *Proceedings of the Fifth National Conference in Strategic and Local Planning for Waste*, 5–6 July, Birmingham: MEL Research. Finally, for more general information about waste and some international comparisons visit www.residue.com which is hosted by Resource Recovery Forum.

PART III

Sustainable Development in Practice

Sue Batty

In many ways, the approaches given here are very different from the arguments and reviews in earlier parts of this book. So far, we have looked at politics, institutions and ethics, law, the philosophies of planning and sustainable development, and the contemporary debates on planning policy. However, to move towards practice and implementation, we must evaluate the actual impact of different urban forms and strategies; we need to enrich the analysis of cities and sustainability with measured and considered scientific evidence. We are also faced with the need to ensure that planning is based on compatible and consistent information that allows efficient and equitable management of land use, urban growth and the internal structure of towns, their centres, and their traffic.

The chapters in this part are thus more technical in nature, and positivist in orientation than previous material introduced in this book. Policy-making in practice requires numerical data and scientific method to support the planning process, to evaluate outcomes and provide guides to best practice. The projects reviewed here aim to contribute to these processes by finding valid ways of developing, monitoring and managing sustainable land use policies.

Three distinct sets of approaches to measuring and planning for sustainability are introduced, followed by an analysis of the conflicts and barriers to the successful implementation of sustainable policies. First, *Helena Titheridge* develops methods to assess changes in the energy use and pollution arising from changes in personal travel demands. These patterns can be measured through the explicit modelling of movements and location, providing a basis for guidance to local decision-makers. Her approach which is based on the ESTEEM model (EStimation of Travel, Energy, and Emissions Model) and the TRANSZ set of models, develops different approaches to travel and trip-making which seek to minimise energy use – in itself a major goal in moving towards sustainable cities. *Jo Williams* then develops a related but more aggregate perspective based on the URBASSS (URBAn Simulation for Sustainable Settlements) collection of models which enable rural settlement patterns to be better planned by locating new housing locations to maximise access and provide increased support for local services. *Mark Thurstain-Goodwin* and *Michael Batty* then develop a series of indicators for measuring the sustainability of town centres. These are the most focal points in western cities where huge concentrations of public and private infrastructure are under threat from changes to the way retailing and commerce as well as government services are being delivered.

David Banister concludes this part with a synthesis of the many different factors which conflict with one another in the design of sustainable settlement patterns and their management. By classifying the barriers to implementation and to good practice, Banister draws our attention to the debates and gaps in our knowledge that we must – and can – urgently address. He calls for the establishment of clear priorities for action, and identifies the crucial role for land use planners as one of translating these visionary ideas into practice.

All of the projects described in these chapters present the results of research projects carried out in UCL's Bartlett School of Planning and the Centre for Advanced Spatial Analysis (CASA). These projects all aim to evaluate alternative and often mutually conflicting development strategies. In the case of sustainable town centres, Thurstain-Goodwin and Batty aim to provide nationally consistent data and models to inform and support their planning and management. Titheridge and Williams also argue the case for good models with all three approaches being developed to provide a new generation of decision-support tools for planners. The authors present and evaluate the use of techniques built around statistical and spatial interaction models, catchment and threshold analysis, and accessibility indices which enable development and service provision strategies to be evaluated. Geographic Information Systems (GIS) and ways of using such techniques across the Internet are also proposed which help users and decision-makers to visualise future land use patterns. GIS allows maps and supporting information to be presented in a variety of ways which can also provide a means of monitoring land use change. The use of indicators to check the health of town centres, for example, provides the potential for planners and developers to quickly see and understand new information. The information is presented in a way that allows users to easily see changes in trends and, because it provides for consistent definitions of town centres across the country, allows local decision-makers to compare their own centre with others. The aim is to ensure timely intervention where sustainability is threatened.

The sustainable development mantra of compact cities, mixed uses, high density and efficient public transport policies is not by any means universally accepted by academics, nor by the public at large. These ideas are now coming under fire and we have already heard arguments in this book by Hall, for example in Chapter 7, to suggest that such patterns are not necessarily sustainable in practice. Titheridge tests these ideas in terms of travel, its volume, its energy use, the choice of mode that potential travellers have to make, and the level of pollutants generated from a range of different strategies. She explores policies based on concentrated land use in compact city forms, decentralisation to smaller communities, and the development of new and efficient communities. Work with the ESTEEM model concludes that although development in compact cities would lead to the lowest increases in travel for the journey to work, New Town development leads to the lowest additional travel for other journeys.

In the examples studied, intensifying densities and land uses were the policies that led to greatest sustainability – but only where trips remained predominantly work-based. If the trend towards greater diversity of trip destinations continues and the decline in the relative importance of work trips continues, then development of new, more efficient town forms to accommodate increased housing would be the most sustainable strategy. Using the TRANSZ models, Titheridge shows how a variety of factors can be studied in her exploration of the critical issues influencing journey length and choice of transport mode (modal split). This allows detailed conclusions about relationships between factors such as journey length, residential densities (urban or rural), and the distribution of employment to be derived. Her research broadly supports the argument that dense urban areas encourage short trips and greater use of public transport. But there are sufficient provisos in her research findings relating to the impact of different distributions of employment on location, the form and type of residential areas, and the distribution of public transport, to suggest the need for serious caution in accepting the idea of intensification.

The chapters on rural sustainability and the sustainable town centre raise similar problems. In both cases, sustainability has become an issue in the light of threats to their continued existence in their current form. The problems of social sustainability raised by Williams mark out the role of local services as the cement which binds rural areas together, providing a focus for the maintenance or the rebirth of a rural society. In the case of town centres, their decline and renaissance have the same effects but in an urban setting, that is providing the glue that holds urban areas together. In both cases, the decline of services accessible to all, such as public transport, leads to social exclusion, and the 'voluntary' migration of those who are able to 'leave' such areas. Such spirals of decline further reduce access to alternative means of travel other than the private car, and consequently access to centralised services is rapidly curtailed. Environmental sustainability is also threatened due to the wasteful neglect of physical and social infrastructures.

In terms of the British planning system and the current policy instruments that guide its operation, specifically Planning Policy Guidance notes (PPG), one important procedure that has been introduced to channel development is the 'sequential test'. This test means that development proposals must show that potential sites have been considered in a particular order; only if there is no site available in the most appropriate locations can the developer look to the next location. For example, retail developers must look for sites in town centres, before considering sites on the edge-of-town. Only if no suitable sites are then found can an out-of-town site be considered. These tests have been introduced for both housing and urban (town centre) sustainability to channel development into sites which meet the objectives of sustainability, defined in the instruments PPG3 for residential purposes and PPG6 for retailing and leisure uses in town centres.

However, two rather different analytical approaches to such questions are offered in these chapters. Williams uses the URBASSS collection of techniques to explore how new housing can be used to maximise access and provision of local services and to maximise levels of sustainability. This suite of methods includes the use of thresholds, catchments and accessibility analysis (in contrast to more explicit gravitational trip distribution models) to identify areas of underprovision and overprovision of services. Under-provision suggests a danger of out-migration and rural decline, while overprovision offers the opportunity to increase housing in the catchment area to ensure economic viability and to support the further development of stable, sustainable communities. The threshold and catchment approaches allow the identification of lower limits for the size of communities to support socially and economically viable services, suggesting settlements of at least 25,000 and no more than 100,000 residents as providing the appropriate lower and upper limits. These approaches use the tests of the viability of housing development based on the sustainable development objectives of accessibility and economic viability. Williams's work, although technical, has strong political implications. The issues she identifies are relevant to recent rural concerns over rapid change in the economic and social framework of the countryside as reflected in the goals of organisations such as the Countryside Alliance and contained in the recent (2000) Government White Paper on Rural Areas.

On the other hand, the problem of town centre sustainability also turns on the issue of balancing the economic and social vitality of towns as reflected in the concept of viable and vital town centres. Thurstain-Goodwin and Batty tackle the issue of identifying town centre boundaries to enable comparative statistics to be collected over time and nationally. They provide an approach to the development and visualisation of indicators that can be used not only to identify the boundaries of town centres but potentially to monitor their health and vitality. Just as the village shop is seen as the lifeblood of the rural community, the town centre provides the focus of social and economic life in urban areas and often the predominant image of what a town is all about. Much of the success of recent initiatives involving an 'urban renaissance' within British cities can be traced to the renewal of town centres which provide an impetus both economically and culturally to the whole town or region through the heart of the city.

Problems of measuring sustainability in town centres also reflect the balance between different types of fixed capital – social, physical and cultural. Social decline is often accompanied by the decline of physical infrastructure, thus suggesting that indicators to monitor the health of the town centre are an essential element in developing plans for their sustainability. The sustainable town centre can only be discussed if a good definition of a town centre is available and this must be based on an approach that can potentially be used to identify indicators of their economic health and vitality. Thurstain-Goodwin and Batty present an index that presumes that town centres are a collection of mixed uses with a measure of diversity and a degree of concentration. These components are central constructs in the measurement of sustainability. As in Williams's chapter, the idea of a threshold is used, acknowledging that a certain concentration of uses and an appropriate size are needed before a grouping of uses is perceived by its users as a 'town centre'.

The definition of what constitutes a town centre and particularly a healthy and sustainable one cannot depend just on measures of economic health, trends and size: its validity also depends on the extent to which people perceive it as a viable and vital unit or area that can provide the image and heart of the community as well as providing the necessary services. The sustainable town centre project, as for all three of the projects, therefore relies both on objective data, local knowledge and perceptions through the monitoring of local user responses to reach a general definition. Such a definition is therefore predicated on the basis of as wide an acceptance as possible under different circumstances, thus providing both a consistent basis for comparable data collection to allow monitoring and national comparisons as well as a general set of indicators that can form the basis for a consistent set of town centre health checks.

One of the implications of all the chapters in this section involves the definition of sustainable urban forms. There is a long tradition in planning and urban studies of developing ideas for the optimal town in terms of its physical structure and size. In urban society, optimal size is inevitably problematic but assuming an urban landscape of many towns which merge into one another, there are still issues relating to the size of centres which provide good and efficient levels of service. Access to such services is all important as is the nature of the transportation system relevant to such forms. The usual arguments about form turn on the extent to which towns should provide opportunities for spacious living – with the implications that optimal cities should reflect more decentralised, lower density forms, in contrast to vibrant urban life which imply more concentrated, higher density living. There is in fact no ideal. It is entirely possible to design highly decentralised town forms which sprawl across the landscape but which are efficient to live within and provide a high quality of life which meet quite severe requirements for sustainability. Higher density forms are often inefficient in that crowding leads to diseconomies of scale. Exactly the opposite argument can be made in each case for much depends upon the micro-organisation and technology of facilities and infrastructure which make up the town. Moreover the ways such towns function and meet requirements of sustainability depend on the cultural responses and behaviour patterns that characterise their residents. Many of the techniques and models in the following chapters are essential instruments in this debate and this section provides the reader with some insights into the methods required for serious analysis of these options.

The research projects which form the basis of these chapters provide contributions to the as yet unresolved debate about the best physical forms for sustainable development. Given that growth, decline, and renewal are inevitable parts of the lifecycle of our rural and urban areas, there are many barriers to sustainable development. In the last chapter in this part, Banister sets out the unresolved debates, the areas of disagreement and limits to our knowledge, the problems of different scales, and the contributions of individuals, from the local to the global which involve issues of international cooperation. Areas of limited knowledge include all the issues we have mentioned which focus on optimal urban forms, means to provide services, agencies and institutions involved in identifying and addressing issues of sustainability, and organisations and controls required to implement plans to meet the appropriate objectives. While recognising that individuals themselves have limited consistency in their preferences, and governments walk a narrow path between popular appeal and long-term viability and sustainability, the message of this part is simple: serious science is required if we are to get to grips with the dilemmas and conflicts that must be resolved in any move towards developing more sustainable cities.

13 The People: Where Will They Travel and How?

Helena Titheridge

Introduction

Between 1971 and 1996 road traffic in Great Britain increased from 208 billion to 438 billion vehicle kilometres. During the same period carbon dioxide emissions, a major greenhouse gas, from road transport almost doubled (ONS, 1999), rising from 17 million tonnes in 1971 to 31 million tonnes by 1996. The transport sector accounts for about 25 per cent of all carbon dioxide (CO_2) emissions, and it is the only sector where emissions are still increasing. If greenhouse gas emissions are to be stabilised, transport must make a major contribution.

At the same time, local authorities are under increasing pressure to find suitable locations for new housing developments. The latest household projections suggest that provision needs to be made for 3.8 million new dwellings (from 1996 to 2021), 1.5 million of which are predicted to be required in London and the South East (DETR, 1999b). The location of new housing and other related development will determine future levels of travel and car dependence. It is therefore important to assess the likely implications of different development strategies in terms of travel distance, energy use, mode choice, and pollution levels. This chapter discusses two quantitative approaches taken to address this problem at the sub-regional level.

ESTEEM[1]

The model

ESTEEM (Estimation of Transport, Energy and Emissions Model) is a computer-based model which aims to assist local authorities in planning new developments in parallel with traffic demand reduction strategies. It can be used to assess the sustainability, in terms of personal travel demand and associated energy consumption and emissions, of new housing and mixed-use developments. ESTEEM not only allows planners to see the effects of different developments on individual modes and purposes, but also allows them to visualise and evaluate the effect on different locations within the county. This visualisation process has been achieved through maps showing the changes in modelled mean trip distance travelled by residents of each enumeration district (ED). ESTEEM has been developed as an extension to ESRI's ArcView GIS (geographical information system) software package. The output includes total and per capita vehicle-km, passenger-km, fuel consumption and emissions.

Travel patterns for education, work, personal business and retail journey purposes, by car and bus modes are simulated, using an origin-constrained gravity model.[2] Journeys by rail and for leisure purposes have recently been added to the model. Approximately 90 per cent of all personal journeys by motorised transport (DETR, 1997b) will be included in the model in its completed form. Each mode is modelled with a generalised cost function based on distance (although other generalised cost functions could also be used). There are no road capacity constraints, thus the complex trip assignment procedures often required by transport models to assess congestion are avoided and travel is estimated on an annual basis.

The modal split between different forms of transport has been incorporated by applying factors (derived from the National Travel Survey 1994/96) to the trip production values. The modal split factors take into account differences in car-ownership and levels of public transport accessibility. All trip purposes use Enumeration District centroids as origins, with appropriate population-based census variables as production units (e.g. the number of four to eighteen year olds for education trips). The number on school roll (NOR) and the number of people with a workplace in each ward are used as destination attraction indices for education and work trips respectively. Footprint floor space was used to generate a destination attraction index for shopping and personal business trip purposes.

ESTEEM calculates energy consumption for each mode of transport and levels of all the main transport-related emissions (CO_2, CO, VOC, NO_x, PM, SO_2).[3] All calculations are made at the same spatial resolution as travel (i.e. at the enumeration district level). The energy and emissions are calculated using equations derived mainly from COPERT II (Ahlvik et al., 1997). Fleet characteristics, such as vehicle age, engine size and type, as well as estimates of average journey speeds and cold start distances are all taken into account. Algorithms for calculating emissions from alternative powered vehicles such as electric, CNG (Compressed Natural Gas) and LPG (Liquid Petroleum Gas) vehicles, are also included. In addition, future emissions limits for cars and buses have been included where possible; for example, the emissions standards for new cars which are proposed for 2001 by the European Commission under the Directive 98/69/EC – CEC (1992).

The application

The ESTEEM model has been tested for two English counties (Leicestershire and Kent) where an additional 10,000 households were located according to four different development strategies which reflect current thinking within many local authorities (Table 13.1).

Results for Kent

Kent is a particularly interesting case as Ashford has been considered as a major growth centre and there is also potential for brownfield development in the Thames Gateway area from Greenwich east to Dartford and the Medway. The 10,000 new households added is equivalent to the stock being increased by 1.61 per cent. In 1995, the population of Kent was 1,546,300, with 620,000 households, but it is likely to need 7,500 new dwellings per year over the next 16 years (GOSE, 1999). So the 10,000 new dwellings modelled in ESTEEM is a relatively modest increase and amounts to about 8.3 per cent of the new housing required for the county over the next sixteen years.

It was assumed that these households would have the same characteristics as the county average. Additional employment and school places were also included, close to the new housing, at a level which would maintain the current (1995) job ratio and availability of school places (i.e. places per child).

Table 13.1 Development strategy descriptions

Development strategy	Description
Intensification (IN)	Housing and employment developments were concentrated within the main urban areas, increasing both the residential and employment densities of the existing towns. No new retail centres were created.
Extensification (EX)	Housing and employment were concentrated around the periphery of the main urban areas. As for the intensification strategy, no new retail centres were created.
Decentralisation (DC)	Housing and employment developments were placed in rural villages throughout the county. Again, no new retail centres were created.
New Town (NT)	All the new housing and employment were placed in a single new settlement located in a relatively rural part of the county. A new retail centre was created to serve the population of the new settlement.

Helena Titheridge

Finally, it was assumed that the development would take place during 1995, and, therefore, the fleet characteristics used in the strategies remained unaltered from the 1995 base model. It was assumed that the bus and road networks would remain largely unaltered and that car ownership levels would reflect typical values for urban and rural areas. The average trip lengths are first modelled by ESTEEM for the base year (1995), and these are shown in Figure 13.1. On the subsequent model runs, each of the four development strategies (Table 13.1) are input and the results are summarised (Table 13.2).

- Intensification resulted in the lowest mean trip length for the journey to work by both car and bus (Table 13.2), and the smallest total increase in

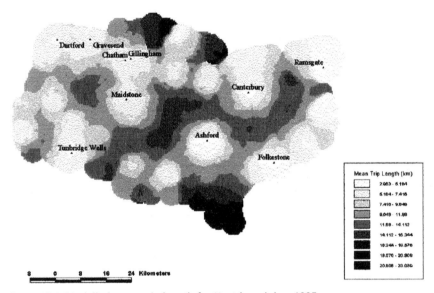

Figure 13.1 Modelled mean trip length for Kent by origin – 1995

Table 13.2 Mean trip distance for internal trips within Kent by mode and by purpose, together with total travel and energy consumption

| | Mean internal trip distance (km) | | | | | | Total annual travel (million passenger km) | Annual energy consumption (TJ) |
| | Education | | Work | | Retail & Personal business | | | |
	Car	Bus	Car	Bus	Car	Bus		
Base	3.66	4.00	10.37	4.29	4.91	4.07	18,236	31,362
IN	3.63	3.96	10.26	4.29	4.88	4.04	18,509	32,091
EX	3.65	3.98	10.34	4.34	4.88	4.05	18,520	32,117
DC	3.69	4.03	10.47	4.30	4.94	4.10	18,554	32,180
NT	3.62	3.95	10.71	4.33	4.77	3.97	18,530	32,168

220

travel (+1.48 per cent), energy consumption and emissions. Most of the major towns in Kent see a reduction in their mean trip lengths, but in rural areas the mean trip length increased, suggesting that more of these trips went to the urban centres (Figure 13.2).

- Extensification resulted in an increase of 1.54 per cent in total passenger kilometres travelled. As with the Intensification option, there is a reduction in trip lengths in the major towns, but a corresponding increase in other trip lengths as these new developments attract trips (Figure 13.3).

- Decentralisation produced a net increase in total travel (+1.74 per cent) and in the total amount of energy used (+2.61 per cent). For the emissions of pollutants, the general picture is one of small improvement, except for CO_2 emissions which increase. Again, there were reductions in rural trip lengths, particularly in the south of the county and to some extent in central Kent (Figure 13.4). This development option has produced more trips to local facilities and jobs in these areas, but the town-based trip lengths increase slightly.

- New Town resulted in the greatest reduction in trip lengths for educational, retail and personal business, for bus and car (Figure 13.5). Here the New Town was located to the south of the centre of the county (near Ashford), in an area associated with high mean trip lengths. Consequently, there were reductions in trip lengths in this part of Kent, but the New Town also generated longer travel distances from other parts of the county (Table 13.2).

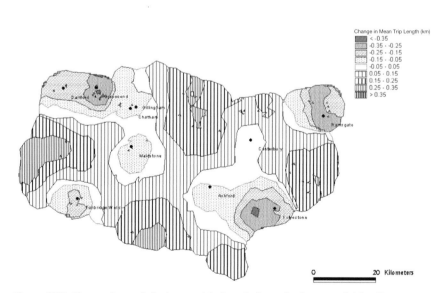

Figure 13.2 Change in modelled mean trip length from the base model for Kent Intensification strategy

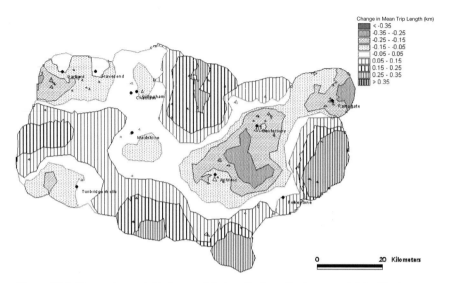

Figure 13.3 Change in modelled mean trip length from the base model for Kent Extensification strategy

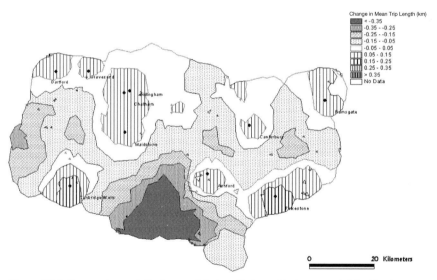

Figure 13.4 Change in modelled mean trip length from the base model for Kent Decentralisation strategy

Results for Leicestershire

The 10,000 new households is equivalent to the stock being increased by 2.86 per cent. In 1995, the population of Leicestershire was 885,000, with 350,000 households. The four development options (Table 13.1) gave the results shown in Table 13.3.

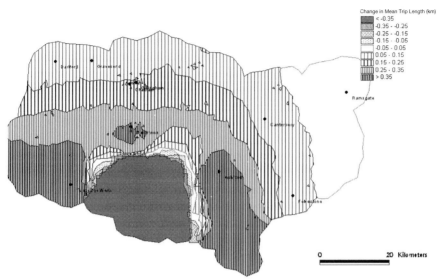

Figure 13.5 Change in modelled mean trip length from the base model for Kent New Town strategy

Intensification resulted in the smallest increase in car travel for the journey to work, as the mean trip length is reduced from 5.31 to 5.26 km. There is also the smallest increase in overall travel (2.7 per cent) and the lowest increase in total energy consumption and emissions. Mapping the distribution showed little change in Leicester itself, but mean trip lengths have reduced in the other main towns, and may have attracted trips away from Leicester (Table 13.3).

- Extensification meant that some reductions in trip lengths for the journey to work by bus (from 4.27 to 4.24 km) were recorded. The shorter journeys were mainly found around the edge of the towns, but there were increases in the trip lengths of those living in central Leicester and Loughborough, perhaps attracted by new out of town employment (e.g. business parks).

- Decentralisation resulted in reduced trip lengths in the rural areas due to the greater availability of local jobs and services, but only a small proportion of the total population was affected.

- New Town reduced the trip lengths for education, retail and personal business trips. But overall passenger kilometres rose by 2.8 per cent and the energy consumption by 2.9 per cent. The New Town location was to the east of Leicester in an area of high mean trip lengths. The settlement was designed to be self-contained, providing jobs, schools, shops and other facilities to residents. Trip lengths within the New Town area decreased substantially, but the trip lengths of those living to the east of the New Town increased substantially as they were attracted to the new centre (Table 13.3).

Table 13.3 Mean trip distance for internal trips within Leicestershire by mode and by purpose, together with total travel and energy consumption

| | Mean internal trip distance (km) | | | | | | Total annual travel (million passenger km) | Annual energy consumption (TJ) |
| | Education | | Work | | Retail & Personal business[1] | | | |
	Car	Bus	Car	Bus	Car	Bus		
Base	1.68	3.51	5.31	4.27	3.90	3.90	11,371	19,352
IN	1.68	3.50	5.26	4.27	3.86	3.86	11,682	19,880
EX	1.67	3.51	5.31	4.27	3.88	3.88	11,689	19,894
DC	1.69	3.53	5.30	4.24	3.96	3.96	11,702	19,912
NT	1.66	3.46	5.52	4.34	3.79	3.79	11,689	19,907

1 For Leicestershire, it was found that for retail and personal business trips, the mean internal trip lengths by bus and car were similar. The calibration process for the Euclidean version of ESTEEM used in this analysis produced very similar distance decay exponents for car and bus modes for this purpose (Titheridge et al., 1998). As Euclidean distance was used rather than network distance, all retail centres were thus inherently treated as equally accessible by car and by bus, producing very similar patterns of trip distribution by both modes.

At first glance, it would seem that in both counties the Intensification policy would be the most sustainable option for adoption, but the results are dominated by work trips. Between 1985 and 1995, the distance travelled per person per year to and from work increased by 18 per cent, whilst the distance travelled per person per year for shopping and personal business purposes increased by 35 per cent (GSS, 1997). During the course of a year, the average person travels nearly as far for these other purposes as they do for work purposes (1,926 km as compared with 2,024km – GSS, 1997). If these trends continue, then the most sustainable option may be the New Town policy rather than the Intensification policy.

The main impact of the policies is on the local area where reductions take place in trip lengths, but travel impacts are also observed over a wider area. In both counties, some of the development options lead to an abstraction effect from other parts of the county. So the benefits of shorter local trips are outweighed by the attractiveness of the development for longer distance travel.

It should also be remembered that this analysis has only looked at the impacts in a single year, and that only 10,000 households have been allocated. The real figures for these two counties are still being finalised, but in both cases will be substantially higher – Leicestershire's target for 2000–2016 will be at least 50,000 new homes, whilst the Kent figure may be over two and a half times that figure or 7,500 new homes each year! We have also assumed that new jobs and facilities will be provided at an appropriate rate to match the new homes. If this is not part of the development strategy, then the trip lengths and energy use will be substantially increased. Decisions now being taken at the national and county levels will determine the distribution of new housing over the next Structure Plan Review period, and by implication this will have a major impact on the travel patterns and car dependence.

The strengths and weaknesses of ESTEEM

The key advantage of ESTEEM is that it has been designed to assess strategies to reduce personal travel through testing alternative land use and development policies in consultation with local practitioners. A number of transport models are commercially available or under development, ranging from complex network flow models to simple spreadsheet models. However, many are expensive and inflexible tools when used for testing the sustainability of possible development patterns and are rarely designed for this purpose. The model stands out from other transport models currently on the market for a number of reasons.

- The model has been designed to use readily available data sets and will not require costly travel surveys and traffic counts to be specially carried out. This minimises data requirements and makes a GIS-based approach attractive to local authorities.
- The model has been designed to link with ArcView GIS, one of the more commonly used GIS packages within local authorities. Thus, minimal data transfer to the model is required.
- The GIS interface also allows visualisation of the resultant travel patterns, allowing changes and hot spots to be identified quickly and easily.
- The model is windows-based and menu driven, and therefore easy to use. Discussions with several local authorities have already produced favourable comments about the timeliness and usefulness of ESTEEM.

As with all models, ESTEEM has a number of weaknesses, which do not necessarily reduce its usefulness as a decision-support tool, but which users need to be aware of when interpreting the output from the model.

- The model assumes that the relationships established within the system are static over time. This may not be the case as the model contains a relatively small number of parameters representing a wide variety of different actors in the system. Because of this and a number of other reasons the model is designed to be comparative rather than predictive. But this can be seen as a strength as much as a weakness as it allows the effect of different development options to be explored, rather than merely projecting current trends forward.
- The model also assumes a simple cause and effect relationship between the land use variables and the resulting travel patterns. In reality, travel

patterns will also have some impact on land-use (e.g. firms relocating to avoid congestion).

ESTEEM allows strategic planners to quickly test a large number of possible options for new developments at an early stage in the structure plan and unitary development plan review processes. By providing a model which uses a familiar windows-based interface, together with the means to link it to their own local data, some of the questions about which settlement options are more or less sustainable in transport terms can be answered.

TRANSZ[4]

The model

The TRANSZ model provides a better understanding of the relationships between the structure of settlements and travel patterns. The models generated should be of use to policy-makers in testing different strategies to accommodate household growth in a more sustainable way. For example, one objective that can be tested in TRANSZ would be to test options to reduce journey to work distances and increase the level of walking, cycling and public transport use for commuting. The models also help create a better understanding of the relative importance of the different forces acting on travel behaviour.

A series of linear regression models were produced for journey to work distance and journey to work modes. The modes studied included rail (overground and underground), bus, car, cycling and walking. The two starting hypotheses for the models were:

- that journey length is related to residential density, accessibility to employment opportunities, occupation and migration history;
- that modal split is related to density, car ownership, access to public transport, occupation and migration history.

The majority of variables included in the analysis were derived from the 1981 and 1991 Censuses of Population. The census Local Based Statistics (LBS) provided data on resident population, car ownership, employment and other socio-economic characteristics such as age, at the ward level. Special Workplace Statistics (SWS) provided detailed journey to work information for place of residence, workplace and flows between wards by mode. A number of additional variables were derived from the census data and other sources. For example, the level of access to bus and rail networks and job opportunity. Table 13.4 gives a full list of the variables included in each of the models.[5]

Table 13.4 The list of variables included in the regression analysis of journey to work by distance and mode

Variable	Tested against		Description
	Distance	Mode	
Car ownership	✓	✓	Four car ownership variables – percentage of residents with access to 0, 1, 2 and 3 or more cars
Socio-economic group	✓	✓	Percentage of employees travelling between each residence and workplace in each socio-economic group
Employment status	✓	✓	Percentage of origin ward residents in part-time employment and percentage unemployed
Migration	✓	✓	Percentage of origin ward residents who moved into the origin ward in the previous year
Children	✓	✓	Percentage of origin ward resident households with children
Age	✓	✓	Percentage of origin ward residents in age groups 16-24, 25-34, 35-54, and 55-64
Residential density	✓	✓	Residential density at the origin
Degree of rurality	✓	✓	Six categories based on percentage of enumeration districts within each origin ward classified as urban
Rail availability	✓	✓	Total number of services departing from stations within 1.5 km of the ward centroid
Rail stations	✓	✓	Number of rail stations within 1.5 km of the ward centroid at the origin and the destination
Bus availability	✓	✓	Number of bus services travelling through the ward
Distance to town centre	✓	✓	Distance from the ward centroid to the nearest centre of a town with a population over 10,000 from the origin and destination wards
Distance to London	✓	✓	Distance from origin ward centroid to London
Access to employment	✓		Number of employees working within 1 km, 2.5 km, 5 km and 10 km from the ward centroid for both the origin and destination wards

The application

An understanding of relationships between urban form and transport is particularly important in the South East where demand for new housing is large, space is at a premium and average distance travelled per person is further than for the UK as a whole (DETR, 1997b). For this reason, the TRANSZ project focused on the South East. An initial analysis of all urban areas within the South East was carried out in order to get an overview of travel to work patterns across the entire area. This was followed by a more detailed study, at ward level, of two transport corridors – running from central London out to the fringes of South East England and beyond, the so-called 'Greater South East' (Hall, 1989).

Both corridors are dominated by strong radial transport links. The first includes the Thames Gateway regeneration area, the London Liverpool Street–Southend line and the London Victoria–Tonbridge–Ashford–Dover line. The second corridor runs northwards from London and is bounded by the East and West Coast Main Line railways. Analysis was also carried out individually for each of the counties within these two corridors at ward level. To provide some comparison with the ESTEEM model, the results from the analysis of Kent data for 1991 are presented here. Results of the analysis on flows between place of residence and workplace are presented for journey distance and three modes (car, bus and rail). The results for Kent are fairly representative of the results for both corridors.[6]

Relationships were tested between journey length and density, car ownership and access to employment opportunities. Socio-economic factors were also taken into account. Regression analyses were carried out using as the dependent variable the distance along the road network between the residence and workplace ward. Of the land-use characteristics tested, most were found to be significant determinants of trip length. The distance a person travels to work was found to be highly dependent on the job opportunities available close to their ward of residence and close to their workplace location. The mean distance travelled to work by residents of a ward was found to be high if low levels of job opportunities existed within a 1 km, 2.5 km and 5 km radii of the ward centroid, illustrating the effect of intervening opportunity on travel patterns.

The location of the home and the workplace in relation to the local town centre is important. The more distant the ward is from the town centre, the longer the likely commute (Figure 13.6). It was found that longer journeys were made to employment opportunities furthest from town centres, suggesting that suburban and out-of-town office developments (in the form of business parks, individual buildings and urban villages) do not necessarily provide employment for the local community.

The analysis found that journey length was unaffected by density, but was influenced by the urban or rural nature of the origin wards. The more rural

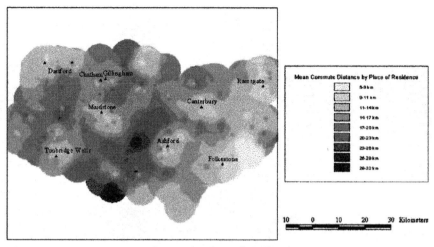

Figure 13.6 Mean commute distance by place of residence, 1991

the ward, the longer the likely commute distances. The most obvious reason why journey length was not related to density but to the degree of urbanisation of the ward was because residential density rather than building density or employment density was measured. Some town centre wards will have lower residential densities than those found in some of the more suburban wards.

Transport availability was also found to be significant in determining travel distances. Trip lengths were found to increase with increasing levels of car ownership. However, the analysis also showed trip lengths decreasing as the level of rail access at both the origin and the destination increased. This is because rail stations tend to be located close to town centres with high employment opportunities.

Distance travelled to work was also affected by a number of socio-economic variables, particularly occupation type which was a strong determinant in all the models. The higher socio-economic groups showed a positive relationship with journey length. The higher the percentage of professional or managerial workers travelling between an origin and a destination, the more likely the origin and destination are far apart. Unskilled and semi-skilled employees tend to live closest to their workplace.

The most important determinant of journey length was the distribution of job opportunities, with people travelling long distances to destinations with a high number of jobs over a wide area and short distances if they live in an area with a high number of jobs spread over a wide area. The effect of London on trip lengths was also very important, with residents in wards furthest from London travelling the longest distances. Socio-economic group was also highly significant, with those in group 3n (skilled – non-manual) being the least likely to travel long distances.

229

Relationships were also tested between modal split and density, car ownership and access to public transport, with types of job and migration history also being taken into account. Regression analyses were carried out using the percentage of total employees travelling by each mode between the residence and workplace ward as the dependent variable. It was found that high residential densities were an important determinant of high levels of travel by bus. High densities were related negatively to rail travel. There are several possible explanations for this. First, the area close to a railway station may exhibit a low density due to a lack of residential premises. Second, the nature of the rail network in Kent (a large number of stations serving relatively small settlements) allows commuters to live in relatively low-density areas. Third, as discussed in relation to the journey length model, high rail access is associated with town centres, high employment opportunities and short journeys, thus decreasing the opportunity/need to travel by rail. Level of car use was unrelated to residential density but was negatively related to the degree of urbanisation. Thus, those living in rural areas were more likely to use the car to travel to work. Again, supporting the argument that residential density is a poor measure of sustainable urban form.

Low levels of car ownership increased travel by bus and by rail, and decreased car travel. However, high percentages of households owning three or more cars were positively related to high levels of train travel, with car ownership perhaps representing the wealth of the area. High rail availability at the workplace increased rail use and decreased car use. Car use also decreased with availability of rail at the origin. Stations tend to be located near employment centres and in places with good bus links, making them accessible to bus users. Conversely, these areas are often associated with high levels of congestion and limited availability of parking providing a disincentive to use the car. Other socio-economic characteristics were also important in determining modal split. Professionals and managers were more likely to travel by car and train, whilst semi-skilled and unskilled manual workers were more likely to travel by bus.

The most important determinant of mode was journey length with the longest journeys made by rail. Socio-economic group was also highly significant, with those in groups 3n and 4 (skilled – non-manual and semi-skilled) being the most likely to travel by bus and least likely to travel by rail. The level of rail access was also important with high levels of rail access being positively related to bus use and negatively related to car use. Finally, car ownership was important in determining levels of car use but much less important in determining bus and rail use, suggesting low car ownership levels being associated with high levels of walking and cycling trips.

These findings seem to support the arguments that dense, urban areas encourage the use of public transport and shorter journey distances. However, the high levels of transport provision associated with these locations also create improved access to more distant employment centres and thus generate a small number of much longer journeys. Although the number of workers making these much longer trips are small, they have a noticeable impact on overall travel distance and thus on energy consumption and emissions. This relationship runs contrary to conventional wisdom that it is more sustainable to concentrate employment where there is strong public transport.

Other limited empirical data also supports this argument. For example, Banister *et al.* (1997) found that within Linford Ward of Milton Keynes, there was substantial variation in energy use per trip. Average energy use per trip was 15.1 MJ (this figure includes both motorised and non-motorised trips). Sixty-six per cent of trips were made by motorised transport. The average energy use for these trips was 22.6 MJ per trip. The vast majority of trips were not found to use much energy, 84 per cent of trips used below the average figure of 15.1 MJ per trip. Those trips using more than the 15.1 MJ per trip threshold had an average energy use of 72.4 MJ per trip. Thus, 24 per cent of the motorised trips used 78 per cent of the total energy consumed. The percentage of trips consuming the majority of energy is even smaller if non-motorised forms are considered. Thus, a few long-distance trips have heavily skewed the data.

The strengths and weaknesses of TRANSZ

The complexity of these results and the difficulties in interpreting them illustrate the problems of this type of analysis. Linear regression analysis not only assumes a simple relationship in the form of $Y = a + bx_1 + cx_2 + dx_3 + \ldots$ but also assumes a cause and effect relationship between the independent and dependent variables, whilst in reality the relationships are much more complex, with high levels of interdependency between the variables. Stead *et al.* (2000: 182) illustrates the point for the interconnectivity between land use characteristics.

The census data on which the models are based only include travel to work data, but they do have the advantage of very high sampling rates (10 per cent and 100 per cent). Using census data provides the added advantage that local authorities have a good understanding of the data and ready access to it. This means that although the models are not transferable across regions, they can be recreated for other regions with relative ease.

There is also no certainty that the model will hold if any of the parameters are moved outside the range of values used to create the model. However, this type of approach does have a strong explanatory value, allowing the relative importance of land-use characteristics at the origin and at the destination, and socio-economic characteristics to be examined, thus providing a better understanding of what affects travel patterns.

Conclusions

Both models are likely to prove useful to planners in solving the problem of where to locate new housing developments in a way that will reduce travel, but in different ways. The TRANSZ model provides a detailed insight into the complex relationships between land use characteristics, socio-economic characteristics and travel patterns for work related travel. ESTEEM allows planners to compare the impact on travel patterns of a large number of possible development sites quickly and with ease and it covers 90 per cent of all travel activities.

Neither model is perfect and both suffer from similar problems. Both models are static, with the relationships between the model parameters assumed to remain constant over time. In addition, neither model takes into account feedback (i.e. the effect of travel patterns on land-use). Both also assume that the input parameters to the model are independent of each other. However, given the limited amount of travel flow data available at the sub-regional level, it is extremely difficult to produce a valid dynamic model at the high levels of spatial disaggregation required to adequately model the effects of location on travel. So despite the limitations of these approaches, some method of assessing the impact of new developments is required. No one approach, be it theoretical or empirical, qualitative or quantitative, provides a perfect picture of the impacts of change in a system. But both models add substantially to the methods available to seek both sustainable corridor and housing development.

As is often the case with both spatial modelling (ESTEEM) and corridor modelling (TRANSZ), it is the lack of data that creates the real limitations as to what can be achieved. In both cases, best use has been made of a range of secondary data sources, some of which are digitally available. Such approaches must be the way forward, so that conceptually and empirically simple methods can be developed for use by planners in trying to understand the complexity of the relationships between land use and development factors, socio-economic variables and travel characteristics, including trips made by purpose, modal choice, trip lengths, energy consumption, and emission of pollutants.

Acknowledgements

I would like to thank the following: Experian Goad, Kent County Council. Essex Data Archive and Manchester Information and Associated Services (MIMAS) for providing data. ESRI (UK) for providing the ArcView and NetEngine software. The TRANSZ and ESTEEM projects are based on data provided with the support of the ESRC and JISC and use boundary material that is copyright of the Crown and the ED-LINE consortium.

Notes

1   ESTEEM was initially developed at the Bartlett School of Planning as part of an EPSRC-funded project under the sustainable cities programme in collaboration with TPK partnership, Leicestershire County Council, West Sussex County Council and Hampshire County Council. The second phase of the ESTEEM development was funded by EPSRC through the LINK – Inland Surface Transport programme in partnership with TPK partnership, ESRI (UK), Experian Goad, West Sussex County Council and Leicestershire County Council.

2   Gravity models are based on Newton's theory that two masses are attracted to each other in proportion to the product of their masses and inversely to the square of their distance apart. Thus the number of trips between an origin and a destination is a function of the size of the trip-making population at the origin, the attractiveness of the destination and the distance between the two. Research has since shown that the inverse square of distance is a poor measure of the deterrence to travel. The size of the exponent (often referred to as the distance decay exponent) has been found to vary according to trip purpose and mode of travel as well as a number of other factors. Other measures for the deterrence to travel have also been experimented with such as travel time or more sophisticated measures based on the overall cost of travel. The part of the equation dealing with the deterrence to travel is referred to as the generalised cost function. Origin-constrained models are used where the number of trips produced by each of the origins is known but the number of trips attracted to each of the destinations needs to be determined. See Ortúzar and Willumsen (1994) for a more detailed explanation.

3   CO_2 = Carbon Dioxide, CO = Carbon Monoxide, VOC = Volatile Organic Compounds, NO_x = Nitrogen Oxides, PM = Particulate Matter, and SO_2 = Sulphur Dioxide.

4   The TRANSZ models were developed at the Bartlett School of Planning as part of an EPSRC-funded project under the sustainable cities programme. The British Academy provided funding for additional research on TRANSZ.

5   The Special Workplace Statistics only provided data on journey distance in bands of uneven widths, i.e. under 2 km, 2 to 4 km, 5 to 9 km, 10 to 19 km, etc. It was felt that a better assessment of the effects of land use, urban form and socio-economic characteristics on the distance people travel to work would be achieved if distance travelled was not banded. Therefore the distance to work variable was calculated as the minimum network distance between the residence and place of work using a 1:250,000 representation of the road network.

6   All the regression models produced for Kent were found to be statistically significant; however, the explanatory power of each of the models varied considerably. The regression model for the percentage of people travelling by rail was the strongest (with an R value of 0.73). The models for journeys by car and for journey distance were slightly weaker, whilst the model describing the percentage of journeys by bus was substantially weaker (R= 0.26). One reason for the relatively low explanatory powers of the models was that the flow data contained a large number of zero and low values and very few large flows.

Helena Titheridge

Further Reading

There are a variety of books available on statistical techniques – try Shaw and Wheeler (1994) for a basic introduction, or Burt and Barber (1996) for a more advanced approach. See Ortúzar and Willumsen (1994) for an explanation of gravity models and other types of transport modelling. For information on using census data see Openshaw (1995). Breheny and Hall (1996) gives a good discussion of the debate around the government's household projections. See Breheny (1992a) for more on the links between urban form, transport and energy.

14 Achieving Local Sustainability in Rural Communities

Jo Williams

Introduction

Rural areas are at present facing a set of complex problems which have reinforced isolation. Migration from rural areas has led to economic and social decay over the past decades. This in turn has reduced provision of local services, facilities and job opportunities in the countryside, which has resulted in poor access for those without cars. Poor local access reinforces social exclusion of certain groups within the countryside and impairs their quality of life. In addition it promotes travel for those groups with access to cars, whilst deterring use of alternative modes, which increases both energy consumption and emissions. Thus the loss of local service centres in rural areas appears to be environmentally and socially unsustainable.

The Rural Development Council for the Countryside Survey of Local Services (1997) highlighted the low levels of provision in the countryside. The survey showed nationally that 42 per cent of the parishes were without a permanent shop, 93 per cent without a public nursery, 91 per cent without day-care facilities for the elderly, 83 per cent without a GP based within the parish, and 75 per cent without a daily bus service. Lack of provision of local facilities has led to an increase in total distances travelled by the rural population. Action with Communities in Rural England (ACRE) notes that rural residents have to travel 50 per cent further than urban residents do and their journeys are 40 per cent longer. These figures include shopping and school trips, as well as work and leisure trips (ACRE, 1998). 'Rural households spend an average of 10 per cent a week more on fuel than their

235

urban counterparts' CPRE (1998). Thus, greater quantities of energy are consumed by travel in rural areas, as larger distances are travelled by motorised, private transport.

Travel poverty has also resulted from a lack of local provision of services, facilities and employment opportunities combined with poor alternatives to private motorised transport. The outcome of these changes is increasing use of the car, increase in distance travelled for all activities and reduction in accessibility. This in turn has had an environmental impact, in terms of transport energy consumption and emissions. Thus travel poverty threatens the sustainability of rural development. Travel poverty specifically affects the elderly, low-income groups, young people and women. All of these groups have poor access to private motorised transport. Nationally, in rural areas 22 per cent of the population are without cars. In addition 33 per cent have low incomes, 40 per cent are retired, unemployed or unoccupied; 14 per cent of adults in rural areas do not possess a driving licence (CPRE, 1998). Thus 'Poor rural households travel half the distance of better-off rural families' (CPRE, 1998). For these groups, access to services, facilities and employment opportunities is limited. In addition, 46 per cent of rural population on average own one car. In larger households, where the car is used for work, the mobility of the rest of the household is effectively reduced. Public transport services are also limited; cycling and walking facilities are poor. Thus the alternatives to car use are very restricted. This reinforces the social exclusion of some groups in rural areas from society, which in turn dramatically reduces their quality of life.

The revised PPG13 highlights the need to 'promote social inclusion and reduce rural isolation, for those without use of a car'. The guidance identifies the need to 'focus development in or near local service centres' and more especially to 'focus rural housing development, to enable it to be accessible to a range of services and to help support the use and quality of local services'. The revised PPG13 suggests that such an approach would 'reduce the need for longer journeys into larger urban areas and help to promote the use of public transport for those journeys which are still required'. The revised draft PPG13 also acknowledges the need to 'create more sustainable patterns of development by building in ways which deliver accessibility by public transport to jobs, education and health facilities, shopping, leisure and local services' (DETR 1999f).

Over the next decade, rapid housing development will take place in rural counties. New house building targets in rural areas could provide the right stimulus for increasing the number and quality of local services, generating more sustainable development patterns. Closure of existing services could also be prevented by using housing development to increase the resident population size in settlements, where local provision is becoming eco-nomically unviable. Thus, rural local authorities are beginning to recognise the potential new housing allocations have for improving local access to services. However, in order to maximise the potential and create more sustainable development strategies, local authorities need to identify areas with poor access to local services or where existing infrastructural capacity is under-utilised.

The draft revised PPG3 suggests that 'local authorities in preparing development plans should adopt a systematic approach to deciding which sites and areas are most suitable for development and the sequence in which development should take place' (DETR 1999g). Thus, PPG3 outlines a sequential approach to determining suitable sites for housing allocation based on the following criteria:

- the accessibility of local services;
- the capacity of existing infrastructure to absorb further development;
- the ability to build communities, to support new physical and social infrastructure and to provide sufficient demand to sustain appropriate local services and facilities;
- physical constraints on development land;
- the availability of previously developed sites and empty or under-used buildings.

The first three criteria acknowledge the importance of ensuring that new residents have local access to services. This suggests that future housing development should be located on sites with good access (in terms of proximity) to existing services or alternatively the site must be of a size that new residents can sustain new services. Methodologies are needed to identify sites with development potential based on these criteria. In this chapter we shall explore these approaches, which have been developed as part of the Urban Sustainability and Settlement Size Project (*URBASSS*), which can be used to guide future housing development in a manner that maximises potential access to local services. The approaches have been developed using data from the rural county of Gloucestershire. Three main approaches used are threshold analysis, catchment area analysis and accessibility analysis (Table 14.1). These approaches are outlined in the following section.

The Approaches

In order to identify suitable sites for future housing development, which either support existing local services or promote the development of local services in isolated rural areas, we must first identify benchmarks for under-and-over provision of services, in terms of size of supporting population. These benchmarks (population thresholds) can be identified using population threshold analysis. The method has been used to calculate the size of resident population required to sustain service provision economically. It calculates

Table 14.1 Methodologies used to determine supporting population, catchment size and accessibility of services

	Threshold analysis	Accessibility analysis	Catchment area analysis
Output	Calculates the size of resident population required to support a service/facility whilst in operation at county, settlement or ward level	Determines the number of residents within accessible distances of services and facilities by foot, cycle or public transport	Determines the number of residents living in the catchment area of specific facilities/services. Also calculates minimum, maximum and average distances travelled to access facilities/services
Methodologies	County analysis, ward analysis, settlement analysis	Accessibility Analysis (AA)	Catchment Area Analysis (CAA) Sectoral Catchment Area Analysis (SCAA)

the minimum number of residents required to patronise a service in order for it to be economically viable (the population threshold). Beneath this threshold the service will be over-provided and not economically viable. In this instance, housing development could be used to boost the size of the population that patronises the service, in order to maintain its economic viability and prevent closure.

Conversely, above the threshold, services are economically viable but could be inadequate for residents' needs. In this instance further development of services will be required, which may need additional expansion of the resident population to ensure economic viability. Thus thresholds provide benchmarks against which the economic viability of services can be tested. These thresholds can be used to determine within a county, district, settlement or catchment, whether service provision is sufficient for the size of resident population within that spatial area. In addition, thresholds can be used to indicate levels of service provision required in new communities, which could be extremely useful in planning a new settlement.

Threshold analysis has been used widely in a range of disciplines for many years (for example, project management, ecology, economics, geography and land use planning). Although some population thresholds for services have been identified, the range studied has been limited. The variation in thresholds estimated has also been substantial. Much of the threshold work is dated and different provision requirements now exist (for example, see GLC, 1963). In addition, some of the more recent work on thresholds has been carried out in urban areas (for example, Milton Keynes Development Corporation, 1992) rather than rural counties. Many surveys, which have been completed to determine population thresholds, have been conducted countywide, at parish level or within settlements (Farthing, 1994; Farthing *et al.*, 1996). In this chapter, three methods for determining thresholds will be outlined: the county method, settlement method, and ward method. There is also a need to determine the accessibility of local services. The decision to support the development or retention of existing services should not be based purely on economic viability. There is also a need to improve provision in currently inaccessible rural areas. Future housing allocations can be used to support the provision of new services in areas where access is poor. Thus, methodologies that can be used to identify areas with poor/good physical access to services are also required. In this chapter, accessibility analysis is the technique used to identify locations with poor/good access to services and those services which are inaccessible/accessible. Accessibility analysis identifies the areas that have access to services within walking, cycling distance or a bus ride away. This information can also be used to determine suitable locations for new housing development and service provision.

A further method which both identifies thresholds and accessibility of services, catchment area analysis, will also be introduced. Catchment area analysis maps existing catchment areas for services and calculates the average distance residents within the catchment area must travel to access the service. This information can then be used to identify areas in which catchments are large and residents must travel greater distances to access services or those with small catchments, where access is good. This enables planners to identify areas with poor access to services and thus determine where the development of new housing could be used to support the provision of extra services. Catchment area analysis can also be used to identify thresholds for services, which again can be used to identify under-and-over provision. The methods introduced here will now be described in greater depth below.

Threshold analysis

Threshold analysis has been broken down into three sub-methods: county, ward and settlement analysis (Table 14.1). Each method calculates thresholds for different boundary sizes: county, wards and settlements. The finer grain technique (sectoral analysis) has introduced socio-economic variables to improve the resolution of all three methodologies. The techniques were applied to Gloucestershire to calculate thresholds and determine whether services were under-or-over provided at a variety of spatial levels. The population thresholds calculated using these different techniques vary. This relates to the assumptions made, the boundaries set and whether the method uses total population or service users. For instance, the variation in boundaries used for analysis influences the size of population considered to be supporting each service. Thus the largest thresholds are found where the county has been used as the boundary and smallest where the ward is used as the boundary.

The most accurate in terms of calculating an average threshold for provision per thousand inhabitants is the county method (Table 14.2). Both the ward and settlement methods are inclined to ignore population lying outside the boundary, which may also be crucial in supporting services. The county method is most accurate in determining population thresholds for services supplying the population within the county. The thresholds calculated for those services with regional or national catchments, or those straddling the border, are less likely to be accurate.

The sectoral methods improve the resolution of the county, settlement and ward techniques by identifying thresholds calculated using user groups rather than total population. Because sectoral analysis specifies user groups, the thresholds calculated are lower.

The population thresholds calculated can provide an indication of service hierarchies. The average population thresholds can be used as benchmarks to determine under-and-over provision at the county level and within settlements. However, the thresholds do not indicate where services are lacking and should be provided. Nor where housing can be built to take advantage of locations in which services are over provided. In order to ascertain where future development of housing and services should take place one needs to define the current catchment areas and how accessible currently provided services are.

Table 14.2 Summary of population thresholds

	Services/facilities and employment opportunities	County Method (CM)
Employment opportunities	Textile manufacturers (e.g. linen, clothing manufacturers)	22015
	Local government offices	66045
	Financial services (e.g. accountants, tax consultants)	1631
Shopping	Convenience stores	4064
	Supermarkets	9784
Leisure	Theatres	66045
	Leisure centres	19569
	Pubs	1129
Education	Primary schools	2056
	Higher Education Colleges	132091
Personal business	Clinics	8129
	Banks	18770
	Garages	1338

Source: Williams (2000a)

Accessibility analysis

Accessibility[1] analysis determines the percentage of potential service users living within walking or cycling distance of/or a local bus ride away from selected services. It can be used to identify variation in the accessibility of services with location. Accessibility analysis can be used to identify sites for housing development with good access to services (as specified by the revised PPG13 (DETR, 1999f) and PPG3 (DETR, 1999g)) or used to identify locations where new housing development could be used to support more accessible services in existing or new communities (as outlined by the revised PPG3 (DETR, 1999g).

Accessibility analysis uses spatial analysis computer applications to calculate the percentage of potential service users living in 'crow fly' walking, cycling distance or a bus ride from services. Table 14.3 outlines the percentages of service users living within walking, cycling or bus ride from the services, investigated in Gloucestershire. The analysis made several assumptions. Accessibility analysis assumes that all residents have equal access to services regardless of mobility and that all services are equally attractive. It also assumes that the distances consumers are prepared to walk, cycle, or

Table 14.3 Percentage of consumers/employees living within walking, cycling or a bus ride away from services, facilities and employment opportunities

	Percentage users / employees living in walking distance					Percentage users / employees living in cycling distance				Percentage users / employees living a bus ride away			
	0-10	10-25	25-50	50-75	75-100	0-25	25-50	50-75	75-100	0-25	25-50	50-75	75-100
Textile manufacturing industries	❋							●					○
Local government services	❋					●					○		
Financial services			❋						●				○
Convenience store			❋						●				○
Supermarket		❋							●				○
Theatre	❋						●					○	
Leisure centre		❋						●					○
Pub			❋						●				○
Primary school				❋					●				○
HE College	❋						●					○	
Clinic		❋						●					○
Bank		❋						●					○
Garage			❋						●				○

Source: Williams (2000a)

travel by bus to services are the same as the average national trip length by mode. The model also assumes that propensity to walk, cycle or use the bus is governed by distance.

The method has various limitations. Estimation of service usage is limited because the mobility of consumers and the attractiveness of the services are ignored. Also there may be variation in the distance people are prepared to travel by foot, bike and bus for different types of people in different geographical locations. By using the national average trip length as an accessibility buffer these variations are overlooked and may need to be reassessed at the local level, using local travel data. The method also presumes that distance is the only factor influencing type of mode used by resident populations, which is unrealistic. In addition, the accessibility method does not take into account actual transport services and networks currently operating in the area which may also increase its limitations as a method to determine relative accessibility.

This methodology could be adapted to determine how the relative accessibility of services alters with increased or decreased provision. It could be used to estimate the percentage of potential consumers in walking/cycling distance or within a local bus ride from services. The method produces a hierarchy of accessibility for the facilities chosen and enables the researcher to determine changes in accessibility patterns relating to the development of services or housing. It also provides a method for determining which services are lacking in the county.

Catchment area analysis

Catchment area analysis (CAA) provides a method which can both identify population thresholds and the relative accessibility of services. It identifies the number of people living within a facility's catchment area, as well as the average, maximum and minimum distances those people must travel to access the facilities. Sectoral Catchment Area Analysis (SCAA) focuses the method further, by identifying potential users. Catchment areas use distance as the determinant of the population threshold rather than settlement or administrative boundaries. However, both CAA and SCAA make the following assumptions:

- no cross-boundary movement;
- that all services are equally attractive;
- that residents will travel to their nearest service.

The first two assumptions are common to all the techniques used; however, the third assumption results from the incorporation of the spatial distribution element into the method. It is feasible that in some instances, residents travel to their closest service. This is certainly true for low order, ubiquitous services or in fact any facility for which distance is the prime factor influencing use (rather than range of products or quality of the service). Where distance and the socio-economic characteristics of the resident population are the key factors influencing use, both catchment area methods are likely to provide accurate thresholds.

The method was applied in Gloucestershire, and the range of catchment areas, in terms of coverage and population size associated with each service studied, is outlined in Table 14.4. Both methods identify a range of population thresholds for all services, based on their spatial distribution and the distribution of residents or user groups. Both methods also calculate the range of distances travelled by residents or user groups within the catchment, to access services. However, neither method uses actual network data to provide more accurate estimates of the range of distance travelled to access services. Thus, the techniques identify differences in the spatial coverage of different catchments for the same type of service, based on patterns of spatial distribution, and they do not identify absolute distances travelled.

Catchment Area Analysis is different from the more traditional population threshold methods in that it determines catchment areas, not the size of population in the county, ward or settlement that may support each service. Thus it improves upon the simple ratio methods previously developed. It analyses information stored on a database, which can be regularly updated and has a wider coverage than the surveys used for analysis previously, by traditional population threshold methods. This technique uses proximity to determine thresholds rather than standards for certain administrative areas. This provides a positive rather than a normative approach. Catchment Area Analysis also calculates population threshold ranges, rather than averages which can be applied to a variety of local situations. Catchment Area Analysis can be used to identify under-and-over provision of services in terms of economic viability (using the population thresholds derived from the method) and accessibility (using catchment coverage). It can also be used to identify suitable locations for future housing development based on proximity to local services. In addition, it can be used to identify sites where housing provision can be used to support an increase in service provision.

This section has provided an overview of some methods that could be used to determine thresholds for services and accessibility. These methods could be used by planners to identify locations for new housing development with good access to local services or where the capacity of existing infrastructure can absorb new housing development. The thresholds developed can also be used to guide service provision in new communities. The following section outlines the application of these methods in identifying suitable sites for housing development in Gloucestershire.

Table 14.4 Summary of catchment areas

	Services/ facilities and employment opportunities	Size of population in catchment	Size of population in catchment by sector	Range of catchment size (metres)	Average catchment size (metres)
Employment opportunities	Textile manufacturers	43226-1661	171-4	15469-658	5234
	Local government offices	211402-161142	2950-201	10304-5876	9384
	Financial services	26415-1147	158-2	4914-66	1796
Shopping	Convenience stores	22350-1264	*	6342-53.5	225
	Supermarkets	40880-1825	*	11000-270	3566
Leisure	Theatres	309223-62099	*	26351-1132	9395
	Leisure centres	60891-5927	*	8856-835	3871
	Pubs	22350-1147	16952-857	4116-58	985
Education	Primary schools	21695-1147	1172-49	4140-57	954
	Higher Education Colleges	309223-60550	241462-48899	15488-4304	11205
Personal business	Clinics	75201-1264	*	10562-480	5084
	Banks	59568-1594	*	9411-42	3901
	Garages	24022-1147	23792-1052	9908-1147	1396

Source: Williams (2000a)

Application in Gloucestershire

The South West region has 8 per cent of the total United Kingdom population, and since 1981 it has had the fastest-growing population among United Kingdom regions. The most recent projections suggest an increase of about 410,000 households in the region between 1996 and 2016. The South West Regional Planning Guidance suggests that 40,000 new dwellings will need to be provided in Gloucestershire between 1996 and 2016. It is proposed that these dwellings will be provided at an average rate of 2,000 per annum.

The County Council used a variety of techniques to test the sustainability of various housing development scenarios including: sieve map analysis, landscape studies, countywide and area-specific transport models and strategic environmental appraisal. At the end of a complicated selection process, the county council decided that most of the new residential development would be provided in the Central Severn Vale, where the majority of services are concentrated (Figure 14.1). Within the Central Severn Vale the county proposed that most of the new housing development would focus in the larger existing settlements; Gloucester, Cheltenham and Cirencester. Outside these larger settlements the council suggested that the majority of development would focus around existing settlements and alongside the M5 corridor. In rural areas the strategy for residential development was to integrate with the existing form of settlements, minimising any adverse impact on the setting of the settlement, or intrusion into the surrounding countryside.

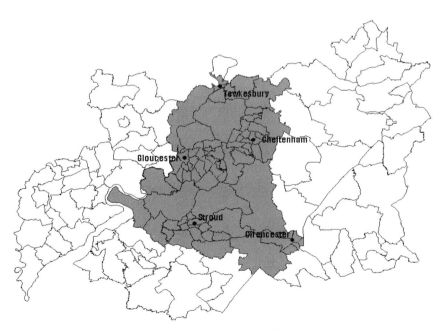

Figure 14.1 Map showing the central Severn Vale in Gloucestershire

245

Accessibility analysis and thresholds derived from catchment area analysis were used to test the sustainability of this development strategy, in terms of increasing local access to services.

Access to local services

Accessibility analysis shows that in Gloucestershire, colleges, theatres and local government services are the least accessible and that primary schools are most accessible (Table 14.3). It also shows that over 50 per cent of primary schools, pubs, garages, convenience stores and financial services are accessible by foot and that 75–100 per cent of financial services, primary schools, pubs, garages, convenience stores and supermarkets are accessible by bike. The analysis finds that most services are accessible to 75–100 per cent of the population by bus. Thus for up to 25 per cent of the population, services are not accessible by any of these modes. Catchment area analysis provides some indication of the variation in accessibility of each service. Largest variations in accessibility can be seen for theatres, manufacturing industries and supermarkets, as they are less numerous and tend to concentrate in the larger urban areas. Least variation in accessibility can be seen for pubs and primary schools as they are more numerous and dispersed throughout the county. It also highlights the fact that households in the north of the Cotswolds and Forest of Dean districts have poorest physical access to services. It is in these areas that access to services by non-car modes is limited.

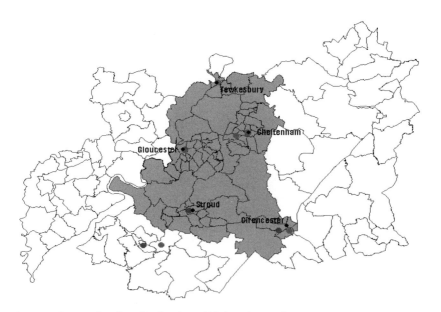

Figure 14.2 Map showing distribution of high-order services

The accessibility of services within the county reflects the relative distribution of residents and service provision. In terms of the distribution, range and scale of services in the county, a definite hierarchy is visible. Analysis has determined that the highest-order services (theatres and higher education colleges) are concentrated in the four main urban areas; Gloucester, Cheltenham, Stroud Urban Area and Cirencester (Figure 14.2). Medium-order facilities are concentrated in the Central Severn Vale; leisure centres, banks, clinics, and textile manufacturing industries (Figure 14.3).

Lower-order services (pubs, schools, convenience stores, garages, and financial services) are decentralised across the entire county (Figure 14.4). These findings suggest that in order to ensure good access for new households to services in Gloucestershire, the majority of new development should focus in the Central Severn Vale, particularly in and around the four main urban areas. This supports the County Council's policy to locate future housing development within this Central Severn Vale.

However, such a policy will mean that for up to 25 per cent of the population, services will still remain relatively inaccessible by non-car modes, which is neither socially nor environmentally sustainable. Dispersal of future housing development into the least accessible areas of the county may provide stimulus for the improved provision of services in outlying areas, also supported by the development plan. Catchment area analysis can be used to identify the outlying settlements in which services are currently under- and -over-provided. This gives some indication of where future housing development can be used to support existing and future service provision and to improve the sustainability of outlying settlements.

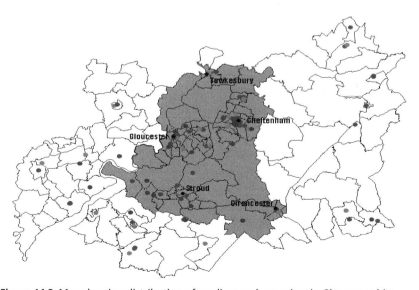

Figure 14.3 Map showing distribution of medium-order services in Gloucestershire

247

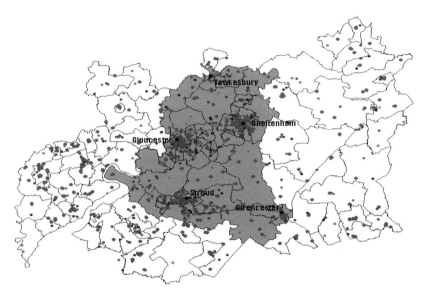

Figure 14.4 Map showing distribution of low-order services in Gloucestershire

Identifying the capacity of existing infrastructure to absorb further housing development

The thresholds identified by catchment area analysis (Table 14.4) can be used to determine whether existing infrastructure can absorb further housing development without expansion of the existing services. Generally, catchment area analysis found that some services were over-provided in smaller settlements (i.e. convenience stores, financial sector services, local government services, pubs, leisure centres, garages, banks and schools). The settlements in which services were over-provided were found in the Central Severn Vale and the more central areas of the Forest of Dean (Figure 14.5). In these settlements, the capacity of the infrastructure is not being fully utilised and housing development could be absorbed without further provision of services. Therefore, the strategic plan could highlight these settlements for future housing development.

In other smaller settlements, services are under-provided (i.e. supermarkets, textile manufacturers, theatres, clinics and colleges). These settlements may benefit from further housing provision which will support existing local services. The settlements in which facilities are under-provided have also been identified. The majority of these settlements can be found around Gloucestershire's periphery (Figure 14.6). All the settlements have less than 10,000 resident population, with the majority having under 2,000 residents. In these instances large-scale housing development could be used to support an increase in service provision in these outlying settlements, which in turn would improve access and increase self-containment. However, in the Forest

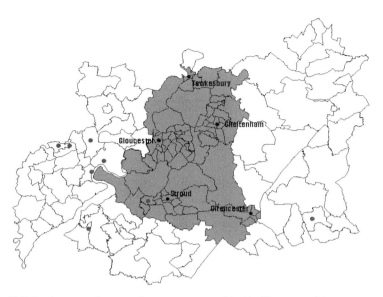

Figure 14.5 Settlement where services are over-provided in Gloucestershire

of Dean and the Cotswolds large-scale development of this kind would be moderated by landscape designations. Thus using catchment area analysis, we have been able to identify specific settlements that would benefit from expansion. This information can now be used in the formulation of the development plan.

Building new communities

The thresholds derived from catchment area analysis can also be used to indicate the quantity of housing required to sustain a variety of services in new communities. Thus, the thresholds can be used to determine economically sustainable mixes of development. Results from further analysis suggest that in settlements of a resident population size of at least 20,000, services representing most low and medium-order activities can be sustained. Previous research completed as part of the URBASSS Research Project also highlighted that in settlements of 25,000–100,000 residents, less total distances were travelled and there was a greater use of non-car modes, than in settlements with a smaller resident population (this observation has also been corroborated by Stead, 1996). This may suggest that travel is more contained in settlements with a population size of 25,000-100,000 residents. In terms of housing development, this finding suggests that new communities should aim to have between 25,000 and 100,000 residents, in order to sustain a mix of services, which allows more sustainable travel patterns.

In Gloucestershire, the concept of large-scale, new communities has to date proved politically unacceptable. Large areas of the county are protected by

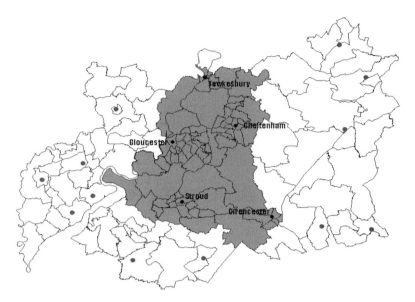

Figure 14.6 Settlements where services are under-provided in Gloucestershire

landscape designations (Areas Of Natural Beauty (AONBs), green belt and conservation areas) which restrict large-scale development, especially in the Forest of Dean and the Cotswolds. In addition, the development of new communities in isolation from existing development can be risky, in terms of attracting services and generating travel. However, it may be possible to develop larger new communities as part of a cluster of existing development, for example the 'Forest Cluster' (Figure 14.7).

Therefore, catchment area analysis and accessibility analysis can be used in combination to identify suitable location, scale and form of new housing development. Both techniques support the fact that access to services is better in the Central Severn Vale. However, catchment area analysis also provides some indication of where further housing development outside the Central Severn Vale could help sustain a wider range of services and encourage self-contained communities. It also indicates the level of service provision required in a new community, in order for it to be self-contained. Thus, both techniques support the presumption for development in central areas, but also provide a range of options for more sustainable housing strategies countywide.

Conclusion

At a strategic level, thresholds derived from Catchment Area Analysis (CAA) can be used to determine the under-or-over provision of services and provide benchmarks for development mix in new settlements. Accessibility analysis (AA) can be used to determine which areas have poor access to services and where cars provide the only option for access. Accessibility analysis can also

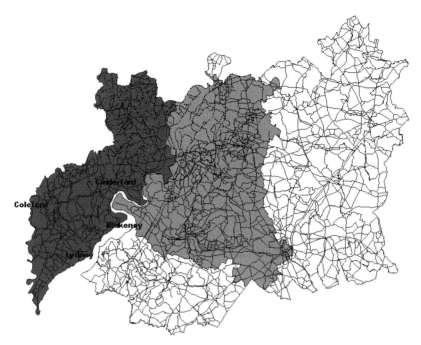

Figure 14.7 The Forest Cluster option

identify which services are less accessible using alternative modes and where increased provision is required. CAA can also be used to identify the impact of new development on current catchment areas as well as the spatial coverage of catchment areas created by new development, which may have economic and travel implications. Accessibility analysis can also be used to determine whether new development is accessible and if it encourages the use of non-car modes.

Thus, in practical terms the techniques developed here could be used to test strategic housing development policies outlined in plans based on accessibility and economic viability, at least two objectives of sustainability. Current methods used to identify the best locations for future housing development are complicated and resource intensive. The methods outlined in this chapter are simpler and less resource-consuming than their traditional counterparts. They are transparent and easily replicated with the correct data and spatial computer applications. They use secondary data sources, which are easily obtainable and require the use of spatial databases and software. Most local authorities now have access to both the secondary data and the spatial database and the software packages. Thus, the methods outlined are relatively user friendly.

However, all the methods identified here are indicative rather than prescriptive and by no means exhaustive. Although in some instances the methods are reasonably flexible and allow for some local variation, the information gained from them can only be used as a guide for future housing development and should not be used as a blueprint. In addition, access to local services, although an important sustainability issue, is by no means the only sustainability issue that needs to be considered when deciding on the location of future housing development. The methods developed here can be legitimately used as tools for determining the future sustainability of housing strategies, but need to be complemented with other tools which test other aspects of sustainability.

Note

1 The use of the term accessibility here refers to physical access (i.e. proximity of services).

Further Reading

Key reading should include the latest policy guidance for housing and transport *Department Transport and Environment* (1999f and 1999g). For a more detailed review and discussion of the methods developed in the chapter refer to Williams, J. (2000a). For greater understanding of the application of these methods refer to Williams, J. (2000b). For an increased depth of understanding of rural development strategies refer to Cloke, P.J. (1983). Read Stead, D., Williams, J. and Titheridge, H. (2000) for a more detailed explanation of the link between settlement size, service provision and travel. For further reading on the link between local service provision and use, refer to Farthing, S. (1994) and Farthing, S., Winter, J. and Coombes, T. (1996). Finally, for the most recent work on thresholds refer to Barton, H., Davies, G. and Guise, R. (1995).

15 The Sustainable Town Centre

Mark Thurstain-Goodwin and
Michael Batty

The Decline of the Town Centre

Our perception of a town is frequently based upon some image of its centre. Ever since settled agriculture began some ten thousand or more years ago, towns have been organised around focal points such as markets or centres of religious and political power. Economic necessity and the need to centralise control have been major forces in the development of town centres throughout history, and only during the past fifty years have these forces begun to change and weaken as the predominant mode of existence has become urban and the economy has become global. Since the world began to industrialise in the mid-eighteenth century, town centres have become focal points for capital investment of many kinds reflecting the diversification of the economy. This intensification of activity has been accompanied by rapid population growth through suburbanisation, and increasing amounts of transportation infrastructure and movement have come to symbolise the function of such centres. In short, the image of the city as being monocentric was reinforced during the industrial era, notwithstanding the fact that large metropolitan areas have been formed as centres and cities have coalesced.

This model of urban structure is no longer sustainable. As cities have grown simply through the accretion of new population, it has become increasingly difficult to develop systems that link the growing population to one major focal point, the centre. Without any of the developments in personal transportation (offsetting the decline of mass transit) which could serve the suburbs, traditional town centres would not have been sustainable. The fact that an increasingly wealthy population demands more space and better personal mobility simply exacerbates the problem of locating all major economic developments in and around town centres. When the industrial revolution began, centres diversified to capture much manufacturing activity as well as retaining and expanding their commercial and political roles; but as the economy itself became more specialised, activities began to decentralise to more suitable locations. In fact, the relative decline in the all-embracing role of the town centre during the past fifty years is as much due to the expansion of the economy into increasingly specialist niches as to the inability of such centres to service an ever-growing population.

One hundred years or more ago, populations were decanting from central cities in search of more space, and once the automobile became affordable, from the 1920s in the United States to the 1970s in Europe, cities began to spread out as industries moved to more accessible locations in the suburbs (Jackson, 1985). But it was not until the 1960s that the traditional role of the town centre as a market place came under real threat. In the United States, downtown areas became increasingly unattractive places in which to shop, as mass transit declined in the face of growing car ownership and as the freeway programme gathered pace, providing highly accessible locations for shopping and other services in and even beyond the suburbs. The old industrial cities of the East Coast of America were severely hit, with those stores traditionally associated with such centres all but disappearing in the early 1990s.

This is perhaps most clearly demonstrated by the decline of the local department store. Often owned by a pillar of the local business community, the department store was usually a symbol of the success and vitality of the town, to the extent that many of these shrines to consumption such as the John Wannamaker department store in downtown Philadelphia, are now national historic landmarks. Before 1940, every town in the US with a population in excess of 100,000 could expect to have its own, locally owned, department store. Over the next twenty-five years, many of these smaller department stores folded due to competition from strip shopping centres and the increasingly ubiquitous suburban shopping mall (Vance, 1987). Of course, a declining downtown merely accelerated the escape to the suburbs: suburban life became the lodestone of Twentieth-Century America. Downtowns continued to decline and were soon unable to sustain sufficient economic, social and cultural infrastructure to reverse the trend. They became increasingly void, characterised by urban decay, high concentrations of urban poor and a general sense of failure and hopelessness.

In contrast, the suburbs bloomed, many of them evolving into fully formed, mixed use ring communities of their own, the so-called 'Edge Cities' (Garreau, 1991). The same kinds of effect have happened in other western cities during the past twenty years. Slower growth in car ownership, less space, polarisation of minority populations in and around the older, inner areas of cities, and lower levels of real disposable income have restrained the process of decentralisation. Nevertheless, European cities in general and British cities in particular have experienced massive change in their town centres and inner areas, with dramatic decentralisation of retailing and office activities, in the face of a disappearing manufacturing sector. The 'donut' effect which is seen in so many American cities with large-scale abandonment of capital and infrastructure in and around their centres, is now characteristic of many British cities – stark evidence that the space economy is now very different from that which led to the development of the industrial city in the first place.

A Revolution in Retailing and Commerce

The kind of urban landscape that characterises North America – edge cities at all levels of the hierarchy, strip malls along major highways, abandoned inner areas and downtowns, decaying inner suburbs, and prosperous exurban residential communities – has not yet reached its apotheosis in the United Kingdom, and it is unlikely to do so. The economy is changing too rapidly now to repeat the kind of forces that have led to suburban America. Agriculture and manufacturing are disappearing as major employment sectors of the economy due to technological change while services of an increasing variety are beginning to dominate employment. This will have very substantial impacts on the location of activities and these are yet to work themselves through the space economy. Before we note these, however, it is worth reflecting on the waves of change in the retail sector which have done most to undermine the traditional sustainability of the British town centre, for these make clear the conflicts between the sustainability of retailing as an economic sector and the traditional locational focus of such activity.

Schiller (1986) identifies three distinct waves of retail development that have engulfed British cities. The first wave began as off-centre retailing – the out-of-town supermarket – during the 1970s. Larger and offering a much greater variety of goods than similar stores in town centres, these supermarkets enabled people to economise on time and cost, in that food shopping for a week or two could be compressed into a single trip. Key to their success was that they were not only readily accessible by car, but also that parking was relatively easy. By the end of the 1970s, supermarkets were firmly established in British retail culture, and their adverse impact on traditional food retailers was already being observed. Furthermore, increasing traffic meant that shopping in town centres became less and less a pleasant experience. As town centres struggled to adapt to these new shopping patterns, the second wave of out-of-town retailing started. This was dominated by Do-It-Yourself and other bulky goods retailers who needed to be large to carry a sufficient number of lines. With high rents in town centres, locations were preferred in peripheral locations where sites were generally cheaper and more accessible by car. Increasingly, these retail warehouses coagulated on parks providing a variety of retail offer and much lower prices than were possible in the town centre.

The influence of the move in government to more market-based policies which in turn led to less planning control during the 1980s is also manifest in Britain's town centres. Traditional employment in manufacturing and related services in and around town centres disappeared or decentralised to suburban locations, while the retailing sector itself was gradually being polarised into larger chains and ownerships. Many town centres fell into a vicious cycle of decline especially those hit hardest by national economic restructuring in old industrial areas such as the Midlands, the North East and South Yorkshire. These were soon to be hit by the third wave of out-of-town retailing – the shopping mall. The first to be opened in the United Kingdom was the MetroCentre in Gateshead, built within an Enterprise Zone (which offered its developers substantial financial incentives). It heralded a wave of mall development, largely on cleared industrial land (such as Meadowhall in Sheffield and Merry Hill in the West Midlands). To arrest the trend, in 1994 the government introduced various policy instruments to bolster town centres and to stem the flow of applications for out-of-town or out-of-centre retailing applications. The key policy instrument, Planning Policy Guidance Note 6 (PPG6) introduced a sequential test which specified that before being allowed to develop off-centre sites, retailer developers must demonstrate that there were no suitable sites in the town centre or in its immediate vicinity which could be developed instead. This sequential test has proved to be a very effective tool in halting the abandonment of town centres but it may prove to be too little, too late as the fundamental changes in the retail hierarchy occurred before its inception. There are other forces in the macro-economy which threaten to change the role of town centres more fundamentally.

New waves of change are now affecting the retail and related commercial sectors. As the population has grown more wealthy, as product lives have shortened and as new products have emerged, the kind of goods and places where they might best be purchased is changing. Time, increasingly, has come to dominate the purchase of goods with little product differentiation. Food shopping is declining in importance while entertainment is a growing function. But the most significant changes are in retailing in unconventional locations. The biggest growth sector is in the location of stores and franchises in other transit locations such as airports, bus and rail stations, petrol filling outlets and so on. There is also now substantial competition from virtual stores due to e-commerce. Online purchases for standard items like books and the reintroduction of home delivery services for those who shop for food on the Web are simply the tip of the iceberg as far as new forms of retailing go. Doubtless there will be some substitution effects which will affect location through e-commerce. Although these may not herald the end of transportation as we know it, they provide yet another competitive factor in our accessibility to the changing opportunity surface of retailing.

Defining Sustainability for Town Centres

Town centres exist, as the earliest economists from Smith to Marshall explained, because of locational economies of scale. Changes in the functions of such centres, their apparent decline, and their occasional growth into other economic niches might simply be taken as evidence of the changing economic milieu, no matter how painful. Much depends upon one's view of the economy. If the view is that the economy effectively adjusts to maximise efficiency, then it might be said that the kind of decentralised, polycentric urban landscape that is emerging, is itself sustainable and that no more needs to be said. The decline of the town centre would then be just a matter of balance within a general system which was optimising itself to remain sustainable (Krugman, 1996).

However, this misses the point in that there is much fixed capital in town centres which has intrinsic value and which has never been part of the economic process *per se*. Town centres historically are meeting places, places where there is social investment, where there is a well-developed infrastructure which has historic and sentimental value, and where there are functions of government which have lasting importance. In short, retailing and commerce are but two sets of activities in a much wider series of functions that need to take place at central locations. Moreover, when places rapidly decline, they become sinks for other problematic features of urban society such as rising crime and ethnic polarisation.

The example of downtown Detroit is instructive. Detroit lost its economic base in the 1960s and 1970s as the automobile industry restructured and as the remaining white population moved *en masse* to the western suburbs. The downtown is now largely abandoned despite some wonderful architecture, some elegant streets, good transportation infrastructure, and the continuing presence of government. These are largely intangible benefits and they have little effect in the face of large-scale movement to better and more spacious housing in the suburbs. Could downtown Detroit ever have been sustainable in the face of these wider forces? The answer is possibly 'yes', for many, if not most, rapid transitions in urban society are path dependent in that they are set off by individual events which consolidate themselves as the phenomenon intensifies. Although the Ford Motor Company's Renaissance Center was not able to reverse the decline, it is possible that with judicious urban management and some strategically timed investment, downtown Detroit might have suffered a better fate and readjusted itself to changed economic circumstances.

In the United States, the International Downtown Association (IDA) is helping to regenerate and revitalise many centres in the country, predominately through supporting initiatives led and funded by local businesses. In the United Kingdom, the public sector has a more dominant role, not only through the development of policy instruments (such as PPG6) but also through funding new ways of thinking about town centres. One of the most noteworthy contributions is URBED's *Vital and Viable Town Centres* Project (DoE, 1994c) which was the first comprehensive review of the state of town centres in the United Kingdom. This focused on the many intangible features of value in town centres, introducing the concept of the town centre health check, and emphasising the need to evaluate town centres across a wide range of indicators, other than those solely measuring economic health.

The health check, later enhanced by other organisations such as the ATCM (Association of Town Centre Management), offers a framework within which town centre stakeholders (local authorities, town centre managers, and local businesses) can measure how well their town centre is faring. Regeneration strategies that would make the town centre more able to withstand the kinds of forces we have identified above – to make the centre 'more sustainable' – should then be able to be developed. Currently, however, there is little consensus as to the range of regeneration strategies that might be adopted, often because the health check is poorly implemented but also, and perhaps more importantly, because the lessons learned from the process are rarely communicated (Thurstain-Goodwin *et al.*, 2000).

As a result, there is no general understanding of what a sustainable town centre might be, and certainly no consensus on how to achieve a required level of sustainability that improves or maintains its economic and social performance within the wider space economy. This is partly because sustainability itself is poorly understood. The widely quoted definition after Brundtland that sustainable development is 'development that meets the needs of the present generation without compromising the ability of the future generation to meet their own needs' (WCED 1987: 23) goes a very little way towards defining what a sustainable town centre might be. In fact, it might be argued that town centres should be left to decline if the needs of future generations are to be best met in terms of giving them greater opportunities to restructure their resources. To understand the sustainable town centre, everything from the environmental to the economic needs to be considered. Although we will offer a good working definition and approach in this chapter, there are perhaps two key reasons why a coherent view has been difficult to formulate. The first is that the processes contingent on the town centres are so complex, acting across a range of spacio-temporal scales, and the second is the dearth of good data or information on which to base any analysis. We will address these before we identify a way forward.

Compounding Sustainability: Questions of Scale and Information

Town centres exist in a wider hierarchy which reflects the spatial organisation of the economy and the extent to which the population is able to support specialist activities in different central places. We do not have a particularly well-worked out theory of central places which is consistent with the modern economy despite the contributions of the German location theorists. The theories that do exist seem to refer to a prior economic system based on market centres in an agricultural landscape rather than the kind of industrial landscape on which our present system of towns and their centres exists. The town centre occupies a pivotal role in the space economy, but the dynamics of the entire system are not well understood and therefore it is difficult to track the impacts of growth and decline on what is a richly connected system of places across many levels of spatial hierarchy. In short, we are unable to answer the question as to what the impact of a declining town centre might be on other centres within the hierarchy or (perhaps more importantly) what impact growth in one centre might have for growth in another. That there are complex inter-relationships there is no doubt.

This problem of scale is compounded by the increasing internationalisation or globalisation of the economy. A recent example in retailing is the decision by WalMart, the world's biggest retailer, to purchase the United Kingdom supermarket chain Asda and to drive prices down in way that is unprecedented in the United Kingdom food sector. The locational implications of this might be substantial but exactly how they pan out will depend on a complex interaction of prices in stores at different locations across a hierarchy of centres. The global scale is undoubtedly where the most fundamental processes that act on town centres currently exist. Notwithstanding the impact of multinationals on location decisions, issues such as a concern for climate change reflect decisions concerning local sustainability and the quality of air which in turn involves policies for reducing the population's dependence on the car. This kind of policy has significant effects on the ability of the population to access the town centre, and any other location, but the effects are not easy to unravel. What might appear to be a policy of increasing the advantage of town centres by increasing the cost of private automobile travel can often misfire for local reasons pertaining to the particular quality of facilities in and out of town centres, as well as complex domestic economics involving time and the ability to transport heavy goods.

Cross-continental influences, such as the location policy of multinational companies, are often more tangible. The closure of a major employer, or the relocation of a new company within the catchment area of a town centre, has major impacts on the potential revenue of that centre. Clearly, the distinction between the global and continental scale is moot (as is that between the continental and the national) and there is no easily definable breakpoint of scale. Retailing in the City of London, for example, is clearly dependent upon a range of scales from the global financial to the very local reflecting a continuum which is hard to cut at any point. Regionally the location of population and employment exerts a significant influence, with the development of new households and their location having a key effect on the sustainability of different town centre and related locations. Indeed, the redistribution of population and employment opportunity in the United

Kingdom over the next decade will change the catchment areas of many towns, and it is even possible that the population drift away from central locations will reverse itself.

As we approach the scale of the town centre, special local conditions become more apparent. At this scale, decisions by the planning authority and the content of the local plan will have a significant impact – housing allocations, the designation of sites for employment, and changes in transportation infrastructure all impinge on the town centre itself. Each local plan has policies laid out for the various town centres that fall within its remit, and at this scale, planners, town centre managers and local business interests must work together, often at the scale of the individual plot, to ensure that town centre development is both sensitive and sustainable. Indeed, it is at this scale, on the street or in the shop where we all, as consumers of the town centre, become aware of the localised expression of the plethora of influences and trends we have discussed. This is the scale at which health checks of town centres must eventually operate.

The relationship between these various trends and forces, both up and down the scale hierarchy, is difficult to identify. This is partly because the relationships are complex, but also because there has been little or no data with which to describe them, or any adequate tools to investigate them. Data in general about the urban economy is hard to assemble. The best data are contained within the decennial Population Census, but employment data on a fine scale are not within the public domain. Data on the financial structure of the space economy are almost non-existent, much of relevance not being collected in any case, despite the increased collection of financial data pertaining to consumers from market research and credit organisations. In fact, as we will report below, a start has been made in the United Kingdom to assemble a comprehensive database on retailing at a very fine spatial scale and our own ideas about the sustainable town centre to be reported here depend on this. But the data are not available at different cross-sections in time. There are no time series and temporal comparisons are essential if changes in the performance of centres are to be evaluated.

We now have available a comprehensive data set on the supply of economic activities at a local level – for unit postcodes which contain around 14–15 addresses. This data set covers floorspace, employment and expenditure of the facilities in question. This means that we are able, for the first time, to make comparisons between different places and agglomerations of places into centres, as well as examining the hierarchy of places and their relative positioning. As yet we are unable to develop measures of change over time which would let us assess changing performance, but this will be possible shortly. These new data sets are driven by the public need to evaluate the sustainability as well as the economic performance of the economy in general at a fine spatial scale and in town centres in particular. This approach was proposed by the Department of the Environment, Transport and the Region's

Retail Statistics Working Group and reiterated in the government response to the Parliamentary Select Committee report on *Shopping Centres and Their Future* (DoE, 1995e). This recommended the development of 'a nationally consistent system of retail data collection to be published at regular intervals', which 'should reduce significantly the costs being incurred in Public Inquiries and impact studies' (page 19).

The key issue in developing such a system involves defining the spatial and sectoral scope of town centres within their hierarchy. In one sense, this is equivalent to defining the sustainable town centre because the objectives of government in developing this census are to apply it to meaningful town centres which in turn reflect a wider range of activities than those which are purely economic (Thurstain-Goodwin and Batty, 1998; DETR, 1998l). The scale issue and the information vacuum which have traditionally plagued the analysis of town centres at long last seem to be resolvable. In the following section, we will outline the way we go about assembling data to define town centres which encompass indicators relating to sustainability. We will then explain how the methods could be applied to develop policies for sustainable town centres.

Sustainability Indicators for Town Centres: The Concept of Town Centredness

To define a town centre, we have identified four key factors, namely: economy (which integrates the various town centre employment types one might expect to find); property (the density of the buildings); diversity of use (based on the mix of employment types) and visitor attractions (which cover the general leisure and entertainment function of town centres). These four factors in themselves are composed of several other layers of data which we consider relevant to their definition. These various data types essentially reflect different components of what we consider a typical town centre to be and in this sense, we consider these data to be key elements in the definition of sustainability. The way we combine these measures or indicators is shown in Figure 15.1.

Our approach is one of representing these data as individual spatial indicators, ensuring that they are commensurate in that they can be compared with one another in their contribution to the fact that a place is a 'town centre', and that they are consistently measurable, hence combinable. The geographic variation of these factors is represented using a 20-metre grid. Surfaces are generated for each of these factors, normalised, and combined into a composite surface, which is an index describing the intensity of 'Town Centredness' at any point in the geographic space. From this, we are able to make different spatial definitions of the town centre as we will now illustrate.

Each indicator is normalised over a standard range and we then essentially compute a weighted average of these indicators, which gives us an average

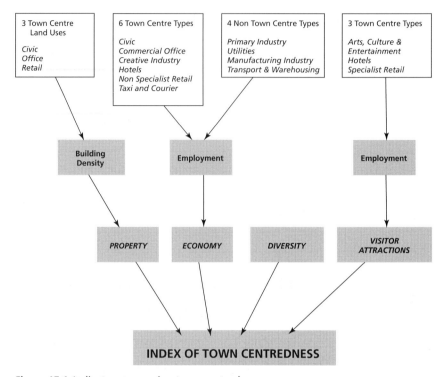

Figure 15.1 Indicators measuring town centredness

for each geographic location.[1] Weights are introduced because each indicator may have a different degree of importance to the definition of town centredness. The resulting weighted average can be interpreted as an index of town centredness. The index is then converted into a surface and by representing the composite surface as a series of contours, it is possible to identify a 'key contour' which best depicts the geographical extent of the town centre; various aggregate statistics can then be compiled for that Central Statistical Area (CSA). This methodology is discussed elsewhere (Thurstain-Goodwin and Unwin, 2000).

As well as being used to define Central Statistical Areas, the Intensity of Town Centredness surface can be interpreted as a combined sustainability indicator. The index was developed to describe the host of different activities that a town centre is expected to provide, although due to the component nature of the model and the linear combination of these components, other indicators could be added, or completely new sustainability indicators developed. As a result, should a particular town centre not contain all the possible activities and facilities that we regard as composing a 'typical' centre, the overall index level for that centre may well be lower than expected. This suggests that the index of a particular town can give us an indication of its overall health.

However, the relationship between the index level and health is not a simple one for the hierarchy of town centres is reflected within this relationship. For example, Figure 15.2 shows the surface for London within the M25. The centre of London is clearly visible as the white-hot core, interspersed with darker areas that correspond to the main parks. Secondary centres, such as Croydon, Bromley, Kingston, Brent Cross and Wood Green (among others) are clearly visible. Smaller centres further down the hierarchy are also clearly visible; as a result, we have identified at least 180 distinct centres within the M25. The mid-grey areas are in fact areas of town centre activity which do not comply with our criteria for a town centre but contain substantial town centre uses such as those found on radial shopping streets and in neighbourhood centres. Any assessment of the absolute value of this index needs to account for the effects of the position of a particular town centre within the retail hierarchy. Nevertheless, were we to consider the index values of two similar centres within the urban hierarchy, for example Kilburn and

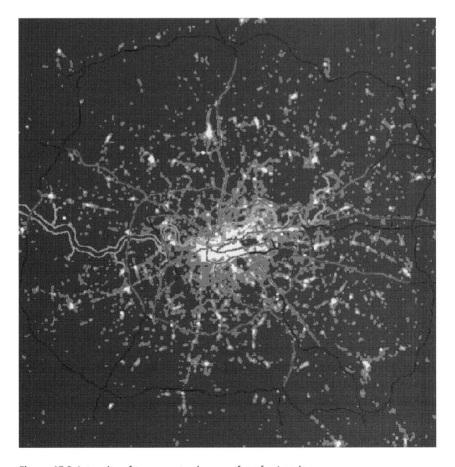

Figure 15.2 Intensity of town centredness surface for London

Cricklewood, we could perhaps begin to make some inferences about their relative health.

Since the index will be updated annually, it will be possible to track the performance of individual town centres through time. We may be able to identify the best centres of a given size or rather ways in which indicators should combine to provide an idealised sustainable centre. Comparing these ideal values to actual values and interpreting the differences provides a means for assessing how near any centre is to its ideal, while computing temporal differences in average sustainability gives some idea as to how the centre is faring with respect to its current condition.

Temporal Sustainability: Looking Back in Space and Time

There are many other questions that this framework enables. We may ask: to what degree does the spatial extent of a town centre vary through time? Does the index increase or decrease through time? Does the overall index for all centres in the system change through time? We can unpack these indicator values to any level of spatial resolution down to the fundamental unit postcode and perform analysis on various spatial (and temporal) slices of the data. We could infer, for example, that a town centre whose geographic extent remains constant through time, yet whose average index is falling, may be a town centre in decline. This sort of analysis is likely to be applicable to the town centres of London, for example, to evaluate the impact of the Bluewater Park Mall. It will be interesting, for example, to see how Central London competes with a development designed to be a direct competitor to it, by offering 'the best and most innovating retail destination in Europe'; a development that considers shoppers 'guests', retailers 'individuals' and which strives not to be a town centre, but rather a 'lifestyle village with a civic atmosphere, designed as a showcase for house, home, and fine food' (Bluewater, 1999).

There is no reason why these generic techniques which we have developed for town centres could not be adopted to explore more general issues of sustainability. Key to the success of this approach is the combination and integration of finely scaled data through their conversion to data surfaces. The techniques employed are more effective than traditional approaches to spatial data analysis (Thurstain-Goodwin and Unwin, 2000). Additionally, the component-based approach to overlay analysis which we have developed enables analysts to explore different aspects of sustainability and to generate new composite sustainability indicators. In this application, we have concentrated almost exclusively on the supply side of urban development but these techniques can be used to represent demand for facilities and ways of bringing demand and supply together. Evaluating mismatches will form an important extension to this approach.

One of the great features of analysing socio-economic datasets as surfaces is that they can be explored using techniques that geomorphologists use to analyse landscapes. The landscape metaphor opens up a host of different techniques that could be used. For example, Dykes *et al.* (1998) have used various landscape techniques to understand population data. Landscape analysis also sheds light on the importance of scale when analysing surfaces. Schumm and Lichty (1965: 110) argue that different geomorphological processes can be seen to act on a landscape at different spatial and temporal scales. More precisely, that 'as the dimensions of time and space change, cause and effect relationships may be obscured or even reversed, and the system itself may be described differently'. Instead of considering geomorphological processes (such as erosion), we can start to identify the geographic processes that act at different spatial scales. For example, linear town centre development on the main arterial routes is clearly discernible in Figure 15.2. This reflects how London developed along its main roads and railways in the nineteenth and early twentieth centuries.

The development of city form is clearly a long-term process, and only becomes manifest when looking at the data at such a large spatial scale. It is likely that other longer-term processes, which can take years to work themselves out and whose impact is deeply embedded within urban form, can only be observed at this spatial scale. In order to understand the broad economic restructuring of the United Kingdom over the past thirty years, for example, it would be necessary to examine the spatial evidence at the regional or national level. Although some of these processes will be evident when looking at the town or town centre in more detail, it is simply not possible to generalise since every space is unique.

This can be illustrated by looking at the town centre of Wolverhampton (which we show in Figure 15.3). The town centre is broadly defined by a ring road which was completed in the 1980s with a covered shopping centre – the Mander Centre – sitting at its heart. When we look at the town centredness surface for Wolverhampton though, we see that the town centre protrudes beyond the ring road to the North West, encapsulating the Chapel Ash area of the town. This does not represent a new strip of development, squeezing out from the constrained town centre, but is rather a vestige of the town centre before the ring road was developed; the town centre originally developed in a linear manner along the main Shrewsbury to Birmingham road, which runs north-west to south-east. Thus, by examining the town centre at this spatial scale, we are able not only to identify the main process that has shaped Wolverhampton's town centre in recent years (the ring road) but also to gain clues about its past. Echoes of the past are preserved in the built form, and can be observed when looking at the data surface at this spatial scale.

Were we to look at the scale of the individual street, or plot, the processes acting on the town centre once again become quite different. Although it is clear that functional scale makes a difference to the role of activities in town

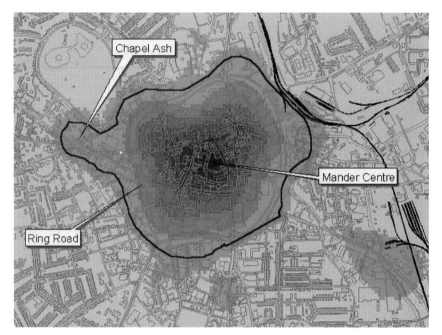

Figure 15.3 The town centredness surface for Wolverhampton with the 'Key Contour'

centres, the more detailed spatial scales within a centre also impact on questions of sustainability; particularly issues involving aesthetics, community, sense of place and environmental quality. In broad terms, we could argue that as the spatial scale of our analysis increases, so does the temporal scale of the process acting on that area. Clearly, this is not always true, since developments that can be observed at the micro scale (such as the development of Bluewater Park) can have impacts at the regional, and indeed national level. However, the advantage of surface analysis within a GIS environment is that it is relatively straightforward to explore effects at different spatial scales. This is its attraction for sustainability analysis in general.

Conclusion

As we have shown, the concept of the sustainable town centre is not new. It can be best understood as a process by which town centres are able to survive in a highly competitive battle with forces in the economy which seek to decentralise activity, primarily for reasons of economic efficiency. Thus the critical issue in this context, like all approaches to sustainability, involves weighing up the importance of non-tangible factors whose value is uncertain, can rarely be quantified, and are likely to be controversial in the political sense. What we have sought to do here is to illustrate a method whereby we can develop an index of sustainability, in this case for town centres or rather for any place that contains town centre-like uses. In this way we can begin to define agglomerations which have distinct meaning as centres and which depend upon the juxtaposition of activities which have economic as well as non-economic returns to scale. In one sense, since our method defines an index of town centredness for every place, it does not prejudge the location of town centres. As a diagnostic tool suggesting the importance of agglomerations and concentrations, it provides a means of assessing the very idea of the town centre itself. It can be used to identify many other kinds of centre, such as retail cores and government centres. The particular combination of factors that we used, however, is geared to identifying what are commonly accepted as being town centres in the United Kingdom.

To use these tools effectively, we need to look at the way town centres are changing through time. Indeed, the threat to town centres posed by the new economy and by very high levels of choice concerning personal mobility is based on the dynamism of the economy. The idea of the sustainable town centre is one which is both pivotal within the urban system, and also responsive to changes within that system. Although we have emphasised how complex the interactions are within such systems, the approach we have demonstrated gives important insights into the way the retail hierarchy is functioning, as well as the way the morphology of town centres is changing in response to new forms of retailing and leisure. Finally, our approach enables us to look more generally at sustainability in time and space, linking other critical urban systems such as transport and population to the retail space economy. In this sense, the sustainable town centre serves as the heartbeat of the sustainable town.

Note

1 Formally we define each indicator as $S^k_i(t)$ where i is the location, k the indicator type, and t the time at which the measurement takes place. Each indicator may have a different degree of importance to the definition of town centredness and thus we introduce weights w^k_i which are then used to compute a weighted average of the form $S_i(t) = \Sigma_k w^k_i S^k_i(t)$ which is the classic form in which sustainability indicators are combined. This weighted average or index of town centredness is then converted and displayed as a surface.

Further Reading

A good contemporary explanation of the forces at work in the modern metropolis which is leading to the continued demise of town centres, sprawl and the rise of the mega-mall is Joel Garreau's *Edge Cities* (1991). This book recounts in vivid detail the explosion of out-of-town retailing in particular in North America. In Britain, the report by URBED (the Urban and Economic Development Consultancy) for the Department of the Environment *Vital and Viable Town Centres: Meeting the*

Challenge in 1994 highlights the problem of raising the quality of town centre environments, while the special issue of the journal *Built Environment* titled 'Town Centres' edited by Christina Tomalin (1998, volume 24) provides a variety of papers which deal with different aspects of the British town centres' problem. Finally, the methodology presented in this chapter is developed in more detail in the report *Town Centres: Defining Boundaries for Statistical Monitoring: Feasibility Study* (DETR, 1998l).

16 Conflicts and Resolutions

David Banister

Introduction

Where does all this leave us? There is the pessimistic view that sustainable development is no more than rhetoric as the economic imperatives will always prevail over the wider concerns of the environment. Perhaps the nearest the economists come to recognising sustainable development is through sustainable growth where there is still a commitment to the narrow concept of growth and value added. Where optimism may prevail is in following Daly (1991) in seeing the economy as part of the wider environment. Yet even here, there are dangers and strong barriers to the effective implementation of sustainable development. This is where planning has a key, perhaps an instrumental role, as some 70 per cent of all energy consumption is influenced by planning (Pinnegar, 1999). In this chapter, we present some of the main barriers to the effective implementation of sustainable development and sketch out the next steps in formulating the means by which they can be overcome. If planning is to take the lead, it is here that it must be in the vanguard of creative discussion and positive action.

All activities consume resources, but cities seem to provide the greatest oppportunities for sustainable development in the United Kingdom and elsewhere (Banister, 1998; Urban Task Force, 1999). Some 70–80 per cent of the world's population lives in cities, yet the total 'ecological footprint' required to sustain a city extends far beyond the physical boundaries of the city itself (Box 16.1).

To keep the use of resources and the production of waste within reasonable limits, the European Environment Agency (1995) proposes a set of five sustainability principles, all of which are central to the new 'look' planning, particularly as it relates to cities:

1 Cities must be designed and managed within the limits imposed by the natural environment – environmental capacity.

David Banister

Box 16.1

In terms of actual daily resources, the average European city of 1 million inhabitants requires:
  2,000 tonnes of food
  11,500 tonnes of fossil fuels
  320,000 tonnes of water
and produces
  1,600 tonnes of solid waste
  25,000 tonnes of CO_2
  300,000 tonnes of waste water

Source: European Environment Agency, 1995

2 Interventions should be reversible so that cities can adapt to new challenges and demands in terms of economic activities without impairing the environmental capacity.

3 Cities should be resilient and be able to respond to external pressures.

4 The maximum economic benefit should be obtained from each unit of resources (environmental efficiency), whilst at the same time ensuring maximum welfare efficiency.

5 Resources and services should be made accessible to all urban inhabitants.

These principles in turn lead to a series of goals that should be achieved if cities are to be sustainable (European Environment Agency, 1995):

- the minimisation of consumption of space and natural resources;
- the rationalisation and efficient management of the urban flows;
- the protection and enhancement of the health of the urban population;
- the maintenance of equal access to resources and services;
- the enhancement of cultural and social diversity.

The first two goals encompass economic and environmental criteria, and the last three address the social dimensions of sustainable development. It should be noted that there is no explicit mention here of the intergenerational issues which commonly form the basis of sustainable development definitions (e.g. see the classic Brundtland definition in the World Commission on Environment and Development (WCED 1987) and Box 16.2).

To achieve these objectives, what must be done in our cities and more generally in the country as a whole, and who is responsible? It is here that planners can take the lead in the achievement of sustainable development, through measures such as the provision of affordable housing, the promotion of strategies that lead to new jobs, encouraging the provision of local services

Box 16.2

Sustainable development has conventionally been seen as comprising three interconnected components (Munasinghe, 1993):

Economic components – Maintaining maximum flows of income, while at least maintaining the stock of assets or capital that yields these benefits. Questions are raised here about maintaining the different types of capital (production, human and natural) and their mutual substitutability. Also needs to address concepts of uncertainty, irreversibility and the possibility of catastrophic collapse.

Ecological components – Preserving the resilience and ability of natural and physical systems to adapt to change, including systems such as cities and city regions. Questions relating to biodiversity and the contribution of small systems to the global ecosystem are critical.

Socio-cultural components – Includes concepts of intragenerational and intergenerational equity, the rights of future generations and the elimination of poverty. Questions here over political stability, the reduction of destructive conflicts and good governance are all crucial.

and facilities, and through the maintenance and enhancement of open space within cities. Through the creation of high quality urban environments with vibrant centres offering a diversity of opportunities, the pressures will return for urban living with people wanting to move back to the cities – this is the only means by which sustainable lifestyles can be achieved (Figure 16.1).

The Barriers

The arguments for sustainable development seem at all levels to be strong and there are no real problems with the introduction of any of the measures outlined, yet real progress has been disappointing. It is here that the problems of implementation become apparent as there is a great uncertainty about priorities and responsibilities at all levels of decision-making. These barriers are not insurmountable, but present real difficulties in achieving sustainable development, with the fear that poor implementation may be counter-productive. Hence, there is a natural caution with decisions being taken incrementally rather than seeing how they might form part of the overall picture. To take the current common parlance, the joined-up thinking on sustainable development is missing.

Some of the barriers to successful implementation of sustainable development are presented here under three headings:

- Barriers 1 – Unresolved debates on the city (Table 16.1);
- Barriers 2 – Unresolved debates on the regions (Table 16.2);

David Banister

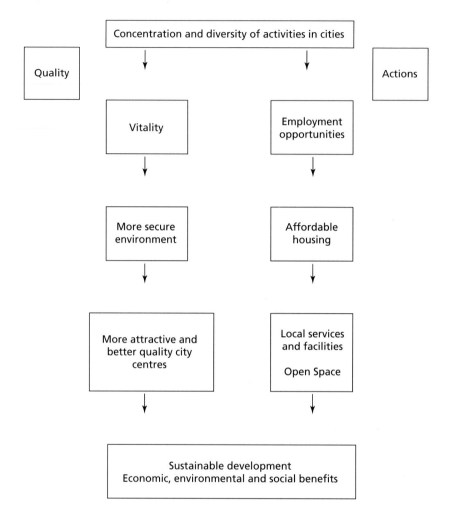

Figure 16.1 The virtuous path towards sustainable development

- Barriers 3 – Institutional and organisational debates (Table 16.3).

It should be made clear that these tables are illustrative and they mainly concentrate on green issues, not on social issues such as affordability, crime, security and safety. Even so, the lists given here may seem formidable and in themselves a clear rationale as to why progress towards sustainable development has not been more rapid. Yet, many of the barriers identified could quite easily be overcome with minor changes in legislation or organisation. For example, there could be a much clearer national policy on renewable energy production (together with the appropriate funding mechanisms) and on incinerator power generation. Development plans could be extended to cover renewable energy, the potential for combined heat and power (CHP), exploitation of the commercial potential of waste management, and new forms of recycling.

In other areas, there needs to be a much closer sharing of responsibilities between the various agencies (e.g. planning and transport), between plan making and implementation, and between different agencies (e.g. planners and developers). These changes can be easily introduced and clear progress can be made. But underlying the relative simplicity of these more cosmetic changes are two fundamental questions that have not yet been resolved or

Table 16.1 Barriers 1 – Unresolved debates on the city

	Importance	Difficulty	Resolution
Land use and reuse in cities and urban areas			
1. Much of the available brownfield land is derelict and the costs of remediation are high, particularly where the land is contaminated.	4	3	No problems
2. Questions relate to liability for pollution of land and its remediation. Balance for developers between risks and returns.	4	4	Primary focus
3. Redevelopment of the first generation of peripheral development sites now being considered	3	2	Second round
4. Availability of greenfield sites in car accessible locations. These are easier and cheaper to develop and are likely to compete successfully with mobile capital.	5	3	No problems
Town centre attractiveness			
1. Debate over densities in town and city centres, and the reuse of existing buildings through conversion and encouragement of mixed use.	4	3	No problems
2. Role of the car (and parking) in creating attractive centres and in encouraging people to take their business elsewhere – abandoning the town centres with loss of trade to competing car access centres.	3	5	Second round
3. Image of the town centre and feeling that there is no ownership of local facilities and mechanisms for co-ordinating and managing change.	3	4	Second round
4. Leaving important principles of detailed design until too late in the planning and development process.	4	2	No problems

Notes: Ratings given on high importance (5) to low importance (1) and levels of difficulty (high = 5 and low = 1).

'No problems' means high importance and low difficulty in implementation.

'Second round' actions means low importance and high (or low) difficulty – less crucial.

'Primary focus' means high importance and high difficulty. It is here that the greatest risks are involved, but also where the greatest returns are to be found.

even seriously addressed – education and learning for sustainable development, and allocation and acceptance of responsibilities for actions. Both are
of crucial importance to planning and to sustainable development.

The purpose of these tables is to give a flavour of the unresolved debates
at the three different levels to which planning has an input, and to give some
indication of the importance and difficulty of action. The resolution column
is the reconciliation of the importance with the difficulty. Actions which can
(or should) have been taken already are in those areas where importance is
high and degree of difficulty is low. Basically, this is where implementation
is relatively easy, but care is needed to ensure that sustainable development
is the main objective. The second group of actions are those of high importance and high difficulty – these should be the primary focus for new
initiatives. They probably include high risk and high return strategies, but
form the basic group of planning policies that must be addressed and resolved

Table 16.2 Barriers 2 – Unresolved debates on the regions

	Importance	Difficulty	Resolution
Regional guidance and responsibilities			
1. Unclear now which agency has responsibility for sustainable development at the regional level – the Regional Development Agencies, the Government Offices, the Regional Planning Agencies, or the Counties.	4	2	No problems
2. Important decisions must be taken on encouraging inward investment, new housing construction and even a new generation of new towns.	5	4	Primary focus
3. Unclear on the key determinants of good practice in terms of settlement size, density and location. Whether town cramming and urban infill (politically unpopular) should be favoured over new development (politically unpopular)	4	4	Primary focus
4. The importance of sustainable development when balanced against other priorities such as employment creation and economic growth, particularly in the less prosperous parts of the country.	5	4	Primary focus

Notes: Ratings given on high importance (5) to low importance (1) and levels of
difficulty (high = 5 and low = 1).

'No problems' means high importance and low difficulty in implementation.

'Second round' actions means low importance and high (or low) difficulty – less crucial.

'Primary focus' means high importance and high difficulty. It is here that the greatest
risks are involved, but also where the greatest returns are to be found.

if sustainable development is to become a reality. The final group of actions are of low importance and high difficulty. Here, the returns are lower and these options could be put in a secondary group where they could be addressed at some time in the future. The key conclusion here is to assess all the options, and to first take action on those strategies that are important and easy to implement, together with those that are important and difficult to implement.

In the three tables, we have identified three resolution types and twenty unresolved debates. Eight of these come in the 'no problem' group, which in principle are not difficult to implement. Clear guidance can be given on reuse of brownfield land in cities, together with the possibilities of a greenfield levy that can then be used to help with the remediation costs. Direction is also required on liability, both in the shorter and the longer term, as this has proved contentious in the United States (see Issue 2 in Table 16.1). Guidance on the sequential approach to development is now clear (through PPG13, PPG12 and PPG3), and the debate on density and mixed use has been clarified through research (e.g. Breheny, 1992b; Banister *et al.*, 1997; and DETR, 1998b), and new advice from government (e.g. PPG13). Even the detailed design issues are being thought about in terms of sustainable development (DETR, 1998b). At the regional level, the main question is over the new responsibilities which have been allocated to the various agencies. In time these will be resolved and PPG11 on regional planning has helped to establish both priorities and responsibilities. The broader institutional and organisational debates (Table 16.3) present a different set of issues on integrated approaches, funding availability and fuel prices. In principle, all these questions can and should be resolved fairly easily with clear direction from national government on standards (e.g. through the Building Regulations), policy on vacant land and land assembly, and a consistent policy on fuel prices and energy efficiency.

A further nine unresolved debates come in the 'primary focus' group. Interestingly, most of them are institutional and organisational concerns (Table 16.3) and regional issues (Table 16.2), rather than actions that can be taken at the city level. At the city level, there is the question of liability for remediation of (contaminated) brownfield land. At the regional level, there are issues relating to housing allocations, the key determinants of sustainable settlements, and the priority allocated to sustainable development objectives when these are set against other policy priorities. Further research is necessary, but the key decisions relate to policy direction and planning actions. If clear and consistent guidance can be given on each of these three questions, then the opportunity for real progress towards sustainable development can be grasped. Decisions made now will determine the land use and development strategies for the next twenty years, which in turn will be instrumental in determining planning's contribution towards the achievement of sustainable development.

But it is at the institutional and organisational level that many of the key changes must be facilitated (Table 16.3). There may be a strong case for a reintegration of responsibilities and powers between and within agencies, to establish common agendas and priorities. All parties must be involved in that process, together with supporting actions related to technical skills, information and advice (including the exchange of data and ideas). In addition, macro economic policy changes may be needed to switch taxation away from labour (production) towards consumption. It is at this level that the key changes are needed if sustainable development is to become central to planning.

The final group of three unresolved issues come in the 'second round' list as being of less importance. Local actions feature here, including the reuse of peripheral development sites, the role of the car in the city and the image of the town centre (Table 16.1). It is through the identification of the main questions, the investigation of their importance and the resolution of the key elements that real progress towards sustainable development can be established. Underlying much of the discussion above is the strong message that education and learning have an instrumental role in the process, and it is these issues that we now address.

Education and Learning for Sustainable Development

Underlying much of the debate above is a healthy professional scepticism about any new radical thinking on the planning and development process. Part of this scepticism is to be welcomed, as there are no clear solutions to sustainable development. But less reassuring is the lack of knowledge about the fundamental nature of some of the thinking required to achieve sustainable development. The opportunities for training and learning about sustainable development are not readily available, the debates are still controversial (see Tables 16.1, 16.2, 16.3), and the necessary supporting skills, both technical and communication, are not present. It is here that institutions of research and education must take a clear lead both in the debates on planning and sustainable development, and in educating planners and others into the new agenda of responsibility and decision-making on sustainable development.

Such a process cannot be achieved overnight, but requires radical innovation, and it must involve all stages in education and learning through schools, universities and continuing professional development. What then are the basic components for any such package?

- Information on the risks and costs of pursuing alternative development paths, whether they address sustainable development or not.
- Involvement in and contributions to the debates from all affected parties.
- Building public support for political action.

At the most simple level, behaviour can be changed through the encouragement of actions which are supportive of change (e.g. recycling), and through clear signals on pricing (e.g. raising taxes on consumption), and capacity (e.g. the landfill tax and the decrease in landfill capacity).[1] More fundamentally, education and learning should be directed at promoting attitudinal changes that are sufficiently strong to generate behavioural change (McKenzie-Mohr, 1999). This level of change is much harder to achieve, as it requires people to switch from just viewing decisions in terms of economic self-interest to an equal concern over the wider environmental and social implications of their decisions (Munasinghe, 1993).

McKenzie-Mohr (1999) sets out what he calls a pragmatic approach to encouraging sustainable behaviour through community-based social marketing (see www.closm.com). The four stages are:

1 Identify barriers to sustainable behaviour, both internal and external.

2 Design a strategy that uses behavioural change tools to encourage commitment and involves direct contact.

3 Pilot the strategy with a small group.

4 Evaluate the impact of the programme.

This approach uses the expert to generate prompts and to establish norms for sustainable behaviour. Its purpose is to gain commitment and create effective messages that can then be applied more generally through a process of social diffusion. Such an approach has been used in schools in Canada to encourage trip reduction programmes and improve safety. This is very much a grassroots approach, tackling the problems of sustainable development from a community perspective and trying to influence short-term (and longer-term) behaviour of school children.

However, one doubts whether such an approach would be equally effective in influencing the location preferences of house builders or the decisions of firms as to whether they should invest in new clean technology to reduce their levels of emissions. Yet the same sorts of involvement must be a feature of all parties as each has a responsibility for action. Effective outcomes will only be achieved if all parties (or at least the key actors) understand and support actions leading towards sustainable development.

In addition to directing change at adults, it is often argued that young people should be directly targeted (Scott and Skea, 1998). There is a wide concern among young people, but programmes in schools and on the media may help to engender a sense of frustration and hopelessness, rather than action. It is the creation of a sense of responsibility that seems to be key to successful change in behaviour, so that young people have the self-confidence to think about solutions rather than the problems.

However, many people are reluctant to change their behaviour and they rationalise this inaction in two ways. Environmental problems are often seen to be of global and national importance rather than something in which individuals can actually have a role to play – their small contribution is insignificant when compared with the scale of action required. So it is not important that they do anything apart from expressing a compassionate concern about the environment. The second element concerns governance and the lack of any respect or social contract between individuals and government. This attitude must be changed so that individual responsibility is taken and encouraged as an integral part of the sustainable development problem and its solution. Equally, there must be respect and co-operation between individuals and governments so that commitment is manifest through action from both the public and private sectors to reinforce the strong verbal commitment to the environment (Harrison *et al.*, 1996).

In their comparative study of the United Kingdom and the Netherlands, Harrison *et al.* (1996) describe the activities of Global Action Plan, where volunteer households undertake a six-month programme of activities to reduce consumption of energy, waste, water, shopping and transport. About 15,000 households in the United Kingdom have participated, but in the Netherlands Global Action Plan has organised groups of eight to ten households into Ecoteams so that they can adopt changes over a six-month period, assisted by experts (Staats and Harland, 1995). The experts suggested some ninety-three behavioural changes, with forty-six of these being accepted to some degree. Better practice has been developed in energy and water consumption and waste production in the home, with reductions of 16 per cent in electricity use, 10 per cent in water use and 27 per cent in waste. They were even able to reduce car kilometres travelled by 18 per cent. These levels of reduction were maintained over a longer monitoring period of a further nine months. The Ecoteam households tend to be already 'greener' than average, so when these results in the Netherlands can be grossed up to the population as a whole, they are even more striking. There would be a reduction in waste production of 70 per cent, with savings of 33 per cent of electricity, 18 per cent on water, and 22 per cent on transport (Staats and Harland, 1995). When these actions were placed in the United Kingdom context, there was less support, particularly on the potential for transport reduction (Harrison *et al.*, 1996). Changes in household travel patterns required strong supporting measures, such as pricing, taxation changes and environmental regulation. In both countries, there was ambivalence about the science of climate change and the health impacts of local pollution, and a great uncertainty over the social problems raised by environmental concerns. There was also a strong perception that industry, the public sector and government should take the lead role and demonstrate their own commitment to environmental improvement through example.

Sustainable Consumption and Building Sustainable Communities

The main conclusions from this chapter are that clear priorities for action need to be established, together with the necessary supporting structures to ensure consistency in approaches. Although the focus has been on actions that should be taken to achieve sustainable development from a planning perspective, it is accepted that pricing policies set at the national, regional and local levels are also instrumental in sending the right messages to all actors. The agenda is sufficiently important to involve the full range of policy measures, including ecological tax measures and tradable permits (Skea and Sorrell, 1999). Actions to achieve sustainable consumption patterns are an essential component of sustainable development and would include:

- The encouragement of real change and best practice in business and industry through changing current practice and the setting of realistic (but challenging) targets so that the appropriate investment decisions can be taken. The achievement of these targets must be linked to advantages in terms of the company's competitive position in the market.

- Individuals need to be given relevant and accurate information so that they can take action, including major purchasing decisions on homes, cars and consumer durables. It is apparent that more detailed information could be made available through ecolabelling and environmental advertising, including the distance that products have travelled and the energy used in distribution. This could be facilitated by local authorities in the form of environmental audits of homes and shops, or through web-based services. There is a new role here for consumer organisations not just to inform, but to be more active in creating change.

- Changing patterns of behaviour in companies and individuals relate to company strategy and lifestyles. The demonstration value of good practice needs to be monitored and disseminated to show what can be achieved in terms of change. This is particularly important at present in terms of patterns of mobility and the growth in unsustainable long-distance travel.

- The power of advertising and brand values is also important (Scott and Skea, 1998), and new opportunities may be available to encourage sustainable consumption patterns. Value must be added to incorporate sustainability into brand marketing, not locking people into unsustainable lifestyles (e.g. in terms of location decisions or car dependence), and in promoting products with small ecological footprints.

- Although many of these actions relate to individuals and firms, it is through the integration of these in the full range of policy measures that progress will be made. All actions must include an environmental element so that these implications can be assessed alongside the conventional economic and social costs and benefits. If there are negative environmental impacts

Table 16.3 Barriers 3 – Institutional and organisational debates

	Importance	Difficulty	Resolution
Institutional and organisational issues			
1. Fragmentation of responsibilities and powers between the different agencies (public and private) and within these agencies.	5	5	Primary focus
2. The different agencies have their own agendas which are increasingly divergent rather than convergent.	4	4	Primary focus
3. Failure of the development industry to respond imaginatively to sustainable development concerns.	3	3	Primary focus
4. Absence of integrated approaches to building standards (including materials, ventilation, lighting, thermal efficiency, and orientation), power generation and recycling.	4	2	No problems
5. Lack of funding and/or tax support to encourage the use of vacant land for housing and other uses, or the powers to allow land assembly for development.	4	2	No problems
6. Lack of professional or political support for energy efficiency – often combined with the lack of technical competence, information and advice, skills and training means that it is a low priority.	5	5	Primary focus
7. Current taxation system taxes production (labour) rather than consumption (resources) – staff levels are minimised rather than material inputs.	4	4	Primary focus
8. Consistently low fuel prices which encourages consumption rather than saving – expenditure on energy efficiency often a prime target for cost savings.	4	2	No problems

Notes: Ratings given on high importance (5) to low importance (1) and levels of difficulty (high = 5 and low = 1).

'No problems' means high importance and low difficulty in implementation.

'Second round' actions means low importance and high (or low) difficulty – less crucial.

'Primary focus' means high importance and high difficulty. It is here that the greatest risks are involved, but also where the greatest returns are to be found.

from policy measures, these must be identified at the decision stage so that mitigating measures can then be taken at the same time as implementation.

Land use planning is a crucial determinant of sustainable development as it actually translates the concepts and ideas into reality. It is really the means by which economic, social and environmental concerns can be realised, but it is more than mere control. The new agenda includes creative thinking and dialogue with all actors concerned with the development process, new forms of partnership, new sources of funding, new structures for organisation, decision-making and implementation, and the creation of support for real action. The planning system has a unique role and opportunity to shape our lives and to move society towards the elusive goal of sustainable development. It is seeing how planners, in conjunction with other decision-makers, can work together to ensure that the effectiveness of all actions is greater than those taken individually. This means that there must be a clear vision of what constitutes a sustainable development for each local authority, and how we can move from where we are now towards that vision. The vision itself is not fixed, but will change over time, but the direction of change must be clear. Not all locations will have the same vision or the same set of solutions, but there needs to be common approaches, the constructive interchange of ideas, and new thinking about how sustainable development can be achieved – this is the new challenge for planning in the twenty-first century.

Note

1   Currently the United Kingdom dumps 27 million tonnes of household waste each year, and this figure is forecast to double in twenty years (to 2020). The vast proportion of this (93 per cent) ends up in landfill sites. The recent EU Directive has stipulated that the amount of United Kingdom household waste put in landfill sites must be cut by 35 per cent to 2020. At present about 7 per cent of household waste is recycled in the United Kingdom as compared with Germany and Canada where between 50 and 80 per cent of household waste is recycled (see www.integra.org.uk).

Further Reading

The following books provide good sources for further reading: Banister, D. (1998) 'Barriers to the implementation of urban sustainability', *International Journal of Environment and Pollution* 10, 1: 65–83; Banister, D. (1999b) 'Planning more to travel less', *Town Planning Review* 70, 3: 313–38. Central Government publications on the subject include: Department of the Environment Transport and the Regions (1999) Review of Sustainable Education Initiatives in the Workplace, Report Commissioned by the Workplace Working Group of the Advisory Panel, London: DETR, available at *www.environment.detr.gov.uk/sustainable/ei/workplace/01.htm*; Department of the Environment Transport and the Regions (2000) Our Towns and Cities: Delivering an Urban Renaissance, London: DETR, available at *www.regeneration.detr.gov.uk/policies/ourtown/cm4911/02.htm* and Urban Task Force (1999) *Towards an Urban Renaissance*, London: E & FN Spon, June.

17 Concluding Remarks: Towards a Sustainable Future

Sue Batty

The idea of planning for a sustainable future, as the contributors in this book have pointed out, has its roots in many different kinds of social intervention which have emerged as distinct perspectives on how to manage the modern world. Indeed, the very concept of planning itself, and certainly institution-alised physical planning which in the West dates from the mid-nineteenth century, is tied up with the general objective of balancing conflicting interests if the collective good is to be realised in terms of a sustainable future. Benton Mackay's 'planning for habitability' which was dominant in the rise of regional planning in North America and Western Europe (Glikson, 1955) from the 1920s was little different from our current concern for 'planning for sustainability'. In fact, historically, physical planning was far closer to a concern for a balanced ecology than it is today although our concern for linking the social with the natural through physical planning is being reawakened once again through this focus on sustainability. It may even be as Meyerson and Rydin (1996) so cogently point out, that this heightened interest in questions of sustainability marks a sea change in the way we think about management of modern global society. This is part and parcel of an increased awareness that the complexities, interdependencies, and possibilities of entirely unanticipated indirect impacts are far greater than they have ever been before.

In this book, we have not attempted to provide a primer on the content of what might constitute sustainable plans. Instead we have focused on the development of the processes through which various institutions might progress the development of sustainable cities and rural areas. We have been largely concerned with how these goals might be articulated and how institutions might respond to their realisation. To this end, we first sketched the institutional context in its social and political setting in the first part of the book, illustrated how this context was responding to particular social and economic issues such as density and congestion in cities in terms of waste, transport, housing, and employment, and only then did we provide examples of how such plans might be measured, modelled and designed in terms of spatial instruments. No book on sustainability in planning can broach all the issues which spin through the natural to the social and economic in different political contexts. But in this conclusion, we will point to where our arguments connect up to issues of sustainability that we have not tackled here.

In general debate, sustainability is often defined in terms of two key themes: first, resource depletion in the face of rapid growth, particularly population growth; and, second, problems of pollution which are associated with the exploitation of resources. In recent years, these two issues are perceived as positively feeding upon one other; rapid growth is clearly leading to resource depletion which appears unsustainable in that alternative sources do not seem feasible, while the very rapidity and carelessness in their exploitation are leading to pollution and climate change that in turn is increasing demand for those very same resources. The image of a polluted urban world depleted of oil and other non-renewable energy sources is an all too real prospect, and in some parts of the world – developing countries and countries of the former second world – is already happening. In this book, we have attempted to sketch the institutions and policies that might be used at a more local scale to deal with how these issues translate into physical changes that are occurring in cities. Housing and transport are significant keys to these problems as several authors argued in Part II, but we are still a long way from developing tools to measure and simulate the way such issues impact on the natural environment.

The models examined in Part III may hold the key but what is sorely lacking are models that link the social and economic structure of cities to their underlying urban ecology, geology and geomorphology, and to urban atmospherics. We urgently need new theory and models which link the spatial structure of the city through its physical form and space-economy to the way natural processes are affected by and affect the city's socio-economic functioning. In the same way, we need to link demographic structure to issues involving health and care. The ultimate goal of planning for a sustainable future is to achieve the greatest quality of life for all and this goal needs to be measured by a range of health indicators. Traffic and housing congestion, the journey to work that links housing to employment, the pollution generated and the resources consumed, must be linked directly to measures of physical and mental health as well as to broader issues of what can and should be afforded. We are currently able to articulate these needs but we are a long distance away from providing ways in which we can trace these inter-dependencies and fashion spatial planning policies to make a real difference in the right direction. The arguments advanced here must thus be set in the context of a much wider urban research agenda which includes urban ecology, pollution and health. In short, the sentiments echoed by Davoudi and Layard in their introduction to this volume that we need firmer, more focused 'processes and methods' are consistent with this wider agenda.

We need better techniques and methods that are effective within a range of planning processes for other reasons that were clearly articulated in Part I. As we enter a world of massive connectivity in which everyone is able to communicate electronically in diverse ways, the prospects for debate over the public good – over issues of collective interest and action – through new ways of public participation are greater than ever before. Of course this brings new questions: although information is more widely available and methods for influencing how it might be used more open, there are new digital divides and the need is ever more urgent for facilitators to help in managing the process of participation. Nevertheless, our abilities to bring structured information into the public domain and to enable the community to be actively involved in using this information, are rapidly increasing. Local planning authorities, for example, have increasing web presence giving access to local development issues, whilst a variety of quangos such as the Environment Agency and non-governmental agencies such as the Friends of the Earth are building effective ways of letting the wider public interact with them through new information technologies. Although we have not reported this formally here, various contributors have been involved in bringing information about pollution and brownfield sites to the public through the development of London Environment Online (LEO: *http://www.leo.ucl.ac.uk/*) and through the development of an information infrastructure for local authorities associated with examining public information about the health of town centres.

The methods that are being used to progress the measurement of sustainability and the design of appropriate plans also need to be judged in terms of their own sustainability. There is rapid change at the present time in such methods in response to new knowledge of how cities are functioning and new ways in which cities might be made to function better. In the same way, the very institutions that are required to promote sustainable development are also in flux. This is a time of very rapid experimentation and it is not at all clear what the best structure of local institutions should now be to develop effective physical planning which focuses explicitly on goals of sustainability. Since the middle of the twentieth century, there have been many changes to the institutions that have been developed to produce and deliver various planning policies. Currently in the United Kingdom, the concern is for devolved government at the national–regional scale as in the Scottish Parliament, and the Welsh and Greater London Assemblies. The need for more grass-roots involvement is clearly driving the move to more accountable local government, but this too is being spurred on by new forms of public participation using Information and Communications Technology (ICT).

In one sense, our current fascination with issues of sustainability is generated by the sense that in a global world, risks have been heightened for us all. The possibility of a grand-scale 'Tragedy of the Commons', very different from the fear of nuclear annihilation in the years of the Cold War, seems ever present, particularly through the uncertainty of global warming. Moreover, there is also a sense in which the world has turned a corner that is probably irreversible. Within the next twenty years, more than half the world's population will live in cities, and by the end of the century, more than 85 per cent will be classed as urban. In the developed countries, the end of agricultural society is in sight whilst most of the demands on the countryside are now urban in origin. How to build an urban world which is somehow more contained physically than current trends imply, is one of the key debates in the West at present as articulated through the issue of urban sprawl. Whether or not we should plan *for* or *against* such an urban world – and either could be envisaged as meeting various goals of sustainability – is the great urban question of our times, and much of the discussion in Part II is structured around this. There is another, less easy, question lurking behind this debate and that is our uncertainty as to the overall impacts of a completely urbanised world on the natural world. Few of us would even hazard a guess at what this might be in terms of the medium-term future, but the sustainability debate as we have presented it in this book, sensitises us to how we might engage in the debate over its impact on more local questions of urban and regional planning.

Conclusions should not necessarily mirror introductions but as we have presented a variety of different viewpoints from contributors who are all connected with the Bartlett School of Planning, it is worth sketching the implications of this debate for education and training in both a narrow and wider context. In the wider context, this debate knows no bounds. Every discipline and every viewpoint have something to contribute to our collective future. As we have been at pains to point out, the methods and technologies required for measuring and modelling sustainability require many sources of expertise across the social, historical, physical, and natural sciences. The administration of plans that articulate related goals requires different varieties of professional expertise and management while the will to implement such plans involves political questions which in the last analysis involve crucial individual and collective trade-offs and choices.

Within this broad context, we need planning professionals who are intellectually aware of these wider issues, but we also need professionals who have a variety of experience, not just of planning processes and institutions but of case studies, contexts, methods, and techniques which enable them to focus their general expertise on specific issues. This new focus on sustainability will clearly change the educational training demands of planners. It would be unusual if this were not the case, for just as planning is bringing sustainability into its core, planning education should also evolve to recognise the multitude of skills required. There needs to be a recognition that this involves something more than can be learnt in the confines of a planning school. Lifelong learning is a cliché of course but if we are to improve our methods, processes, institutions, and communication, we have to understand that they will evolve over longer time scales and over broader ranges of disciplines than those to which we have previously become accustomed. The chapters in this book have suggested what some of these key issues might be.

Bibliography

ACRE (1998) ACRE's *Detailed Comments on Comprehensive Spending Review for the Department of the Environment, Transport and the Regions*, London: ACRE.

Adams, J. (1997) 'Alternative policies for reducing dependence on the car', in R. Tolley (ed.) *The Greening of Urban Transport*, London: Wiley, pp. 239–50.

Adams, T. (1996) 'Gridlock in waste planning', *Waste Planning* 18 (March): 3–5.

Adams, W.M. (1990) *Green Development – Environment and Sustainability in the Third World*, London: Routledge (cited in Backstrand *et al.*, 1996).

Ahlvik, P., Eggleston, S., Gorißen Hassel, D., Hickman, A., Joumard, R., Ntziachristos, L., Rijkeboer, R., Samara, Z. and Zierock, K. (1997) *COPERT II: Computer Programme to Calculate Emissions from Road Transport: Methodology and Emission Factors*, Final Draft Report, European Environment Agency.

Altshuler, A.A. (1965) *The City Planning Process*, Ithaca, NY: Cornell University Press.

Anderson, J.R. (1985) 'Assessing the impact of farming systems research: Framework and problems', *Agricultural Administration*, Vol. 20.

Axelrod, R.S. and Vig, N.J. (1999) 'The European Union as an environmental governance system', in R.S. Axelrod and N.J. Vig (eds) *The Global Environment: Institutions Law and Policy*, London: Earthscan.

Backstrand, K., Kronsell, A. and Soderhol, P. (1996) 'Organisational challenges to sustainable development', *Environmental Politics* 5, 2: 209–30.

Ball, M.J. (1983) *Housing Policy and Economic Power*, London: Methuen.

Banister, D. (1998) 'Barriers to the implementation of urban sustainability', *International Journal of Environment and Pollution* 10, 1: 65–83.

—— (1999a) 'Sustainable development and transport', in German, Bundesamt für Bauwesen und Raumordnung, *Urban Future: Preparatory Exercises (Overviews) for the World Report on Urban Future for*

the Global Conference on the Urban Future URBAN 21, pp. 41–59,
Bonn: Bundesamt für Bauwesen und Raumordnung, (Forschungen, Heft
21).

—— (1999b) 'Planning more to travel less: land use and transport', *Town
Planning Review* 70, 3: 313–38.

—— (1999c) 'Some thoughts on a walk in the woods', *Built Environment*,
25, 2: 162–7.

Banister, D. and Marshall, S. (2000) *Encouraging Transport Alternatives:
Good Practice in Reducing Travel*, London: The Stationery Office.

Banister, D., Stead, D., Aackerman, J., Steen, P., Dreborg, K., Nijkamp, P.
and Schleicher-Tappeser, R. (2000) *European Transport Policy and
Sustainable Mobility*, London: E & F. N. Spon.

Banister, D., Watson, S. and Wood, C. (1997) 'Sustainable cities: transport,
energy and urban form', *Environment and Planning B: Planning and
Design*, 24, 2: 125–43.

Barton, H. (1996) 'Going Green by design', *Urban Design Quarterly*, Issue
57, (January): 13–18.

Barton, H., Davies, G. and Guise, R. (1995) *Sustainable Settlements: A Guide
for Planners, Designers and Developers*, Luton: University of the West
of England and Local Government Management Board.

Bates, R. (1981) *Markets and States in Tropical Africa*, Berkeley, CA:
University of California Press.

Batty, M. (1979) 'On planning processes', in B. Goodall and A. Kirby (eds)
Resources and Planning, Oxford: Pergamon.

Baum, H. (1997) 'Social science, social work, and surgery', *Journal of the
American Planning Association*, 63, 2: 180–8.

Beck, U. (1992) *Risk Society: Towards a New Modernity*, London: Sage.

—— (1996) 'Risk society and the provident state', in Szerszynzki, B., Lash,
S. and Wynne B. (eds) *Risk, Environment and Modernity: Towards a
New Ecology*, London: Sage.

—— (1998) *Democracy Without Enemies*, Cambridge: Polity Press.

Beck, U., Giddens, A. and Lash, S. (1994) *Reflexive Modernisation: Politics,
Tradition and Aesthetics in Modern Social Order*, Cambridge: Polity
Press.

Beckerman, W. (1992) 'Economic growth and the environment: whose
growth? Whose environment?'. *World Development*, 20, 4: 481–96.

—— (1995) *Small is Stupid: Blowing the Whistle on the Greens*, London:
Duckworth.

Bell, S. and McGillivray, D. (2000) *Ball and Bell on Environmental Law*,
5th edition, London: Blackstone Press.

Bentley, I. (1990) 'Ecological urban design', *Architects' Journal*, 192, 24
October: 69–71.

Bentley, I., Alcock, A., Murrain, P., McGlynn, S., Smith, G. (1985) *Responsive
Environments: A Manual for Designers*, Oxford: Butterworth Architecture.

Berneri, M.L. (1982) *Journey through Utopia*, London: Freedom Press.

Bhatti, M. (1996) 'Housing and environmental policy in the UK', *Policy and Politics*, 24, 2: 159–70.

Birnie, P.A. and Boyle, A.E. (1992) *International Law and the Environment*, Oxford: OUP.

—— (eds) (1995) *Basic Documents on International Law and the Environment*, Oxford: Clarendon Press.

Blowers, A. (1993) *Planning for a Sustainable Environment*, London: Earthscan.

—— (1997) 'Society and sustainability, the context of change for planning', in M. Blowers and B. Evans (eds), *Town Planning into the 20th Century*, London: Routledge.

Blowers, A. and Evans, B. (eds) (1997) *Town Planning into the 20th Century*, London: Routledge.

Bluewater (1999) *Welcome to Bluewater*, advertising brochure available at Bluewater Park, Kent, UK.

Boléat, M. (1997) 'The politics of home ownership', in P. Williams (ed.) *Directions in Housing Policy: Towards Sustainable Housing Policies for the UK*, London: Paul Chapman Publishing, pp. 54–67.

Breheny, M. (1990) 'Strategic planning and urban sustainability', in Town and Country Planning Association, *Planning for Sustainable Development, 1990 Annual Conference, Proceedings*, London: Town and Country Planning Association.

—— (ed.) (1992a) *Sustainable Development and Urban Form*, London: Pion.

—— (1992b) 'The contradictions of the compact city', in Breheny, M. (ed.) *Sustainable Development and Urban Form*, London: Pion, pp. 138–59.

—— (1997) 'Urban compaction: feasible and acceptable?', *Cities*, 14: 209–17.

—— (1999) 'People, households and houses: the basis to the great housing debate in England', *Town Planning Review*, 70, 3: 275–93.

Breheny, M., Gordon, I., Archer, S. (1998) 'Building densities and sustainable cities', Engineering and Physical Sciences Research Council (EPSRC), Sustainable Cities Programme, *Project Outline No. 5*, June 1998.

Breheny, M, and Hall, P. (eds) (1996) *The People – Where Will They Go? National Report of the TCPA Regional Inquiry into Housing Need and Provision in England*, London: TCPA.

Brinkerhoff, D.W. and Goldsmith, A.A (eds) (1990) *Institutional Sustainability in Agriculture and Rural Development: A Global Perspective*, New York: Praeger.

—— (1992) 'Promoting the sustainability of development institutions: a framework for strategy', *World Development*, 20, 3: 369–83.

British Medical Association (BMA) (1998) *Health & Environmental Impact Assessment: An Integrated Approach*, London: Earthscan.

Brownlie, I. (1995) *Basic Documents in International Law*, Oxford: Oxford University Press.

Buckingham-Hatfield, S. and Evans, B. (eds) (1996) *Environmental Planning and Sustainability*, New York: John Wiley.

Buckingham-Hatfield, S. and Matthews, J. (1999) 'Including women: addressing gender', in Buckingham-Hatfield, S. and Percy, S. (eds) *Constructing Local Environmental Agendas: People, Places and Participation*, London: Routledge.

Buckingham-Hatfield, S. and Percy, S. (1999) *Constructing Local Environmental Agendas: People, Places and Participation*, London: Routledge.

Burt, J.E. and Barber, G.M. (1996) *Elementary Statistics for Geographers*, 2nd edition, London: Guildford Press.

Cabinet Office, The (2000a) *Social Exclusion Unit Leaflet*, London: Cabinet Office.

—— (2000b): London Cabinet Office.

CAG Consultants (1997) *Sustainability in Development Control: A Research Report*, London: Local Government Association.

—— (1998) *National Barriers to Local Sustainability*, London: Friends of the Earth.

Calthorpe, P. (1993) *The Next American Metropolis: Ecology, Community and the American Dream*, New York: Princeton Architectural Press.

Campbell, S. (1999) 'Planning, green cities, growing cities, just cities? Urban Planning and the contradictions of sustainable development', in Satterthwaite, D. (ed.) *Sustainable Cities*, London: Earthscan.

Carley, M. and Christie, I. (1992) *Managing Sustainable Development*, London: Earthscan.

Carley, M. and Spapens, P. (1998) *Sharing the World: Sustainable Living and Global Equity in the 21st Century*, London: Earthscan.

Carmona, M. (1996) 'The local plan agenda', *Urban Design Quarterly*, Issue 57 (January): 18–23.

Carson, R. (1962) *Silent Spring*, Boston: Houghton Mifflin.

Castells, M. (1996) 'An interview with Manuel Castells', *Cities*, 13, 1: 3–9.

—— (1997) *The Information Age: Economy, Society and Culture, Volume II: The Power of Identity*, Oxford: Blackwell.

CEC (Commission of the European Communities) (1989) *EC Strategy on Waste Management*, CEC (89)934, Luxembourg: CEC.

—— (1990) *Green Paper on the Urban Environment*, EUR 12902, Brussels: CEC.

—— (1992) *Towards Sustainability: a European Community Programme of Policy and Action in Relation to the Environment and Sustainable Development*, COM 92 (23), Brussels: CEC

Chadwick, G. (1971) *A Systems View of Planning: Towards a Theory of the Urban and Regional Planning Process*, Oxford: Pergamon.

Chambert, H. (1997) *Urban Development and Metropolitan Housing Construction: a Spatial Analysis Approach*, Stockholm: Chamberts förlag.

Champion, A., Atkins, D., Coombes, M. and Fotheringham, S. (1998) *Urban Exodus: A Report for CPRE*, London: Council for the Protection of Rural England.

Chaney, P. and Sherwood, K. (2000) 'The resale of Right to Buy dwellings: a case study of migration and social change in rural England', *Journal of Rural Studies*, 16, 1: 79–94.

Cheshire, P. (2000) 'Building on brown fields: the long term price we pay', *Planning in London*, 33: 34–5.

Child, M. (2000) 'Interview with the author', Edinburgh: City of Edinburgh Council, 6th January.

Clapp, B.W. (1994) *An Environmental History of Britain since the Industrial Revolution*, London: Longman.

Clifford, S. and King, A. (1993) *Local Distinctiveness: Place, Particularity and Identity*, London: Common Ground.

Cloke, P.J. (1983) *An Introduction to Rural Settlement Planning*, London: Methuen.

Cobb, J. and Daly, H. (1989) *For the Common Good*, London: Green Print.

Colenutt, B. (1997) 'Can town planning be for people rather than property?', in Blowers, M. and Evans, B. (eds) *Town Planning into the 20th Century*, London: Routledge.

COMEAP (1992) *Towards Sustainability: A European Community Programme of Policy and Action in Relation to the Environment and Sustainable Development*, COM 92(23), Brussels: CEC.

—— (Committee on the Medical Effects of Air Pollutants) (1998) *Quantification of the Effects of Air Pollution on Health in the United Kingdom*, Department of Health, London: The Stationery Office.

Commission of the European Union (2000) *White Paper on Environmental Liability*, Brussels: CEU.

Connelly, J. and Smith, G. (1999) *Politics and the Environment: From Theory to Practice*, London: Routledge.

Costanza, R. and Daly, H.E. (1992) 'National capital and sustainable development', *Conservation Biology*, 1: 37–45.

Countryside Commission (1998) *Planning for Countryside Quality*, London: CC.

Coveney, P. and Highfield, R. (1995) *Frontiers of Complexity: The Search for Order in a Chaotic World*, London: Faber & Faber.

Cox, J. and Cadman, D. (2000) *Commercial Property Markets in a Sustainable Economy*, London: University College London School of Public Policy.

CPRE (Council for Protection of Rural England) (1997) *Waste and the Countryside*, London: CPRE.

—— (1998) *Rural Transport Policy and Equity*, CPRE with RDC and Countryside Commission, London: CPRE.

Croall, J. (1999) 'Local, mutual, voluntary and simple: the power of local exchange trading schemes', in Worpole, K. (ed.) *Richer Futures: Fashioning a New Politics*, London: Earthscan.

Cullingworth, B. and Nadin, V. (1994) *Town and Country Planning in Britain*, London: Routledge.

Dafis, C. (Member of Parliament for Ceredigion) (1998) *Hansard*, at col. 410.

Dagenhart, R. and Sawicki, D. (1992) 'Architecture and planning: the divergence of two fields', *Journal of Planning Education and Research*, 12: 1–16.

Daly, H. (1991) *Steady State Economics*, Washington, DC: Island Press.

DANTE Consortium (1998) *Encouraging Travel Alternatives: A Guide to Good Practice in Reducing Travel*, London: The Bartlett School of Planning.

Davidoff, P. (1965) 'Advocacy and pluralism in planning', *Journal of American Institute of Planners*, 31: 186–97.

Davison, I. (1995) 'Viewpoint: do we need cities any more?', *Town Planning Review*, 66, 1: iii–vi.

Davoudi, S. (1997) 'Environmental considerations in minerals planning, theory versus practice', in D. Borne, A. Khakee and C. Lacirignola (eds), *Evaluating Theory-Practice and Urban-Rural Interplay in Planning*, Netherlands: Kluwer Academic Publisher.

—— (1999) 'A quantum leap for planners', *Town and Country Planning*, 68, 1: 20–4.

—— (2000) 'Planning for waste: changing discourse and institutional relationships', *Progress in Planning*, 53, 3: 165–216.

Davoudi, S. and Cadman, D. (1997) 'The changing face of planning in the 90s', *Planning*, 4 April: 16–17.

Davoudi, S. and Petts, J. (2000) 'How to involve the public in waste planning', *Proceedings of the Fifth National Conference in Strategic and Local Planning for Waste*, 5–6 July, Birmingham: MEL Research.

Davoudi, S., Hull, A. and Healey, P. (1996) 'Environmental concerns and economic imperatives in strategic plan-making', *Town Planning Review*, 64, 4: 421–36.

DoE (Department of the Environment) (1974) *War on Waste: A Policy for Reclamation*, Green Paper, cmnd.5727, London: HMSO.

—— (1985) *Town and Country Planning Circular 14/85*, London: HMSO.

—— (1992a) *PPG12 (Planning Policy Guidance Note 12)*, London: HMSO.

—— (1992b) *This Common Inheritance: Britain's Environmental Strategy*, (Cmnd 1200), London: HMSO.

—— (1992c) *Waste Management Paper No 1: A Review of Options*, London: HMSO.

—— (1994a) *Sustainable Development: The UK Strategy*, Cmnd 2426, London: HMSO.

—— (1994b) *PPG23: Planning and Pollution Control*, London: HMSO.

—— (1994c) *Vital and Viable Town Centres: Meeting the Challenge*, London: HMSO.

—— (1995a) *RPG9a: Supplement to Regional Planning Guidance*, London: HMSO.

—— (1995b) *Projections of Households in England to 2016*, London: HMSO.

—— (1995c) *Making Waste Work: The UK Strategy for Sustainable Waste Management*, London: HMSO.

—— (1995d) *Our Future Homes: Opportunity, Choice, Responsibility*, London: HMSO.

—— (1995e) *Shopping Centres and Their Future*, London: HMSO.

—— (1996a) *Reclamation of Damaged Land for Nature Conservation*, London: HMSO.

—— (1996b) *Revision of PPG23 'Planning and Pollution Control' on Waste Issues, Consultation Draft*, London: Doe.

DoE/DoT (Department of the Environment and Department of Transport) (1993) *Reducing Transport Emissions through Planning* (ECOTEC Research and Consulting Ltd. in association with Transportation Planning Associates), London: HMSO.

—— (1995) *PPG13: Guide to Better Practice – Reducing the Need to Travel Through Planning*, London: HMSO.

DETR (Department of Environment, Transport & Regions) (1997a) *Smog Information Made Clear*, Press Release No. 463, 19th November 1997.

—— (1997b) *National Travel Survey 1994/96*, London: The Stationery Office.

—— (1998a) *Sustainable Local Communities for the 21st Century: Why and How to Prepare an Effective Local Agenda 21 Strategy*, London: DETR.

—— (1998b) *The Use of Density in Urban Planning*, Report from the Planning Research Programme by the Bartlett School of Planning and Llewelyn Davies Planning, London: The Stationery Office (June 1998). Online. Available HTTP: http://*www.detr.gov*.

—— (1998c) *Guidance on Local Housing Strategies*, London: DETR. Online. Availabl http://*www.housing.detr.gov.uk/local/guidance/index.htm*.

—— (1998d) *Planning for Communities of the Future*, London: DETR.

—— (1998e) *Modernising Planning*, London: DETR.

—— (1998f) *Transport Statistics Great Britain 1998*, London: The Stationery Office.

—— (1998g) *A New Deal for Transport – Better for Everyone*, London: The Stationery Office.

—— (1998h) *Planning for Sustainable Development*, London: The Stationery Office.

—— (1998i) *Places, Streets and Movement: A Companion Guide to Design Bulletin 32, Residential Roads and Footpaths*, London: DETR.

—— (1998j) *Draft PPG10: Waste Disposal and Management*, London: HMSO.

—— (1998k) *Less Waste More Value, Consultation Paper on the Waste Strategy for England and Wales*, London: HMSO.

—— (1998l) *Town Centres: Defining Boundaries for Statistical Monitoring: Feasibility Study*, London: The Stationery Office.

—— (1999a) *Towards a Better Quality of Life: A Strategy for Sustainable Development for the United Kingdom*, London: The Stationery Office. Online. Available *http://www.detr.gov.uk/sustainable/quality/index.htm*.

—— (1999b) *Projections of Households in England to 2021: 1996-Based Estimates*, London: DETR.

—— (1999c) *A Way With Waste: A Draft Waste Strategy for England and Wales, Part One*, London: DETR.

—— (1999d) *A Way With Waste: A Draft Waste Strategy for England and Wales, Part Two*, London: DETR.

—— (1999e) *Planning Policy Guidance Note 10: Planning and Waste Management*, London: DETR.

—— (1999f) *Planning Policy Guidance Note 13: Transport (Revised)*, London: HMSO.

—— (1999g) *Draft Planning Policy Guidance Note 3: Housing (Revised)*, London: HMSO.

—— (2000a) *Guidance on Preparing Regional Sustainable Development Frameworks*, London: DETR.

—— (2000b) *Regional Planning Guidance RPG9: Draft Regional Planning Guidance*, London: The Stationery Office.

—— (2000c) *Planning Policy Guidance Note 3: Housing*, London: DETR.

—— (2000d) *North West Regional Housing Need and Demand Research*, London: DETR.

—— (2000e) *Waste Strategy 2000: England and Wales Parts One and Two*, London: The Stationery Office.

—— (2000f) *White Paper on Rural Areas*. London: The Stationery Office.

DETR Property Advisory Group (1998) *Sustainable Development and Buildings*, London: DETR.

Dimitriou, H.T. (1988) 'Urban transport and manpower development and training needs for Asian cities', *Habitat International*, 12, 3: 65–90.

—— (1998) 'Concept of sustainable development', in *Sustainable Urban Development and Transport: Toward a Strategy for Policy-making*,

Planning and Project Implementation, Supporting Technical Report No. 2, Prepared for UNDP Programme for Economic Reform through Enhanced Transport and Communication Services, Transport Division of Transport, Water & Urban Development Department, Washington, DC: World Bank, pp. 13–17.

Doyle, T. and McEachern, D. (1998) *Environment and Politics*, London: Routledge.

Drabble, M. (1990) *Safe as Houses: An Examination of Home Ownership and Mortgage Tax Relief*, London: Chatto & Windus.

Dupuis, A. and Thorns, D.C. (1996) 'Meanings of home for older home owners', *Housing Studies*, 11, 4: 485–501.

Dykes, J.A., Fisher, P.F., Stynes, K., Unwin, D. and Wood, J. (1998) 'The use of the landscape metaphor in understanding population data', *Environment and Planning B, Planning and Design*, 26, 281–95.

Eckersley, R. (1996) 'Environmentalism and political theory', in W.M. Lafferty and J. Meadowcroft (eds) *Democracy and the Environment: Problems and Prospects*, Cheltenham: Edward Elgar, pp. 86–101.

Ecologist, The (1972) *Blueprint For Survival*, Harmondsworth: Penguin.

—— (2000a) *The Economist*, 18 November.

—— (2000b) 'The World Bank's muddled prescriptions', *The Economist*, 30 September.

Edwards, M. (2000a) 'City design: what went wrong at Milton Keynes?', *Journal of Urban Design*.

—— (2000b) 'Towards a joined-up London', *Planning in London*, 32, (Jan–Mar): 41–2.

—— (2000c) 'Property markets and the production of inequality', in S. Watson and G. Bridge (eds) *The Blackwell Companion to the City*, Oxford: Blackwell, 599–608.

—— (2000d) 'Sacred cow or sacrificial lamb? Will London's green belt have to go?' *CITY*, 4, 1:105–12.

Ehrlich, P. (1972) *The Population Bomb*, London: Pan/Ballantine.

Elliot, L. (1998) *The Global Politics of the Environment*, Basingstoke: Macmillan.

ENDS (1995) 'Health studies point the finger at industrial air pollution', *ENDS Report*, May, 244: 22.

—— (1998) 'SEPA's report leaves accountability gap', *ENDS Report*, 287: 5–6.

—— (1999a) 'LAAPC inspections below par despite improvement', *ENDS Report*, 291: 15.

—— (1999b) 'Agency staff's "no confidence" vote in top management', *ENDS Report*, 292: 7–8.

—— (2000) 'Consultation begins on sustainability scheme for Wales', *ENDS Report*, 300: 41.

English Heritage (1997) *Sustaining the Historic Environment: New Perspectives in the Future*, London: English Heritage.

EPA (1990), *Environmental Protection Act*, London: HMSO.

Ettema, D.F. and Timmermans, H.J.P. (eds) (1997) *Activity-based Approaches to Travel Analysis*, Oxford: Pergamon.

European Environment Agency (1995) *Europe's Environment – The Dobříš Assessment*, edited by D. Stanners and P. Bourdeau, Copenhagen: the European Environment Agency. Online. Available *http://org.eea.eu.int/document*).

Evans, A.W. (1998) 'Dr Pangloss finds his profession: sustainability, transport and land use planning in Britain', *Journal of Planning Education and Research*, 18, 2: 137–44.

Evans, B. (1997) 'From town planning to environmental planning', in A. Blowers and B. Evans (eds) *Town Planning into the 21st century*, London: Routledge.

Evans, B. and Rydin, Y. (1997) 'Planning, professionalism and sustainability', in A. Blowers and B. Evans (eds) *Town Planning into the 21st Century*, London: Routledge.

Evans, R. (1998) 'Tackling deprivation on social housing estates in England: an assessment of the housing plus approach', *Housing Studies*, 13, 5: 713–26.

Fairlie, S. and This Land is Ours (1996) *Low Impact Development: Planning and People in a Sustainable Countryside*, Charlbury, Oxon: Jon Carpenter Publishing.

Faludi, A. (1973) *Planning Theory*, Oxford: Pergamon.

Farthing, S. (ed.) (1994) *Co-ordinating Facility Provision and New Housing Development: Impacts on Car and Local Facility Use*, Towards Sustainability Conference Papers, Bristol: University of West England.

Farthing, S., Winter, J. and Coombes, T. (1996) 'Travel behaviour and local accessibility to services and facilities', in M. Jenks, E. Burton and K. Williams (eds) *The Compact City: A Sustainable Urban Form*, London: E & FN Spon, pp. 181–90.

Ford, J. and Wilcox, S. (1998) 'Owner occupation, employment and welfare: the impact of changing relationships on sustainable home ownership', *Housing Studies*, 13, 5: 623–38.

Forrest, R. and Murie, A. (1992) *Residualisation and Council Housing: A Statistical Update*, Bristol: School for Advanced Urban Studies.

Frey, H. (1999) *Designing the City: Towards a More Sustainable Urban Form*, London: E & FN Spon.

Friedmann, J. (1998) 'Planning theory revisited', *European Planning Studies*, 6, 3: 245–53.

Friends of the Earth (2000) *Pollution Injustice*. Online. Available http://www.foe.co.uk/pollution-injustice/

Gandy, M. (1994) *Recycling and the Politics of Urban Waste*, London: Earthscan.

Garreau, J. (1991) *Edge Cities: Life on the New Frontier*, New York: Doubleday.

Geddes, P. (1915) *Cities in Evolution*, London: Williams & Norgate.

Giddens, A. (1998) *The Third Way: The Renewal of Social Democracy*, Cambridge: Polity Press.

GLC (Greater London Council) (1963) *The Planning of a New Town: Data Design Based on Study for a New Town of 100,000 at Hook, Hampshire*, London: GLC.

Glikson, A. (1955) *Regional Planning and Development*, Leiden, The Netherlands: A.W. Sijthoff Uitgeversmaatshappij NV.

Gloucestershire County Council (1996) *Structure Plan: Second Review*, May 1996.

—— (1999) *Examination in Public*, February 1999.

Goodin, R.E. (1996) 'Enfranchising the earth, and its alternatives', *Political Studies*, XLIV, 835–49.

GOSE (Government Office for the South East) (1999) *Regional Planning Guidance for the South East of England: Public Examination, May–June 1999: Report of the Panel*, Guildford: GOSE.

Goss, S. and Blackaby, B. (1998) *Designing Local Housing Strategies: A Good Practice Guide*, Coventry and London: Chartered Institute of Housing and the Local Government Association.

GOSW (Government Office for the South West) (1999) *Draft Regional Planning Guidance for the South West*, Bristol: GOSW.

Gouldson, A. and Murphy, J. (1997) 'Ecological modernisation: restructuring industrial economies', in M. Jacobs (ed.) *Greening the Millennium*, Political Quarterly, pp. 74–85.

Graham, S. and Marvin, S. (1996) *Telecommunications and the City*, London: Routledge.

Greenpeace (1995) *The European Union Fails to Take Effective Measures Against Nigeria*, press release, London: Greenpeace.

Grubb, H. *et al.* (1993) *The Earth Summit Agreements: A Guide and Assessment*, London: Earthscan.

GSS (Government Statistical Service) (1997) *National Travel Survey 1994–1996*, London: The Stationery Office.

Guardian, The (2000) 'Incinerator cancer threat revealed', 18 May, p. 3.

Gurney, C. (1997) 'Half of me was satisfied: making sense of home through episodic ethnographies', *Women Studies International Forum*, 20, 3: 373–86.

Guy, S. (1998) 'Developing alternatives: energy, offices and the environment', *International Journal of Urban and Regional Research*, 22, 2: 264–82.

Hague, C. (1996) *Planning Places For People*, Proceedings of the Town and Country Planning Summer School, 6–17 September, London: TCPA.

Haigh, N. (1998) *Manual of Environmental Policy: The EC and Britain*, London: Longman

Haigh, N. and Lanigan, N. (1995) 'Impact of the European Union on U.K.

policy making', in T. Gray (ed.) *U.K. Environmental Policy in the 1990's*, London: Macmillan.

Hajer, M. (1992) 'The politics of environmental performance review: choices in design', in E. Lykke (ed.) *Achieving Goals: The Concept and Practice of Environmental Performance Review*, London: Belhaven.

—— (1996) 'Ecological modernisation as cultural politics', in B. Szerszynzki, S. Lash and B. Wynne, *Risk, Environment & Modernity: Towards a New Ecology*, London: Sage.

—— (1997) *The Politics of Environmental Discourse*, Oxford: Oxford University Press.

Hall, P. (1988) *Cities of Tomorrow*, London: Blackwell.

—— (1989) *London 2001*, London: Unwin Hyman.

—— (1992) *Urban and Regional Planning*, London: Routledge.

—— (1994) *Cities of Tomorrow*, Oxford: Blackwell.

—— (1995) 'Planning and urban design in the 1990s', *Urban Design Quarterly*, Issue 56: 14–21.

—— (1997) 'The next fifty years: 1997–2047', paper presented at the Royal Town Planning Institute's National Planning Conference, Edinburgh, 7–9 July.

—— (2000) *Thames Gateway – Nine Years On*, Occasional Paper No. 1, London: Thames Gateway London Partnership.

Hall, P., Thomas, R., Gracey, H. and Drewett, R. (1973) *The Containment of Urban England*, 2 volumes, London: George Allen and Unwin.

Hall, P., Edwards, M. and Robson, D. (1999) *London's Spatial Economy: The Dynamics of Change*, London: London Development Partnership (LDP) and the Royal Town Planning Institute.

Hall, P. and Ward, C. (1998) *Sociable Cities: The Legacy of Ebenezer Howard*, Chichester: Wiley.

Hardin, G. (1968) 'The tragedy of the Commons', *Science*, 162: 1243–8.

Harris, D.J. (1998) *Cases and Materials on International Law*, London: Sweet & Maxwell.

Harrison, C. and Burgess, J. (1994) 'Social construction of nature: a case study of conflicts over the development of Rainham Marshes', *Transactions of the Institute of British Geographers*, 33: 253–68.

Harrison, C., Burgess, J. and Filius, P. (1996) 'Rationalising environmental responsibilities: a comparison of lay publics in the UK and the Netherlands', *Global Environmental Change*, 6, 3: 215–34.

Harvey, D. (1996) 'Cities or urbanisation?', *City*, 1: 38–61.

Haughton, G. and Hunter, C. (1994) *Sustainable Cities*, London: Regional Studies Association.

Hawkins, K. (1989) 'Rule and discretion in comparative perspective: the case of social regulation', *Ohio State Law Journal*, Vol. 50, 663–82.

Hayward, T. (2000) 'Constitutional environmental rights: a case for political analysis', *Political Studies*, 48: 558.

HC (House of Commons Environmental, Transport and Regional Affairs Committee) (1998) *Sustainable Waste Management*, HC 484–1, London: The Stationery Office.

HCEC (House of Commons Environment Committee) (1989) *Toxic Waste*, 2nd Report (Session 1988–89, HC 22), London: HMSO.

Healey, P. (1997) *Collaborative Planning: Shaping Places in Fragmented Societies*, London: Macmillan.

Healey, P. and Barrett, S. (1990) 'Structure and agency in land and property development processes: some ideas for research', *Urban Studies*, 27, 1: 89–104.

Healey, P. and Davoudi, S. (1998) 'Participation in waste planning: theoretical considerations', *Proceedings of the Third National Conference on Strategic and Local Planning for Waste: Priorities, Participation and Planning Practice*, 15–16 July, Birmingham: MEL Research.

Healey, P., Khakee, A., Motte, A. and Needham, B. (eds) (1997) *Making Strategic Spatial Plans: Innovation in Europe*, London: University College London Press.

Healey, P. and Shaw, T. (1993) 'Planners, plans and sustainable development', *Regional Studies*, 27: 769–76.

Hebbert, M. (1998) *London: More by Fortune Than Design*, Chichester: Wiley.

Hedges, B. and Clemens, S. (1994) *Housing Attitudes Survey*, London: HMSO, pp. 209–17.

Hencke, D. (2000a) 'MPs accuse Whitehall of cover-up on incinerators', *The Guardian*, 1 November.

—— (2000b) 'Watchdog admits ignorance of incinerator health risks', *The Guardian*, 28 November.

Henneberry, J. (1995) 'Developers, property cycles and local economic development: the case of Sheffield', *Local Economy*, 10, 2: 23–5.

Hill, R. (1991) 'Homeless women, special possessions, and the meaning of home – an ethnographic case-study', *Journal of Consumer Research*, 18, 3: 298–310.

Hillman, M. (1997) 'The potential of non-motorised transport for promoting health', in R. Tolley (ed.) *The Greening of Urban Transport*, Chichester: Wiley.

Hobsbawm, E. (1994) *The Age of Extremes: The Short Twentieth Century, 1914–1991*, London: Michael Joseph.

Honadle, G. and Van Sant, J. (1985) *Implementation for Sustainability: Lessons from Integrated Rural Development*, West Hertford, Connecticut: Kumarian.

Hough, M. (1984) *City Form and Natural Process*, London: Routledge.

Houghton-Evans, W. (1975) *Planning Cities: Legacy and Portent*, London: Lawrence & Wishart.

HRF (Housing Research Foundation) (1998) *Home Alone*, Report by A.

Hooper, K. Dunsmore and M. Hughes, London: National House-Building Council.

Howard, E. (1898) *To-morrow: A Peaceful Path to Real Reform*, London: Swan Sonnenschein.

Huntington, S.P., (1968) *Political Order in Changing Societies*, New Haven: Yale University Press.

Hutton, W. (1995) *The State We're In*, London: Cape.

IHT (Institution of Highways and Transportation) (1997) *Transport in the Urban Environment*, London: IHT.

INURA (1998) *Possible Urban Worlds: Urban Strategies at the End of the 20th Century*, Basel: Birkhäuser Verlag.

IPCC (Intergovernmental Panel on Climate Change) (2000) *Report to the Sixth Conference of the Parties of the United Nations Framework Convention on Climate Change by Robert T. Watson, Chairman of the Intergovernmental Panel on Climate Change*, Geneva: IPCC.

IUCN (International Union for the Conservation of Nature) (1980) *World Conservation Strategy: Living Resource Conservation for Sustainable Development*, Gland: IUCN.

Ive, G. (1995) 'Commercial architecture in 1980s London: value engineering or conspicuous investment', in I. Borden and D. Dunster (eds) *Architecture and the Sites of History: Interpretations of Buildings and Cities*, London: Butterworth, pp. 372–86.

Jackson, K.T. (1985) *Crabgrass Frontier: The Suburbanization of the United States*, New York: Oxford University Press.

Jacobs, A.B. and Appleyard, D. (1987) 'Toward an urban design manifesto', *Journal of the American Planning Association*, 53: 112–20.

Jacobs, M. (1996) 'Real world', *Environmental Politics*, 5, 4: 744–51.

—— (1999) *Environmental Modernisation: The New Labour Agenda*, London: Fabian Society.

Jacobs, M. and Stott, M. (1993) 'Sustainable development and the local economy', *Local Economy*, 7: 261–72.

Jenks, M., Button, E. and Williams, K. (1996) *The Compact City: A Sustainable Urban Form?*, London: E & FN Spon.

JMP Consultants (1995) *Travel to Food Superstores*, London, JMP Consultants.

Karn, V., Wong, C., Gallent, N. and Allen, C. (1999) *Housing Requirements in Bolton: Current Patterns and Future Concerns*, Manchester: Manchester Housing Research Group, University of Manchester.

Katz, P.R. (1989) 'The real meaning of home in nursing-homes', *Journal of the American Geriatrics Society*, 37, 7: 665.

—— (1994) *The New Urbanism: Toward an Architecture of Community*, New York: McGraw-Hill.

Kean, J.A., Turner, A., Wood, D.H. and Wood, J.M. (1988) *Synthesis of AID*

Evaluation Reports: FY 1985 and 1986, Evaluation Paper No. 16, DC: USAID.

Kiss, A. and Shelton, D. (1997) *Manual of European Environmental Law*, Cambridge: Cambridge University.

Krugman, P. (1996) *The Self-Organizing Economy*, Cambridge, Massachusetts: Blackwell.

Kuhn, T. (1962) *The Structure of Scientfic Revolutions*, Chicago: University of Chicago Press.

Kunzman, K. (1997) 'The future of planning education in Europe', unpublished response to survey by the Bartlett School of Planning, University College, London.

Lafferty, W.M. (1996) 'The politics of sustainable development: global norms for national implementation', *Environmental Politics*, 5, 2: 185–208.

Lafferty, W.M. and Meadowcroft, J. (eds) (1996) *Democracy and the Environment*, Cheltenham: Edward Elgar.

Lang, J. (1994) *Urban Design: The American Experience*, New York: Van Nostrand Reinhold.

Layard, A. (1997) 'The GATT, health and cows: finding the link', *World Competition: Law and Economics Review*, 21, 1, September 1977.

—— (1999) 'Environmental justice: the American experience and its possible application to the United Kingdom', in J. Holder and D. McGillivray (eds) *Locality and Identity*, Aldershot: Ashgate Press.

Leonard, S. (1992) 'Geddes – the green pioneer', *Edinburgh Review*, No. 88.

Levett, R. (1999) 'Planning for a change' *Town and Country Planning*, September.

Local Government Management Board (1998) *Corporate Approaches to Local Agenda 21 through the Implementation of EMAS*, London: LGMB.

Lowe, R. and Bell, M. (1998) *Towards Sustainable Housing: Building Regulation for the 21st Century*, York: Joseph Rowntree Foundation.

LPAC (London Planning Advisory Committee) (1997) *Supplementary Advice on Planning for Waste in London*, London: LPAC.

Luithlen, L. (1994) *Office Development and Capital Accumulation in the UK*, Aldershot: Avebury.

McCormick, J. (1991) *British Politics and the Environment*, London: Earthscan.

McGranahan, G., Songsore, J. and Kjellen, M. (1999) 'Sustainability, poverty and urban environmental transitions', in D. Satterthwaite (ed.) *Sustainable Cities*, London: Earthscan.

McHarg, I. (1969) *Design with Nature*, New York: Doubleday & Company.

McKenzie-Mohr, D. (1999) 'Fostering sustainable behaviour: online guide to community-based social marketing', St Thomas University. Online. Available http://*www.cbsm.com*.

McLoughlin, J.B. (1969) *Urban and Regional Planning: A Systems Approach*, London: Faber & Faber.

McMahon, M. (1985) 'The law of the land: property rights and town planning in modern Britain', in M.J. Ball, V. Bentivegna, M. Edwards and M. Folin (eds) *Land Rent, Housing and Urban Planning: A European Perspective*, London: Croom Helm, pp. 87–106.

Madanipour, A. (1996) *Design of Urban Space: An Inquiry into a Socio-spatial Process*, Chichester: Wiley.

Mandic, S. and Clapham, D. (1996) 'The meaning of home ownership in the transition from socialism: the example of Slovenia', *Urban Studies*, 33, 1: 83–97.

Mandix (1996) *Energy Planning: A Guide for Practitioners*, London: Royal Town Planning Institute.

Marsh, C., Lucas, K. and Jones, P. (2000) *Research Report on Sustainability and Property Development*, London: The Rees Jeffreys Road Fund.

Marshall, S. (1999) 'Restraining mobility while maintaining accessibility: an impression of the "City of Sustainable Growth"', *Built Environment*, 25, 2: 168–79.

Marshall, T. (1996) 'British land use planning and the European Union', in S. Buckingham-Hatfield and B. Evans (eds), *Environmental Planning and Sustainability*, Chichester: Wiley.

Maslow, A. (1943) *Motivation and Personality*, New York: Harper & Row.

Massey, D. and Catalano, A. (1978) *Capital and Land: Land Ownership by Capital in Great Britain*, London: Edward Arnold.

Mathers, S. (1999) 'Reducing travel in the City of Bristol: promoting bus use through complementary measures', *Built Environment*, 25, 2: 94–105.

Meadows, D.H., Meadows, D.L., Rander, J. and Behrens, W.W. (1972) *The Limits to Growth: A Report for the Club of Rome's Project on the Predicament of Mankind*, London: Pan.

Meen, G. (1998) 'Modelling sustainable home-ownership: demographics or economics?', *Urban Studies*, 35, 11: 1919–34.

Mehta, A. and Hawkins, A. (1998) 'Integrated pollution control and its impact: perspectives from industry', *Journal of Environmental Law*, 10: 61–74

Merrett, S. (1979) *State Housing in Britain*, London: Routledge & Kegan Paul.

—— (1994) 'New age of planning', *Town and Country Planning*, June, 164–5.

Meyerson, M. and Banfield, E.C. (1955) *Politics, Planning and the Public Interest*, New York: Free Press.

Meyerson, M. and Rydin, Y. (1996) 'Sustainable Development' in S. Buckingham-Hatfield and B. Evans (eds) *Environmental Planning and Sustainability*, Chichester: John Wiley.

Milton Keynes Development Corporation (1992) *Milton Keynes Planning Manual*, Milton Keynes: MKDC.

Mittler, D. (1997) 'What, how and why? Local Agenda 21', *LINK*, No. 76, January/February.

—— (1998a) 'A belated boom: Local Agenda 21 in Germany', *EG, Local Environment News*, 4: 2, February.

—— (1998b) 'Good national and international practice: Local Agenda 21 and local sustainability', mimeo, London: Friends of the Earth.

—— (1999a) 'Sustaining Edinburgh: The Lord Provost's Commission on sustainable development for the City of Edinburgh', *Scottish Affairs*, No. 29, Autumn.

—— (1999b) 'Environmental space and barriers to local sustainability: evidence from Edinburgh, Scotland', *Local Environment*, 4, 3: 353–65.

Morphet, J. (1997) 'There'll be planning, but not as we know it', *Town and Country Planning*, 66, 4: 122–3.

Morris, W. (1912 edition) *News from Nowhere: A Dream of John Ball*, London: Williams and Norgate.

MoT (Ministry of Transport) (1963) *Traffic in Towns* (The Buchanan Report), London: HMSO.

Muellbauer, J. and Murphy, A. (1997) 'Booms and busts in the UK housing market', *Economic Journal*, 107, 445: 1701–27.

Mulholland Research Associates Ltd (1995) *Towns or Leafier Environments? A Survey of Family Home Buying Choices*, London: House Builders Federation.

Munasinghe, M. (1993) *Environmental Economics and Sustainable Development*, World Bank Environment Paper No. 3, Washington, DC: World Bank.

Nagpal, T. (1995) 'Voices from the developing world: progress towards sustainable development', *Environment*, 37, 8: 10–15 and 30–33.

New Economics Foundation (1998) *Participation Works! 21 Techniques and Community Participation for the 21st Century*, London: New Economics Foundation.

New Scientist (1998) 'Burn me', 22 November: 31–4.

Newby, H. (1990) 'Ecology, amenity and society', *Town Planning Review*, 61, 1: 3–13.

Newman, P. and Kenworthy, J. (1989) *Cities and Automobile Dependence: A Sourcebook*, Aldershot and Brookfield, Vermont: Gower.

—— (1999) *Sustainability and Cities: Overcoming Automobile Dependence*, Washington, DC: Island Press.

Oels, A. (1997) 'Wege zum Konsens', *Politische Ökologie*, 15, 52, July/August.

Offer, A. (1981) *Property and Politics, 1870–1914*, Cambridge: Cambridge University Press.

Office for National Statistics (1999) *Social Trends 29*, London: The Stationery Office.

Openshaw, S. (ed.) (1995) *Census User's Handbook*, Cambridge, UK: GeoInformation International.

O'Riordan, T. (1992) 'Shaping environmental science for effective public participation', in E. Lykke (ed.) *Achieving Environmental Goods: The Concept and Practice of Environmental Performance Review*, London: Belhaven.

—— (1995) *Environmental Science for Environmental Management*, Harlow: Longman Scientific & Technical.

O'Riordan, T. and Voisey, H. (1998) *The Transition to Sustainability: The Politics of Agenda 21 in Europe*, London: Earthscan.

—— (2000) *Environmental Science for Environmental Management*, 2nd ed., Hanlow: Pearson Education.

Ortúzar, J. de D. and Willumsen, L.G. (1994) *Transport Modelling*, Chichester: Wiley.

Owens, S.E. (1984) 'Spatial structure and energy demand', in D.R. Cope, P.R. Hills and P. James (eds) *Energy Policy and Land Use Planning*, Oxford: Pergamon, pp. 215–40.

—— (1994) 'Land, limits and sustainability: a conceptual framework and some dilemmas for the planning system', *Transactions of the Institute of British Geographers, NS19*, 430–56.

—— (1997) 'Giants in the path: planning, sustainability and environmental values', *Town Planning Review*, 68, 3: 293–305.

Paehlke, R. (1996) 'Environmental challenges to democratic practice', in W.M. Lafferty and J. Meadowcroft (eds) *Democracy and the Environment*, Cheltenham: Edward Elgar.

Parker, J. and Selman, P. (1999) 'Local government, local people and Local Agenda 21', in S. Buckingham-Hatfield and S. Percy, *Constructing Local Environmental Agendas*, London: Routledge.

Pateman, C. (1970) *Participation and Democratic Theory*, Cambridge: Cambridge University Press.

Patten, C., Lovejoy, T., Browne, J., Brundtland, G., Shiva V. and HRH The Prince of Wales (2000) *Respect for the Earth* (The Reith Lectures), London: BBC with Profile Books.

Paul, S. (1982) *Managing Development Programmes: The Lessons of Success*, Boulder, Colorado: Westview.

Paul, S. (1990) *Institutional Development in World Bank Projects: A Cross Sectoral Review*, Research and External Affairs Working Paper No. WPS 392, washington, DC: World Bank.

Pearce, D. (ed.) (1993) *Blueprint 3, Measuring Sustainable Development*, London: Earthscan.

Pearce, D. and Barbier, E. (2000) *Blueprint for a Sustainable Economy*, London: Earthscan.

Pearce, D., Markandya, A. and Barbier, E. (1989) *Blueprint for a Green Economy: Report for the Department of the Environment*, London: Earthscan.

Pepper, D. (1984) *The Roots of Modern Environmentalism*, London: Routledge.

Peters, T. and Waterman, R. (1982) *In Search of Excellence*, New York: Harper & Row.

Petts, J. (1995) 'Waste management strategy development, a case study of community involvement and consensus building in Hampshire', *Journal of Environmental Planning and Management*, 38, 4: 519–36.

Pharaoh, T. and Apel, D. (1995) *Transport Concepts in European Cities*, Studies in Green Research, Aldershot: Avebury.

Pickrell, D. (1992) 'A desire named Streetcar', *Journal of the American Planning Association*, 58, 2, Spring, 158–76.

Pinnegar, S. (1999) 'A review of urban sustainability', a joint paper of the Public Policy and the Jackson Environment Institute, edited by David Cadman. Online. Available e-mail: *environgov@dial.pipex.com*.

Planning (1997a) 'Minister defends brownfield targets', *Planning*, 1245, 21 November, p. 3.

—— (1997b) 'Fifty years of planning', *Planning, Journal of the Royal Town Planning Institute*, 8 and 22 August, 5 and 19 September, 3 and 17 October, 14 November.

—— (1999) 'Negative response to waste strategy', *Planning*, 1 October, p. 7.

Power, A. (1993) *Hovels to High Rise: State Housing in Europe since 1850*, London: Routledge.

—— (1997) *Estates on the Edge: The Social Consequences of Mass Housing in Northern Europe*, London: Macmillan.

—— (1999) 'High-rise estates in Europe: is rescue possible?', *Journal of European Social Policy*, 9, 2: 139–163.

Pratt, D. (1998) 'Urban compactness, social labour and planning', *Proceedings of the International Summer School on the Production of the Built Environment, Biss 17*: 195–208.

Raemaekers, J. (2000) 'Planning for sustainable development', in P. Allmendinger, A. Prior and J. Raemaekers (eds) *Introduction to Planning Practice*, London: Wiley.

Rasmussen, S.E. (1937) *London: The Unique City*, London: Jonathan Cape.

RCEP (Royal Commission for Environmental Protection) (1988) *Best Practicable Environmental Options, 12th Report*, London: HMSO.

—— (1996) *Sustainable Use of Soil, 19th Report*, London: HMSO.

Redclift, M. (1989) *Sustainable Development: Exploring the Contradictions*, London: Routledge.

—— (1992) 'Sustainable development and global environmental change', *Global Environmental Change*, 2, 32: 32–42.

Rees, W.E. (1990) 'The ecology of sustainable development', *The Ecologist*, 20, 1: 18–23.

—— (1999) 'Achieving sustainability: reform or transformation?', in D. Satterthwaite (ed.) *Sustainable Cities*, London: Earthscan.

Reid, D. (1995) *Sustainable Development: An Introductory Guide*, London: Earthscan.

Richmond, J.E. (1998) 'The mythical conception of rail transit in Los Angeles', *Journal of Architectural and Planning Research*, 15, 4, Winter 1998, pp. 294–320 (forthcoming as book, Akron Press).

Roberts, J. (1989) *Quality Streets: How Traditional Urban Centres Benefit from Traffic Calming*, London: TEST.

—— (1990) 'The use of our streets', *Urban Design Quarterly*, issue 35, June.

Robinson, N. (1993) *Agenda 21: Earth's Action Plan*, New York: Oceania.

Rogers, R. (1997) *Cities for a Small Planet*, London: Faber & Faber.

Rowan-Robinson, J. and Ross, A. (1994) 'Enforcement of environmental regulation in Britain: strengthening the link', *Journal of Planning and Environmental Law*, p. 200.

Rowley, A. (1994) 'Definitions of urban design: the nature and concerns of urban design', *Planning Practice and Research*, 8, 3: 179–97.

Royal Commission on Environmental Pollution (1998) *Twenty-First Report: Setting Environmental Standards*, London: The Stationery Office.

—— (1999) *The Use of the Land Use Planning System to Achieve Non-land Use Policy Objectives*, Background Paper 2, London: Landuse Consultants.

Rudden, B. and Wyatt, D. (eds) (1999) *Basic Community Laws*, 7th Edition, Oxford: Oxford University Press.

Rudlin, D. (1998) *Tomorrow: A Peaceful Path to Real Reform: The Feasibility of Accommodating 75 per cent of New Homes in Urban Areas*, London: Friends of the Earth.

Rudlin, D. and Falk, N. (1999) *Building the 21st Century Home: The Sustainable Urban Neighbourhood*, Oxford: Architectural Press.

Rural Development Council for the Countryside (1997) *Survey of Local Services*, Salisbury, RDC.

Rydin, Y. (1998) *Urban and Environmental Planning in the United Kingdom*, London: Macmillan.

—— (1999) 'Environmental governance for sustainable urban development: a European model?', *Local Environment* 4, 1: 61–5.

Sachs, W. (1995) *Global Ecology: A New Arena of Political Conflict*, London: Zed Books.

Salletmaier, C. (1993) 'The development and superimposition of tourism – second homes and recreation within the rural fringe of an urban center', *Mitteilungen der Österreichischen Geographischen Gesellschaft*, 135: 215–242.

Salomon, I., Bovy, P. and Orfeuil, J. (eds) (1993) *A Billion Trips a Day: Tradition and Transition in European Travel Patterns*, Dordrecht: Kluwer Academic Press.

Sands, P. (1995) *Principles of International Environmental Law*, Manchester: Manchester University Press.

Saunders, P. (1990) *A Nation of Home Owners*, London: Hyman Unwin.

Schiller, R. (1986) 'The coming of the third wave', *Estates Gazette*, 279, 16 August, pp. 648–51.

Schipper, Y. (1999) *Market Structure and Environmental Costs in Aviation: A Welfare Analysis of European Air Transport Reform*, Tinbergen Institute Research Series, Amsterdam: Tinbergen Institute.

Schumm, S.A. and Lichty, R.W. (1965) 'Time, space and causality in geomorphology', *American Journal of Science*, 265: 110–99.

Scott, A. and Skea, J. (1998) 'Implementing sustainable development: research insights', special briefing paper prepared for the ESRC Global Environmental Change Programme, Number 3, September. Online. Available http://*www.gecko.ac.uk*.

Selman, P. and Parker, J. (1999) 'Tales of local sustainability', *Local Environment* 4, 1: 47–60.

Shaw, G. and Wheeler, D. (1994) *Statistical Techniques in Geographical Analysis*, 2nd edition, London: David Fulton Publishers.

Shiva, V. (1992) 'Recovering the real meaning of sustainability', in D.E. Cooper and J.A. Palmer (eds) *The Environment in Question*, London: Routledge.

—— (2000) 'Poverty and globalisation', in C. Patten *et al. Respect for the Earth* (The Reith Lectures), London: BBC with Profile Books.

Skea, J. (1999) 'New governance, new hope?', *EG, Local Environment News*, 9: 2–4.

Skea, J. and Sorrell, S. (1999) *Pollution for Sale: Emissions Trading and Joint Implementation*, Cheltenham: Edward Elgar.

Smith, A. (1997) *Integrated Pollution Control*, Aldershot: Ashgate.

Smith, M., Whitelegg, J. and Williams, N. (1998) *Greening the Built Environment*, London: Earthscan.

Smolka, M. (1984) 'Towards a view of the internal structuring of Brazilian cities: The Rio de Janeiro case', *Proceedings of the Bartlett International Summer School on the Production of the Built Environment, Biss 5*, 2: 4–10.

Somerville, P. (1992) 'Homelessness and the meaning of home – rooflessness or rootlessness', *International Journal of Urban and Regional Research*, 16, 4: 539–56.

Soussain, J.G. (1992) 'Sustainable development', in A.M. Mannion and S.R. Bowlby (eds) *Environmental Issues in the 1990s*, Chichester: Wiley.

Southworth, M. and Ben Joseph, E. (1997) *Streets and the Shaping of Towns and Cities*, London: Methuen.

Staats, H.J. and Harland, P. (1995) *A Longitudinal Study of the Effects of the Ecoteam Programme on Environmental Behaviour and its Psychological Backgrounds*, The Netherlands: Centre for Energy and Environmental Research, Leiden University.

Stead, D. (1996) 'Density, settlement size and travel patterns', unpublished research note on the National Travel Surveys 1985/86, 89/91 and 92/94, Bartlett School of Planning, University College London.

Stead, D., Williams, J. and Titheridge, H. (2000) 'Land use change and the people – identifying the connections', in K. Williams, E. Burton and M. Jenks (eds) *Achieving Sustainable Urban Form*, London: E & FN Spon, pp. 174–86.

Stone, C. (1972) 'Should trees have standing?', in M.A. Cahn and R. O'Brien (eds) (1996) *Thinking About the Environment: Readings on Politics, Property and the Physical World*, Armonk, New York: M.E. Sharpe.

—— (1993) *The Gnat is Older than Man: Global Environment and Human Agenda*, Princeton, NJ: Princeton University Press.

Stopher, P. and Lee-Gosselin, M. (1997) *Understanding Travel Behaviour in an Era of Change*, Oxford: Pergamon.

Stroud, D. (1995) 'Higher education and planning: towards a better relationship', *Town Planning Review*, 66, 2: 183–99.

Sustainable Property Consultants (1999) *Research on Sustainable Development for the Transport and Development Working Party*, London: London Planning Advisory Committee (LPAC).

Taylor, M. (1998) 'Combating the social exclusion of housing estates', *Housing Studies*, 13, 6: 819–32.

Terence O'Rourke plc (1998) *Planning for Passive Solar Design*, Watford: BRECSU.

Thomas, A. and Dittmar, H. (1995) 'The experience of homeless women – an exploration of housing histories and the meaning of home', *Housing Studies* 10, 4: 493–515.

Thomas, V. (2000) 'Why quality matters', *The Economist*, 7 October: 142.

Thomas, V. *et al.* (2000) *The Quality of Growth*, Oxford: World Bank and Oxford University Press.

Thornley, A. (1993) *Urban Planning under Thatcherism: The Challenge of the Market* (2nd edition), London: Routledge.

Thurstain-Goodwin, M. and Batty, S. (1998) 'GIS and town centres: exploratory environments involving experts and users', *Built Environment*, 24: 43–56.

Thurstain-Goodwin, M. and Unwin, D. (2000) 'Defining and delineating the central areas of towns for statistical monitoring using continuous surface representations', Working Paper 18, Centre for Advanced Spatial Analysis, University College London. Online. Available. http://*www.casa.ucl.ac.uk/towncentres.pdf*.

Thurstain-Goodwin, M. *et al.* (2000) *An Evaluation of Health Checks for Town Centres in London*, a report for the National Retail Planning Forum, London.

Tibbalds, F., Colbourne, Karski, and Williams, K. (1990) *City of*

Birmingham, City Centre Design Strategy, Birmingham: Birmingham City Council.

Titheridge, H., Hall, S. and Gardner, R. (1998) 'Sustainable settlements – a model for the estimation of transport, energy and emissions, model development and calibration', ESTEEM Working Paper 3, Bartlett School of Planning, University College London, October. Online. Available e-mail: h.titheridge@ucl.ac.uk.

Tolley, R. (ed.) (1997) *The Greening of Urban Transport*, Chichester: Wiley.

Topalov, C. (1985) 'Prices, profits and rents in residential development: France 1960–80', in M.J. Ball, V. Bentivegna, M. Edwards and M. Folin (eds) *Land Rent, Housing and Urban Planning: A European Perspective*, London: Croom Helm, pp. 25–45.

Turner, R. (1997) 'Sustainability and practice', in L. Owen and T. Unwin (eds) *Environmental Management: Readings and Cases*, Cambridge, MA: Blackwell.

UNEP (United Nations Environment Programme) (1999) *Global Environment Outlook 2000*, London: Earthscan.

UNEP (United Nations Environment Programmes' Report) (2000) *Global Environment Outlook 2000*, New York: United Nations.

Urban Design Group (1998) *Urban Design Source Book*, Blewbury, Oxon: UDG.

Urban Task Force (1999) *Towards an Urban Renaissance*, London: Spon.

Urban Villages Group (1992) *Urban Villages*, London: Urban Villages Group.

URBED (Urban and Economic Development Group) (1997) 'The model sustainable urban neighbourhood?', *Sun Dial*, Issue 4: 2–5.

Vance, J.E. (1987) 'Revolution in American space since 1945 and a Canadian contrast', in R.D. Mitchell and P.A. Groves (eds) *North America: The Historical Geography of a Changing Continent*, London: Hutchinson, pp. 438–61.

Vigar, G., Healey, P., Hull, A. and Davoudi, S. (2000) *Planning, Governance and Spatial Strategy in Britain*, London: Macmillan.

Wackernagel, M. and Rees, W.E. (1995) *Our Ecological Footprint: Reducing Human Impact on the Earth*, Gabricola (Canada): New Society Publishers.

Warbarton, D. (ed.) (1998) *Community and SD Participation in the Future*, London: Earthscan.

Ward, H. (1996) 'Green arguments for local democracy', in D. King and G. Stoker (eds) *Rethinking Local Democracy*, Basingstoke: Macmillan.

Ward, S. (1994) *Planning and Urban Change*, London: Paul Chapman.

—— (1997) 'The IGC and the current state of EU environmental policy: consolidation or rollback?', *Environmental Politics*, 6: 178–84.

Waste Planning (1993) 'Waste planning decision', *Waste Planning* 9: 42–4.

—— (1996) 'Waste planning decision', *Waste Planning* 18: 30.

—— (1999) 'The landfill directive', *Waste Planning* 32: 7.

WCED (World Commission on Environment and Development) (1987) *Our Common Future*, Oxford: WCED.

Weal (1993) 'Ecological modernisation and the integration of European environmental policy', in J.D. Liefferink, P.D. Lowe and A.P. Mol (eds) *European Integration and Environmental Policy*, London: Belhaven.

Webber, M. (1968–69) 'Planning in the environment of change', *Town Planning Review*, 39, 179–95 and 277–95.

Webster, K. (1999) 'Hopes and fears for Local Agenda 21', in S. Buckingham-Hatfield and S. Percy (eds), *Constructing Local Environmental Agendas*, London: Routledge.

Weisacker, E., Lovins, A.B. and Lovins, L.H. (1997) *Factor Four: Doubling Wealth – Halving Resource Use*, London: Earthscan.

Wells, G. (1970) *Land Transport Tomorrow*, Brighton: Clifton Books.

Werksman, J. (ed.) (1996) *Greening International Institutions*, London: Earthscan.

Whatmore, S. and Boucher, S. (1993) 'Bargaining with nature: the discourse and practice of "Environmental planning gain"', *Transactions of the Institute of British Geographers*, 18: 166–78.

Whittick, A. (1987) *F.J.O. – Practical Idealist: A Biography of Sir Frederic J. Osborn*, London: Town and Country Planning Association.

Williams, J. (2000a) 'Achieving sustainability – tools for determining sustainable provision of facilities and services in rural Gloucestershire', (forthcoming in *Planning Practice and Research*).

—— (2000b) 'Sustainable rural development strategies in Gloucestershire', unpublished research paper, Bartlett School of Planning, University College London.

Williams, P. (ed.) (1997) *Directions in Housing Policy: Towards Sustainable Housing Policies for the UK*, London: Paul Chapman Publishing.

Winch, G. (ed.) (2000) *Building Research and Information (special issue on the construction business system in Europe)*.

Winter, J., Farthing, S. and Coombes, T. (1995) 'Compact but sustainable', *Planning Week*, 8: 15–17.

Wolsink, M. (1994) 'Entanglement of interests and motives: assumptions behind the NIMBY-theory on facility siting', *Urban Studies*, 31, 6: 851–66.

World Bank (1990) Evaluation Results for 1988: *Issues in World Bank Lending Over Two Decades*, Washington, DC: Operations Department.

World Bank (1999) *Entering the 21st Century: World Development Report 1999/2000*, New York: World Bank and Oxford University Press.

WWF (World Wildlife Fund) (2000) *Living Planet Report 2000*, Geneva: WWF.

Index

Index